Learning RSLogix 5000 Programming
Second Edition

Build robust PLC solutions with ControlLogix, CompactLogix, and Studio 5000/RSLogix 5000

Austin Scott

BIRMINGHAM - MUMBAI

Learning RSLogix 5000 Programming
Second Edition

Commissioning Editor: Vijin Boricha
Acquisition Editor: Rohit Rajkumar
Content Development Editor: Alokita Amanna
Senior Editor: Arun Nadar
Technical Editor: Dinesh Pawar
Copy Editor: Safis Editing
Project Coordinator: Neil Dmello
Proofreader: Safis Editing
Indexer: Rekha Nair
Production Designer: Shankar Kalbhor

First published: August 2015
Second edition: July 2020

Production reference: 1020720

Published by Packt Publishing Ltd.
Livery Place
35 Livery Street
Birmingham
B3 2PB, UK.

ISBN 978-1-78953-246-3

`www.packt.com`

To my son, Ryker, for his unquenchable thirst for knowledge, and for continuing to teach me as I teach him.

- Austin Scott

Contributors

About the author

Austin Scott (GICSP, CISSP, OSCP) has nearly 20 years of industrial automation experience and is a principal industrial penetration tester at Dragos Inc., where he identifies cyber risks within industrial control networks. Prior to Dragos, Austin worked as part of the industrial cybersecurity team at Sempra, Shell, and as an industrial cybersecurity consultant at Accenture. Austin is a SANS Cybersecurity Difference Maker (2015) winner for his industrial cybersecurity contributions. In August 2018, Austin won the DEFCON ICS Village HACK THE PLAN(3)T competition and was awarded the DEFCON UBER black badge.

Thanks to my wife and kids, for their love and support during this book's creation; to Dragos inc, for their continued support; Tetranex Solutions Inc., for their support over the years; the terrific Packt editorial team, including Alokita Amanna and Suzanne Coutinho; and Gus Serino, for bringing his decades of PLC programming experience to the technical reviewing and editing of this book.

About the reviewers

Gus Serino is currently an Industrial Control System (ICS) / Operational Technology (OT) cybersecurity consultant; the bulk of his career has focused on the engineering of industrial controls systems. Gus is a mechanical engineer who holds a professional engineering license in control systems and 20 years of experience in the design, implementation, management, and security of industrial controls systems. He has extensive experience in PLC programming, HMI development, ICS/OT networking, advanced troubleshooting, facility startup and testing, and implementing ICS cybersecurity controls. He holds an MA Water Treatment Operator's License, multiple GIAC Cyber Security certificates, is a member of the GIAC advisory board, and is passionate about controls systems and the security of critical infrastructure.

Javeria Parwani is an electronics engineer with 6 years of experience in the field of industrial automation. One of the few female engineers in this field, she has gained her experience by working in different parts of the world as an automation engineer, such as the UK, the Middle East, and Asia. She is a certified SCADA designer and a trained PLC engineer. As part of her job, she has delivered various projects for the Allen Bradley, Siemens, and Schneider PLCs. Having worked for many different industries, such as aerospace, manufacturing, district cooling, railways, and energy management, she has gained a great deal of experience.

Packt is searching for authors like you

If you're interested in becoming an author for Packt, please visit `authors.packtpub.com` and apply today. We have worked with thousands of developers and tech professionals, just like you, to help them share their insight with the global tech community. You can make a general application, apply for a specific hot topic that we are recruiting an author for, or submit your own idea.

Table of Contents

Section 3: Advanced Logix Programming

Preface

In 1997, Rockwell Automation launched its current generation control platform, Logix. Logix represented decades of technical advancement in automation for robust, large-scale solutions. The RSLogix 5000 programming software (from version 21 and above, it is referred to as Logix Designer within the Studio 5000 software package) provides a unified IEC61131-3 control platform featuring user-friendly interfaces and workflows. Ultimately, the Logix platform reduces programming complexity, eases troubleshooting, and increases plant reliability.

RSLogix 5000 provides intuitive access to real-time information, easy-to-follow runtime logic animations, and a comprehensive suite of online change capabilities. Rockwell's market share is second only to Emerson in North America. Moreover, due to Rockwell Automation's continued success and the glacial speed at which most plants switch platforms, it will be the market leader for the foreseeable future. Globally, Rockwell Automation is the fifth-largest automation manufacturer (behind Siemens, ABB, Emerson, and Schneider). Rockwell Automation's total global install base is well over 2 million programmable controllers. Needless to say, as an automation professional, learning the Logix platform suite is an excellent investment of your time.

Rockwell Automation has provided a wealth of knowledge in their web-based Literature Library, which is the ultimate source of all Logix platform knowledge. Rockwell has created a library of over 10,000 documents that are often difficult to navigate for beginners. *Learning RSLogix 5000 Programming, Second Edition* is in no way a replacement for this resource (this book would need to be 100,000 pages longer) but provides newcomers with a solid foundation in the Logix platform features and Rockwell Automation terminology. By the end of each chapter, links to the relevant Literature Library resources are provided to allow you to dive deeper into the topics covered. The final chapter of this book crystalizes what has been learned in a working control-system example that you can build at home. The final project of this book details all the steps required to create a Rockwell-powered robot bartender from the ground up. By the end of this book, you will have a clear understanding of the capabilities of the Logix platform and be able to quickly navigate the Rockwell Automation Literature Library resources. Moreover, you will have the unique experience of purchasing, building, wiring, and programming a control system from end to end. *Learning RSLogix 5000, Second Edition* provides a gentle introduction to RSLogix 5000/Studio 5000 and the Logix platform. If you are new to **Programming Logic Controller** (**PLC**) programming or have experience with programming other PLC platforms, then this book will provide you with the knowledge of the Rockwell family of controllers and teach you how to become proficient at implementing Logix solutions from the ground up.

Who this book is for

The purpose of this book is to explore the hardware, software, and programming of the Logix platform so that electricians, instrumentation technicians, automation professionals, industrial control system network defenders, and students who are familiar with automation can get up to speed with a minimal investment of time. I intentionally focus on the essential requirements for selecting, configuring, and programming a modern Logix application to get you working with the platform as quickly as possible. Once you have a solid foundation in the Rockwell Automation Integrated Architecture system, you will be able to further your knowledge of any topic using the online Literature Library.

What this book covers

`Chapter 1`, *History of the Rockwell Automation Technologies,* provides a history of industrial control systems and the Rockwell Automation ecosystem. It is important to understand the legacy systems provided by Rockwell Automation because some of them can still be found operating in the field today. Also, it is important to understand the overall Rockwell Automation offering, terminology, and how the platforms we focus on in the book fit into that world. Rockwell Automation's Integrated Architecture system is outlined, as is where ControlLogix fits into their larger strategy.

`Chapter 2`, *Understanding ControlLogix,* introduces the flagship controllers available within Rockwell Automation's Integrated Architecture system. We cover the controller solutions available within the Integrated Architecture system and learn how to make solution architecture decisions. We explore the physical features and diagnostic information available on the ControlLogix cards and investigate the evolution of the platform's firmware. Finally, we learn the differences between the traditional synchronous PLC scan and the Logix asynchronous operating cycle.

`Chapter 3`, *Understanding CompactLogix,* introduces the full line of CompactLogix controllers available within Rockwell's Integrated Architecture system. We learn about the CompactLogix 5480 hybrid controllers, and their unique position in the industrial marketplace. We gain an understanding of the controller solutions available within Integrated Architecture and learn to make CompactLogix architecture decisions. We also learn how to use Rockwell's online resources to identify the modules that are compatible with our solution.

`Chapter 4`, *Understanding SoftLogix,* teaches us about the SoftLogix 5800 controllers, which enable us to create a PC-based Logix controller rack. We learn how to create a virtual rack that houses our virtual controllers and virtual communication modules. We also learn that SoftLogix is another component of Rockwell Automation's Integrated Architecture system and can interface with the other Logix controllers, communication modules, and I/O modules. We also learn that by taking advantage of the computing power of modern PCs, the SoftLogix controllers are capable of processing larger volumes of data and at a higher speed than even the most powerful Logix controller.

`Chapter 5`, *Understanding the Logix Emulate 5000,* teaches us how to leverage a virtual Logix controller and rack to facilitate debugging Logix program code using features such as breakpoints and tracepoints. In this chapter, we create a virtual test rack using similar modules to a physical rack and create a simple test. We learn the critical differences between Emulate 5000 and SoftLogix 5800. We learn how to create a RSLogix Emulate 5000 solution containing modules that are configured in a virtual Logix rack to mimic the end solution.

`Chapter 6`, *Industrial Network Communications,* introduces the various communication technologies available for the Logix platform. The focus of this book is the current state of Rockwell Automation's ControlLogix and CompactLogix controllers; however, we will touch on some legacy communication protocols that you may still find running in the field today. Communications allow us to interface with controllers, racks, and devices on our network. Establishing communications is an important step that enables us to connect with a device and transfer configuration changes and programs. In completing this chapter, you will be familiar with all the Rockwell Automation communication technologies that have been used in the past and that are actively used in the field today.

`Chapter 7`, *Configuring Logix Modules,* enumerates the available modules for the Logix platform, how to configure them, and their usage in a Logix project. We will also include methods for identifying module features by their Logix module catalog numbers and introduce the address tree that a typical I/O module creates. After completing this chapter, you will be able to select and add I/O modules to your projects, modify the module configurations, and reference their real-time values using the recommended best practices.

`Chapter 8`, *Writing Ladder Logic,* looks at the history of ladder logic and the development of the IEC standard programming languages. Then, it jumps into ladder logic programming by creating a simple pump control program. We demonstrate how to buffer inputs and outputs in our ladder logic code and discuss the importance of this process. At the end of the chapter, you will be able to read and write IEC ladder logic for the Logix platform and for multiple other vendors that support IEC standard programming languages.

`Chapter 9`, *Writing Function Blocks,* explores the origins of **Function Block Diagrams** (**FBDs**) in systems engineering and introduces the basic concepts of IEC FBD programming. We learn how to create FBDs by dragging and dropping elements into a sheet in a routine. The way Logix compiles IEC languages down to bytecode is also explored in this chapter. We learn how to wire input and output references to Function Block pins and identify digital and analog connections before monitoring their values online. By the end of the chapter, you will understand how to read and write Function Blocks and be able to apply this knowledge to Rockwell products or products from other industrial automation vendors that conform with the IEC standards.

`Chapter 10`, *Writing Structured Text,* introduces you to the best uses for **Structured Text** (**ST**) within an automation solution. We start by exploring the ST editing environment and then introduce some of the new editing features available in Studio 5000 version 31 and higher. We create a simple ST routine and learn about the powerful syntax of ST code. Then we explore the full range of operators, expressions, instructions, and constructs available in the ST language. You will gain a solid foundation to help you read and write ST code within Logix and within other products that implement the IEC standard ST language.

`Chapter 11`, *Building Sequential Function Charts,* introduces you to **Sequential Function Charts** (**SFCs**) and typical usages within an automation solution. The core elements that make up an SFC are covered, and you will create a simple backwash process routine. We will learn how the usage of SFC varies from industry to industry. You are also shown that there are certain cases where leveraging the IEC SFC construct can greatly simplify the creation and debugging of a program. As with the previous IEC languages covered in this book, we will learn that selecting the appropriate language for your application is like selecting the correct tool to solve the problem you are facing. Although some programmers will only ever write in ladder logic, we learn that there are many advantages of using the full range of IEC languages where appropriate.

`Chapter 12`, *Using Tasks and Programs for Project Organization,* investigates the project organizational units used throughout this book. It details the way a Logix controller executes tasks and how the CPU divides its time based on priority. It introduces the overhead time slice and emphasizes its importance when optimizing a Logix application. Finally, it investigates methods within the Logix platform to monitor and troubleshoot performance issues. By the end of the chapter, you will be able to troubleshoot and optimize Logix project performance on larger solutions.

`Chapter 13`, *Faults and Troubleshooting in Logix,* provides recommendations for improving your troubleshooting capabilities in the Logix platform. It teaches us how to identify and troubleshoot the various types of faults that can occur in a Logix solution. In this chapter, we will use ladder logic to trigger a major fault, and then learn how to trap the major fault and prevent the controller from stopping when it occurs. Finally, we will highlight the FactoryTalk TeamONE app provided by Rockwell Automation for troubleshooting the Logix issues while in the field from a mobile device. By the end of the chapter, you will be comfortable investigating issues and will know where to find additional support if required.

`Chapter 14`, *Understanding Cybersecurity Practices in Logix,* introduces some of the industrial control system cybersecurity resources provided by Rockwell Automation and the tools that can be used to prevent unauthorized views or edits of projects. Rockwell has invested heavily in its cybersecurity practice over the past decade and has come to the table with numerous products, services, and guidance to help protect their customers from cyber threats. By the end of the chapter, you will be familiar with the Rockwell cybersecurity solution landscape and the features that can be enabled in a Logix solution to protect the process and code base.

`Chapter 15`, *Building a Robot Bartender in Logix,* combines the skills we have learned throughout this book into a sample application. This chapter steps through building a complete robot bartender control system from scratch, including configuring the modules, writing the code, and downloading it into our PLC. At the end of this chapter, you will understand how to select the components required for a simple ControlLogix industrial control solution. You will also learn how to wire digital input and output cards for a small control system project. After completing this project, you will gain a deeper understanding of the entire industrial control system building, tuning, and troubleshooting process and will be able to apply this knowledge to real-world control environments.

To get the most out of this book

To get the most out of this book, you should create a Rockwell Support account by visiting the following URL:

`https://www.rockwellautomation.com/account/create-account`

The account is free, and the material we will be reviewing in this chapter is publicly available to anyone who has registered with Rockwell Automation.

You will also need a copy of RSLogix or Studio 5000 to program your project. You can either purchase this from your local distributor or request a time-limited trial version. You can find a local distributor for Rockwell products at the following URL:

`https://locator.rockwellautomation.com/`

Software/hardware covered in the book	OS requirements
Rockwell Automation Studio 5000 Logix Designer v20 - v32	• Windows® 7 Professional (64-bit) with Service Pack 1 • Windows 8.1 Professional (64-bit) with April 2014 Update Roll-up • Windows 10 Professional (64-bit) version 1607 • Windows Server 2008 R2 Standard Edition with Service Pack 1 • Microsoft Windows 8.1 Professional (64-bit) • Windows Server 2012 Standard Edition • Windows Server 2016
Rockwell Automation RSLogix 5000 v10 - v19	• Microsoft Windows XP Professional with Service Pack 2 • Microsoft Windows Server 2003 R2 Standard Edition with Service Pack 1 • Microsoft Windows 2000 Professional with Service Pack 4 • Microsoft Windows XP Home • Microsoft Windows Server 2003 Standard Edition with Service Pack 1 • Microsoft Windows 2000 Professional with Service Pack 1, 2, or 3
ControlLogix CPUs	• 1756-L55 ControlLogix 5555 • 1756-L61 ControlLogix 5561 • 1756-L62 ControlLogix 5562 • 1756-L63 ControlLogix 5563 • 1756-L71 ControlLogix 5571 • 1756-L72 ControlLogix 5571 • 1756-L73 ControlLogix 5571 • 1756-L81 ControlLogix 5581 • 1756-L82 ControlLogix 5582 • 1756-L83 ControlLogix 5583 • 1756-L84 ControlLogix 5584 • 1756-L85 ControlLogix 5585
CompactLogix CPUs	Any CompactLogix controller CPU

To complete the robot bartender build in the last chapter of this book, you will also need to have several tools and purchase some Rockwell Automation equipment. The tools and parts are listed in the final chapter of the book, `Chapter 15`, *Building a Robot Bartender in Logix*.

Download the color images

We also provide a PDF file that has color images of the screenshots/diagrams used in this book. You can download it here: `http://www.packtpub.com/sites/default/files/downloads/9781789532463_ColorImages.pdf`.

Conventions used

There are a number of text conventions used throughout this book.

`CodeInText`: Indicates code words in text, database table names, folder names, filenames, file extensions, pathnames, dummy URLs, user input, and Twitter handles. Here is an example: "Mount the downloaded `WebStorm-10*.dmg` disk image file as another disk in your system."

A block of code is set as follows:

```
(* IF THEN ELSEIF ELSE Example *)
if (TankLevel >= 50) then
   Pump1Permissive [:=] 1;
elseif (TankLevel >= 100) then
   Pump1Permissive [:=] 1;
Pump2Permissive [:=] 1;
else
   Pump1Permissive [:=] 0;
Pump2Permissive [:=] 0;
end_if
```

When we wish to draw your attention to a particular part of a code block, the relevant lines or items are set in bold:

```
(* CASE Example *)
case sequence_number of
   1: StartPump [:=] 1;
      OpenValve [:=] 1;
   2: StartBlower [:=] 1;
   3,4: StartMixer [:=] 1;
   4..10: StartAuger [:=] 1;
else
   StartPump [:=] 0;
end_case;
```

Bold: Indicates a new term, an important word, or words that you see onscreen. For example, words in menus or dialog boxes appear in the text like this. Here is an example: "Click on the **Finish** button, or in RSLogix 5000, click on **OK**."

Warnings or important notes appear like this.

Tips and tricks appear like this.

Get in touch

Feedback from our readers is always welcome.

General feedback: If you have questions about any aspect of this book, mention the book title in the subject of your message and email us at `customercare@packtpub.com`.

Errata: Although we have taken every care to ensure the accuracy of our content, mistakes do happen. If you have found a mistake in this book, we would be grateful if you would report this to us. Please visit `www.packtpub.com/support/errata`, selecting your book, clicking on the Errata Submission Form link, and entering the details.

Piracy: If you come across any illegal copies of our works in any form on the Internet, we would be grateful if you would provide us with the location address or website name. Please contact us at `copyright@packt.com` with a link to the material.

If you are interested in becoming an author: If there is a topic that you have expertise in and you are interested in either writing or contributing to a book, please visit `authors.packtpub.com`.

Reviews

Please leave a review. Once you have read and used this book, why not leave a review on the site that you purchased it from? Potential readers can then see and use your unbiased opinion to make purchase decisions, we at Packt can understand what you think about our products, and our authors can see your feedback on their book. Thank you!

For more information about Packt, please visit `packt.com`.

1
Section 1: Introduction to RSLogix

This section starts by describing the history of the evolution of industrial control systems and of Rockwell Automation. You will then be introduced to the ControlLogix and CompactLogix families of controllers, which utilize RSLogix/Studio 5000 for programming purposes. Finally, we will introduce two virtual controllers that also leverage RSLogix/Studio 5000 for development.

This section comprises the following chapters:

- `Chapter 1`, *The History of the Rockwell Automation Technologies*
- `Chapter 2`, *Understanding ControlLogix*
- `Chapter 3`, *Understanding CompactLogix*
- `Chapter 4`, *Understanding Softlogix*
- `Chapter 5`, *Understanding Logix Emulate 5000*

1

The History of Rockwell Automation Technologies

This book begins with some background history of industrial control systems and the Rockwell Automation ecosystem. It is essential to understand the legacy systems provided by Rockwell Automation because some of them can still be found operating in the field today. Also, it is important to understand the overall Rockwell Automation offering, the terminology, and how the platforms we focus on in this book fit into that world.

In this chapter, we will introduce Rockwell Automation and provide a history of the evolution of their technologies, right up to the Logix platform. Due to the 15- to 20-year industrial controller lifespan, it is not uncommon to encounter older versions of hardware and firmware and so it is critical to understand their evolution.

The following topics will be covered in this chapter:

- Controlling equipment with water, air, and power
- A brief history of Rockwell Automation
- Understanding Integrated Architecture

In the first section of this chapter, we will look at the earliest examples of control systems in history.

Controlling equipment with water, air, and power

The earliest control systems can be traced back to the float regulator mechanisms that were used in Greece around 270 BC. The need for accurate time tracking inspired the Greek water clock (*clepsydra*), which leveraged the simple float regulator to maintain a constant flow of water. The float regulator would maintain the water level in a primary tank at a constant depth; water kept at a constant depth maintained a constant water pressure.

Constant pressure resulted in a constant flow of water through a tube that would fill a secondary tank at a constant rate. The level of the second tank was used to measure time, which was displayed on a dial using a second float. A similar float regulator mechanism is still used in our toilets today. A construct that uses input from another device (float) to maintain a value (water level) is called a feedback controller.

The following diagram details the components of a simple Greek water clock (*clepsydra*):

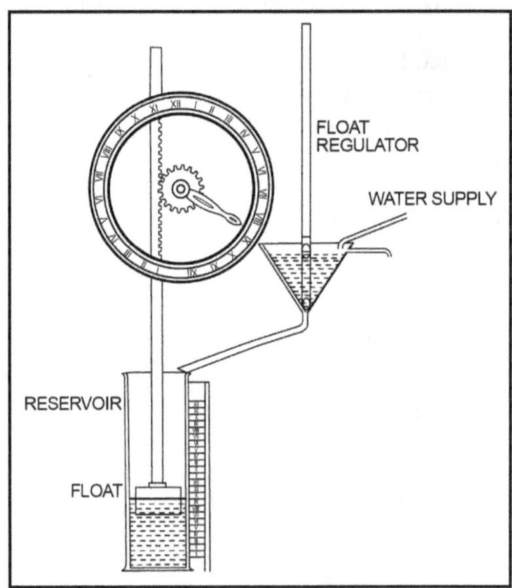

In the next section, we will discuss the advent of pneumatics and its place within industrial control systems.

The rise of pneumatics

The Greeks also invented a more sophisticated feedback control mechanism that utilized steam or compressed air, rather than water, called **pneumatics**. The Greek mathematician Hero of Alexandria created inventions that were powered by steam or the wind. German physicist Otto von Guericke (1602 – 1686) was the first to invent a vacuum pump that can draw out air or gas from the attached vessel. After the industrial revolution, the air pressure from pneumatics was used as a method of activation and signal transmission within control systems. In the 1950s and 1960s, pneumatics signal transmission started to be replaced by electric signal transmission, which gave rise to the modern control systems we see today. However, it is not uncommon to see pneumatics still used today in a wide range of applications. Today, pneumatics are still a ubiquitous part of many **Heating Ventilation and Air Conditioning** (**HVAC**) systems.

The following diagram illustrates a typical pneumatic HVAC heating system (*image courtesy of Spirax Sarco Limited*):

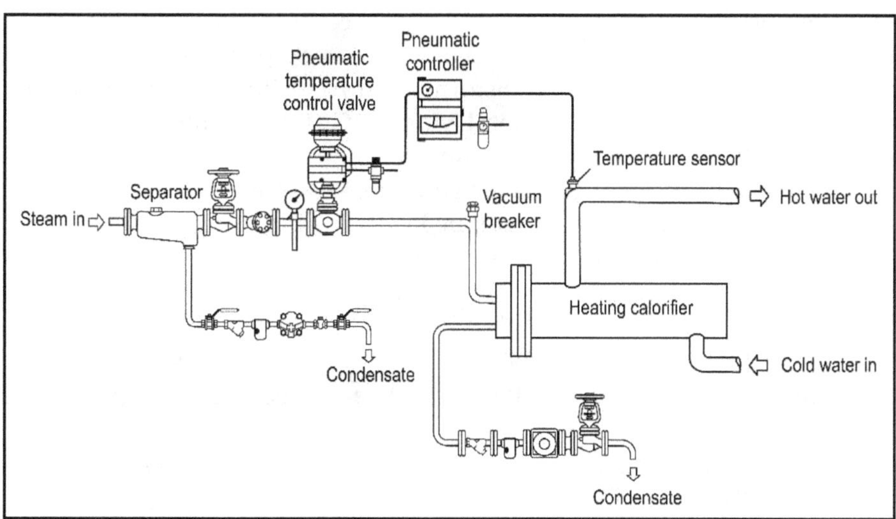

The preceding diagram shows how a pneumatic controller is used to regulate the temperature of a steam heating system using a pneumatic temperature control valve based on the feedback loop from the temperature sensor.

In the next section, we will introduce the electromechanical relay and discuss how it changed industrial automation forever.

Understanding electric relay logic

The electromechanical relay was first created in 1835 by Joseph Henry (1797 – 1878). Although Joseph Henry built and demonstrated the first mechanical relay, he had no intention of applying it to a practical application. The relay was used to demonstrate the phenomenon of self-inductance and mutual inductance to his students. In 1836, when Samuel F. B. Morse learned of the electromechanical relay, he began to consider its potential application for communications and controlling machinery.

Samuel Morse soon used Henry's relay device to carry morse code signals over long distances of wire. As electromechanical relays began to be widely adopted to control electrical equipment, a standard method of documenting the relay wiring was required. This led to the advent of ladder diagrams, which were used to document the convoluted logic of these systems so that they could be maintained and upgraded.

Control systems evolved into a complex mixture of industrial relays, rotary drum sequencers, pneumatic plunger timers, counters, motors, push buttons, selector switches, limit switches, and valves, all connected together and controlled using hundreds or thousands of failure-prone electromechanical relays. As complex control systems evolved and were maintained, they inevitably transformed into a *rat's nest* of wires, leading to outages and extended turnarounds. **General Motors** (**GM**) had grown tired of the shortcomings of hardwired relay logic within their automotive factories and were aware of advances in solid-state computers. So, as the story goes, on New Year's Day 1968, they detailed a specification for what would later be known as the **Programmable Logic Controller** (**PLC**). GM's requirements were as follows:

- Competitively priced with a traditional relay logic system
- Leveraging a solid-state system that is flexible, such as a computer
- Programmed in a manner that aligns with accepted relay ladder engineering diagrams
- Robust enough to work in industrial environments where they would be exposed to dirt, moisture, electromagnetism, and vibration
- Modular and expandable to support a wide range of process sizes and types

We have now covered the past 2,000 years of industrial automation evolution. In the next section, we will introduce Rockwell Automation and detail their contributions to the automation industry.

A brief history of Rockwell Automation

In 1901, while working for Milwaukee Electric, Lynde Bradley (a teenager at the time) devised a better way to build the controllers that regulate motor speed. He soon quit his job, secured a small $1,000 investment from his lifelong friend, Dr. Stanton Allen, and co-founded the Allen-Bradley company with his brother, Harry Bradley, in 1903. The primary focus of Allen-Bradley was, for several decades, motor controllers, until they received an unusual request from GM in 1968 to build a system to replace their hardwired relay logic with something more dynamic—a standard machine controller.

Program Data Quantizer II and the Programmable Matrix Controller

Allen-Bradley responded to GM's request with two solutions—first, a large, difficult-to-program, expensive minicomputer-based **Program Data Quantizer** (**PDQ**) II in 1970 and later, the smaller and easier-to-program **Programmable Matrix Controller** (**PMC**) in 1971. The PMC was an early precursor to the modern PLC, and Allen-Bradley later adopted the term *PLC* for future releases of their automation products.

Allen-Bradley used the term PLC, rather than **programmable controller**, which was the previously used industry-accepted term. PLC became the standard moving forward as PCs became incorporated into control systems.

Although Allen-Bradley did not win the GM bid, the PMC continued to evolve until the release of the PLC-2. GM awarded the contract to Dick Morley and his company, Bedford and Associates. Dick Morely spun off a new company, named Modicon, and started to sell a PLC product called the Modicon 084 (named because it was prototype #84) based on this initial design.

PLC-2 controllers

Allen-Bradley introduced their very first PLC (PLC-1) in 1970, and it continued to evolve until the release of the PLC-2 in 1978. The PLC-2 played a vital role in the Space Shuttle program as Rockwell International was a primary contractor. The PLC-2/20 and many other AB controls were used in the manufacturing and testing of the 153-foot one-time-use tank, which fueled and provided structure to the shuttle.

The PLC-2 family of processors featured three versions:

- PLC-2/10
- PLC-2/20
- PLC-2/30

The more-powerful PLC-2 processors ran on a 1772-LP3D4 processor running at 47 to 63 Hz and supporting up to 16 K (16 data bits) of memory capacity.

The following diagram depicts the original PLC-2/30 controller:

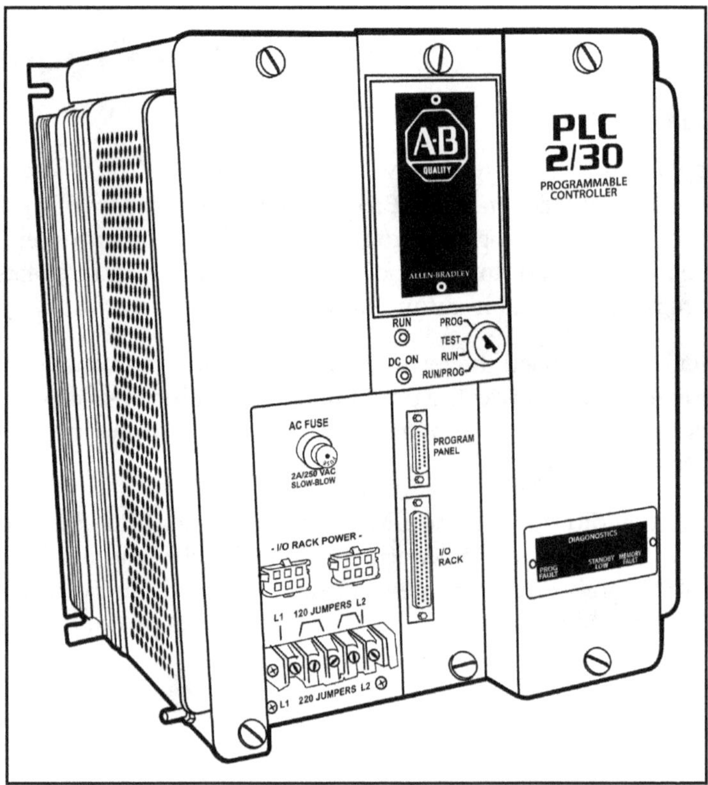

It is possible that a few PLC-2/30s or PLC-2/20s could still be found in the field today. The PLC-2 can be programmed using 32-bit operating systems, such as Windows 8. The PLC-2 can be programmed using the 6200 programming terminal or **Application Interface** (**AI**) programming version 6.24 and a serial interface. The Rockwell AI software is an MS-DOS-based programming interface that provides a text-based graphical interface for viewing and editing ladder logic.

In the next section, we will discuss the third PLC created by Allen-Bradley—the PLC-3.

PLC-3 controllers

The PLC-3 was introduced in 1981 (the same year that the first Space Shuttle launched) and provided significant scalability increase for control systems. The PLC-3 was usually packaged with a programming terminal, much like the PLC-2. The PLC-3 supported up to 128 K (16 data bits) of memory capacity.

The following diagram depicts the Allen-Bradley PLC-3 controller unit, which featured a numeric keypad for programming and adjustments:

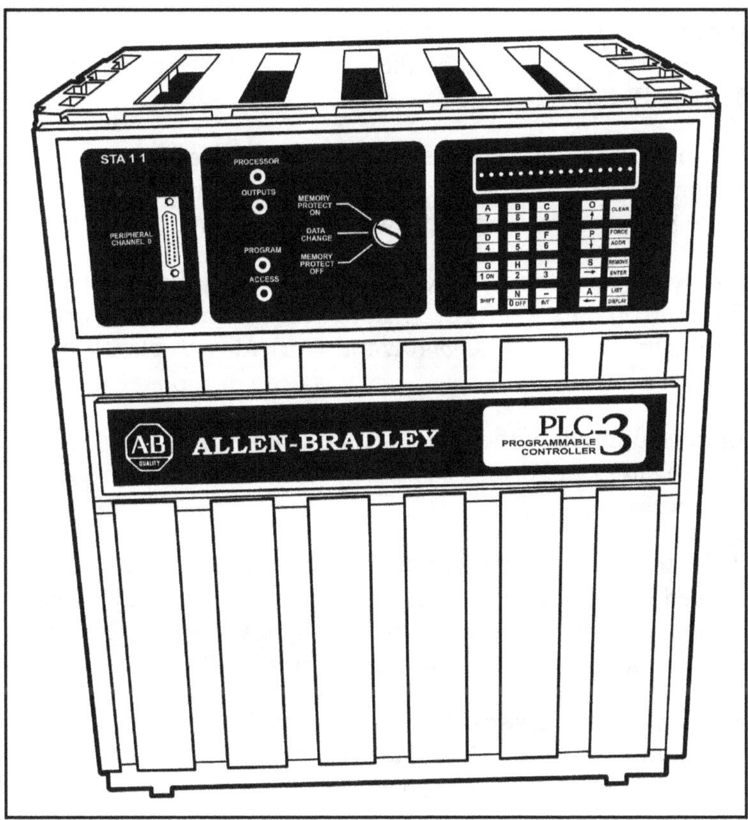

In the following section, we will introduce the robust PLC-5 platform, which replaced the PLC-3 and can still be found operating in some plants today.

PLC-5 controllers

The 1785 catalog number PLC-5 was launched in 1986 based on the Motorola 68000 32-bit CISC microprocessor and was designed to scale and support both centralized and distributed control architectures. Allen-Bradley defined a centralized architecture design as one that featured a single processor managing a plant where a distributed architecture contained multiple processors and user interfaces to manage a plant.

At the time of its release, a PLC-5 network would likely be managed by a VAX/VMS host or a panel-view operator terminal and programmed using dedicated programming terminal computers engineered by Allen-Bradley. As the PLC-5 platform evolved, it later adopted Ethernet connectivity (PLC-5/20E, PLC-5/40E, and PLC-5/80E) using a 15-pin Ethernet port, the first Allen-Bradley PLCs to do so.

Around the same time as the PLC-5 release in 1985, Allen-Bradley was acquired by Rockwell International (now known as Rockwell Automation), but the Allen-Bradley name and logo can still be found on many of Rockwell Automation's products.

The PLC-5 was an extremely robust platform and although it has been discontinued and replaced with the ControlLogix platform by Rockwell, it continues to operate in many plants. I have personally owned a PLC-5/40E and worked with plants that still operate these devices today.

Over the years of development of the PLC-5, Allen-Bradley released 15 versions of the platform, which were later categorized by Rockwell as Classic PLC-5 processors and Enhanced PLC-5 processors.

PLC-5 processors that contain an *E* after the series number are Ethernet-enabled (for example, PLC-5/20E, PLC-5/40E, and PLC-5/80E). PLC-5 processors that contain an *L* after the series number also support an extended local I/O connection (for example, PLC-5/40L and PLC-5/60L).

The PLC-5 Classic family of processors leveraged **DataHighway Plus** (**DH+**) and remote I/O for its communications. The PLC-5 Enhanced family of processors also had serial communications and Ethernet communications. Although the early programming software for the PLC-5 was DOS-based, Allen-Bradley eventually created a Windows-based programming environment for the PLC-5, called RSLogix5. The PLC-5 rack was entirely made of metal, making it very heavy and giving it an industrial feel. The following diagram depicts the PLC-5 rack with a processor and some I/O cards:

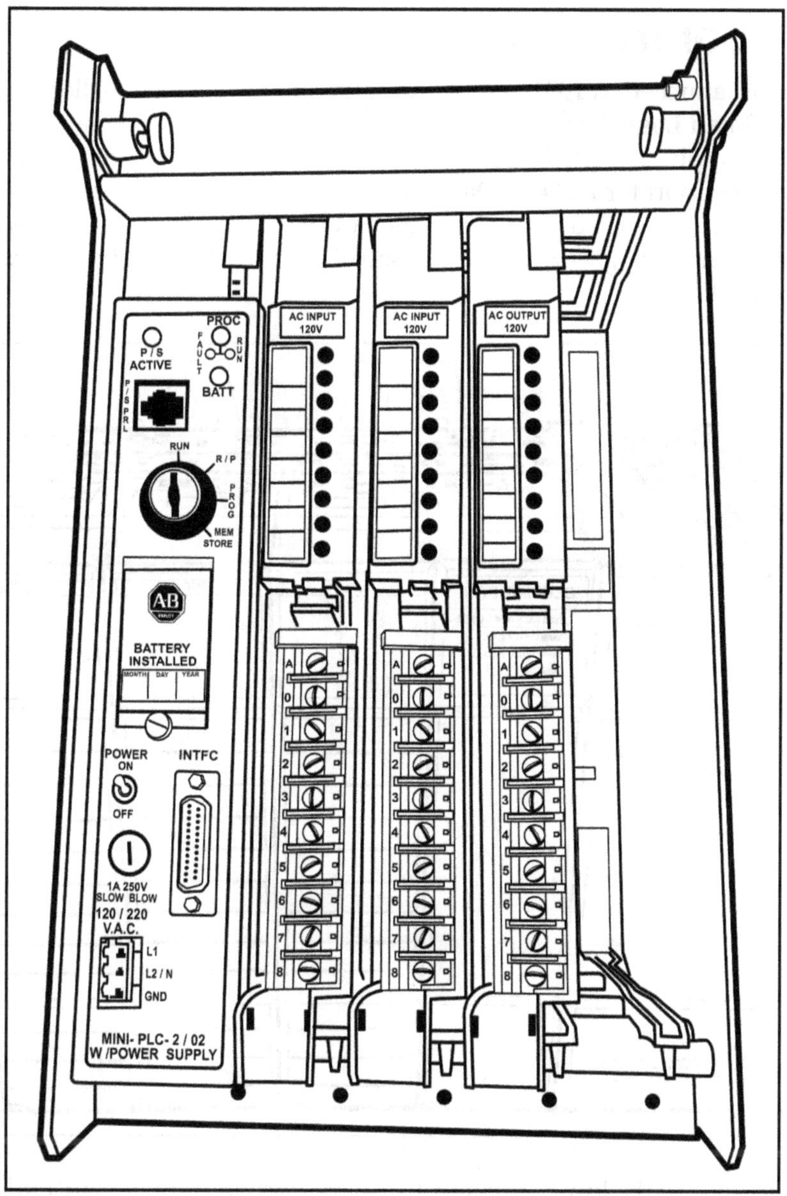

In the next section, we will discuss Allen-Bradley's first foray into the midsize control system market with the SLC-500 controller.

SLC-500 controllers

The SLC-500 was launched in 1991 and was designed to be used in smaller plants; in fact, **SLC** stands for **Small Logic Controller**. The SLC-500 is an integrated platform that contains the CPU, power supply, and I/O in a single unit. The SLC-500 platform eventually received communications support for DH485 (Data Highway) and Ethernet. The Allen-Bradley RSLogix 500 software was used to program the SLC-500s. The SLC-500 has been replaced with the newer CompactLogix 5370 or 5380 control platforms. The following is a diagram of the SLC-500 controller:

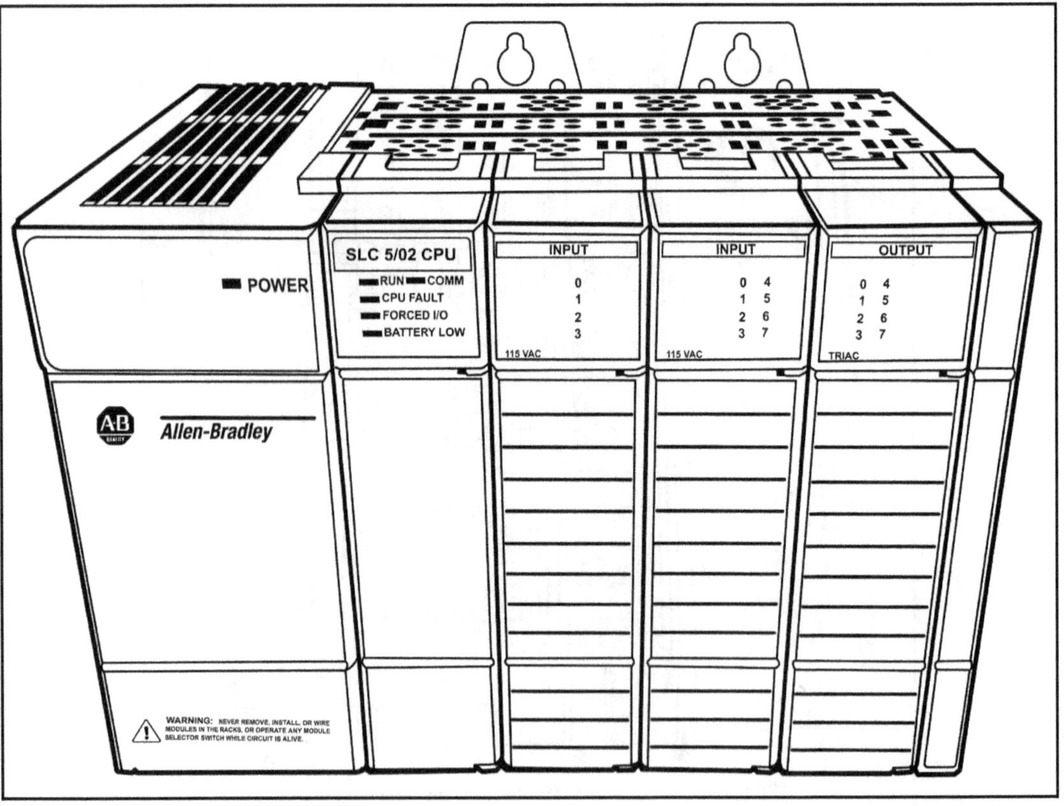

Next, we will introduce the low-cost control system solution from Allen-Bradley, the MicroLogix controller.

MicroLogix

MicroLogix and Flex I/O were launched in 1994. MicroLogix used the RSLogix 500 software for programming their PLCs (the same software used for the SLC controller family). The first MicroLogix unit to be introduced was the MicroLogix 100 PLC, which was released with several different combinations of I/O. Its creation was a response to the need for a low-cost automation solution with a limited feature set. The MicroLogix controller did not originally use a rack and modular cards, but rather a fixed set of input and output channels.

The following is a diagram of a Rockwell MicroLogix controller:

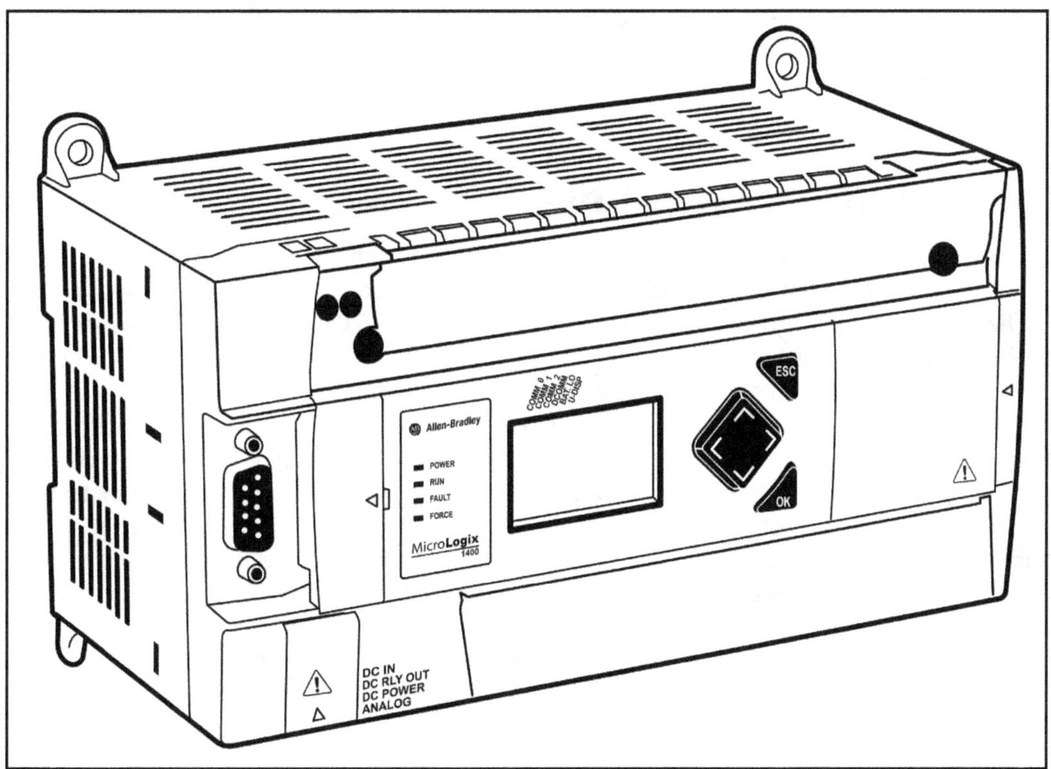

Over the years, Rockwell also introduced other new MicroLogix controllers, such as the Bulletin 1763 MicroLogix 1100, the Bulletin 1762 MicroLogix 1200, and the Bulletin 1766 MicroLogix 1400 series. The 1100, 1200, and 1400 series controllers have reached their end of life and have been replaced with the Micro800 series or CompactLogix series of controllers.

What is a Rockwell Bulletin number? A Bulletin is a brief posting of public information. Product lines within Rockwell are associated with a Bulletin number. A Bulletin and its associated number are posted when a new semiconductor product starts development within Rockwell. The Bulletin number is the internal project number associated with a product line during research and development within Rockwell. The Bulletin number is maintained after the product is released.

You can always check the end-of-life status of a particular product by going to the Rockwell product life cycle page at `https://www.rockwellautomation.com/global/support/product-compatibility-migration/lifecycle-status/overview.page`.

Now, we are ready to introduce the ControlLogix line of controllers, which are the primary focus of this book.

ControlLogix controllers

The ControlLogix controller was first launched in 1997 as a replacement for Allen-Bradley's previous large-scale control platform—the PLC-5. The ControlLogix platform includes the Bulletin 1756 ControlLogix 5550 controller, the Bulletin 1756 ControlLogix I/O modules, and the RSLogix 5000 programming software platform (now referred to as Logix Designer). ControlLogix represented a significant technological step forward, which included a 32-bit ARM-6 RISC-core microprocessor and the ABrisc Boolean processor combined with a bus interface on the same silicon chip. At launch, the Series 5 (also referred to as L5 and ControlLogix 5550) ControlLogix controllers were able to execute code *three* times faster than the PLC-5. The L5 controller is considered to be a **Programmable Automation Controller** (**PAC**), rather than a traditional PLC, due to its modern design, power, and capabilities beyond a traditional PLC (such as motion control, advanced networking, batching, and sequential control). The ControlLogix platform is built on the ControlBus backplane, which performs like a mini-network and allows devices to be **Removed or Inserted Under Power** (**RIUP**).

Warning – removing modules while under power can create an arc and have disastrous consequences in explosive environments.

The L5 has since been retired from the lineup, so we will focus on the newer L6 and L7 controllers in this book. Throughout this book, we will refer to the ControlLogix controllers as PACs, which are the modern-day equivalent of PLCs. In 2002, the Bulletin 1756 ControlLogix L6 processor was released with a more powerful processor, more memory, and the CompactFlash non-volatile memory card was added to the lineup.

Even though the ControlLogix platform is approaching its 20th birthday, it is still in the early stages of its product life cycle. For example, Allen-Bradley's 1747 series SLC-500 family, which was introduced in 1989, is still available for sale today. Although it is no longer actively developed, the SLC-500 represents a product life in excess of 25 years.

ControlLogix represents a standard control engine with a standard development environment and tight integration between the programming software, controller, and I/O modules. This close integration greatly reduces the automation engineering development time and cost. The following diagram is of the L5 (Logix5550) controller, which was the very first ControlLogix processor card:

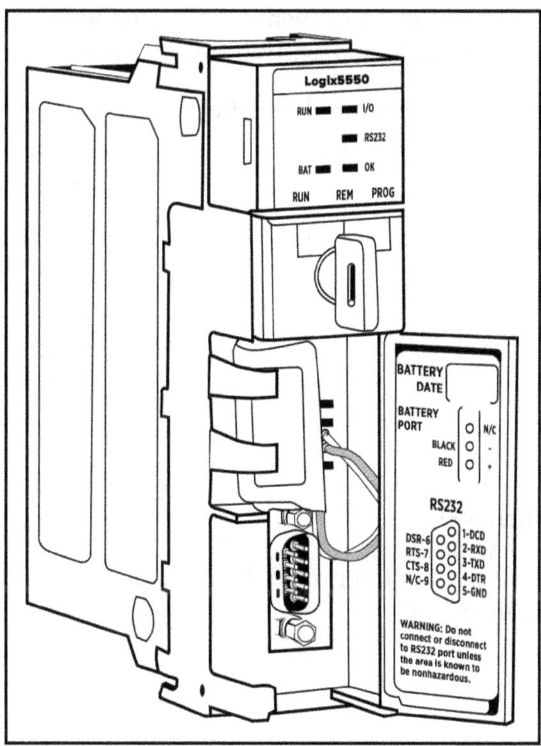

In the following section, we will introduce Rockwell Automation's Integrated Architecture product strategy and show you how the ControlLogix family fits into this bigger picture.

Understanding Integrated Architecture

Like many other vendors, Rockwell Automation has recently rebranded and reorganized its offering. The ControlLogix family is part of Rockwell Automation's larger solution offering, called Integrated Architecture. Integrated Architecture is a relatively new term in the world of Rockwell Automation, but the concept has been in place for quite some time. It represents a convergence of the control and information systems within an operating environment. We have seen a continuous increase in demand for operational information to be provided to the corporate information system in real time to fulfill maintenance needs, environmental reporting, accounting, and other corporate requirements. At the same time, we have seen operational technology move from proprietary protocols and data access technology to traditional IT technologies, such as TCP/IP and Ethernet. The promise of Integrated Architecture is the ability to implement plant-wide optimization quickly, reduce technical project risk, increase machine performance, and improve long-term reliability.

The five core technologies of the Integrated Architecture PAC product line include the following:

- ControlLogix
- CompactLogix
- GuardLogix
- DriveLogix
- SoftLogix
- MicroLogix/Micro800

The following diagram outlines the Integrated Architecture structure and where ControlLogix fits into the mix:

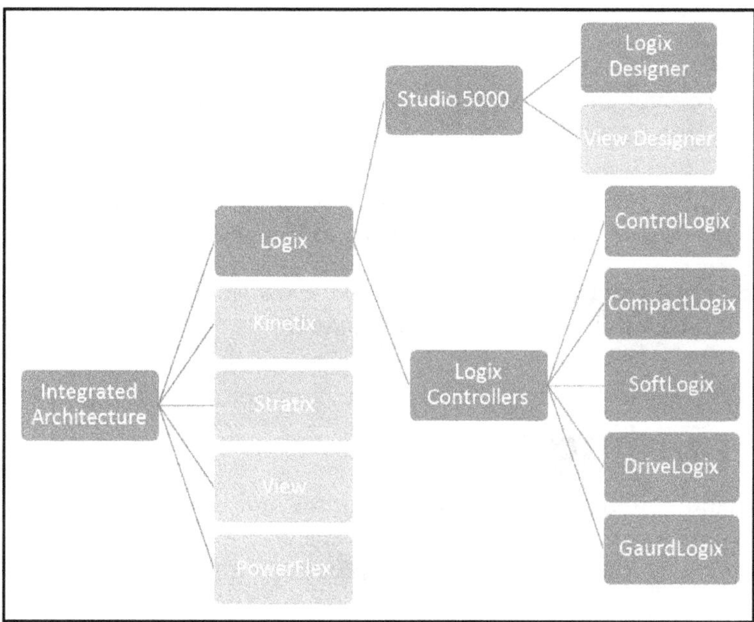

FlexLogix (Bulletin 1794) controllers were also part of the Logix PAC family that was used to communicate PLC-5 and SLC-500 Flex I/O blocks. However, FlexLogix has now been retired from the lineup, so it will not be covered in this book. However, 1794 Flex I/O racks continue to be supported, so these will be discussed.

The product formally known as RSLogix 5000 (used for programming ControlLogix and CompactLogix controllers) is now included within the Automation Engineering and Design software suite called Studio 5000 and is now referred to as Logix Designer. For the remainder of this book, we will refer to Logix Designer, which is essentially just the newest version of RSLogix 5000.

Rockwell's rebranding of Studio 5000 has also generated several other products and features. One such feature is the Connected Components Workbench software, which aims to streamline the development of the overall control system by incorporating PLC programming, device configuration, and HMI editing into a single product offering. We will not touch on the Connected Components Workbench software in this book, but it is important to be aware of its role in the Rockwell product ecosystem.

Summary

In this chapter, we delved into the history of industrial automation, starting with the Greek water clock and moving right up to modern control systems. We learned about the controllers and product lines that were developed by Allen-Bradley and Rockwell Automation over the years and discussed their evolution. We also touched on the modern controller solutions that are part of Studio 5000 and Integrated Architecture.

In the next chapter, we will take a deep dive into the ControlLogix platform and start to work with modern Rockwell Automation controllers.

Further reading

For more information on the history of Allen-Bradley and Rockwell Automation, take a look at the *Our History* section of the Rockwell website at `https://www.rockwellautomation.com/en_NA/about-us/overview.page?pagetitle=Our-History`.

Questions

The following questions can be used to test your retention of the concepts introduced in this chapter. You can find the answers to these questions in the back of the book under *Assessments*:

1. What device is considered to be one of the first control systems?
2. What device did Samuel F. B. Morse create in 1836 that is still widely used in automation systems today?
3. What was the name of the company started by Lynde Bradley and Harry Bradley in 1903?
4. What was the name of the device created as a result of the GM request for information to replace hardwired relay logic in 1968?
5. What PLC platform was launched in 1991 that was designed to be used in smaller plants and stands for Small Logic Controller?
6. What PLC platform was launched in 1997 as a replacement for Allen-Bradley's previous large-scale control platform, the PLC-5?
7. What is the Rockwell Automation umbrella term for integrated convergence of the control and information systems within an operational environment?

2 Understanding ControlLogix

When the ControlLogix controller was launched in 1997, it represented a significant technological step forward for industrial control systems. The ControlLogix platform is built on the ControlBus backplane, which performs like a mini-network and allows devices to be **Removed or Inserted Under Power** (**RIUP**). The L5 has since been discontinued (as has the L6) from the lineup, so we will focus on the newer L7 and L8 controllers in this book. Throughout this book, we will refer to the ControlLogix controllers as PACs, which is the modern-day equivalent of PLCs.

This chapter will cover the following topics:

- Introducing ControlLogix controllers
- Selecting a ControlLogix controller
- Introducing GuardLogix safety controllers
- Introducing extreme environment controllers
- Understanding the ControlLogix operating cycle

In the first section of this chapter, we will review the evolution of the ControlLogix platform over the years.

Technical requirements

To complete this chapter, you need to create a Rockwell Automation support account by going to `https://www.rockwellautomation.com/account/create-account`.

Creating an account is free, and the material we will refer to in this chapter is publicly available to anyone who has registered with Rockwell Automation.

You will also need a copy of RSLogix or Studio 5000 to program your project. You can either purchase this from your local distributor or request a time-limited trial version. You can find a local distributor for Rockwell Automation products at `https://locator.rockwellautomation.com/`.

Introducing ControlLogix controllers

ControlLogix consists of a common control engine with a common development environment and tight integration between the programming software, controller, and I/O modules. This close integration greatly reduces the automation engineering development time and cost.

Even though the ControlLogix platform is over 20 years old, it is still in the early stages of its product life cycle. For example, Allen-Bradley's 1747 series SLC-500 family, which was introduced in 1989, is still under support today. Although it is no longer actively developed, the SLC-500 represents a product life in excess of 25 years.

The following is a diagram that details the look of a typical ControlLogix L5 processor card:

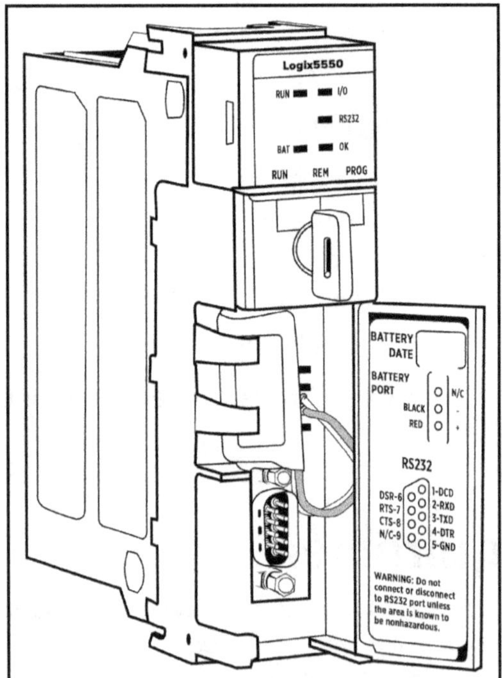

We will next discuss the following ControlLogix controllers in the upcoming subtopics:

- ControlLogix Series 6 controllers (L6)
- ControlLogix Series 7 controllers (L7)
- ControlLogix Series 8 controllers (L8)

ControlLogix Series 6 controllers (L6)

In 2002, the Bulletin 1756 ControlLogix L6 processor was released with a more powerful processor and more memory, and the CompactFlash non-volatile memory card was added to the lineup. The ControlLogix L6 came in two different flavors—**Series A** and **Series B**. Series A processors used volatile memory and required a battery to maintain the program and user memory when power to the controller was disconnected. The Series B processor had internal non-volatile memory, which did not require a battery to maintain the current program.

The following photo shows a typical ControlLogix L6 processor card:

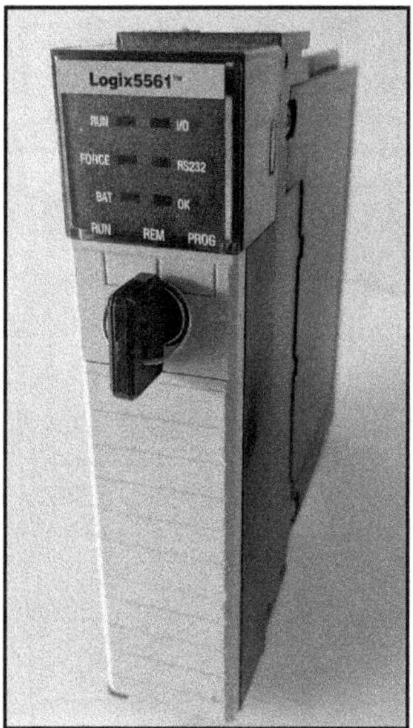

In the next section, we will introduce the Series 7 ControlLogix controller, also known as the L7.

ControlLogix Series 7 controllers (L7)

In 2010, Rockwell Automation launched the Series 7 (also referred to as L7 and ControlLogix 5570) controllers.

The following is a diagram of the ControlLogix 5573 controller, featuring the four-ASCII-character LCDs and an SD card slot:

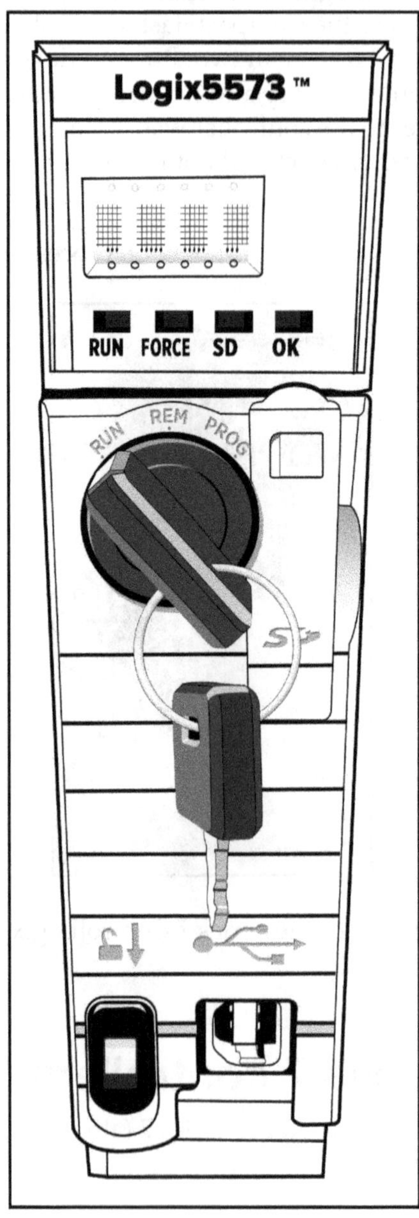

The ControlLogix Series 7 controller featured the following enhancements over the Series 6 (L6) controllers:

- Twice the performance capability due to a more powerful dual-core CPU.
- Adoption of modern **Synchronous Dynamic Random Access Memory (SDRAM)** memory.
- The replacement of the nine-pin serial port with a USB 2.0 port (programs transfer 200 times faster over USB 2.0 than serial).
- The replacement of the CompactFlash memory card with an SD memory card.
- The replacement of the lithium battery with the capacitor-based **Energy Storage Module** (**ESM**). The ESM provides power to the controller in the event of a power loss to allow it to copy the contents of its memory from volatile memory to the onboard non-volatile memory. The ESM eliminates the issue with L6 series controllers where they would lose the program after a few weeks without power once the battery was completely drained.
- The ability to store program comments and tag descriptions on the controller (firmware v21 and higher).
- Addition of the onboard four-character display.

We have learned in this section that there are many improvements in the L7 controllers over the L6, providing more power and reliability. In the following section, we will introduce the latest ControlLogix controller series, known as the L8.

ControlLogix Series 8 controllers (L8)

In 2015, Rockwell Automation released a new series of faster controllers called Series 8 (also referred to as L8 and ControlLogix 5580). The L8 model provides several improvements over the L7 series of controller, including the following:

- A CPU performance increase in the range of 5 to 20 times compared to the L7 series
- 20% more memory over the L7 series
- Larger memory cards (SD cards), with 2 GB cards as opposed to the 1 GB models that come with the L7 series
- A 10-fold increase in network speed with support of up to 1 GB (compared to the 100 MB connection supported by the L7 series)
- Support for CIP Security (more information on this is covered in `Chapter 14`, *Understanding Cybersecurity Practices in Logix*)

Finally, because the L8 controllers have an Ethernet/IP card integrated into the controller itself, there is no need to purchase a separate 1756-ENBT (Ethernet/IP card), which makes the L8 slightly cheaper than purchasing an L7. The following diagram is of a ControlLogix 5585E and features the front connection ports for Ethernet and USB:

In the next section, we will cover some of the data points you will need when selecting a ControlLogix controller.

Selecting a ControlLogix controller

In this section, we will detail the Logix software versions that are compatible with the various ControlLogix series and the currently active series.

When selecting a ControlLogix controller, it is important to consider the following:

- The supported Logix Designer software versions
- The processing requirements of your current application and future expansion
- The memory requirements of your current application and future expansion

ControlLogix Series 6, 7, and 8 controllers and their software version compatibilities are detailed as follows:

Controller	Memory	Minimum Version	Maximum Version	Product Status
Series 5 (L5)				
1756-L1	2 MB	v4	v13	Discontinued
1756-L53	2 MB	v6	v11	Discontinued
1756-L55	2 MB	v6	v16	Discontinued
Series 6 (L6)				
1756-L61	2 MB	v12	v20	Discontinued
1756-L62	4 MB	v12	v20	Discontinued
1756-L63	8 MB	v10	v20	Discontinued
1756-L64	16 MB	v16	v20	Discontinued
1756-L65	32 MB	v17	v20	Discontinued
Series 7 (L7)				
1756-L71	2 MB	v18		Active
1756-L72	4 MB	v19		Active
1756-L73	8 MB	v18		Active
1756-L74	16 MB	v19		Active
1756-L75	32 MB	v20		Active
Series 8 (L8)				
1756-L81	3 MB	v29		Active
1756-L82	5 MB	v29		Active
1756-L83	10 MB	v28		Active
1756-L84	20 MB	v29		Active
1756-L85	40 MB	v28		Active

Rockwell classifies their products' life cycle statuses using the following terminology:

- **Active**: Most current/latest offering within a product category.
- **Active Mature**: A product that is still fully supported, but a newer product or family exists that can directly replace it.
- **End of Life**: A product discontinued date has been announced and the customer should consider migrations and last-time buys. The product can still be purchased until the official discontinued date, although inventory outages on specific items may occur.
- **Discontinued**: The product is no longer manufactured and it is unlikely that you can purchase the product (and if you can, it will be very expensive). Support, repair, or exchange services may still be available.

As you can see, the Series 6 (L6) controller has been discontinued. However, I will continue to reference this model as I still personally use this model in my own lab. Furthermore, it is relatively easy to find these controllers on eBay for your own testing and development projects.

It is important to note that the Series 6 (L6) controllers are not supported in version 21 and higher of Studio 5000 Logix Designer.

Now that we have covered the various Logix controller hardware at a high level, let's take a look at the supporting software and firmware versions in the following section.

ControlLogix software and firmware

Due to the long lifespan of most industrial PACs, it is common to encounter controllers that still run legacy firmware. Controller firmware versions and RSLogix 5000 and Logix Designer versions go hand in hand. If you are working on ControlLogix or a CompactLogix controller that is running firmware version 13.03, you should use RSLogix 5000 version 13.03 to program it. As updating firmware can introduce process downtime, it is important to understand and work with the capabilities of older firmware and software versions of RSLogix 5000 and Logix Designer.

The following table details some of the major changes with each firmware release over the past two decades of ControlLogix:

Version	Year	Notes
1	1997	Cross-reference support, RSLinx Version 2.0 support, and L5x.
2	1998	Trending, position and time camming, 1794 FLEX I/O, and RSWho.
3 and 4	1998	Internal builds, not released to the public.
5	1998	SERCOS, the **Quick View** pane, function block diagrams, and FLEX EX.
6	1999	FlexLogix support and SoftLogix support.
7	2000	Windows 2000 support, CompactLogix support, and Ethernet/IP support.
8	2001	ControlLogix redundancy, DH485, and non-volatile memory L55.
9	2001	SERCOS drive support with the 1756-M08SE module.
10	2002	ControlLogix 5563 controller support.
11	2002	**Sequential Function Chart** (**SFC**), **Structured Text** (**ST**), **Function Blocks Diagram**(**FBD**) online editing, SoftLogix 5800, and point I/O support.
12	2003	RSLogix Emulate 5000, event tasks, CompactLogix support, and **Compare**.
13	2004	SFC online editing, ST online editing, and LD Import/Export.
14	2004	GM-only build.
15	2005	S88, adds 1756 I/O modules during runtime, and **User-Defined Data Type** (**UDT**).
16	2007	User-defined **Add-On Instructions** (**AOI**) and ControlLogix 1756-L64.
17	2008	Windows Vista free-to-download demo and advanced process control.
18	2010	The 1756-L73 and 1756-L75 controllers, CIP motion, CIP SYNC, and CompactLogix safety.
19	2010	Windows 7 support, 1756-L72, 1756-L74, and integrated motion Ethernet/IP.
20	2012	1756-L71, support to 200 to 10,000 I/O points, and GuardLogix.
		Studio 5000–Logix Designer
21	2013	Logix Designer, alarm log, and comments and descriptions stored in PAC.

22	2014	Internal build, not released to the public.
23	2014	Controller firmware updates and fixes.
24	2014	Windows 8, the **Logical Organizer** view, the **Program** parameter, and merge improved.
25	2015	Internal version only.
26	2015	Primarily bug fixes.
27	2015	The **Motion Coordinate Linear Move** (**MCLM**) instruction **Merge All** changed and **HMI Button Control** (**HMIBC**) allows tighter integration with PanelView.
28	2015	Added support for L83 and L85. The ISA-88 batch sequence manager was added.
29	2016	Added support for L81, L82, and L84. `CIP MSG to SELF` to disable diagnostic features, and improved capacity calculations and instruction-based alarms.
30	2016	Added a simplified method for counting controller Ethernet/IP resources.
31	2018	CIP energy for monitoring energy usage and tag-based alarms.
32	2018	Enhanced diagnostics on controller web pages, new thermal fault code 37, and CIP security enhancements.

Now that we have covered a brief overview of the changes introduced in each Logix firmware version, in the next section, we will detail the meaning of the lights, key switches, and LED displays on the controller CPUs.

Key switches, lights, and character displays

All of the ControlLogix family controllers have status lights and keys, and the L7 and L8 series even have four character displays. Let's now take a look at what the various status codes and messages mean and what information they provide to operators.

The following diagram shows the L5 controller status lights and key positions:

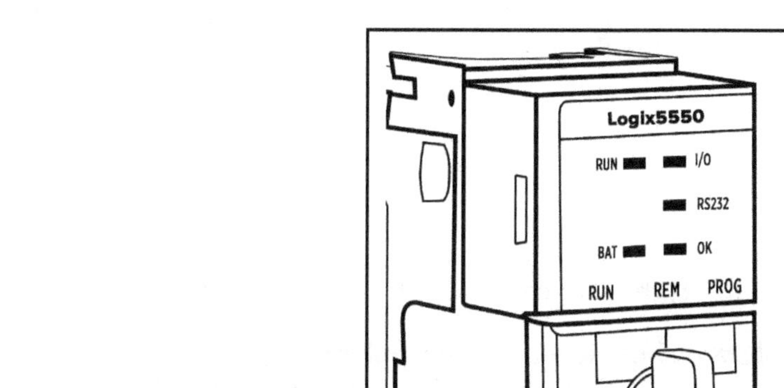

In the next section, we will detail the meaning of each of the three key position values illustrated in the previous diagram (**RUN**, **REM**, and **PROG**).

Key switches

Key switches control the operating mode of a PLC. A key is used to change the operating mode because changing the mode can potentially interrupt a running process.

All ControlLogix controllers have a key switch with the following three positions:

- **RUN**: While the key switch is in **RUN** mode, logic is executing, inputs are being read, logic is being scanned, and outputs are actively being controlled. Values in the program can be changed through the data monitor or by using the I/O force table. The program and operating mode and program logic cannot be changed remotely while the key switch is in **RUN** mode.
- **REM (remote)**: Selecting **REM** mode allows the processor run mode and logic to be changed remotely using an Ethernet or serial connection while the PLC is online. The controller still continues to run as it would normally in **RUN** mode.
- **PROG (program)**: When the key switch is in **PROG** mode, the program logic stops executing, outputs are not controlled, and the program can be edited remotely using a serial or Ethernet connection. The health LED will flash green on any output module in your rack when the CPU is in **PROG** mode.

Internally, within the Studio 5000 software, there is also a test mode, where inputs are read, logic is scanned, and outputs are controlled but are ignored by the actual I/O modules.

Turning the key from **RUN** or **REM** to **PROG** will cause the PLC to stop the running process. This could have disastrous consequences depending on the nature of the process being controlled. It is best to avoid turning the key while working on a running process just in case you accidentally bump it to **PROG** mode. Furthermore, it is also possible, when you switch to **PROG** mode, that the output that is currently active will remain on.

Lights

There are several different status lights that appear on ControlLogix controllers:

- **RUN**: When the **RUN** status light is off, the controller is in program or test mode. When the **RUN** status light is steady green, the controller is in **RUN** mode.
- **I/O**: When the **I/O** light is off, this means that either there are no I/O devices configured in the controller's program or no program has been loaded into the controller. When the **I/O** light is solid green, the controller is communicating with its configured I/O devices. When the **I/O** light flashes green, this indicates that one or more of the configured I/O devices are not responding. A flashing red **I/O** light indicates that a chassis fault exists and it may need to be replaced.
- **RS232**: The **RS232** indicator shows whether the serial port is in use. The indicator light will be off if there is no serial activity but will flash green when a serial connection is active.
- **BAT**: The **BAT** indicator shows the charge of the battery and the status of the program that is saving to non-volatile memory. The **BAT** indicator will shine green when the program is being stored in non-volatile memory during power down. The **BAT** indicator will glow red when the battery is not installed or is 95% discharged.
- **FORCE**: The **FORCE** indicator shows whether I/O forces are active or enabled within the controller. A forced value is a value within the program that is being overwritten and disregarding any changes made to it by the program logic. When the indicator glows a steady amber, this means that I/O forces are active and enabled. A flashing amber light indicates that a force is active but not enabled.
- **OK**: The **OK** indicator shows the state of the controller and, when it is glowing solid green, this means that the controller is in a normal state. When the **OK** indicator is flashing red, the controller either requires a firmware upgrade or a major fault has occurred that has stopped the logic from executing. When the **OK** indicator is solid red, this usually means that the controller is powering up, is unable to power up, or a program is being loaded in memory.

- **SD**: The **SD** indicator light shows whether the SD card is in use.
- **NET**: The **NET** and **LINK** indicators show the state of the Ethernet/IP port on the L8 controller. When the **NET** light is off, the controller does not have an IP address, or the link has been disabled. When the indicator is flashing green, the controller has an IP address, but no connections have been established. When the indicator light is steady green, the controller has an IP address and at least one active connection. A steady red color means that a duplicate IP address exists or that there is an invalid network configuration.
- **LINK**: When the **LINK** light is off, this means there is no physical Ethernet/IP connection to the controller or the port has been disabled. A flashing green light indicates network activity on the port.

Character displays

The four-character display that appears on the L7 and L8 series controllers can provide a plethora of information about the controller.

The following is a diagram of the four-character display on the L7 controller:

The following is a diagram of the four-character display on the L8 display:

The following modes display on the four-ASCII-character display found on the L7 and L8 controllers:

- **TEST**: The controller is in **TEST** mode.
- **PASS**: Power-up testing has completed successfully.
- **SAVE**: A ControlLogix project is being saved to the SD card.
- **LOAD**: A ControlLogix project is being loaded from the SD card.
- **UPDT**: A firmware upgrade is being performed.
- **CHRG**: The capacitor-based ESM module is being charged.
- **REV**: Displays the major and minor versions of the firmware running on the controller.
- **No Project**: No ControlLogix project is currently loaded on the controller.
- **Project Name**: The name of the currently loaded ControlLogix project.
- **BUSY**: The I/O modules are not fully online yet.
- **Fault Code Information**: Major faults and I/O module faults will also be displayed on the four-character LCD panel.

Now that we have a solid understanding of the features, capabilities, and display functions of ControlLogix controllers, we will introduce an online tool to help you select compatible components and download firmware. This tool is called the Rockwell Automation Compatibility and Download Center and we will explore it in the following section.

The Rockwell Automation Compatibility and Download Center

Rockwell has released an online tool that makes it much easier to find and download compatible firmware for your ControlLogix controller. Using the Rockwell website, you can enter in a product model number and search for all the compatible firmware versions that are supported for it. The Compatibility Center also provides details about the specific changes between each version of firmware, including the following:

- Features
- Alarms and events
- Redundancy
- Safety
- Security

The Rockwell Automation Compatibility and Download Center can be accessed from `https://compatibility.rockwellautomation.com`.

For example, if I want to check the compatible firmware versions with my 1756 L81E, I can enter the model number into the search bar.

The following is a screenshot taken from the Rockwell Automation's web-based **Compatibility & Downloads** tool:

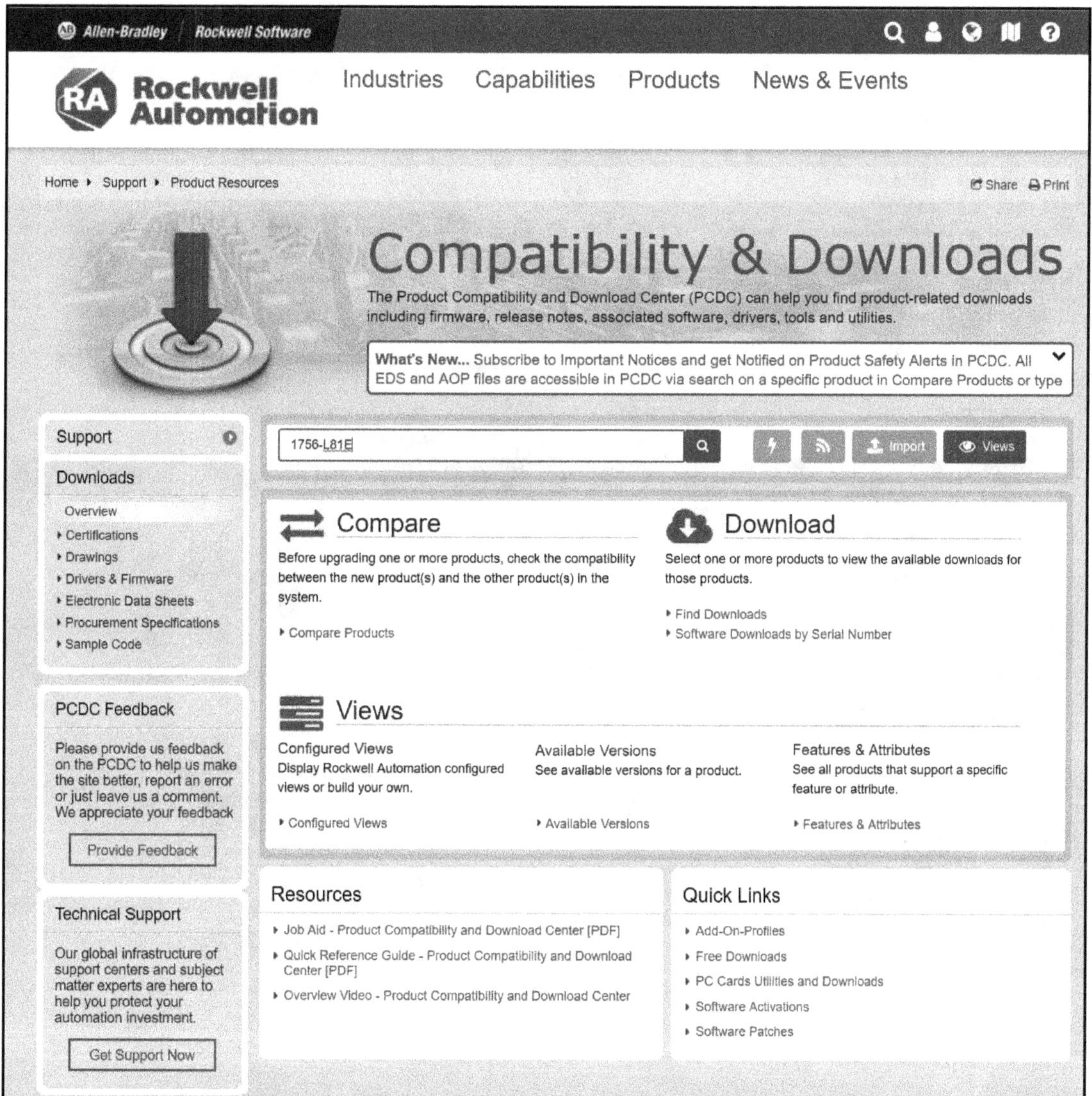

I can review all the compatible firmware versions for this specific controller and compare how the features change between different software versions.

The following screenshot demonstrates the product compatibility comparison feature of the Rockwell Automation compatibility tool:

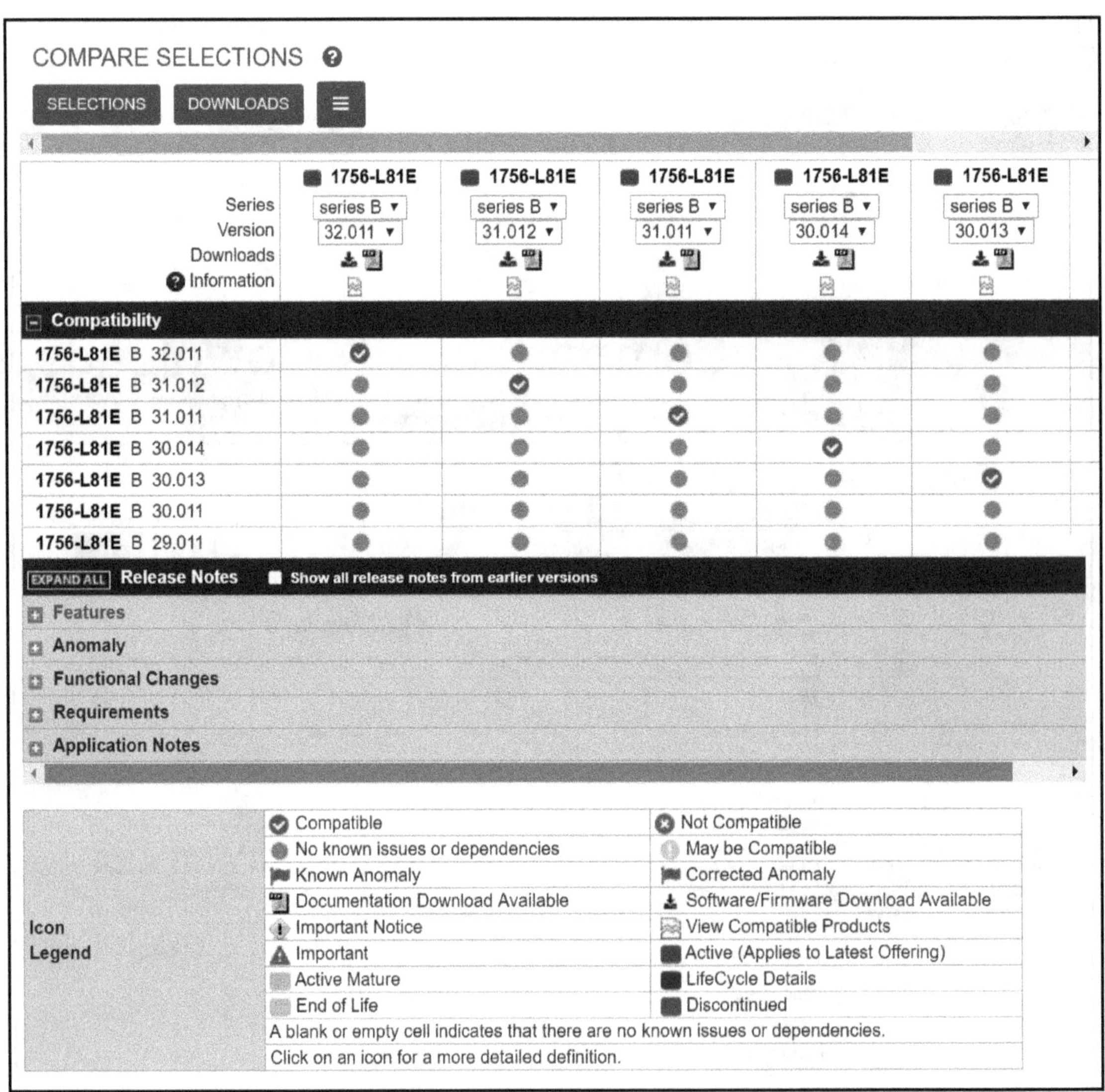

In the following section, the GuardLogix controller safety system will be briefly covered.

Introducing GuardLogix safety controllers

With the launch of the (Bulletin 1756) GuardLogix controller in 2005, the ControlLogix platform supported both standard and safety system control in the same chassis. The GuardLogix controller system is designed for use in safety applications, including SIL 3 (IEC 61508) and applications up to and including PLe/Cat.4 (ISO 13849-1).

The GuardLogix safety controller is part of a failsafe (de-energize to trip) system. This means that when a fault is detected, all of its outputs are set to `0`. In the event of a faulty input or input module, the GuardLogix safety controller automatically sets any input values associated with them to `0`. The Series 6 (L6), Series 7 (L7), and Series 8 (L8) controllers are all available in the GuardLogix form factor.

Physically, the GuardLogix controllers are usually installed in pairs—the primary controller and the safety partner controller. GuardLogix controllers closely resemble normal controllers, except they are typically red. GuardLogix controllers are only supported in version 18 and higher of RSLogix 5000 and Studio 5000 Logix Designer. When programming safety-related functions, GuardLogix only supports the Ladder logic programming language. However, GuardLogix controllers are fully capable of performing non-safety related functions using the other IEC languages, similar to a normal Logix controller.

In the next section, we will briefly touch on the extreme environment controller series of ControlLogix processors, which are designed to withstand harsh operating conditions.

Introducing extreme environment controllers

Rockwell Automation's extreme environment controllers (Bulletin 1756 ControlLogix-XT) share the same features and programming interfaces as standard ControlLogix controllers but are certified to operate in extreme conditions. ControlLogix-XT modules are a darker gray in color than the ControlLogix modules and are spaced in every other slot to provide improved ventilation/isolation. In addition, the ControlLogix-XT modules are treated with a conformal coating, which improves the resistance of the product to corrosive environments.

ControlLogix-XT controllers and modules are rated for temperatures ranging from -20 °C to 70 °C (-4 °F to 158 °F) and have the cULus, Class 1, Div 2, C-Tick, CE, ATEX Zone 2, SIL 2, IEC 61131-2, ANSI-ISA-S71.04-1985, Class G1, G2, and G3, Series 6 (L6) and Series 7 (L7) environmental certifications. The standard controllers and GuardLogix controllers are all available in extreme environment form factors.

At the time of writing, extreme environment controllers are not available for Series 8.

In the next section, we will discuss the ControlLogix operating cycle, how it differs from other PLCs, and the impact it has on the logic you will write.

Understanding the ControlLogix operating cycle

Historically, PLCs such as the SLC-500 and PLC-5, and even ControlLogix controllers such as the Series 5 (L5), execute sequentially in a predictable, single-threaded manner, as illustrated here:

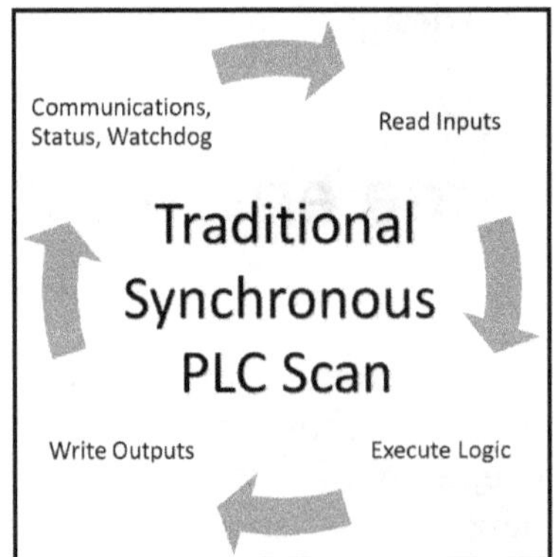

Newer models of the ControlLogix family, such as Series 6 (L6), Series 7 (L7), and Series 8 (L8), perform much differently than the previous synchronous PLC scan example. Newer ControlLogix versions take advantage of the performance increases afforded by the multithreaded asynchronous operation.

Asynchronous operation simply means that the controller will execute multiple tasks at the same time and will not wait for a previous task to complete before continuing to the next task (as the following diagram illustrates):

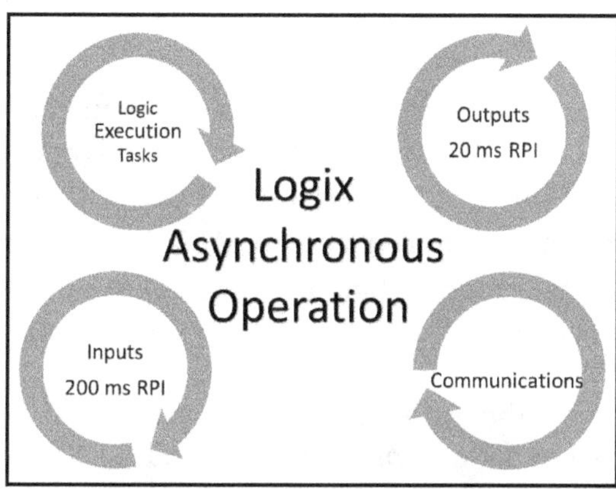

The trade-off for the performance gained, however, is some level of unpredictability, where the inputs and outputs are now continuously scanned while the logic executes. This has the potential to create a situation where the state of the process can change midway through the logic execution. We will look into this in `Chapter 8`, *Writing Ladder Logic*, in more detail, and also discuss a commonly used buffering technique to protect code from unpredictable state changes.

Summary

In this chapter, we learned about the controllers available within Rockwell Automation's Integrated Architecture. We now have an understanding of the controller solutions available within Integrated Architecture and are capable of selecting components for a ControlLogix solution. Furthermore, we explored the physical features and diagnostic information available on the ControlLogix cards and investigated the evolution of the platform's firmware. Finally, we touched on the differences between the traditional synchronous PLC scan and the Logix asynchronous operating cycle.

In the next chapter, we will introduce the CompactLogix series of controllers, just as we covered the ControlLogix series in this chapter.

Questions

The following questions can be used to test your retention of the concepts introduced in this chapter. You can find the answers to these questions in the back of the book under *Assessments*:

1. Which bus technology is the ControlLogix platform backplane built on that allows it to act like a mini-network, as well as devices to be RIUP?
2. What was the first processor released in the ControlLogix controller family?
3. What processor first introduced the four-ASCII-character LCD display?
4. What is the processor mode where the program logic stops executing, outputs are not controlled, and the program can be edited remotely using a serial or Ethernet connection?
5. Which mode allows the processor run mode and logic to be changed remotely using an Ethernet or serial connection while the PLC is online?
6. Which series of ControlLogix controllers are designed for use in safety applications, including SIL 3 (IEC 61508), and applications up to and including PLe/Cat.4 (ISO 13849-1)?
7. Which series of ControlLogix controllers are rated for temperatures ranging from -20 °C to 70 °C (-4 °F to 158 °F) and have the cULus, Class 1, Div 2, C-Tick, CE, ATEX Zone 2, SIL 2, IEC 61131-2, ANSI-ISA-S71.04-1985, and Class G1, G2, and G3 environmental certifications?
8. Newer ControlLogix controllers execute programs on which type of operating cycle?

Further reading

For more information on the ControlLogix control system, please refer to the ControlLogix system Rockwell Automation documentation: `https://literature.rockwellautomation.com/idc/groups/literature/documents/sg/1756-sg001_-en-p.pdf`

3 Understanding CompactLogix

In this chapter, we will introduce the CompactLogix platform by exploring its genesis and evolution since its initial launch in 2001. We will explore the myriad different versions and form factors that are available within the CompactLogix product line and their typical use cases. The CompactLogix product line is by far the most confusing of the Rockwell Automation family due to the wide range of low-cost products and confusing naming conventions. I will attempt to unravel this product line throughout this chapter.

This chapter will cover the following topics:

- Introducing CompactLogix controllers
- Navigating the CompactLogix controller family
- CompactLogix deprecated controllers
- CompactLogix 5370 controllers
- CompactLogix 5380 controllers
- CompactLogix 5480 controllers
- Identifying compatible products

In the first section of this chapter, we will introduce the CompactLogix family of controllers and provide an overview of its history.

Technical requirements

To complete this chapter, you need to create a Rockwell Automation support account by going to `https://www.rockwellautomation.com/account/create-account`.

Creating an account is free, and the material we will refer to in this chapter is publicly available to anyone who has registered with Rockwell Automation.

You will also need a copy of RSLogix or Studio 5000 to program your project. You can either purchase this from your local distributor or request a time-limited trial version. You can find a local distributor for Rockwell Automation products at `https://locator.rockwellautomation.com/`.

Introducing CompactLogix controllers

In 2001, Rockwell Automation first shipped the L43 CompactLogix (Bulletin 1768) controllers, targeted at small- to medium-size automation solutions. At launch, the CompactLogix Controller was intended as the long-term replacement for the SLC-500 controller family. The CompactLogix control platform was designed with an emphasis on the controller software. As the CompactLogix hardware evolves with improved performance and additional features, the logic can easily be migrated to new hardware and firmware versions.

Unlike the SLC-500 platform, the CompactLogix controllers can be programmed using the same RSLogix 5000 (Logix Designer) software suite that is used with ControlLogix. In 2006, the CompactLogix L43 was launched with integrated motion support. In 2008, Rockwell Automation released the low-cost CompactLogix L23 (Bulletin 1769) controllers with embedded I/O and the L3x modular (Bulletin 1769) controllers.

In 2009, Compact GuardLogix, an SIL 3 certified controller with the L43S and L45S CPU supporting integrated safety was added to the Logix family. The 1769 CompactLogix modules do not have a chassis like the ControlLogix modules do. The 1769 CompactLogix modules can connect together using a **DIN** rail (which stands for "**Deutsches Institut fur Normung rail**") can be screwed in directly to a panel. In 2016, the latest generation of CompactLogix controllers was announced, the Bulletin 5069 CompactLogix 5380 Controllers.

The following table provides a high-level overview of the evolution of the CompactLogix family of controllers:

Controller	**Year**	**Description**
Bulletin 1768 CompactLogix L43	2001	Replacement for the SLC-500 controller family
Bulletin 1768 CompactLogix L43 with Motion Control	2006	Added integrated motion control
Bulletin 1769 CompactLogix L23	2008	Low-cost controller with embedded I/O
Bulletin 1769 CompactLogix L3x	2008	CompactLogix controller with modular cards
Bulletin 1769 Compact GuardLogix L43S and L45S	2009	CompactLogix SIL 3 rated safety controllers
Bulletin 5069 CompactLogix 5380	2016	The next generation of CompactLogix controllers

In the next section, we will discuss the various form factors and features that comprise the CompactLogix family of controllers in greater detail.

Navigating the CompactLogix controller family

CompactLogix embodies a wide-ranging series of controller solutions, which can be a challenge to navigate for those who are new to the platform. CompactLogix controllers represent a low-cost solution for industrial automation problems that still have the power of the Studio 5000 development environment behind them. CompactLogix controllers come in many different fit-for-purpose form factors that we will detail in this chapter.

There are more factors to consider when selecting a CompactLogix controller due to their modular nature and the wide range of form factors available, such as the following:

- Supported Logix Designer software versions
- Cabinet size restrictions
- CompactLogix form factors/I/O module scalability
- Processing requirements of your current application and future expansion
- Memory requirements of your current application and future expansion

The CompactLogix product line is broken down into the following five categories:

- 1768 CompactLogix controllers
- 1769 CompactLogix L3x controllers
- 1769 CompactLogix 5370 controllers
- 5069 CompactLogix 5380 controllers
- 5069 CompactLogix 5480 controllers

The various model numbers for CompactLogix don't follow an incremental model numbering scheme, which is often a point of confusion.

The following CompactLogix controller table illustrates the release timeline of the various CompactLogix controller model numbers:

Bulletin 1768 CompactLogix controllers (no longer supported by Rockwell Automation):

Controller	Memory	Minimum version	Maximum version
1768-L43	2 MB	v16	v20
1768-L45	3 MB	v16	v20

Bulletin 1769 L23x packaged controllers with embedded I/O (no longer supported by Rockwell Automation):

Controller	Memory	Minimum version	Maximum version
1769-L23	512 KB	V16	V20

Bulletin 1769-L3x modular controllers (no longer supported by Rockwell Automation):

Controller	Memory	Minimum version	Maximum version
1769-L3x	1.5 MB	v16	v20

Bulletin 1769 CompactLogix 5370 controllers:

Controller	Memory	Minimum version	Maximum IP nodes
5370 1769-L16	384 KB	V20	4
5370 1769-L18	512 KB	V20	8
5370 1769-L24	750 KB	V20	8
5370 1769-L27	1 MB	V20	16
5370 1769-L30	1 MB	V20	16
5370 1769-L33	2 MB	V20	32
5370 1769-L36	3 MB	V20	48
5370 1769-L37	4 MB	V31	64
5370 1769-L38	5 MB	V31	80

Bulletin 5069 CompactLogix 5380 controllers:

Controller	Memory	Minimum version	Maximum IP nodes
5380 5069-L306	0.6 MB	V28	16
5380 5069-L310	1 MB	V28	24
5380 5069-L320	2 MB	V28	40
5380 5069-L330	3 MB	V29	60
5380 5069-L340	4 MB	V29	90
5380 5069-L350	5 MB	V30	120
5380 5069-L380	8 MB	V30	150
5380 5069-L3100	10 MB	V30	180

Bulletin 5069 CompactLogix 5480 controllers:

Controller	Memory	Minimum version	Maximum IP nodes
5480 5069-L430	3 MB	V32	60
5480 5069-L450	5 MB	V32	120
5480 5069-L4100	10 MB	V32	180
5480 5069-L4200	20 MB	V32	250

It is also important to consider that some of the CompactLogix 5370 controllers are slated as direct replacements for some of the older CompactLogix controllers (although the older controllers are still available for purchase):

- 5370 1769-L24 replaces 1769-L23.
- 5370 1769-L3x replaces 1769-L3x.

In the next section, we will explore the various CompactLogix deprecated controller series.

CompactLogix deprecated controllers

Now that we have introduced the CompactLogix product line, it is time to dive into the wide range of form factors and varying features available. In this first section, we will discuss the CompactLogix controllers that have reached the end of their life cycle and are no longer supported by Rockwell Automation. It is important to identify these controllers as it is still quite common to encounter them operating in the field today.

First, we will introduce the L43 and L45 controllers in the following section.

Bulletin 1768 – L43 and L45

The CompactLogix L43 and L45 controllers were first introduced in 2001 and have subsequently been replaced by the 5370 and 5380 CompactLogix controllers. The L43 and L45 platforms featured the following:

- A compact flash memory card
- An Ethernet port
- A serial RS-232 port
- 1769/1768 modules (can only be placed to the right of the power supply)
- A power supply module

The following illustration depicts the L43 and L45 CompactLogix series controller with power supply and I/O modules:

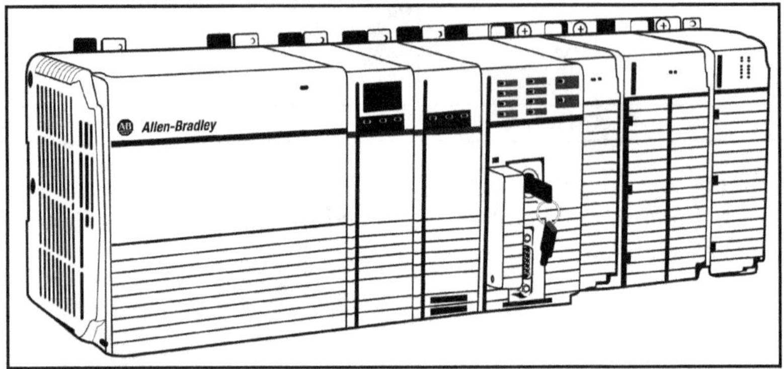

As of July 2020, the Bulletin 1768-L43 and 1768-L45 CompactLogix controllers have been discontinued and are no longer available for sale. Rockwell Automation recommends migrating to the newer CompactLogix 5370 or CompactLogix 5380 control platform.

In the next section, we will detail the L23x controller, which is also no longer being produced by Rockwell Automation.

Bulletin 1769 – L23x

The L23x CompactLogix controller is a highly compact controller featuring embedded I/O. The L23x controller has been discontinued and replaced by the 5370 and 5380 CompactLogix controllers.

The L23x platform featured the following:

- A serial RS-232 port
- An Ethernet port (only on E models)
- Embedded I/O
- An embedded power supply module

The following illustration shows the L23E featuring an embedded network card and its embedded I/O points:

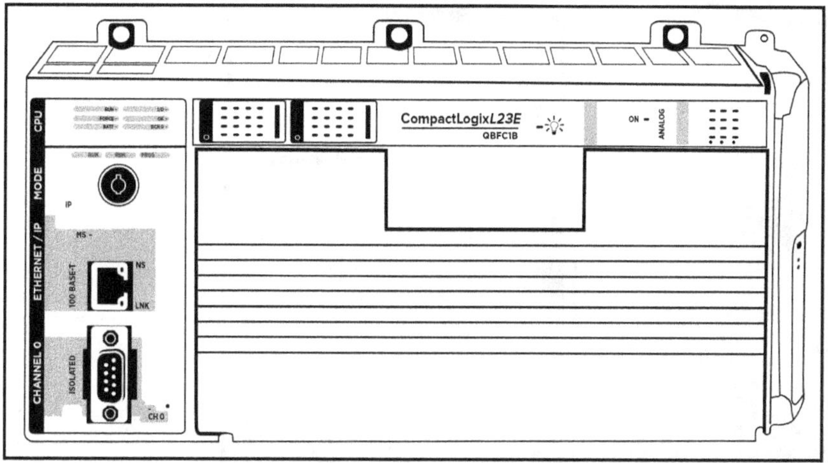

L23x CompactLogix controllers have been discontinued and are no longer available for sale. Rockwell Automation recommends migrating to the newer CompactLogix 5370 or CompactLogix 5380 control platform.

In the next section, we will discuss the CompactLogix L3x modular controllers.

Bulletin 1769 – L3x modular controllers

The L3x CompactLogix controller is a modular controller platform featuring replaceable I/O cards similar to the ControlLogix platform. The L3x controller has been discontinued and replaced by the 5370 and 5380 CompactLogix controllers.

The L3x platform featured the following:

- A CompactFlash memory card
- A serial RS232, or ControlNet, or Ethernet port
- 1769 modules that can be placed to the left or right of the power supply module
- A power supply module

The following illustration depicts the L3x controller, its power supply, and I/O modules:

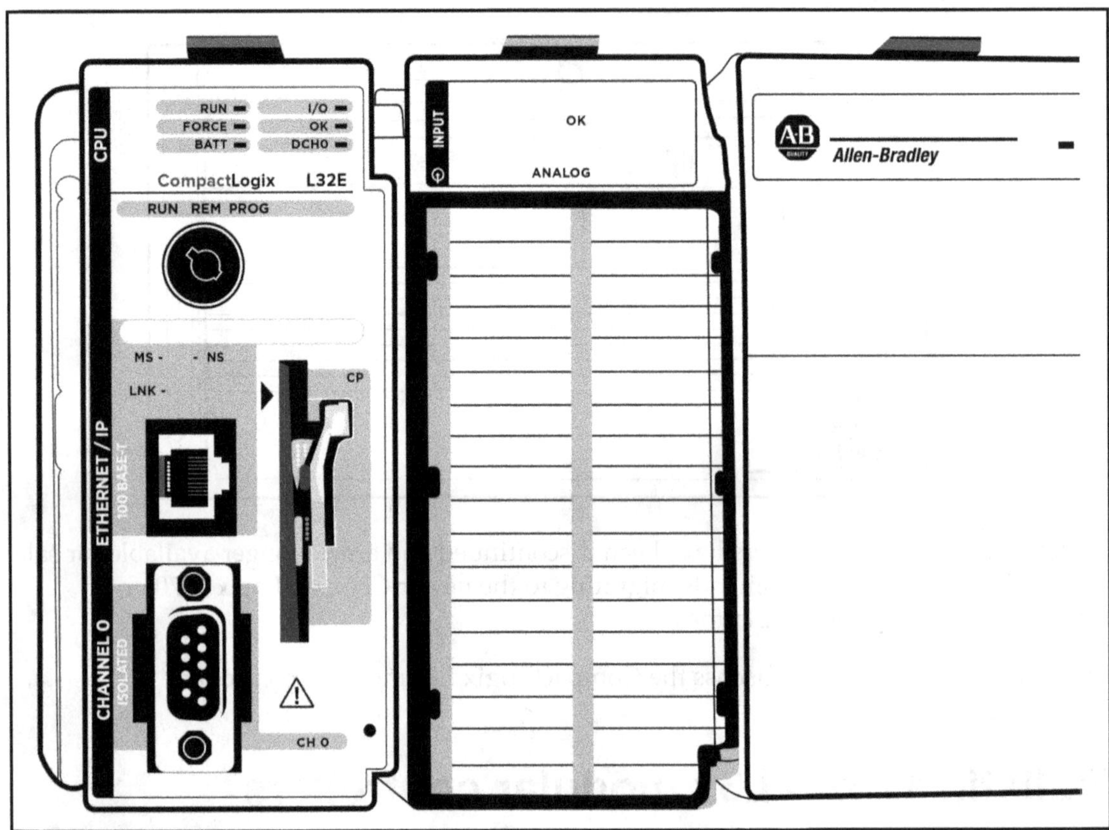

L3x CompactLogix controllers have been discontinued and are no longer available for sale. Rockwell Automation recommends migrating to the newer CompactLogix 5370 or CompactLogix 5380 control platform.

In the following section, we will introduce the modern line of embedded I/O CompactLogix controllers, the 5370 controllers.

CompactLogix 5370 controllers

In 2012, Rockwell Automation released the 5370 L1, L2, and L3 (Bulletin 1769) controllers, which provided a low-cost, Ethernet/IP-enabled, high-performance controller in a 40 percent-smaller form factor. The 5370 CompactLogix controllers represent the fourth-generation CompactLogix series release. The CompactLogix 5370 series controller provides many of the same enhancements that the ControlLogix 5570 (Series 7, L7) provided over the ControlLogix 5560 (Series 6, L6), including the following:

- Twice the performance capability due to a more powerful dual-core CPU
- Adoption of modern SDRAM memory
- The replacement of the 9-pin serial port with a USB 2.0 port (programs transfer 200 times faster over USB 2.0 than the serial port)
- The replacement of the CompactFlash memory card with a Secure Digital (SD) memory card
- Added the Energy Storage Module (ESM) and removed the need for a lithium battery
- Makes use of existing 1769 I/O modules
- Integrates motion control over Ethernet

The ability to store program comments and tag descriptions on the controller (with firmware V21 and above)

Now that we have introduced the newer 5370 line of CompactLogix controllers, we will explore the L1, L2, and L3 form factors that are available.

Bulletin 1769 5370 – L1

The CompactLogix 5370 L1 controller is a significantly smaller direct replacement for the L23 CompactLogix controllers with embedded I/O. One of the more interesting aspects of the L1 is that its embedded I/O module is only available with the built-in digital I/O.

The L1 CompactLogix controller features the following:

- An SD memory card
- Two Ethernet ports
- A USB 2.0 port
- Embedded point I/O modules
- Expandable with 6- or 8-point I/O modules

- Embedded power supply
- Integrated motion control

The following is an illustration of the L1 form factor CompactLogix 5370 controller with embedded I/O terminals:

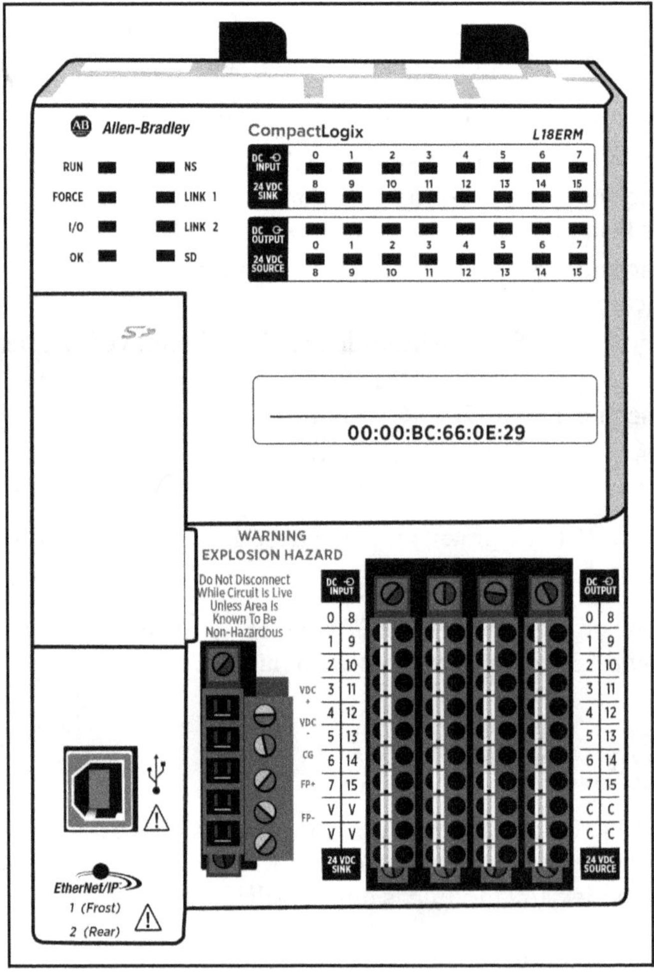

In the next section, we will introduce the L2 form factor of the fourth generation CompactLogix controller.

Bulletin 1769 5370 – L2

The CompactLogix 5370 L2 controller is another direct replacement for the CompactLogix controllers with embedded I/O. Unlike the L1 controller, the L2 controller comes in multiple embedded I/O form factors: digital inputs, combination digital and analog inputs, high-resolution analog inputs, and universal inputs.

The L2 CompactLogix Controller features the following:

- An SD memory card
- Two Ethernet ports
- A USB 2.0 port
- Embedded 1769 I/O modules
- Expandable with 4 x 1769 I/O modules
- Embedded power supply
- Integrated motion control

The following is an illustration of the L2 CompactLogix form factor:

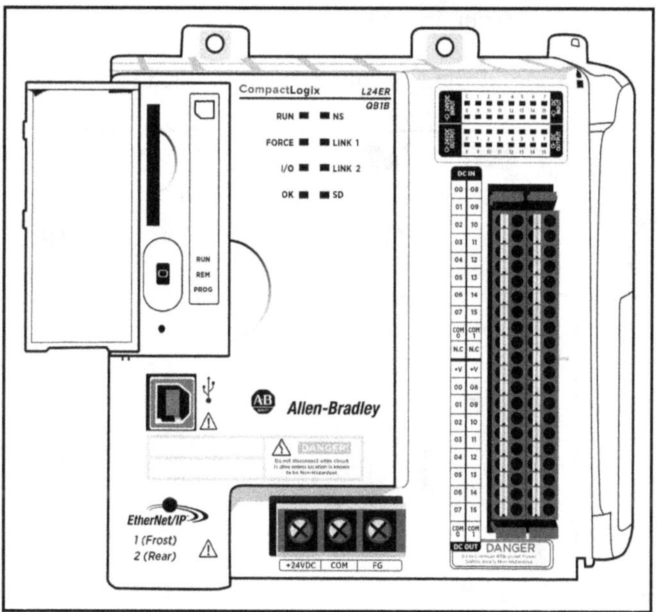

In the next section, we will introduce the L3 form factor of the CompactLogix 5370.

Bulletin 1769 5370 – L3

The fourth generation CompactLogix 5370 L3 controllers are a direct replacement for the CompactLogix L3x line. The CompactLogix L3 form factor supports all of the 1769 I/O modules, power supplies, and cables previously used with the L32E and L35E controllers.

The L3 series controller features the following:

- An SD memory card
- Two Ethernet ports
- A USB 2.0 port
- 8 to 30 1769 I/O modules
- 1769 modules can be placed to the left or right of the power supply
- A power supply module
- Comes in 1 MB, 2 MB, and 3 MB versions
- Safety version available
- Phase Manager supported
- Alarm instructions supported (ALMA, ALMD)
- Supports Studio 5000 version 20+

The following is an illustration of the L3 CompactLogix form factor:

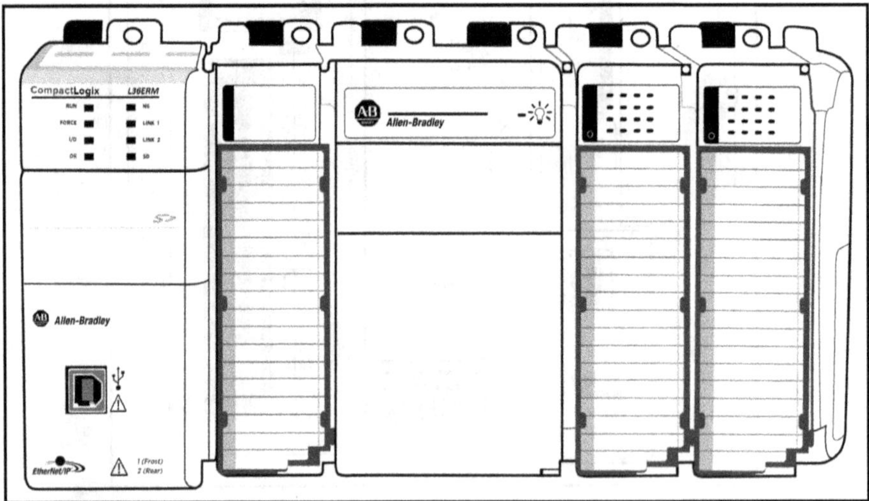

In the next section, we will introduce the L8 processor-based CompactLogix 5380 controllers.

CompactLogix 5380 controllers

In 2016, Rockwell Automation introduced the 5380 CompactLogix (Bulletin 1769) controllers, which feature the same processor as the ControlLogix L8 series controllers.

The 5380 series controllers feature the following improvements over the 5370 series:

- A 20% increase in memory capacity
- 5-20 times faster scan times and task switching
- The task monitor is now built into 5380 web pages
- Safety, Phase Manager, and **Application lifecycle management** (**ALM**) support to be added in future
- Supports Studio 5000 version 28+

The following illustration depicts a CompactLogix 5380 L3 CPU:

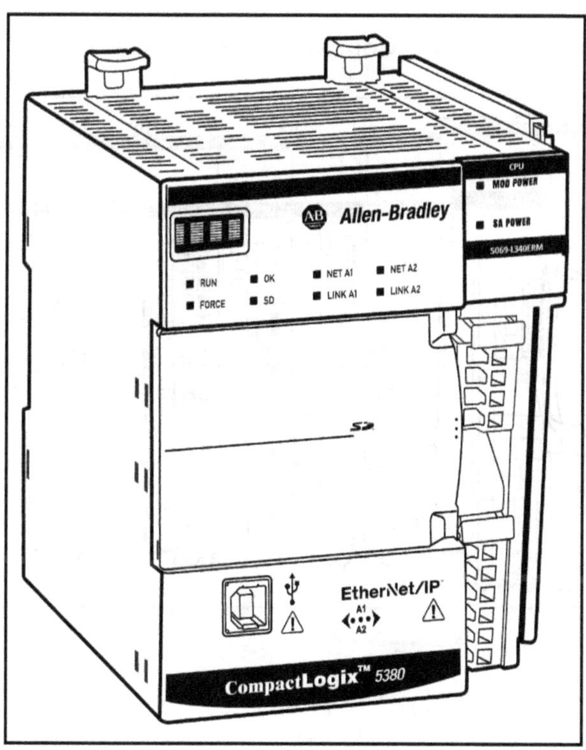

In the next section, let's take a look at the powerful 5380-L3 controller.

Bulletin 1769 5380 – L3

The CompactLogix 5380 series represents the fifth generation of CompactLogix controllers. The CompactLogix 5380 L3 controller is a powerful, expandable, and compact form factor **Process Automation Controller** (**PAC**).

The 5380 series features include the following:

- LED status indicators
- A run mode switch
- An SD card slot
- A USB port
- A four-digit digital status display
- Processor and field power connections
- Comes in 1 MB, 2 MB, 3 MB, and 4 MB versions
- No memory reserve required – 100% of the memory can be used for applications

The following is an illustration of the CompactLogix 5380 controller:

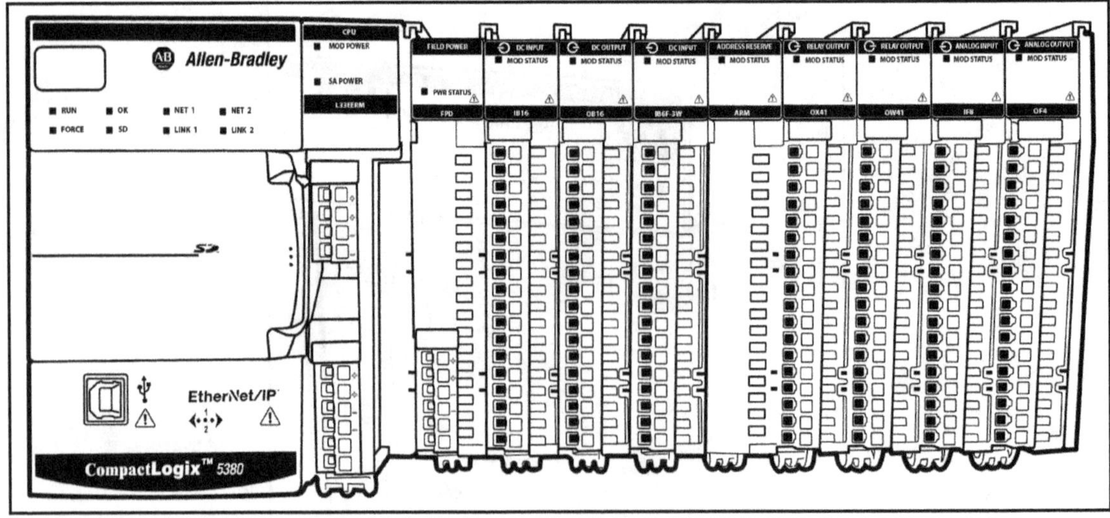

In the following section, we will introduce the Compact GuardLogix controller.

CompactLogix GuardLogix

The Compact GuardLogix form factor of the 5370 L3 controllers provides integrated safety and integrated motion in a single compact controller. The GuardLogix L3 controllers support integrated safety up to SIL 3, PLe Cat.4. Safety systems and GuardLogix are outside the scope of this book, but it is important to know they are available and their function within control systems.

The following is an illustration of the CompactLogix GuardLogix controller:

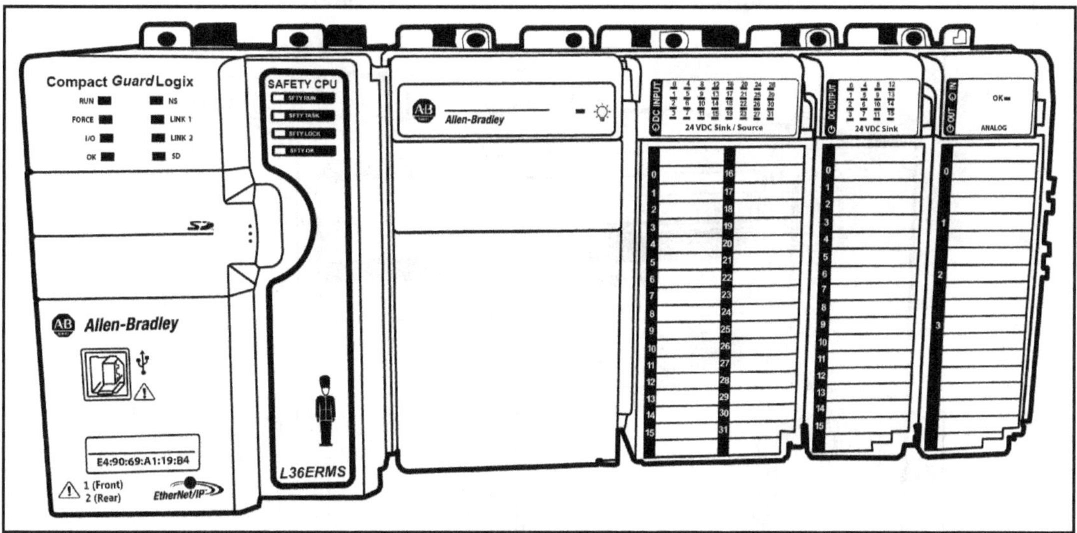

When programming safety-related functions, CompactLogix GuardLogix only supports ladder logic. However, CompactLogix GuardLogix controllers are fully capable of performing non-safety-related functions using the other **International Electrotechnical Commission** (**IEC**) languages similar to a normal CompactLogix controller.

In the next section, we will introduce the CompactLogix 5480 hybrid controller and Windows-based solution in a compact form factor.

CompactLogix 5480 controllers

The CompactLogix 5480 controllers provide a unique hybrid controller and an industrial computer running Windows 10 (IoT Enterprise) in a single device. The 5480 controller features many of the same features of the L3 series controller, with the added benefit of also being able to run Windows 10 to support a **Human Machine Interface** (**HMI**) (such as FactoryTalk), run Studio 5000, or connect data to the Microsoft Azure IoT cloud. A monitor, mouse, and keyboard can be plugged directly into the controller thanks to the integrated display port and USB 3.0 connections. The CompactLogix 5480 controller utilizes the same powerful ControlLogix L8 processor that the ControlLogix L8 and the CompactLogix 5380 controllers take advantage of.

The following illustration depicts the hybrid CompactLogix 5480 controller:

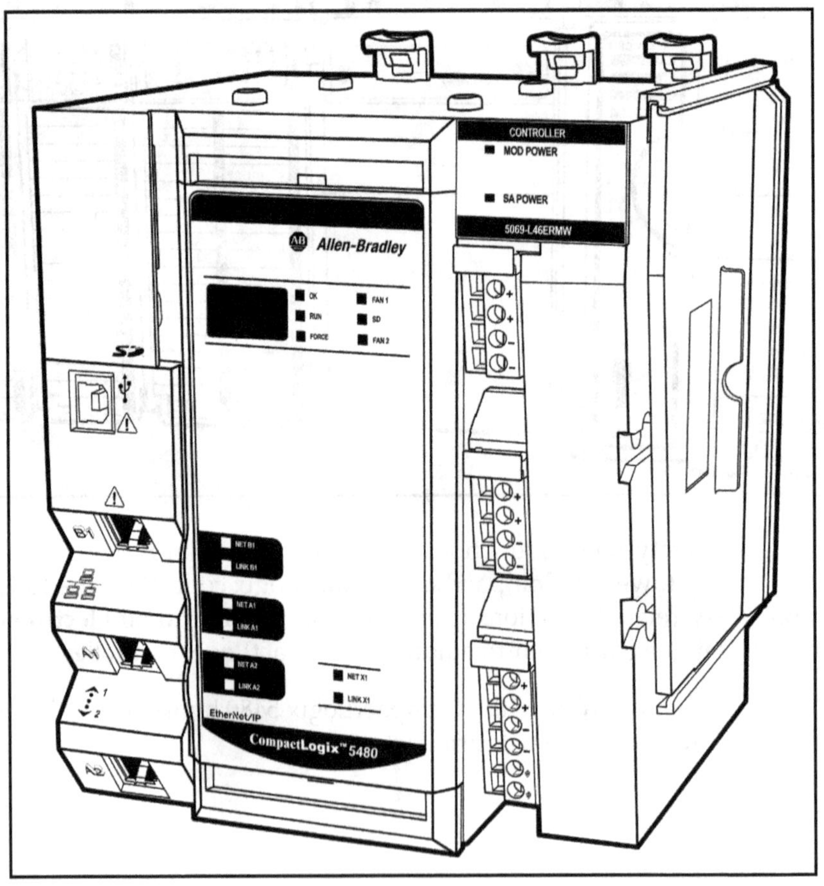

The CompactLogix 5480 features the following:

- An instance of Windows 10 IoT Enterprise running on an integrated industrial PC
- A 64 GB SSD drive for running Windows 10 IoT Enterprise
- Supported in Studio 5000 Logix Designer version 32
- Includes three 1 GB Ethernet/IP ports
- Includes a 1 GB Ethernet port as a dedicated Windows 10 network interface
- Supports up to 31 local Bulletin 5069 compact I/O modules
- Integrated DisplayPort for high-definition industrial monitor connectivity
- Two USB 3.0 ports for OS peripherals and expanded data storage capabilities

Now that we have covered the wide range of CompactLogix devices that are compatible with Logix/Studio 5000, in the next section, we will review how to identify compatible products using the tools available on the Rockwell Automation website.

Identifying compatible products

As we have highlighted in this chapter, there are several different product lines of CompactLogix, each with its own unique set of controller, modules, and chassis. One challenge that integrators are faced with is selecting components that are compatible with their CompactLogix product line. Fortunately, Rockwell Automation has come to the rescue in the form of a compatibility listing feature on their website.

Next, we will take a quick look at how to find compatible products for any of the CompactLogix controllers using the **Compatibility & Downloads** section of the Rockwell Automation website:

1. First, let's navigate to `https://compatibility.rockwellautomation.com`.
2. Next, we enter in the Bulletin number and model of the CompactLogix controller we wish to search for in the **Search PCDC** text field and then click the search icon. Let's enter the Bulletin number `5069-L330` and then press the search icon:

3. The search results will display a number of different models of the 5069-L330 CompactLogix controller. We will focus on the 5069-L330ER controller. The green square icon beside the 5069-L330ER tells us that this model is still fully supported by Rockwell Automation.
4. A gray icon would tell us that there are some life cycle messages related to this product to be aware of. A red icon would indicate that this product is no longer supported by Rockwell Automation.
5. Click on the **Show More** link:

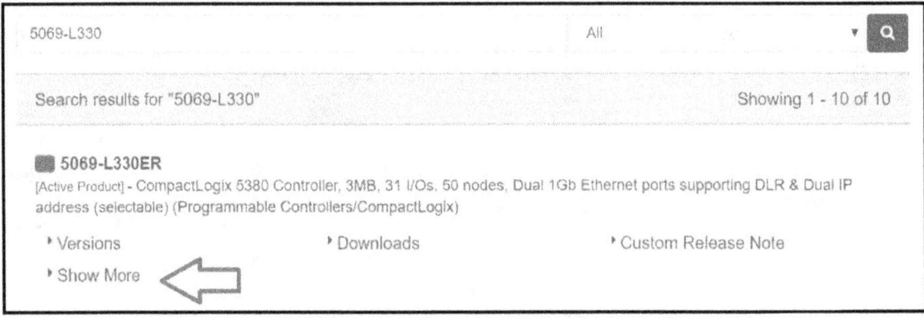

6. Next, click on the **Compatible Products** link.
7. We can now view the Rockwell Automation products, I/O modules, and software compatible with the 5069-L330ER model:

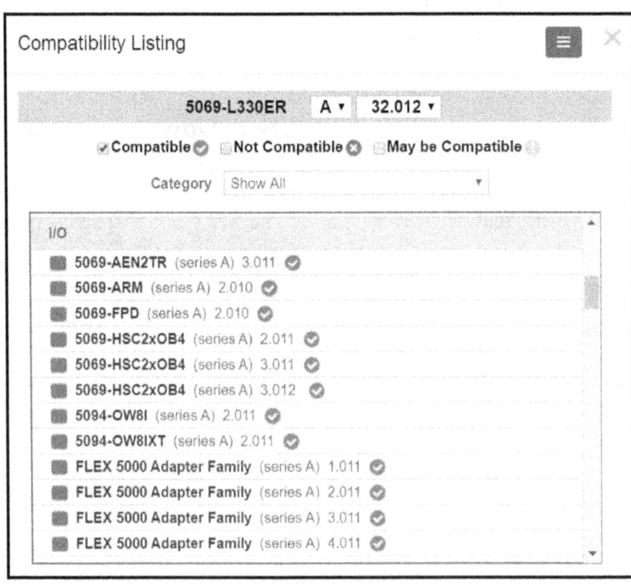

We have now learned how to use the **Compatibility & Downloads** section of the Rockwell Automation website to find software and products that are compatible with a particular Compact Logix controller.

Summary

In this chapter, we learned about the full line of CompactLogix controllers available within Rockwell Automation's Integrated Architecture system. We learned about the CompactLogix 5480 hybrid controllers and their unique position in the industrial computing marketplace. We now have an understanding of the controller solutions available within the Integrated Architecture system and are capable of making solution architecture decisions. We have also learned how to use Rockwell Automation's online resources to identify the modules that are compatible with our solution.

In the next chapter, we will introduce Rockwell Automation's SoftLogix platform, a PC-based ControlLogix controller.

Further reading

For more information about the CompactLogix series of controllers and modules, please refer to the Rockwell Automation documents:

- CompactLogix 5380, Compact GuardLogix 5380, and CompactLogix 5480 Controllers Specifications: `https://literature.rockwellautomation.com/idc/groups/literature/documents/td/5069-td002_-en-p.pdf`
- Legacy 5370 1769 Series CompactLogix Controller Specifications: `https://literature.rockwellautomation.com/idc/groups/literature/documents/td/1769-td005_-en-p.pdf`

Questions

The following questions can be used to test your retention of the concepts introduced in this chapter. You can find the answers to these questions in the back of the book under *Assessments*.

1. What size of automation system does the CompactLogix series of controller target?
2. In what year was the CompactLogix series of controller first launched?
3. Which series of ControlLogix controller features an integrated industrial computer offering a display port connection, two USB 3.0 connections, and a dedicated 1 GB Ethernet connection?
4. Where can we find products and I/O modules that are compatible with a particular controller?
5. Which series of CompactLogix controller replaced controllers such as the 1769-L23 and 1769-L32?
6. In what year did Rockwell Automation introduce the (Bulletin 1769) 5380 CompactLogix controllers that feature the same processor as the ControlLogix L8 series?
7. What CompactLogix controllers support safety systems with integrated safety up to SIL 3, PLe CAT 4?

4
Understanding SoftLogix

In this chapter, we will introduce the Rockwell Automation SoftLogix 5800 controller and virtual chassis. We will go through the setup of the SoftLogix chassis monitor and the configuration of our SoftLogix controller within Logix. Finally, we will investigate the techniques for simulating I/O using the 1784-SIM module.

This chapter will cover the following elements of the SoftLogix platform:

- Learning about SoftLogix
- Understanding SoftLogix controllers
- Understanding the components of a SoftLogix solution
- Working with SoftLogix

The first section of this chapter will provide an overview of the Rockwell Automation SoftLogix system.

Technical requirements

To complete this chapter, you need to create a Rockwell Automation support account by going to `https://www.rockwellautomation.com/account/create-account`.

Creating an account is free, and the material we will refer to in this chapter is publicly available to anyone who has registered with Rockwell Automation.

You will also need a copy of RSLogix or Studio 5000 to program your project, as well as a license for SoftLogix. You can either purchase this from your local distributor or request a time-limited trial version. You can find a local distributor for Rockwell Automation products at `https://locator.rockwellautomation.com/`.

Learning about SoftLogix

SoftLogix 5800 controllers enable you to create a PC-based Logix controller rack. By using the SoftLogix application, you can create a virtual rack that houses your virtual controllers and virtual communication modules. SoftLogix is another component of Rockwell Automation's Integrated Architecture (as discussed in `Chapter 1`, *The History of Rockwell Automation Technologies*) and can interface with the other Logix controllers, communication modules, and I/O modules. By taking advantage of the computing power of modern PCs, SoftLogix controllers are capable of processing larger volumes of data at a higher speed than even the most powerful Logix controller.

Furthermore, SoftLogix controllers support the 1784-SIM (I/O simulator) modules, which emulate the real-world I/O modules for debugging, operator training, acceptance testing, and simulation. Studio 5000 allows you to build custom C++-based **Dynamic Link Libraries** (**DLLs**), called external routines, that can be executed by the SoftLogix. External routines allow you to take control of all the aspects of Windows-based PCs and perform resource-intensive program execution.

In the next section, we will review the three SoftLogix processors that are available.

Understanding SoftLogix controllers

There are three Bulletin 1789 SoftLogix controllers—1789-L10, 1789-L30, and 1789-L60. They are all fully integrated into the Logix platform. SoftLogix controllers can be incorporated into any Logix control system solution. They are also capable of running the Logic programs designed for standalone Logix controllers on a Windows-based PC. When running a SoftLogix controller on a PC, up to 32 configurable tasks can be run simultaneously. Communication modules can be added to PCs using the PCI cards available from Rockwell Automation.

The following table details the three SoftLogix controllers and their distinguishing features:

ControllerMemoryAvailable Slots1784-SIMPCI cards

Controller	Memory	Rack Size	1784-SIM	PCI Cards	Third-party support
1789-L10	2 MB	3	1	N/A	No
1789-L30	64 MB	5	5	5	Yes
1789-L60	64 MB	16	16	16	Yes

In the next section, we will detail the components that comprise a SoftLogix solution.

Understanding the components of a SoftLogix solution

In this section, we will explore the software and hardware components that interact with SoftLogix. The following diagram displays a typical SoftLogix solution architecture:

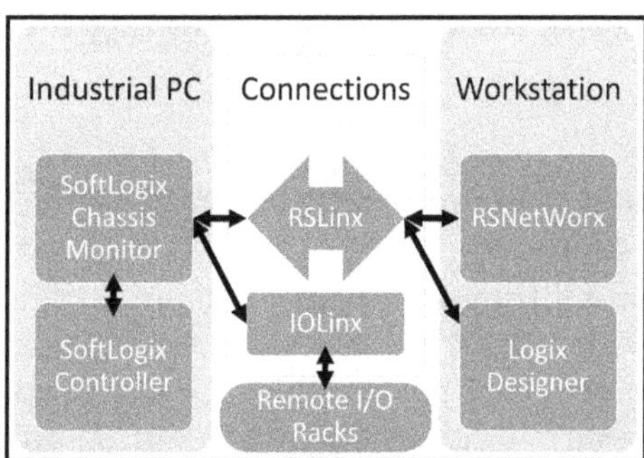

The assets in the preceding diagram are as follows:

- **SoftLogix Chassis Monitor**: This application is the virtual software-based rack that runs on the PC. It allows you to manage the virtual rack modules, monitor the status of the controllers and modules (just like a physical rack), and configure your virtual controllers.
- **SoftLogix Controller**: This application is a virtual controller process running on a Windows-based PC. The virtual controller runs the RSLogix 5000/Logix Designer programs, such as ladder logic and function block diagrams, that would usually run on a physical controller. It is also capable of running C++-based external routines.
- **RSLinx**: As discussed in `Chapter 6`, *Industrial Network Communications*, RSLinx is a communications gateway that allows PCs to communicate with the Logix controllers.
- **IOLinx**: This application is an API that allows SoftLogix controllers to read the I/O data from a physical I/O module.

In the following section, we will explore the similarities and differences between SoftLogix 5800 and Logix Emulate 5000.

SoftLogix 5800 versus Logix Emulate 5000

Although we will cover Logix Emulate 5000 in more detail in the next chapter, let's take a look at the differences between the two products. Both of the PC-based controller products provide a virtual rack and controller.

You cannot install SoftLogix on a PC that already has RSLogix Emulate 5000 installed on it. In order to install SoftLogix, you must first uninstall RSLogix.

Logix Emulate 5000 is a virtual Logix controller and rack that is designed to allow you to debug your Logix program code using features such as breakpoints and tracepoints. Using Emulate 5000, you can create a virtual test rack using similar modules to a physical rack and even test your project with an HMI. Unlike SoftLogix, Emulate 5000 is not capable of controlling real I/O. Also, communication modules are not supported by Emulate 5000. A typical Logix Emulate 5000 solution consists of modules that are configured in a virtual Logix rack to mimic the end solution. The logic is downloaded and monitored using Logix Designer/RSLogix 5000 in order to troubleshoot it.

The following table outlines some significant differences between these two products:

SoftLogix 5800	Logix Emulate 5000
Fully featured PC-based Logix controller	Emulated controller for Logix debugging
Full network module support	No networking modules supported
Normal Logix controller features	Advanced debugging features

For simulation and testing, you can easily use either SoftLogix or Emulate 5000. However, if you are looking for advanced debugging/logging features, Emulate 5000 is the better option.

Now that we have introduced the basic elements of SoftLogix and detailed its differences from Emulate, in the following section, we will start to work with a simple SoftLogix program.

Working with SoftLogix

SoftLogix controllers are capable of processing larger volumes of data at a higher speed than even the most powerful Logix controller as it utilizes the computing power of modern PCs.

In the following exercises, we will perform the following tasks:

- Configuring the SoftLogix 5800 chassis monitor
- Configuring the RSLinx virtual-backplane driver
- Creating a Logix Designer SoftLogix project
- Simulating values using the 1789-SIM module

In the next section, we will learn how to configure the SoftLogix 5800 chassis monitor application, which is a virtual, Windows-based controller rack.

Configuring the SoftLogix 5800 chassis monitor

In this exercise, we will configure a SoftLogix controller in the SoftLogix chassis monitor.

SoftLogix 5800 is part of the annual release of the Rockwell Automation toolkit. It can also be found on the Rockwell Automation website for approved customers and system integrators. SoftLogix controllers need to be licensed in order to run, and the Rockwell Automation activation manager will also need to be installed.

To configure a SoftLogix controller, perform the following steps:

1. Start the SoftLogix 5800 chassis monitor software.
2. Open the drop-down menu option by navigating to **Slot | Create Module...**.
3. The **Select Module** dialog box appears and allows us to add the communication modules, the 1789-SIM I/O simulation modules, or the SoftLogix 5800 controller modules to the slot we specify.
4. Select **1789-L60 SoftLogix5860 Controller** and `1` for the **Slot** number field using the numeric selector. Then, click on the **OK** button, as in the following screenshot:

5. The **General** dialog box appears. Next, we will configure the SoftLogix controller we added to slot `1` in our virtual chassis.

The **General** dialog box allows us to specify the following options:

- **Startup Mode**: This option allows you to select the SoftLogix run mode state when the controller first starts up (equivalent to the key position on a physical controller). The options are **Remote Program** or **Last Controller State**.
- **Memory Size (KB)**: This option is the amount of memory (RAM) that the controller is allowed to use on the PC.
- **Periodic Save Interval**: This option stores all the current tag values in the SoftLogix controller to the PC's hard disk drive. This value runs at a higher processor priority than other tasks on your PC and can impact the performance of other processes. Having a modern multi-core processor helps to reduce this risk.

6. We are going to keep the default options in the **General** dialog box, so click on the **Next >** button, as in the following screenshot:

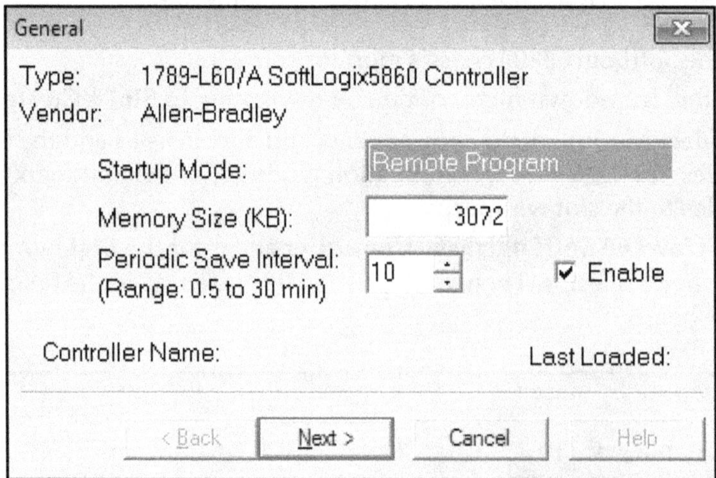

7. Now, the **NT System** dialog box appears and provides us with the following options:
    - **Continuous Task Dwell Time (ms)**: This option is the breathing room you offer the PC to handle other tasks running on the system. It is essential to provide the CPU with a slice of time to handle Windows-related system tasks; otherwise, you may find your CPU pegged at 100 percent utilization and your PC system unresponsive.
    - **CPU Affinity**: This option is the CPU core used for the SoftLogix controller.
    - **Channel 0 Serial Port**: This option is the COM port used for serial communication by the SoftLogix controller.
8. We are going to keep the default options, as in the **General** dialog box, so click on the **Finish** button, as in the following screenshot:

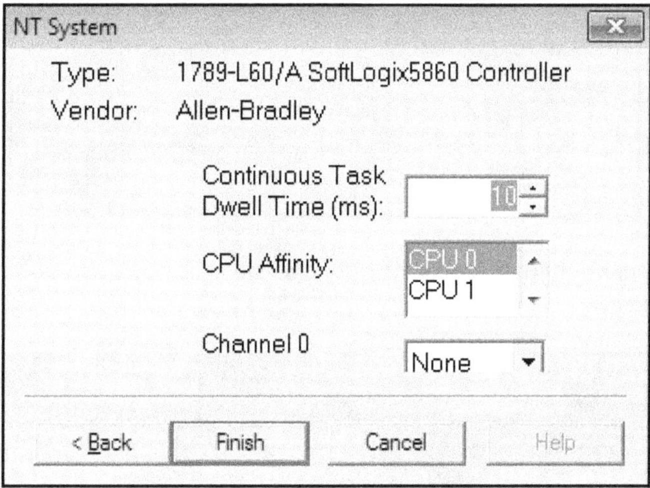

Adding a 1789-SIM I/O module will allow us to simulate input values and monitor output values. We can add the 1789-SIM module using the same process we used to add the SoftLogix controller module.

9. Open the drop-down menu option by navigating to **Slot** | **Create Module...**.
10. In the **Select Module** dialog box, select **1789-SIM 32 Point Input/Output Simulator** in the **Module Type** field, select **2** in the **Slot** field, set the **Label** option to **Simulated Points**, and click on the **OK** button.

11. Now that we have a 1789-SIM module added to our virtual backplane, we can toggle inputs and monitor the outputs. You can toggle the digital points by right-clicking on the 1789-SIM module and selecting **Properti**
12. You can toggle the digital input values by selecting the **I/O Data** tab and toggling the input boxes. You can also see the output values by clicking on the module on the virtual chassis to open the module door:

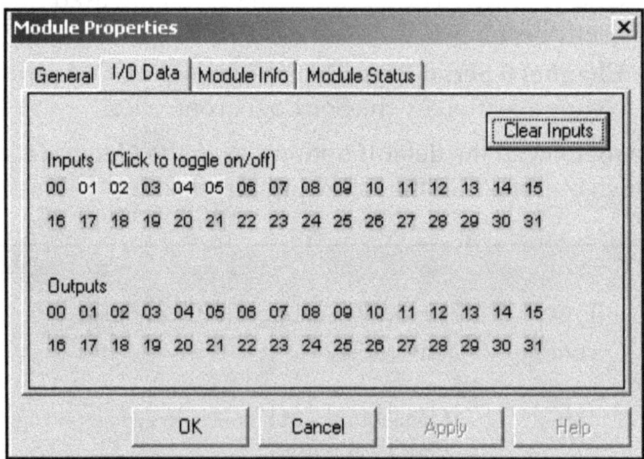

The following screenshot shows the SoftLogix chassis monitor that contains the SoftLogix CPU we have added:

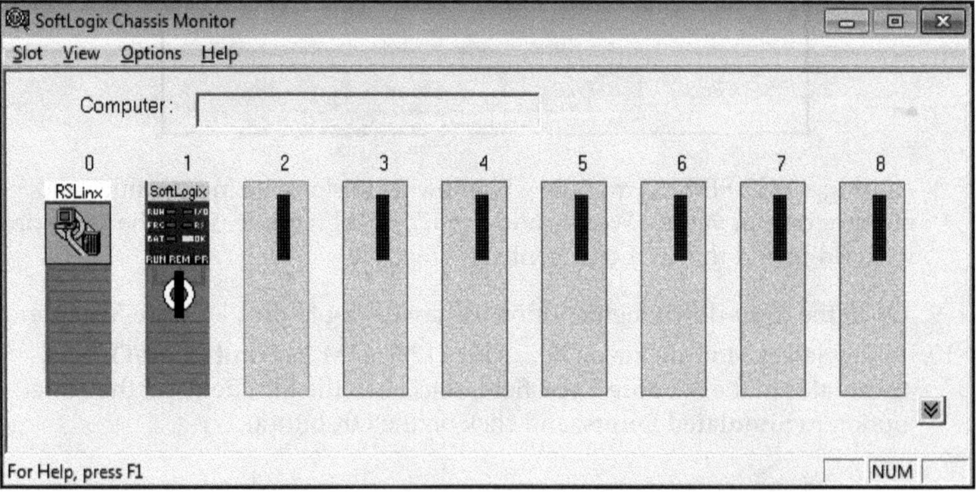

Now, we have completed the configuration of our SoftLogix controller and the chassis monitor. We have also learned how to create and configure a virtual rack for our SoftLogix controllers and cards.

Next, we will set up our RSLinx driver to allow Logix Designer/RSLogix 5000 to communicate with the SoftLogix controller.

Configuring the RSLinx virtual-backplane driver

The RSLinx virtual-backplane driver is the communication gateway used by Logix Designer/RSLogix 5000 to program and monitor the SoftLogix controllers. To configure the RSLinx virtual-backplane driver, follow these steps:

1. Run **RSLinx Classic** and navigate to **Communications** | **Configure Drivers**.
2. In the **Configure Drivers** window, click on the **Available Driver Types** dropdown and select **Virtual Backplane (SoftLogix58xx, USB)**.
3. Then, click on the **Add New...** button, as in the following screenshot:

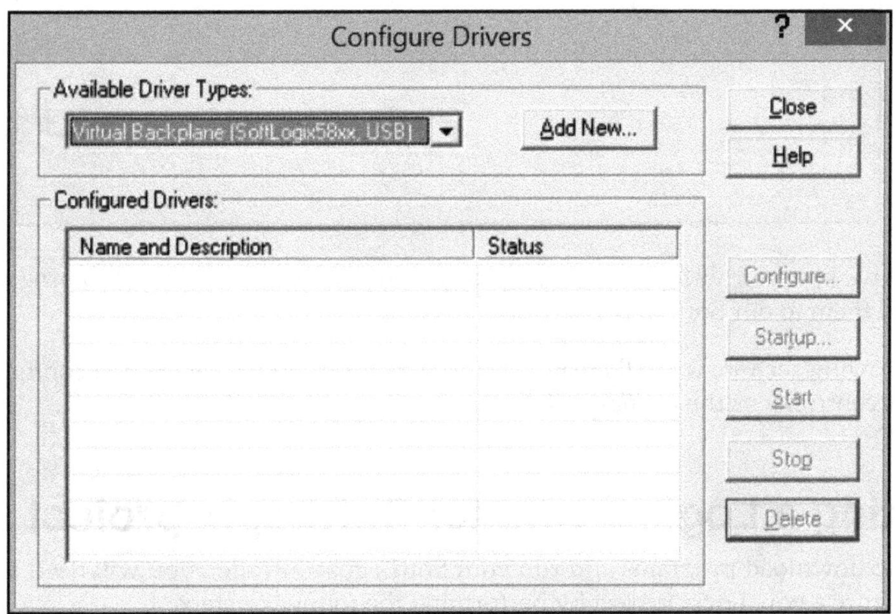

4. A Windows dialog box will appear with an **Add New RSLinx Driver** title. Enter `VirtualBP_1`.

5. Next, the **Configure VirtualBackplane** dialog box will allow us to select the slot number where the RSLinx module will reside. By default, the module will be positioned in slot `0`. Only in Logix Designer version 2.1 and higher can you select a slot position that isn't `0`.
6. Our virtual backplane drive is now configured and running, and we can close the dialog box by clicking on the **Close** button:

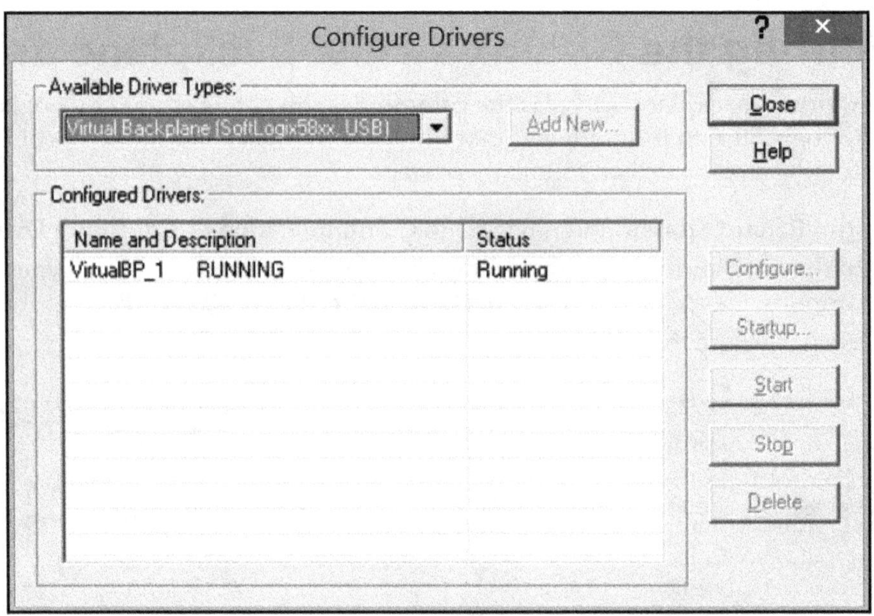

Now that we have our virtual backplane configured, we can start to develop programs and download them to our SoftLogix controller.

In the following section, we will create a new Logix program where we will configure our SoftLogix controller as the primary controller for the project.

Creating a Logix Designer SoftLogix project

In order to download programs and run your SoftLogix controller, you will need to create and configure a new Logix project by performing the following steps:

1. First, open Logix Designer/RSLogix 5000 and create a new project by selecting **New Project** from the Studio 5000 splash screen in Studio 5000, or by opening the drop-down menu option after navigating to **File | New...** in RSLogix5000.

2. In Studio 5000 Logix Designer, there is another **New Project** wizard step, but in RSLogix 5000, there is only a single dialog box for creating a new project.
3. In the **New Project** dialog box, navigate to **SoftLogix™ 5800 Controller** | **1789-L60 SoftLogix™ 5800 Controller** and set the **Name** field to `NewSoftLogixProject`. Then, click on the **Next** button:

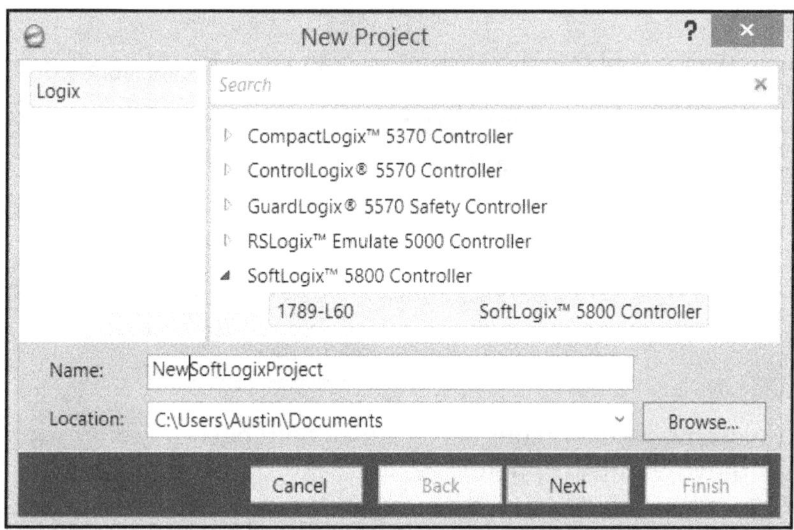

4. Set the **Chassis** field to **1789-A17 17-Slot SoftLogix Virtual Chassis** and the **Slot** field to **1**. Set the **Security Authority** field to **No Protection**:

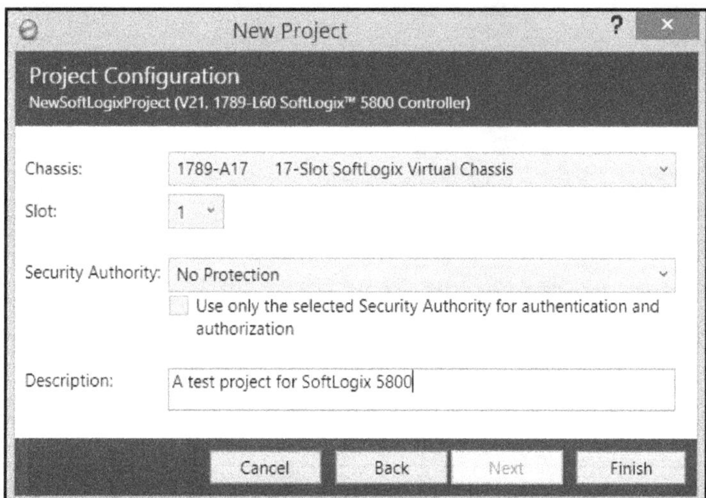

5. Specify a useful project description and then click on the **Finish** button or, in RSLogix 5000, click on **OK**.

   In later versions of Logix, you can specify a value in the **Security Authority** field, which must be present on a `FactoryTalk Network` directory in order to go online with a controller. Projects that are secured to a specific security authority cannot be recovered if that security authority is lost.

6. In the **Control Organizer** pane, we can see our SoftLogix controller listed:

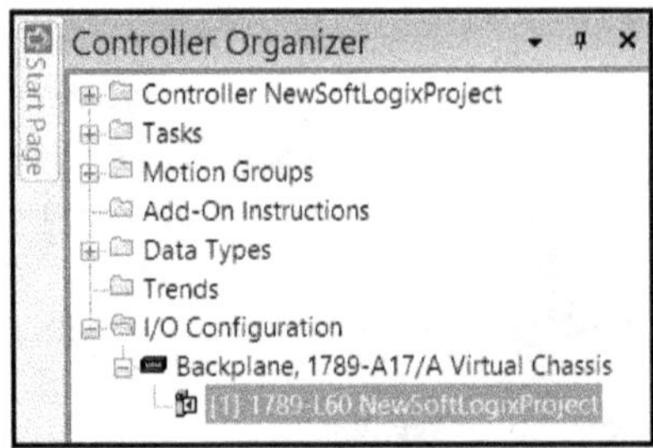

7. Next, right-click on our newly added SoftLogix controller and select the **Properties** menu option:
8. The **Controller Properties** window allows us to configure the controller to suit the needs of our application.

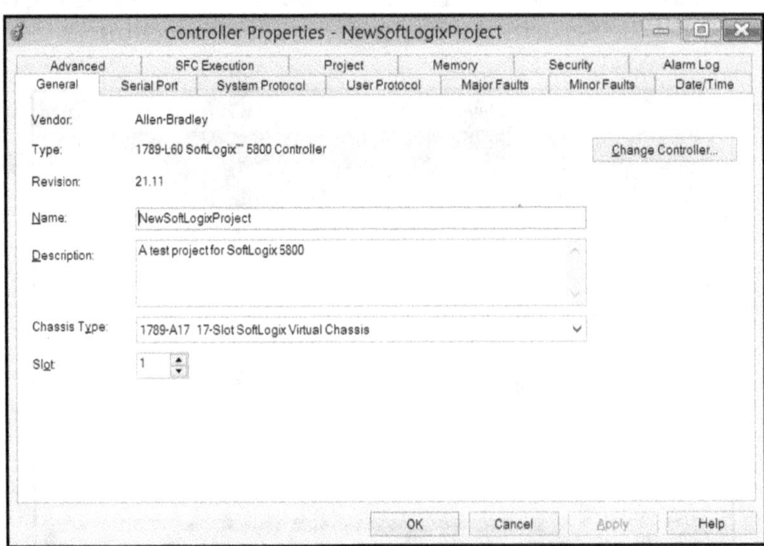

Now that we have configured our SoftLogix controller, we can add modules and begin downloading programs to it.

In the next section, we will utilize our newly configured SIM module within a Logix program.

Configuring the 1789-SIM module in the Logix Designer project

To use our 1789-SIM module within our program, we will need to load and configure the module in our Logix Designer project:

1. Open Logix Designer/RSLogix 5000 and open the project we previously added our SoftLogix controller to.
2. In Logix, right-click on the `I/O Configuration` folder and select **New Module**:

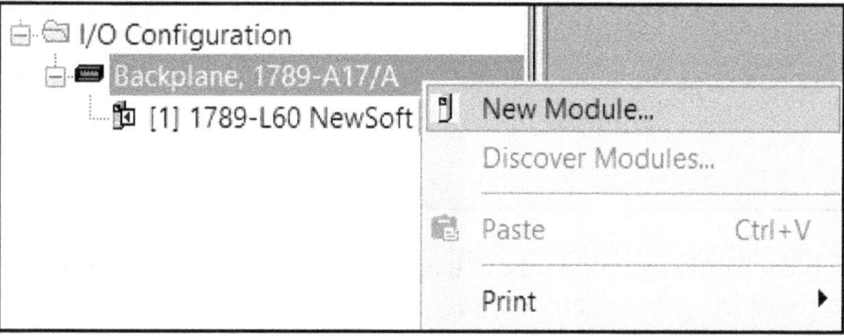

3. The **Select Module Type** dialog box will appear. Use the dialog box to find the **1789-MODULE Generic 1789 Module** module (under **Other** in Logix Designer), then click on the **Create** button:

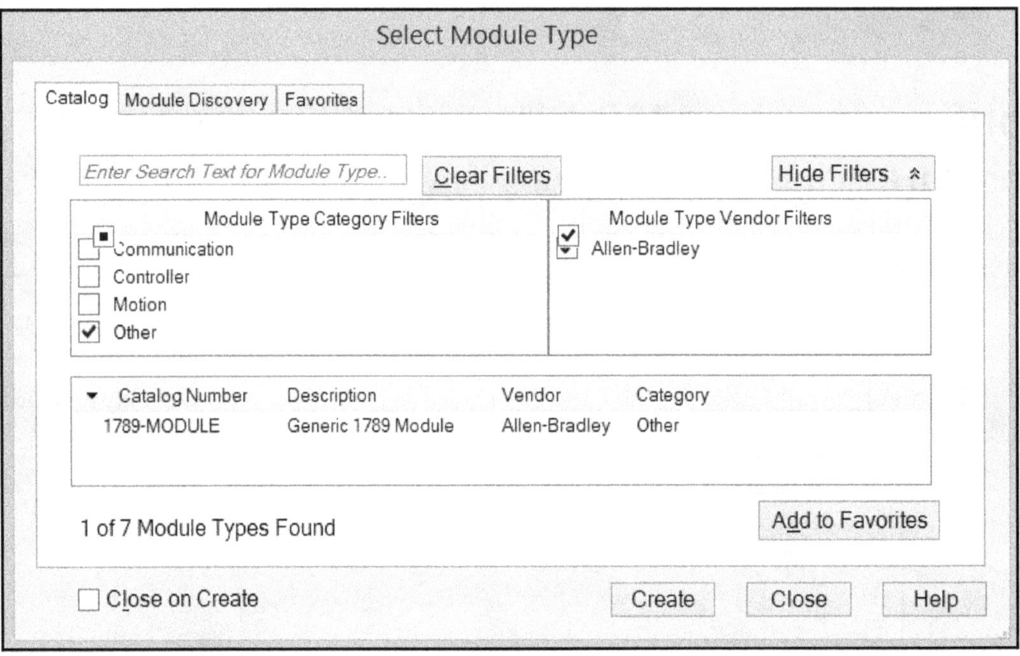

4. The **New Module** dialog box will appear and allows us to configure the 1789-SIM module's general properties.
5. The **Assembly Instance** field values represent the configuration modes for the 1789-SIM module. The **Status Input** and **Status Output** values are disabled when the **Comm Format** field that does not support the status information is selected. I have only ever seen two different configuration modes here, which are detailed in the following table:

Assembly Instance	Read/Write	Listen Only
Input	1	1
Output	2	3
Configuration	4	4
Status Input	5	5
Status Output	6	6

As you can see from the preceding table, the **Assembly Instance** values will always stay the same, except for the case of **Listen Only** mode, where the **Output** field value changes to `3`.

The **Size** property for each **Assembly Instance** field value is used to specify the number of channels for **Input**, **Output**, **Status Input**, and **Status Output**. The **Configuration** field size is always `400`, regardless of the value entered in the **Size** property.

6. Set the properties of the 1789-SIM module, as in the following screenshot:

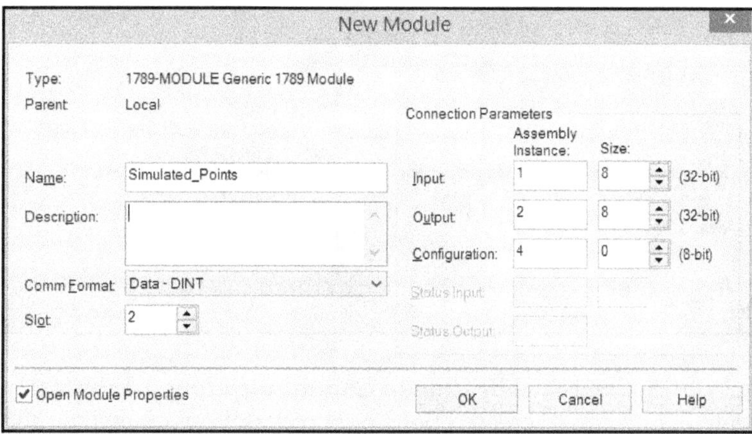

The preceding configuration will create the following input, output, and configuration controller tags:

Name	Value	Force Mask	Style	Data Type
- Local:2:I	{...}	{...}		AB:1789_MODULE_DIN...
+ Local:2:I.Data	{...}	{...}	Decimal	DINT[8]
- Local:2:O	{...}	{...}		AB:1789_MODULE_DIN...
+ Local:2:O.Data	{...}	{...}	Decimal	DINT[8]
- Local:2:C	{...}	{...}		AB:1789_MODULE:C:0
+ Local:2:C.Data	{...}	{...}	Hex	SINT[400]

Had we selected the **Comm Format** field with **Status**, we would also have the **Input Status** and **Output Status** controller tags appear in the **Controller Tag** list.

7. Click on the **OK** button. The **Module Properties** window will appear and allows us to modify the module connection configuration.
8. Set the **Requested Packet Interval (RPI)** value for the 1789-SIM module to `50.0` ms and click on the **OK** button. Setting an RPI value to less than 50 ms can cause the 1789-SIM module to fail.

Now, we can connect and download our program to the SoftLogix controller, just like a regular physical controller:

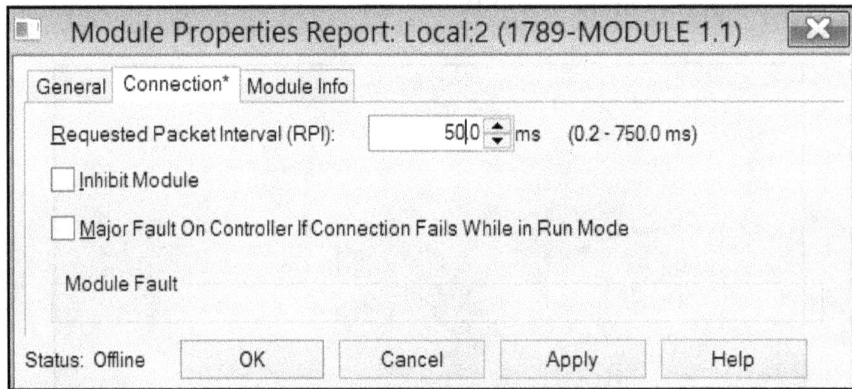

9. Open **Who Active** by navigating to **Communications** | **Who Active**, and then navigate to our newly created SoftLogix controller and click on the **Download** button.
10. Finally, ensure that you are online with your SoftLogix controller so that, in the next exercise, we can start to simulate some values.

Now that we have added our SIM module to our Logix project, we will begin to simulate values in the exercise in the next section.

Simulating values using the 1789-SIM module

Now that we have configured our virtual chassis, RSLinx, our controller, and the 1789-SIM module, as well as downloaded our program, we can start to simulate input and monitor output values by performing these steps:

1. Open **SoftLogix Chassis Monitor**, right-click on the 1789-SIM module, and select **Properties**.
2. Click on the **I/O Data** tab under **Module Properties**.

3. The **I/O Data** tab allows us to toggle digital inputs by clicking on them and monitoring the digital outputs, as shown:

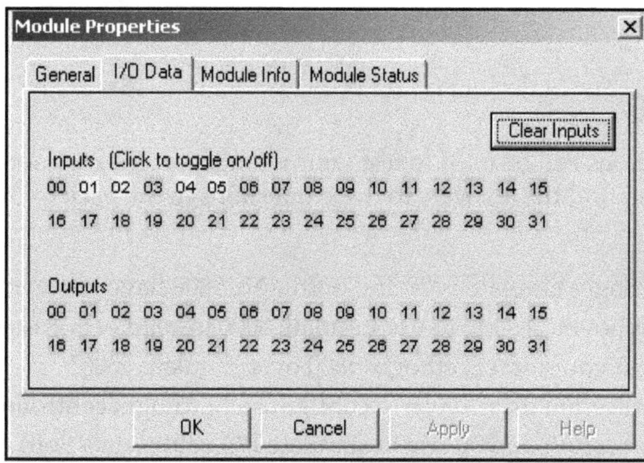

4. When you toggle a digital input and return to your online program in RSLogix/Logix Designer, you will see that the corresponding value has changed in the **Controller Tags** monitor.

In the previous exercise, we learned how to configure a SoftLogix controller, set it up in a Logix program, and simulate I/O data values.

Summary

In this chapter, we introduced the virtual controller options on the Rockwell Automation Integrated Architecture platform, including SoftLogix 5800. We learned how to configure our SoftLogix controller's virtual chassis and RSLinx application and how to create a new project based on the SoftLogix platform. In this chapter, we learned about SoftLogix 5800 controllers, which allow us to create a PC-based Logix controller rack.

We learned how to create a virtual rack that houses our virtual controllers and virtual communication modules. We also learned that SoftLogix is another component of Rockwell Automation's Integrated Architecture and can interface with the other Logix controllers, communication modules, and I/O modules. We also learned that by taking advantage of the computing power of modern PCs, SoftLogix controllers are capable of processing larger volumes of data at a higher speed than even the most powerful Logix controller.

Finally, we learned the power of the 1789-SIM I/O cards and their use with the SoftLogix controller. In the next chapter, we will introduce the Logix Emulate 5000 virtual controller and discuss how to create a new project based on it.

Questions

The following questions can be used to test your retention of the concepts introduced in this chapter. You can find the answers to these questions in the back of the book under *Assessments*:

1. What do Logix Emulate 5000 and SoftLogix 5800 have in common?
2. When might you decide to use Emulate 5000 instead of SoftLogix?
3. Why might you select SoftLogix 5800 over Emulate 5000?
4. What application do you use to configure a SoftLogix controller?
5. What application do you use to simulate I/O values on a SoftLogix controller?

Further reading

You can learn more about SoftLogix by referring to the following Rockwell Automation documents:

- The SoftLogix 5800 system: `https://literature.rockwellautomation.com/idc/groups/literature/documents/um/1789-um002_-en-p.pdf`
- The SoftLogix selection guide: `https://literature.rockwellautomation.com/idc/groups/literature/documents/sg/1789-sg001_-en-p.pdf`

5
Understanding Logix Emulate 5000

In this chapter, we will introduce Rockwell Automation Logix Emulate 5000. We will go through the setup of an Emulate chassis monitor and the configuration of our Logix Emulate 5000 controller within Logix. We will also learn how to configure our controller's virtual chassis and the required communication settings in the RSLinx application. Finally, we will investigate the techniques for simulating I/O using the 1789-SIM module.

This chapter will cover the following aspects of the Emulate platform:

- Learning about Logix Emulate 5000
- Working with Logix Emulate 5000

In the first section, we will provide an overview of the Emulate 5000 solution from Rockwell Automation.

Technical requirements

To complete this chapter, you will need to create a Rockwell Automation support account by visiting `https://www.rockwellautomation.com/account/create-account`.

Creating an account is free, and the material we will be reviewing in this chapter is publicly available to anyone who is registered with Rockwell Automation.

You will also need a copy of RSLogix or Studio 5000 that has a license for Emulate 5000 to program your project. You can either purchase this from your local distributor or request a time-limited trial version.

You can find a local distributor for Rockwell Automation products at `https://locator.rockwellautomation.com/`.

Learning about Logix Emulate 5000

Much like the SoftLogix solution, Logix Emulate 5000 controllers enable you to create a PC-based Logix controller rack. RSLogix Emulate 5000 is a virtual Logix controller and rack, designed to allow you to debug your Logix program code using advanced features such as breakpoints and tracepoints:

- **Breakpoints**: Breakpoints can be added to a program by using the breakpoint (`BPT`) instruction. A `BPT` instruction will cause the executing program to stop once energized and a prompt to appear. The values that caused the `BPT` instruction to energize are displayed in the prompt.
- **Tracepoints**: Tracepoints can be added to a program using the tracepoint (`TPT`) instruction. When a `TPT` instruction is energized, it writes a trace entry to a trace window or log file.

Breakpoint and tracepoint instructions monitor the state of a program's logic when the logic is in specified conditions. When the specified condition for the rung is true, breakpoints stop program emulation and the tracepoints log specified data.

Using Emulate 5000, you can create a virtual test rack using similar modules to a physical rack, and even test your project with a **Human Machine Interface** (**HMI**). However, Emulate 5000 is not capable of controlling real I/O. Also, the communication modules are not supported by Emulate 5000. A typical RSLogix Emulate 5000 solution consists of modules that are configured in a virtual Logix rack to mimic the end solution. The logic is downloaded and monitored using Logix Designer/RSLogix 5000 in order to troubleshoot it. Logix Emulate 5000 is packaged with the Professional edition of Studio 5000 or RSLogix 5000. However, it can also be purchased separately if you are not currently using the Professional edition. Emulate works very similarly to SoftLogix, as we will see in the following sections.

Working with Logix Emulate 5000

Now that we have covered some of the use cases for Logix Emulate 5000, we will work toward setting up a project that utilizes it. In the following exercises, we will complete the following tasks:

1. Configure a Logix Emulate 5000 chassis monitor.
2. Configure the RSLinx virtual backplane driver.
3. Create a Logix Designer Emulate 5000 project.
4. Configure the 1789-SIM module in the Logix Designer project.
5. Simulate values using the 1789-SIM module.

A license for Logix Emulate 5000 is required to complete the following exercises. Emulate 5000 is a software product that is sold separately from Studio 5000. Emulate 5000 is included in the Professional edition of Studio 5000.

In the following section, we will complete an exercise to configure an Emulate 5000 chassis monitor for use in our project.

Configuring a Logix Emulate 5000 chassis monitor

Emulate 5000 uses a virtual controller that is configured using the Logix Emulate 5000 Chassis Monitor software. It works in a similar manner to a real-world chassis and allows us to add and remove cards and CPUs to different slots in the rack. In this exercise, we will configure a controller in Logix Emulate 5000 Chassis Monitor.

To configure a Logix Emulate 5000 controller, you need to perform the following steps:

1. Start the **Logix Emulate 5000 Chassis Monitor** software.
2. In the **Virtual Chassis** window that appears, open the drop-down menu option by navigating to **Slot** | **Create Module...**. The following screenshot shows the virtual controller added to **RSLogix Emulate 5000 Chassis Monitor**:

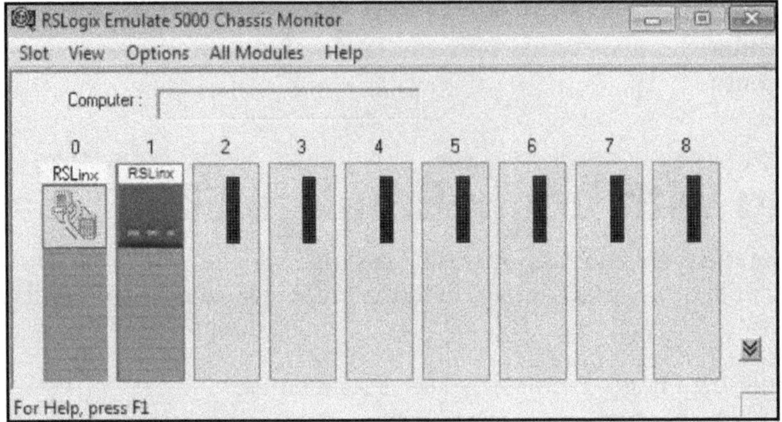

3. The **Select Module** dialog box appears and allows us to add the following modules to the slot we specify:
   - **Emulator RSLogix Emulate 5000 Controller**
   - **1789-SIM 32 Point Input/Output Simulator**
4. Select **Emulator RSLogix Emulate 5000 Controller**, as well as 2 for the **Slot** field using the numeric selector. Finally, press the **OK** button, as in the following screenshot:

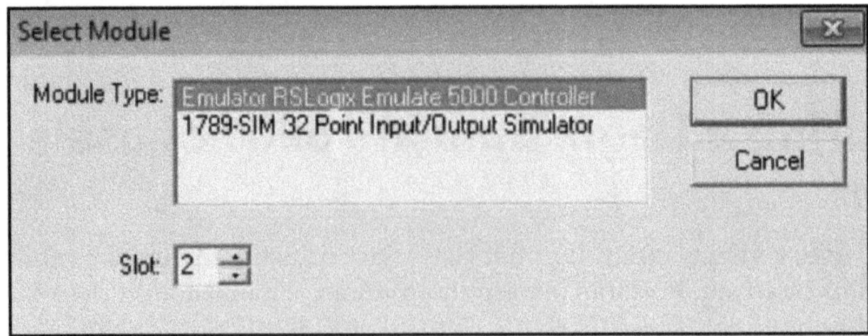

5. After pressing **OK**, we can now see that the RSLogix Emulate 5000 controller appears on our virtual chassis:

Adding a 1789-SIM I/O module allows us to simulate input values and monitor output values. We can add the 1789-SIM module using the same process we used to add the Emulate controller module:

1. Open the drop-down menu option by navigating to **Slot** | **Create Module...**.
2. When we added the controller in *Step 3* of the previous set of steps using the **Select Module** dialog, you may have noticed the 1789-SIM card option that was available (you can see the SIM module option in the screenshot following *Step 4* of the preceding steps). In the **Select Module** dialog box, select **1789-SIM 32 Point Input/Output Simulator** for the **Module Type** field, select `3` for the **Slot** field, set the **Label** option to **Simulated Input**, and click on the **OK** button.

We now have our Emulate controller and a simulated input card added to our virtual chassis, as in the following screenshot (note that slot `0` and slot `1` are automatically pre-populated with RSLinx modules):

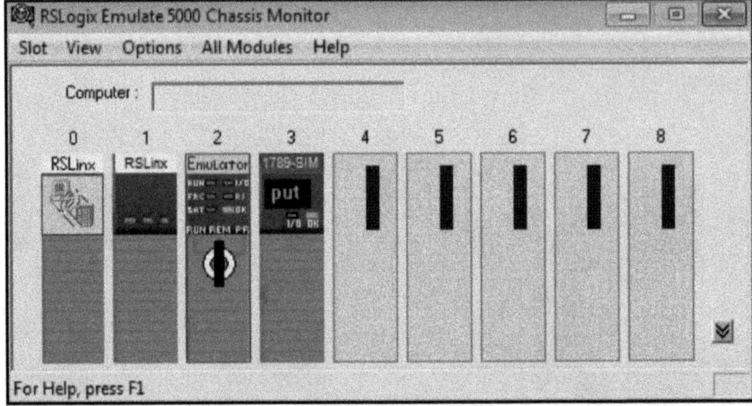

Now that we have a 1789-SIM module added to our virtual backplane, we can toggle the inputs and monitor the outputs. You can toggle the digital points by right-clicking on the 1789-SIM module and selecting **Properties**, which will take you to the following screen:

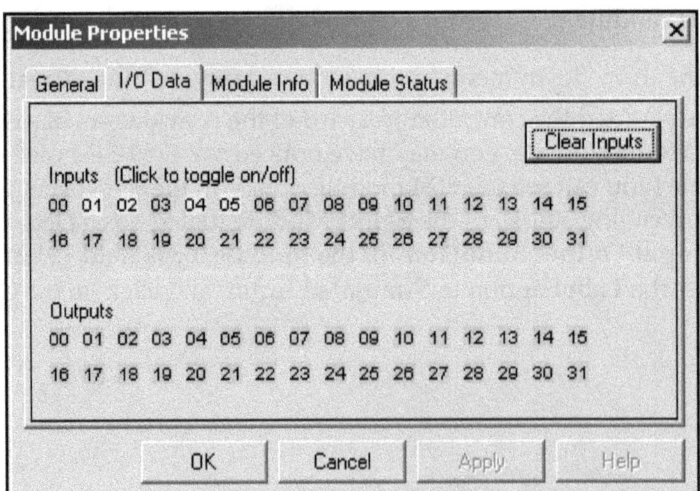

We have now completed the configuration of our Logix Emulate 5000 virtual chassis.

Next, we will set up our RSLinx driver to allow Logix Designer/RSLogix 5000 to communicate with the Logix Emulate 5000 virtual controller.

Configuring the RSLinx virtual backplane driver

The RSLinx virtual backplane driver is the communication gateway used by Logix Designer/RSLogix 5000 to program and monitor the Emulate 5000 controllers. When configuring RSLinx, we will use the same SoftLogix virtual backplane driver that we used in the previous chapter, `chapter 4`, *Understanding Softlogix*. There is no dedicated Emulate 5000 driver—both SoftLogix and Emulate 5000 use the SoftLogix virtual backplane driver.

In the following steps, we will configure the RSLinx virtual backplane driver. Configuring the driver will enable us to program and communicate with the Emulate 5000 controller in our Logix project.

We will need to have this driver in place when it is time for us to download our program to the Emulate 5000 virtual CPU:

1. Run **RSLinx Classic** and navigate to **Communications** | **Configure Drivers**.
2. In the **Configure Drivers** window, click on the **Available Driver Types** dropdown and select **Virtual Backplane (SoftLogix58xx, USB)**. Then, click on the **Add New...** button, as in the following screenshot:

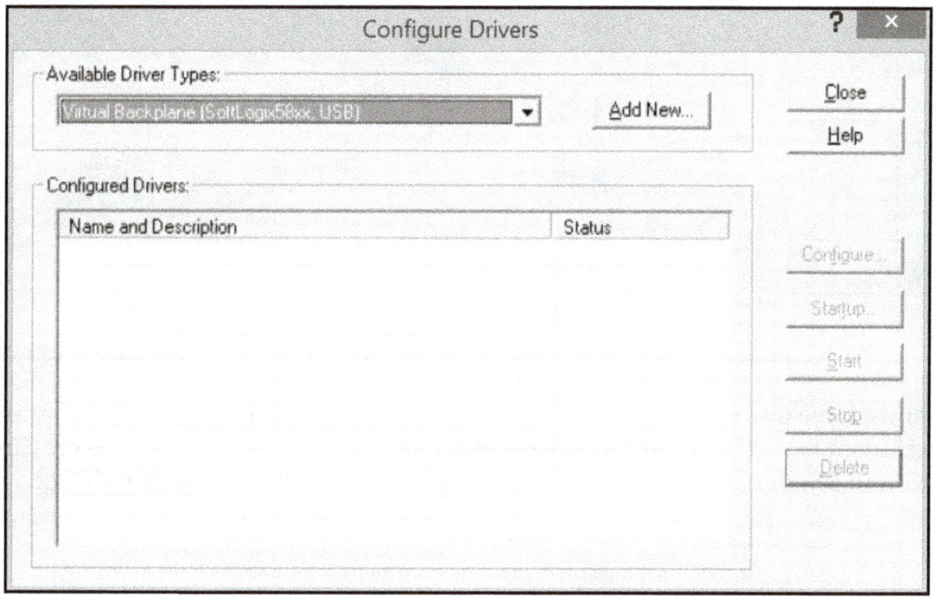

3. A windows dialog box will appear, entitled **Add New RSLinx Driver**. Enter `VirtualBP_1` for the title.

4. Next, a **Configure Virtual Backplane** dialog box will allow us to select the **Slot** number where the RSLinx module will reside. By default, the module will be positioned in **Slot 0**.

Only in Logix Designer version 21 and higher can we select a slot position other than `0`.

5. Our virtual backplane driver is now configured and running, and we can close the dialog box by clicking on the **Close** button:

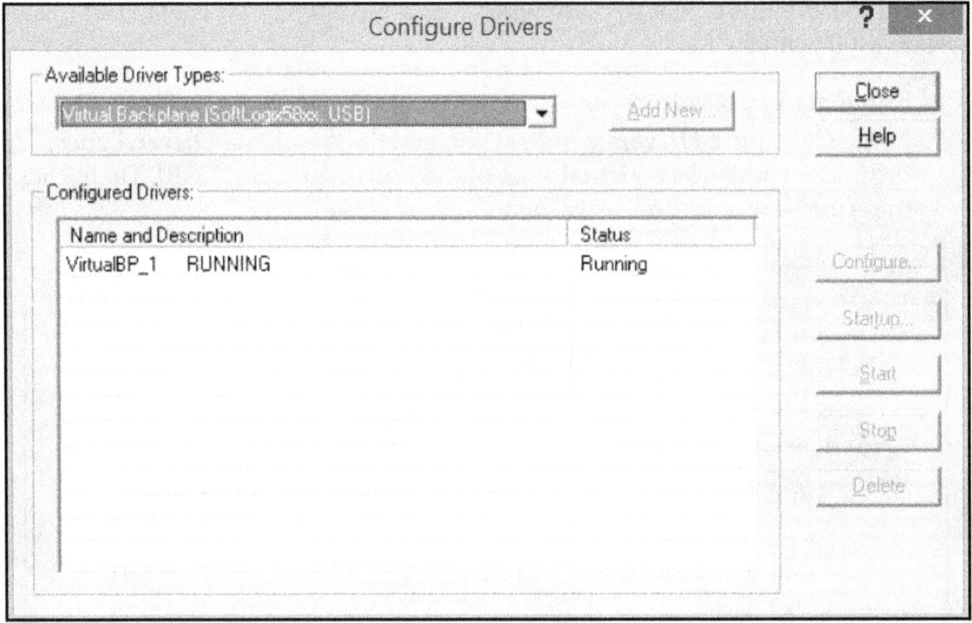

Now that we have our virtual backplane configured, we can start to develop programs and download them to our Emulate 5000 controller. In the next section, we will be creating a new project in RSLogix 5000 and downloading a sample application to our virtual controller.

Creating a Logix Designer Emulate 5000 project

In order to download programs and run your Emulate 5000 controller, you will need to create and configure a new Logix project.

Here are the steps that will help us create and configure the new Logix project:

1. First, open **Logix Designer/RSLogix 5000** and create a new project by selecting **New Project** from the Studio 5000 splash screen in Studio 5000, or by opening the drop-down menu option by navigating to **File** | **New...** in RSLogix 5000.

In Studio 5000 Logix Designer, there is another **New Project** wizard step, but in RSLogix 5000, there is only a single dialog box for creating a new project.

2. In the **New Project** dialog box, navigate to **RSLogix Emulate 5000 Controller** and set the **Name** field to `NewEmulateProject`:

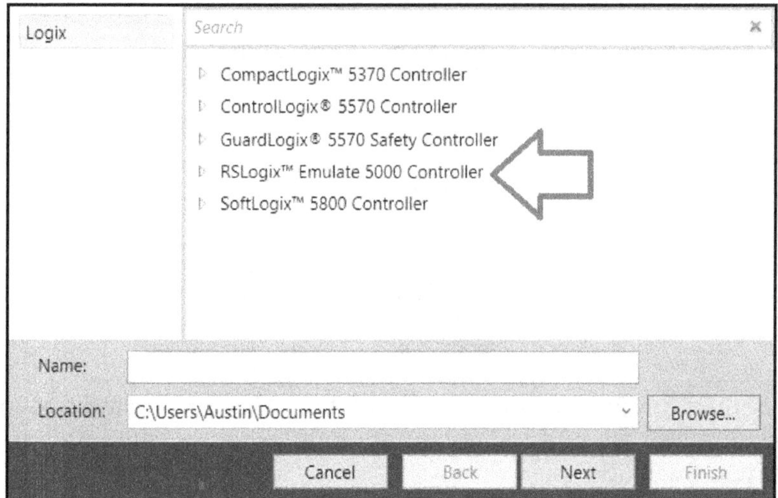

3. In Logix Designer, click on the **Next** button.
4. Set the **Chassis** field to **1789-A17 17-Slot ControlLogix Virtual Chassis**.
5. Next, set the **Slot** field to `2` to match the slot we selected on our virtual chassis.

The firmware revision here must also match the firmware revision you configured on the controller on the virtual chassis.

6. Set the **Security Authority** field to **No Protection**.
   In later versions of Logix, you can specify a value in the **Security Authority** field, which must be present on the `FactoryTalk Network` directory in order to go online with a controller.

Projects that are secured with a specific security authority cannot be recovered if that security authority is lost.

7. Specify a useful project description.
8. Then, in Logix Designer, click on the **Finish** button. If you are using RSLogix 5000, click on **OK**.
9. In the **Controller Organizer** pane, we can see our Emulate 5000 controller listed:

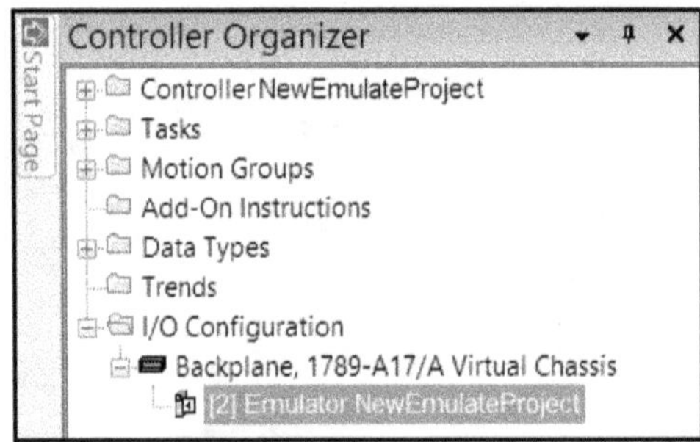

We have successfully configured our Logix Emulate 5000 controller in RSLogix 5000/Studio 5000. In the next exercise, we will add the input module that we configured in the virtual chassis that we just created.

Configuring the 1789-SIM module in the Logix Designer project

In this exercise, we will add a SIM module that can be used to toggle digital values and manipulate analog values to our Emulate 5000 project.

To use our 1789-SIM module within our program, we will need to load and configure the module in our Logix Designer project:

1. Open **Logix Designer/RSLogix 5000** and open the project we previously added our Emulate controller to.
2. In Logix, right-click on the **I/O Configuration** folder and select **New Module...**:

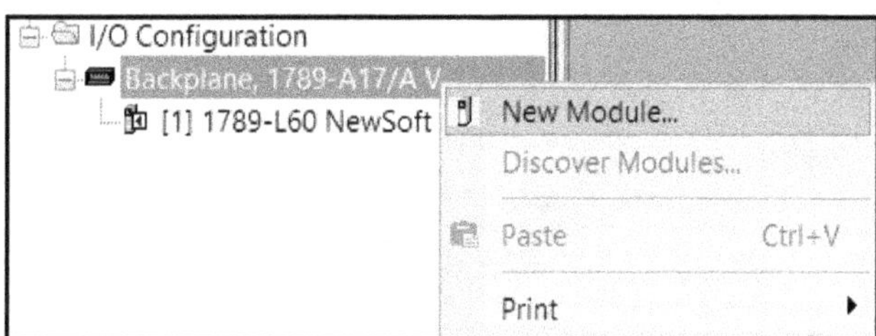

3. The **Select Module Type** dialog box will appear. Use the dialog box to find the **1789-MODULE Generic 1789 Module** module (under **Other** in Logix Designer), and then click on the **Create** button:

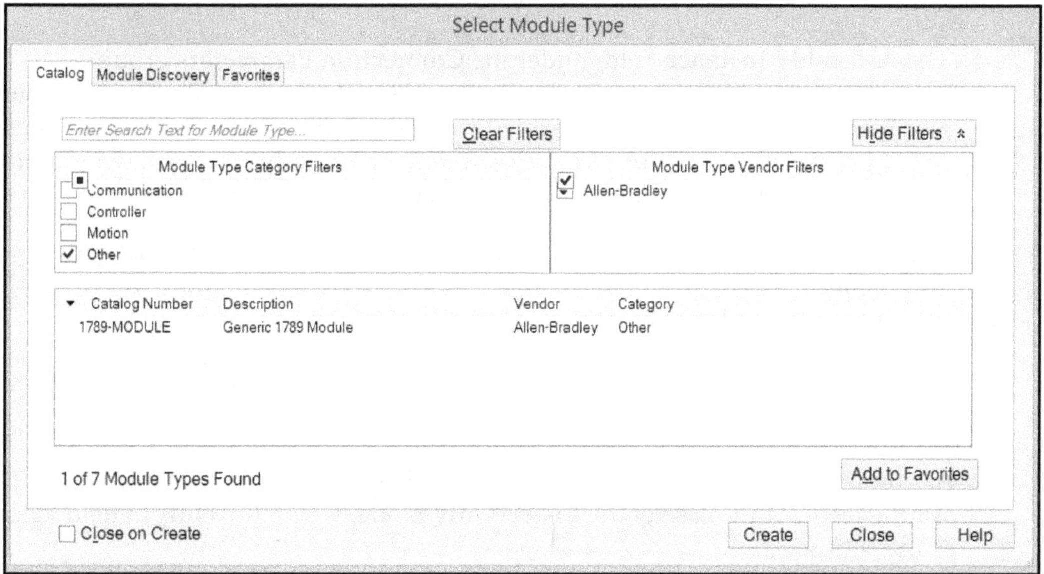

4. The **New Module** dialog box will appear and allows us to configure the 1789-SIM module's general properties. The following is a screenshot of the **New Module** dialog box:

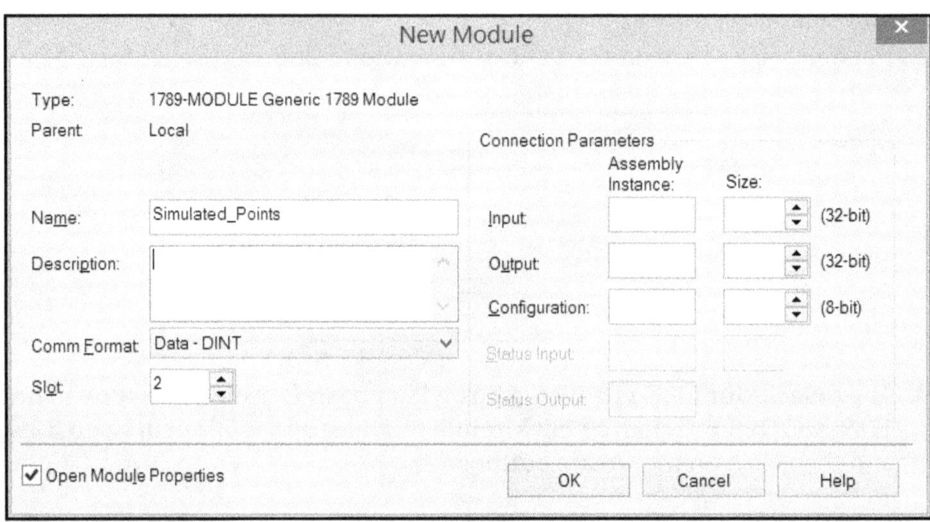

5. The **Assembly Instance** field, under the **Connection Parameters** group, represents the configuration modes for the 1789-SIM module. The **Status Input** and **Status Output** values are disabled when the **Comm Format** field that does not support the status information is selected. I have only ever seen two different configuration modes here, which are detailed in the following table:

Assembly Instance	Read/Write	Listen Only
Input	1	1
Output	2	3
Configuration	4	4
Status Input	5	5
Status Output	6	6

As you can see from the table, the **Assembly Instance** values will always stay the same, except for the case of the **Listen Only** mode, where the **Output** field value changes to `3`.

The **Size** property for each **Assembly Instance** field value is used to specify the number of channels for **Input**, **Output**, **Status Input**, and **Status Output**. The **Configuration** field is always **4**, regardless of the value entered in the **Size** property.

6. Set the properties of the 1789-SIM module, as in the following screenshot:

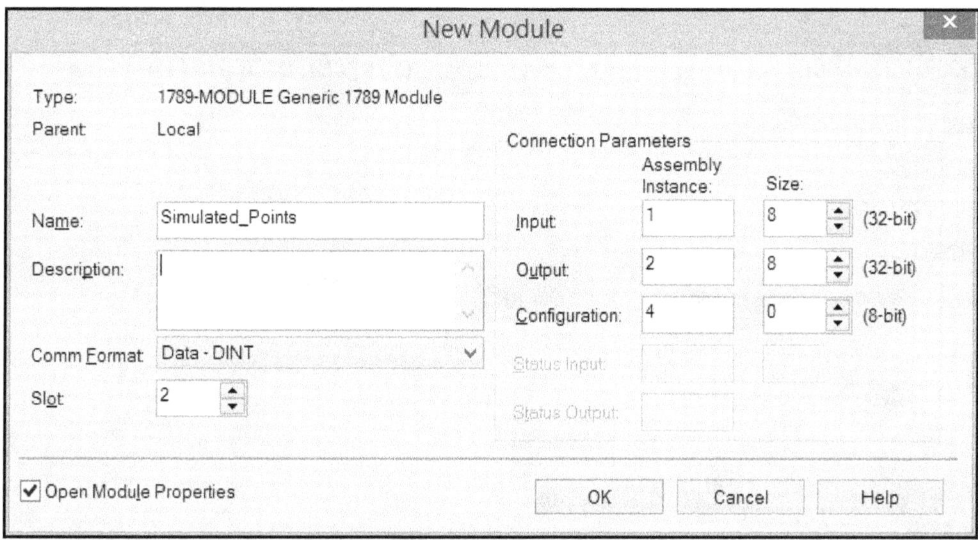

7. The preceding configuration will create the following input, output, and configuration controller tags:

Name	Value	Force Mask	Style	Data Type
- Local:2:I	{...}	{...}		AB:1789_MODULE_DIN...
+ Local:2:I.Data	{...}	{...}	Decimal	DINT[8]
- Local:2:O	{...}	{...}		AB:1789_MODULE_DIN...
+ Local:2:O.Data	{...}	{...}	Decimal	DINT[8]
- Local:2:C	{...}	{...}		AB:1789_MODULE:C:0
+ Local:2:C.Data	{...}	{...}	Hex	SINT[400]

8. Had we selected a **Comm Format** field with **Status**, we would also have the **Input Status** and **Output Status** controller tags appear in the **Controller Tag** list.
9. Click on the **OK** button.

10. The **Module Properties Report** window will appear and allows us to modify the module connection configuration:

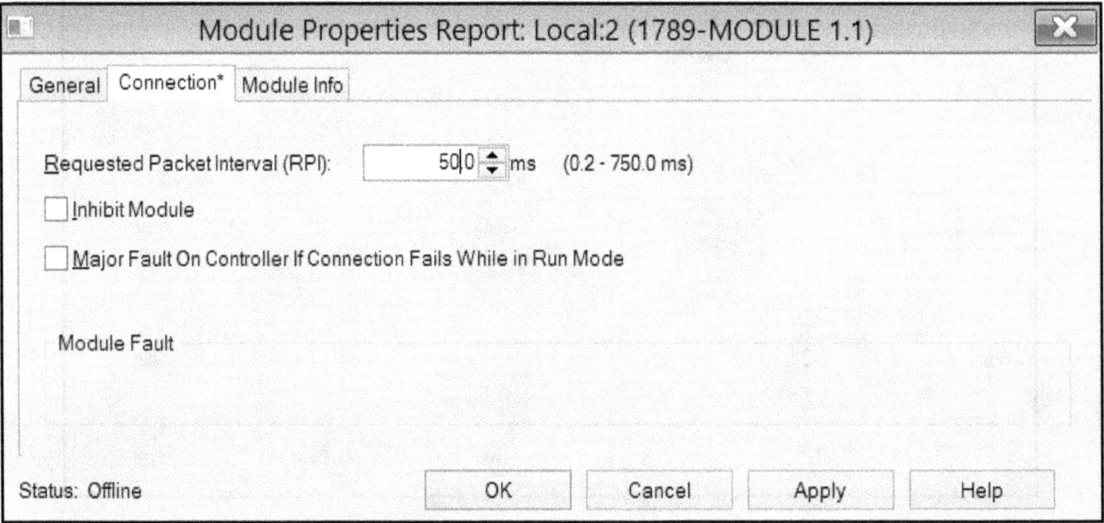

11. Set the **Requested Packet Interval (RPI)** value for the 1789-SIM module to `50.0` ms and click on the **OK** button.

Setting an RPI value to less than `50` ms can cause the 1789-SIM module to fail.

12. Now, we can connect and download our program to the Emulate controller, just as with a regular physical controller.
13. Open **Who Active** by navigating to **Communications** | **Who Active**, then navigate to our newly created Emulate controller and click on the **Download** button.
14. Finally, ensure that you are online with your Emulate controller by looking for the spinning gears in the icon next to the path selector in Studio 5000 or RSLogix 5000.

In the next exercise, we will leverage our emulated controller to simulate input values.

Simulating values using the 1789-SIM module

Now that we have configured our virtual chassis, RSLinx, our controller, and our 1789-SIM module, as well as downloaded our program, we can start to simulate input and monitor output values by performing the following steps:

1. Open **Emulate Chassis Monitor**, right-click on the 1789-SIM module, and select **Properties**.
2. Click on the **Module Properties** tab, which is labeled **I/O Data**.
3. The **I/O Data** tab allows us to toggle digital inputs by clicking on them, and also allows us to monitor digital outputs. The following screenshot shows the **Module Properties** pop-up window that appears:

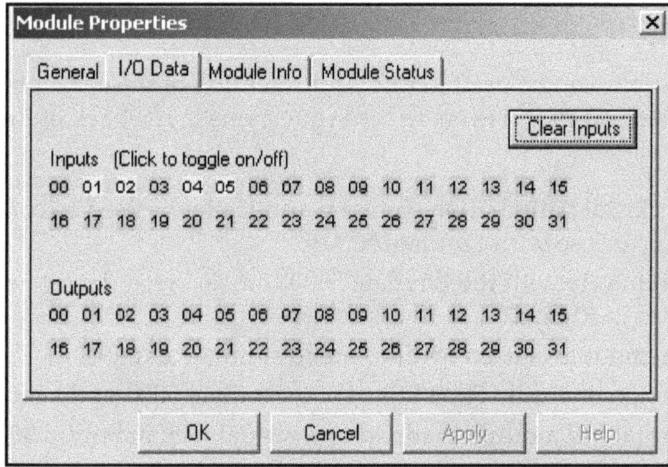

When you toggle a digital input and return to your online program in RSLogix/Logix Designer, you will see that the corresponding value has changed in the **Controller Tags** monitor. Forcing inputs allows us to test the different states of our process without having to hardwire our input cards.

We have now completed the setup of our Logix Emulate 5000. We can now create ladder logic based on the input cards we have created and fully simulate the logic execution based on the inputs from our virtual chassis.

Summary

In this chapter, we introduced the Logix Emulate 5000 virtualized controller and learned how to configure our controller's virtual chassis and the required communications in the RSLinx application. We also learned how we can create a new project on the Logix Emulate 5000 platform. Finally, we learned the power of the 1789-SIM I/O cards and their use within the Logix Emulate 5000 controller.

In the next chapter, we will introduce multiple types of Rockwell Automation network communications technologies that are available and some of the tools that can streamline network planning.

Questions

The following questions can be used to test your retention of the concepts introduced in this chapter. You can find the answers to these questions in the back of the book under *Assessments*:

1. What Rockwell Automation software application is used to configure the backplane for use with Emulate 5000?
2. To communicate with the Emulate 5000 chassis, what driver needs to be configured in RSLinx?
3. What I/O module is used by Emulate to simulate data?
4. What edition of Studio 5000/RSLogix is Emulate 5000 packaged with?
5. What virtual I/O module is added to a virtual rack in Studio 5000/RSLogix?

Further reading

For more information on Emulate 5000, take a look at `https://literature.rockwellautomation.com/idc/groups/literature/documents/gr/lgem5k-gr016_-en-p.pdf`.

2

Section 2: Logix Programming Basics

This section allows you to start developing IEC languages within the Logix platform. You will be exposed to industrial networking and the various Rockwell Automation PLC modules, and you will learn to interact with them using Ladder Logic, Function Block, Structured Text, and Sequential Function Chart programming.

This section comprises the following chapters:

6
Industrial Network Communications

In this chapter, we will discuss the various communication technologies available on the Logix platform. The focus of this book is the current state of Rockwell Automation's **ControlLogix** and **CompactLogix** controllers; however, we will touch on some legacy communication protocols, that you may still find running in the field today.

Communications allow us to interface with controllers, racks, and devices on our network. Establishing communications is an important step that enables us to connect with a device and transfer configuration changes and programs. After completing this chapter, you will be familiar with all the Rockwell Automation communication technologies that are actively used in the field today.

This chapter will cover the following key areas of industrial network communications in the Logix platform:

- Understanding the key terms in industrial communications
- Learning about modern network communication technologies
- Understanding legacy network technologies
- Comparing network communication technologies
- Working with EtherNet/IP Capacity Tool
- Using RSLinx Classic and FactoryTalk Linx
- Using Rockwell Automation Integrated Architecture Builder

We will start this chapter by covering some of the basic terminologies for industrial networking.

Technical requirements

To complete this chapter, you need to create a Rockwell Support account by visiting `https://www.rockwellautomation.com/account/create-account`.

Creating an account is free, and the material we will be reviewing in this chapter is publicly available to anyone who is registered with Rockwell Automation.

You will also need a copy of RSLogix or Studio 5000 to program your project that has a license for Emulate 5000. You can either purchase this from your local distributor or request a time-limited trial version. You can find a local distributor of Rockwell products at `https://locator.rockwellautomation.com/`.

Understanding the key terms in industrial communications

Communications enable the exchange of data between devices on an industrial control network. Without communications, controllers are unable to see the values coming from field devices and operators are unable to see the values coming from controllers. Here are some of the key terms we will use when talking about industrial networking and communications:

- **Media**: Communication requires wires, cables, or fiber-optic connections between devices. The connections used for communication are called the media, which differ from one another by properties such as the maximum distance for each connection and the maximum data transmission speed.
- **Node**: Each device on the network is called a node.
- **Node address**: Each node will typically have a unique identifier called a node address.
- **Network**: When multiple devices are connected under a common device address space, we call this a network.
- **Topology**: The physical structure of the network is called the topology.
- **Bridge**: This device creates a connection between two separate networks.
- **Router**: This device can forward data between two or more networks.
- **Hub**: This device can channel data between multiple nodes within a single network.

- **Switch**: This device can channel data from one node to another. Unlike a hub, a switch will intelligently route only the data destined for a device and is not prone to data loss due to network packet collisions.
- **Segment**: This device divides a localized section of the network with bridges, routers, or switches.
- **Protocol**: The language used to communicate data between each node across a network is called a protocol.

The following diagram illustrates a typical Rockwell automation **Industrial Control Systems** (**ICS**) network:

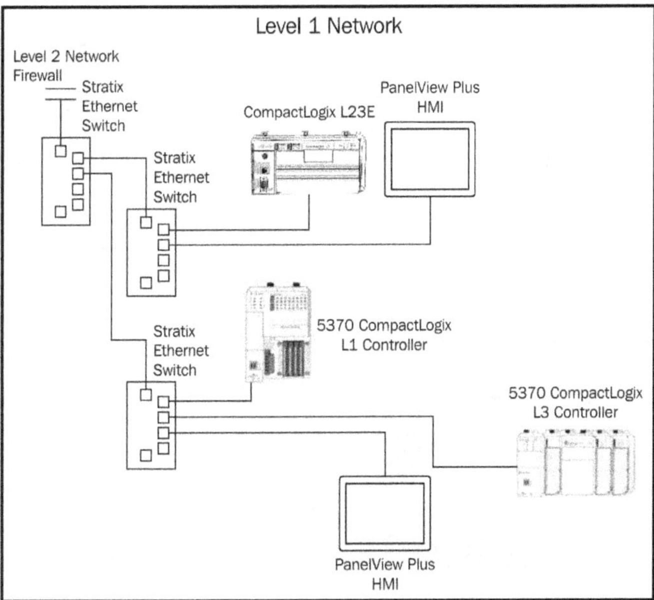

In networks that use a coaxial cable as media, such as ControlNet, you will find the following terminology:

- **Tap**: This device is small and *T*-shaped and connects a trunk-line cable (the top of the *T*) to a drop-line cable (the bottom of the *T*).
- **Terminating resistor**: This device is a 75 Ohm resistor that can be connected to a trunk-line connection, which absorbs energy and prevents electrical signal reflection.
- **Trunk line**: This device is the main cable that connects to the taps and drop line cables. A trunk line will have a terminating resistor at either side and one or more drop lines attached to it.

- **Drop line**: This device is a cable connection from a tap that connects down to a node.
- **Repeater**: This device is a two-port device that connects two trunk lines together and boosts the signal. It is helpful for connecting segments across longer distances or boosting the signal for a long network segment.

The following diagram illustrates a typical coaxial cable network:

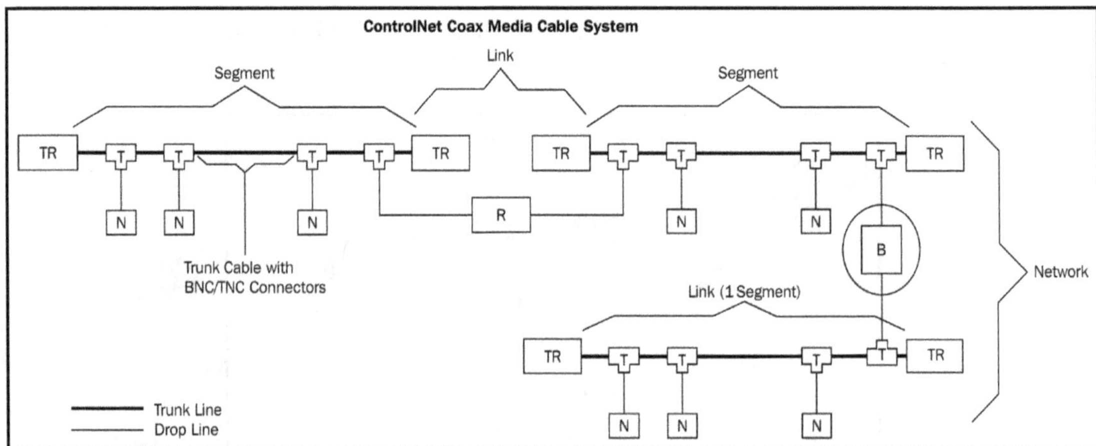

Now that we have covered some of the basic terms, let's look at the various communication solutions used by Rockwell Automation.

Learning about modern network communication technologies

Communications plays a vital role in most industrial automation solutions and Rockwell Automation's Integrated Architecture offers a variety of options.

Rockwell communication technologies can be categorized by the primary network technologies (those that are actively used in modern implementations of a Logix system) and legacy network technologies (those that have been used frequently in the past but are not installed on the new Logix control systems).

In the next section, we will introduce some of the primary network technologies we see today in Rockwell Automation-based networks.

Primary network technologies

Logix relies on the following three primary technologies for network communication:

- DeviceNet
- ControlNet
- EtherNet/IP

DeviceNet and ControlNet were developed by Rockwell Automation and are based on the **Common Industrial Protocol** (**CIP**). They are maintained by the **Open DeviceNet Vendors Association** (**ODVA**). EtherNet/IP (note the capitalized *N* and that **IP**, in this case, stands for **Industrial Protocol**) was developed by ODVA in 2001 and was adopted by Rockwell Automation.

Let's discuss each of these in more detail in the following subsections.

DeviceNet

DeviceNet is explicitly designed to communicate with and provide power to the lowest-level field devices. It can communicate with intelligent devices that support a DeviceNet module, such as sensors, **Variable-frequency drive** (**VFDs**), valves, motors, and distributed I/O blocks. DeviceNet is convenient as it provides both signal and power to the device. However, it's not designed to handle high volumes of network traffic. DeviceNet networks must be configured using Rockwell Automation's RSNetworx for DeviceNet software. DeviceNet allows selectable data rates (such as 125, 250, or 500 KBaud), which enables system integrators to potentially trade speed for communication-run distances. DeviceNet devices are not required and do not necessarily support all the data rate ranges, but many do.

In this book, we will primarily focus on EtherNet/IP networking, but links to further DeviceNet resources are available at the end of this chapter.

In the next section, we will introduce the Rockwell I/O backbone protocol, known as ControlNet.

ControlNet

ControlNet is a deterministic network technology that acts as the I/O communication backbone for a control system. Deterministic data collection guarantees that new data arrives within a predefined interval. It enables the interconnection of multiple DeviceNet networks and shares data with other controllers. It is capable of full network redundancy, so if a redundant ControlNet network is configured and one cable is broken, the network can continue operating normally.

Connections over ControlNet are configured as **scheduled** or **unscheduled**. The ControlNet **Network Update Time** (**NUT**) is the millisecond interval for collecting updated data in a ControlNet network. ControlNet is a highly repeatable deterministic communications method—albeit slow (locked at 5 Mbits/s), but deterministic nonetheless. Deterministic networks are ideal for processes that require continuous synchronized data and cannot tolerate any data update delays, such as motion control.

The ControlLogix backplane, ControlBus, is nearly identical to the ControlNet networking. It is based on an open standard for industrial network protocols known as **Fieldbus** and is based on the same Fieldbus **IEC 61158** communication standard as **Foundation Fieldbus**, **PROFIBUS**, and **Interbus**. The Fieldbus architecture provides the skeleton that ControlNet is based on. However, due to fundamental implementation differences, it is not able to directly communicate with any other Fieldbus protocols. On top of the Fieldbus architecture, at the protocol application layer, ControlNet uses the CIP to provide its functionality. ControlNet can upload and download programs, perform I/O forcing and online editing, and communicate with the remote I/O racks.

ControlNet uses a **Quad Shield RG6 coaxial cable** as the networking media, which requires it to use network taps for each drop and terminating resistors at the end of each segment. In this book, we will primarily focus on EtherNet/IP networking, but more ControlNet resources are available in the appendix.

We will introduce EtherNet/IP in the next section.

EtherNet/IP

EtherNet/IP is the most widely used communications technology in the Integrated Architecture ecosystem today because of its speed, scalability, and ease of integration with enterprise-level network hardware. EtherNet/IP is the primary communication method used in the examples in this book. It combines the IEEE 802 standard Ethernet technology stack with the object-based CIP. Basing the communications on Ethernet allows ease of integration with the existing enterprise IT networks.

The CIP application-layer protocol also allows the Logix controllers to communicate control, safety, synchronization, motion, configuration, and diagnostic information with devices from hundreds of different vendors. CIP enables EtherNet/IP to upload a program, download a program, force I/O values, monitor code, perform online edits, and connect to the remote I/O racks.

In the legacy I/O systems, the **Programmable Logic Controller (PLC)** would poll (request data at a set interval) digital input modules for new data. The CIP protocol on EtherNet/IP digital input modules can perform the following tasks:

- Return data on **Change of State** (**COS**).
- Return data at a **Request Packet Interval** (**RPI**), scheduled in milliseconds.

One notable difference from the other methods of data collection is that EtherNet/IP is non-deterministic. Deterministic, in the context of communications, means the delays in delivering a packet of data across a network are known in advance and are not subject to change. Non-deterministic data collection does not guarantee that the new data will arrive within the RPI. IEEE 802 standard Ethernet is fundamentally non-deterministic as it is not scheduled within a set time window. However, the speed of EtherNet/IP with a modern full-duplex switch almost negates this fact.

EtherNet/IP uses **User Datagram Protocol** (**UDP**) to communicate the basic I/O and non-critical information on the network. UDP does not perform any error checking or handshaking mechanisms, so the delivery of information is not guaranteed and the data is susceptible to any network-related data loss. UDP is ideally suited for real-time information as it trades speed for guaranteed data delivery. In real-time systems, dropped packets are preferable to waiting for delayed packets. It is far better to get the next most-recent value than circling back for a packet that is already stale. Using UDP, EtherNet/IP is capable of collecting data by polling cyclic and change-of-state monitoring. EtherNet/IP makes use of UDP port number `2222`.

Transmission Control Protocol (**TCP**) is used by EtherNet/IP for critical data, in tasks such as writing set points, parameters, and recipes and uploading and downloading programs. TCP has a built-in error checking and a three-way handshake mechanism that ensures that no packets are lost during the data transfer. TCP sacrifices data transfer speed for guaranteed delivery of information. EtherNet/IP makes use of TCP port number `44818`.

Stratix is a line of industrial networking and security solutions from Rockwell Automation that has been engineered specifically for EtherNet/IP (and is based on the ubiquitous Cisco hardware platform). However, because EtherNet/IP is based on the IEEE 802.x standards, it is possible to use normal network switchgear with EtherNet/IP. Rockwell Automation recommends that you use robust industrial-grade networking equipment with the Logix controllers. Furthermore, Stratix switches seamlessly integrate with the Logix platform and can easily provide health and status information as the native Logix tags.

In `Chapter 15`, *Building a Robot Bartender in Logix*, we will go through the process of selecting an EtherNet/IP card (ENBT, EN2T, and so on) for our Robot Bartender project.

Now that we have covered the three primary network communications used in modern Rockwell solutions, we will cover some of the legacy network technologies in the next section.

Understanding legacy network technologies

There are a few other communication technologies that you may also encounter in a Rockwell Automation solution. Some are legacy networks, while others are solution-specific technologies:

- **Data Highway Plus** (DH+)
- **Universal Remote I/O** (RIO)
- **Serial Real-time Communications System** (SERCOS)
- SynchLink
- DF1
- DH-485

In the following sections, we will introduce each of the legacy network technologies listed here.

Data Highway Plus

DH+ was used by older controllers (such as PLC-2, PLC-3, PLC-5, and SLC 500) for networking. It was developed as a proprietary protocol in the late '70s by Allen-Bradley. There are Logix communication modules available that can connect to the DH+ networks and can save customers from having to rip out and replace their older DH+ networks. DH+ supported remote programming and messaging over the network.

Specifically, it enabled uploading and downloading programs, forcing values, monitoring, and online edits. It is common to encounter DH+ networks still used in the field today, but it is obsolete, so we will not cover it in detail in this book.

In the following section, we will cover another legacy Rockwell network technology, called RIO.

RIO

RIO was also used by older controllers (such as PLC-2, PLC-3, PLC-5, and SLC 500) to communicate with the remote I/O chassis. There are Logix communication modules available that can connect to RIO and save the cost of replacing the RIO networks. Using a remote rack allows you to place the I/O modules closer to the actual devices with which they are communicating. The RIO rack connected back to the main controller using a two-wire Belden 9463 cable, also known as a **blue hose cable**. Although it is common to encounter RIO networks in the field today, it is also obsolete, so we will not cover it in detail here.

In the next section, we will introduce another serial communication protocol, called SERCOS.

SERCOS

SERCOS, or IEC 61491, is a communication technology created for real-time motion control. It provides high-speed serial communication over an electrical noise-immune fiber-optic cable and is commonly used in the manufacturing industry. It was developed by an international consortium of companies called **Interest Group SERCOS**, which included Siemens, ABB, AEG, AMK, Robert Bosch, and Indramat. Logix communication modules that can communicate with SERCOS devices for motion control are available. However, we will not touch on motion control in this book, so we will not explore this communication technology in detail.

In the following subsection, we will briefly cover the SynchLink fiber-optic communication technology.

SynchLink

SynchLink is a fiber-optic communication technology for interfacing with **PowerFlex 700** products. It is a streamlined protocol focused on high-speed drive and motion control. It does not transmit diagnostic information and should be used in conjunction with a standard control network, such as ControlNet or EtherNet/IP.

Next, we will cover the DH-485 and DF1 protocols in the following subsection.

DH-485 and DF1

The **DH-485** and **DF1** networks are legacy serial technologies that provided communication for the PLC-5, SLC 500, and MicroLogix controllers, as well as **Human Machine Interface** (**HMI**) terminals and computers. There are third-party communication modules available from ProSoft that allow DH-485 and DF1 to communicate with Logix devices. Although it is common to encounter DH-485 and DF1 in the field today, they have both been retired and so will not be covered in this book.

Now that we have introduced a myriad of Rockwell Network communication technologies, we will compare their capabilities in the next section.

Comparing network communication technologies

In this section, we will show a side-by-side comparison of the properties of Rockwell's industrial networking technologies.

The following table compares the media, maximum distances, maximum nodes, maximum speeds, and topologies of these communication technologies:

Protocol	**Media**	**Distance**	**Nodes**	**Speed**	**Topology**
EtherNet/IP	Ethernet CAN/CIP over IP	100 m/328 ft	Many	100 Mbits/s (1 Gbits/s)	Star, linear, and ring
ControlNet	Quad Shield RG-6 coaxial cable and CIP	1,000 m/3,280 ft	99	5 Mbits/s	Star, trunk line, drop line, tree, and ring

DeviceNet	4 wires—2 signal and 2 power—and CIP	100 m/328 ft to 380 m/1,246 ft	64	125 Kbits/s to 500 Kbits/s	Trunk line, drop line, and star
DH+	Twinaxial cable, peer-to-peer, and token-based	Trunk line: 3,050 m/10,000 ft Drop line: 30 m/100 ft	64	57.6 Kbits/s half-duplex	Daisy chain, trunk line, and drop line
RIO	Twinaxial cable and scanner-based	Trunk line: 3,050 m/10,000 ft Drop line: 30 m/100 ft	32	230.4 Kbits/s	Trunk line and drop line
SERCOS	Fiber-optic serial-based	250 m/820 ft	254	16 Mbits/s	Ring
SynchLink	Fiber-optic	250 m/820 ft	257	10 Mbps	Star, daisy chain, and ring
DF1	RS-485 serial	1,219 m/4,000 ft	255	19.2 Kbits/s	Trunk line and drop line
DH-485	RS-485 serial	1,219 m/4,000 ft	32	19.2 Kbits/s	Trunk line and drop line

Listed in the preceding table are the properties of each Rockwell Automation communication technology. However, there are fiber-optic converters for most communications technologies that can extend their maximum distances.

As we design our process control networks, it is important to understand the limitations of our network infrastructure. Rockwell has provided some tools to help solve this problem, which is covered in the following section.

Working with EtherNet/IP Capacity Tool

Rockwell Automation has provided a tool called **EtherNet/IP Capacity Tool** that is designed to help you calculate the resources required to support a control network. The tool takes a conservative approach to estimate the requirements of your network usage based on a few data points you provide it.

EtherNet/IP Capacity Tool is used to measure the networking capacity of a single **scanner processor**. A scanner processor is either an EtherNet/IP module, such as the ControlLogix ENBT, or a Logix controller with a built-in EtherNet/IP port, such as the CompactLogix L32E. If a scanner processor is at maximum capacity, in most cases, an additional EtherNet/IP module or controller can be added to the control solution. A separate EtherNet/IP Capacity Tool report can be created for each scanner processor network.

When you calculate your capacity, the tool provides you with the available CIP connections, TCP connections, I/O **Packets Per Second** (**PPS**), and HMI PPS. EtherNet/IP Capacity Tool is designed to highlight potential design issues early on in the network architecture process.

CIP connections are the real-time implicit (scheduled at a set RPI) UDP data connections. You have a limited number of CIP connections, which varies according to the scanner processor you select.

TCP connections are explicit (unscheduled request, response) data communications.

Here are a few common scenarios that use a CIP connection:

- Each I/O rack added to the network for reporting the optimized digital values will use a CIP connection.
- Each analog I/O module added to a rack consumes an entire CIP connection.
- Each produced tag and each consumed tag processed from another Logix controller consumes an entire CIP connection.

Here are a few common scenarios that use TCP connections:

- Each I/O rack uses a TCP connection (used for writing set points or setting digital values).
- Each controller uses a TCP connection (used for uploading and downloading programs).
- Each HMI uses a TCP connection (the HMI MSG statements between the Logix controllers).

I/O PPS is the volume of data moving through the network. There is a maximum amount of PPS that any particular scanner processor is capable of handling. The PPS value is proportional to the CIP and TCP connections and EtherNet/IP Capacity Tool creates a conservative estimate of the traffic.

In the following exercise, we will demonstrate how to use EtherNet/IP Capacity Tool.

Using EtherNet/IP Capacity Tool

You will need to have a copy of the freely available Rockwell Automation EtherNet/IP Capacity Tool in order to complete the following exercise.

EtherNet/IP Capacity Tool is included in the annual release of the Rockwell Automation toolkit. It can also be found in the Integrated Architecture tools on the Rockwell website as a free download for approved customers and system integrators.

Let's begin by opening **EtherNet/IP Capacity Tool** and performing these steps:

1. Select the scanner processor for this exercise. In the center of the window, you will see a group box with a **Scanner Processor** label. Click on the drop-down box in the **Scanner Processor** group box and select the ControlLogix EtherNet/IP module's **ControlLogix ENBT** option from the list:

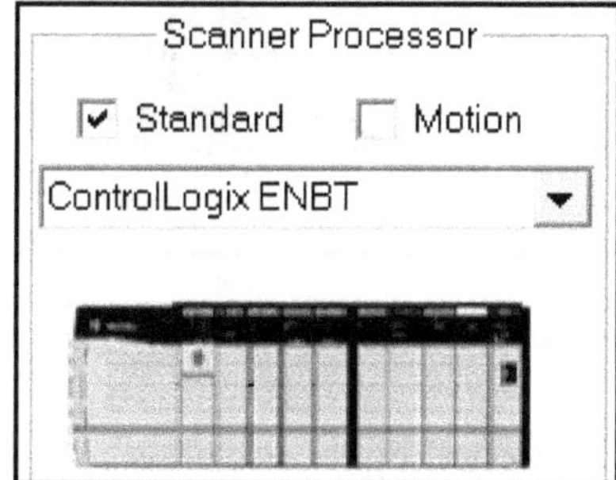

2. Now, we will add some node group devices to our network and compute the network usage they add. Find the box that contains the **Node Group 2** label to the left of the scanner processor.
3. Next, we will add a ControlLogix I/O rack by selecting **1756 I/O Rack** from the **Node Group 2** drop-down list.
4. Set the number of ControlLogix I/O racks on our network by setting 3 for the **No.Racks** numeric field.

5. Click on the checkbox labeled **Analog/Specialty Modules** to indicate that we have analog modules on our I/O rack. Add analog modules for each I/O rack by setting the **No. of Analog Modules** value in the first column to `2`, as in the following screenshot:

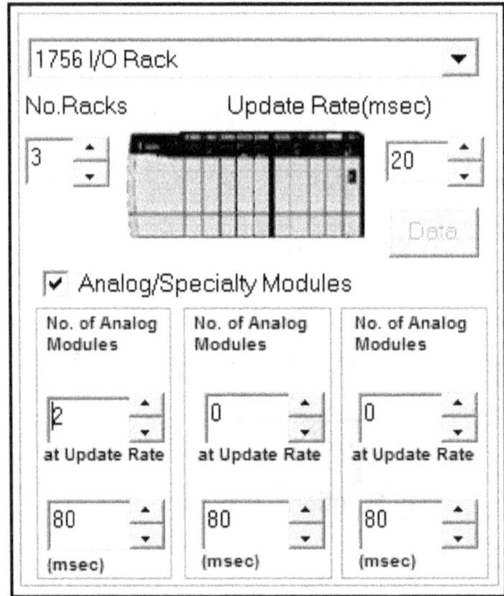

6. Now, let's hit the **Compute** button to see our current EtherNet/IP usage in the center of the screen.
7. Next, we will add a CompactLogix controller, which we will communicate with using produced and consumed tags. Using produced and consumed tags is a method of passing values from one controller to another every RPI.

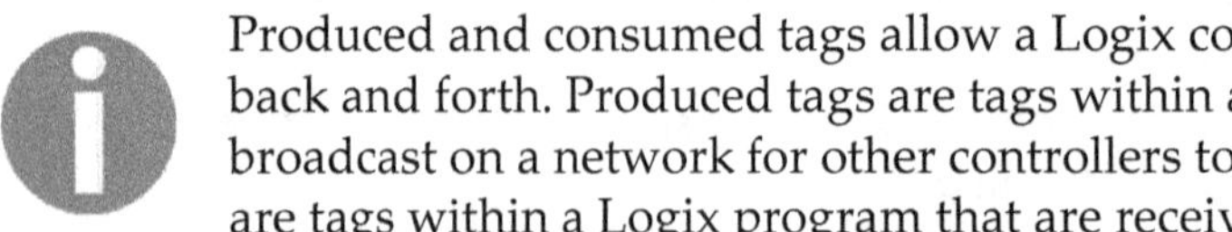

Produced and consumed tags allow a Logix controller to pass information back and forth. Produced tags are tags within a Logix program that are broadcast on a network for other controllers to receive. Consumed tags are tags within a Logix program that are received from other controllers.

8. In the **Node Group 1** box, select **CompactLogix ENBT V1**. Next, set the number of produced tags to `16`. Set the number of consumed tags to `16` (32 is the maximum number of produced tags and consumed tags for our scanner processor):

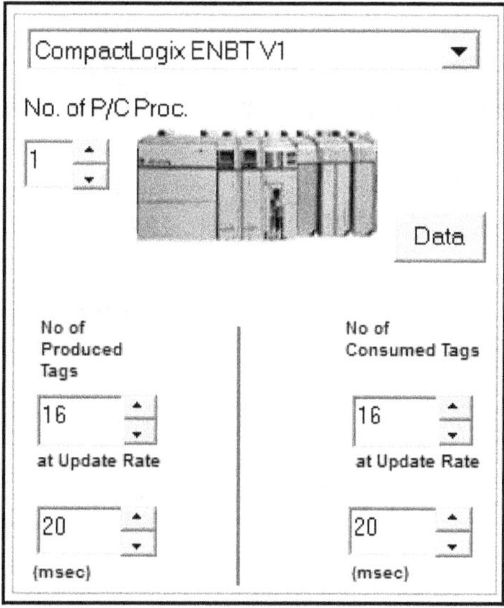

9. Our control system needs a window into the process so that the operator can control and monitor it. Next, we will add our FactoryTalk HMI.
10. In **Node Group 3**, select **FactoryTalk HMI** from the drop-down list to add an HMI to our network.
11. Set the **No. Std Tags** field to `1000` and the **No. CIP Cxns** field to `5`:

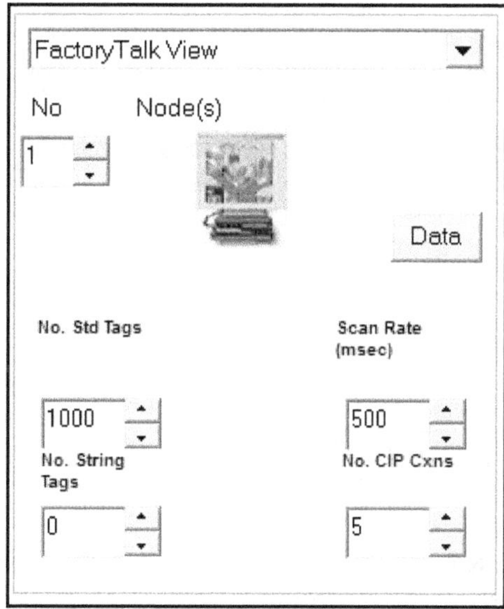

12. Next, we will hit the **Compute** button to see how many network resources we have left.
13. Now, we increase the size of our network to exceed the capacity of our scanner processor and view the results.
14. In **Node Group 2**, where we have set up our 1756 I/O rack, change the **Update Rate(msec)** field to `2`, then hit the **Compute** button. You will notice that the network connections have turned red and our I/O PPS now exceeds the limit for our scanner processor. As you can now see, adjusting the **Update Rate(msec)** field greatly impacts the PPS:

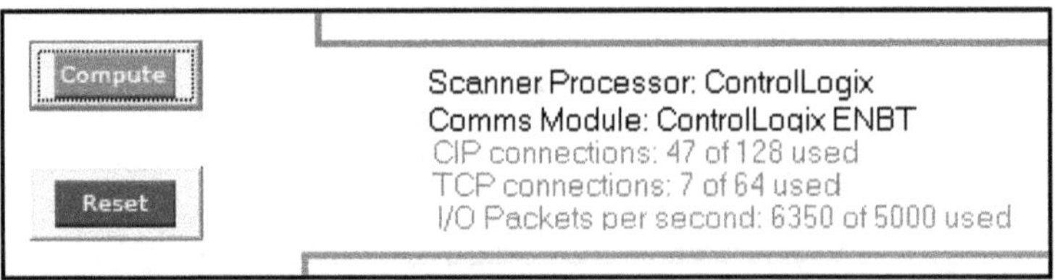

15. Finally, let's change the **Update Rate(msec)** field back to `80` msec, but update the **No. Racks** field for **1756 I/O Rack** to `25`.

16. As you can see from the results, increasing the number of racks increased the CIP connections, TCP connections, and the I/O PPS values:

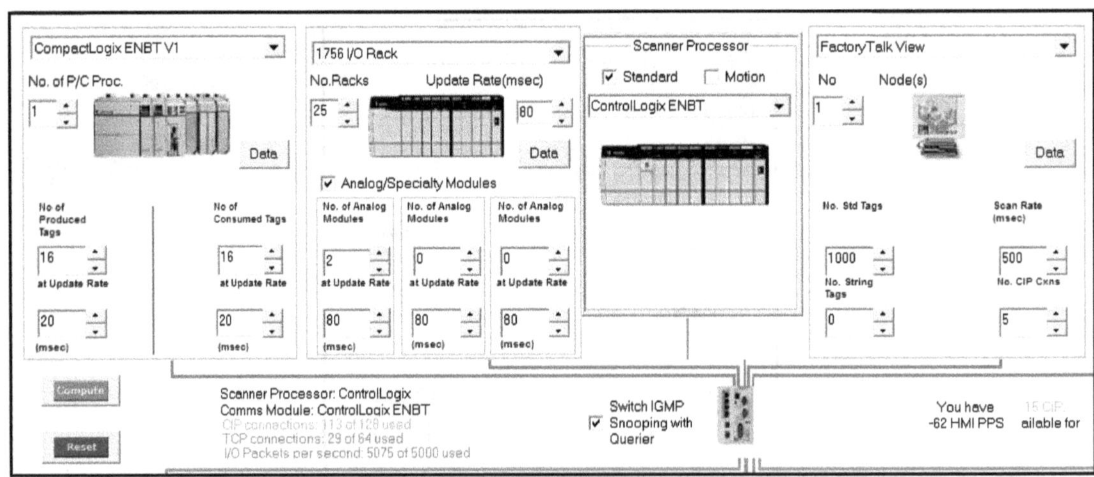

Now that we have explored Rockwell's Ethernet/IP Capacity Tool, we will introduce another important tool for Rockwell Automation networks—RSLinx.

Using RSLinx Classic and FactoryTalk Linx

RSLinx Classic and **FactoryTalk Linx** are the communication server applications in the Rockwell Automation product line. The original RSLinx communication server evolved over time into two separate products:

- RSLinx Classic
- FactoryTalk Linx (formally known as RSLinx Enterprise)

FactoryTalk Linx is typically packaged with the FactoryTalk HMI software.

FactoryTalk Linx is an HMI communications gateway that also provides the following properties:

- Diagnostics
- Security
- Auditability
- Redundancy

FactoryTalk Linx collects data from Rockwell Automation controllers and delivers data to FactoryTalk-enabled applications via **Live Data**, which is the communication protocol used in the FactoryTalk suite of software products through FactoryTalk services.

For more information on FactoryTalk Linx, refer to the relevant links in the *Further reading* section of this chapter.

RSLinx Classic is typically packaged with RSLogix 5000 and Studio 5000 and is a communication gateway that also provides the following properties:

- Batch sequencing
- Firmware updates
- Uploading and downloading programs to controllers

In this chapter, we will work with RSLinx Classic to create the communications gateway between our computer and our controller. Before we start working with RSLinx Classic, we will define some key terms regarding controller communications:

- **Upload**: This term is used to copy a program from the controller to the computer.
- **Download**: This term is used to copy a program from the computer to the controller.

- **Equal**: This term is used when the computer and the controller both have the same program loaded. When a program is equal, you will be able to go online and view the program's current values and make changes.
- **Online**: This term is used while working on a program that is currently residing on the controller.
- **Offline**: This term is used while working on a program that is currently residing on the computer.

There are many combinations of the communication methods and the Logix controllers that can be configured using RSLinx Classic, and most of the combinations follow a similar setup procedure.

In the next exercise, we will establish communications between RSLinx Classic and a ControlLogix L7X controller using a USB connection.

Using BOOTP/DHCP

The BOOTP/DHCP tool from Rockwell allows you to set the IP address of a new EtherNet/IP device. Most new Rockwell EtherNet/IP devices are configured to use BOOTP/DHCP to assign an initial IP address.

The **Dynamic Host Configuration Protocol** (**DHCP**) is a network management protocol used to automate the process of assigning a device IP address.

The Rockwell BOOTP/DHCP tool can be installed as an add-on to RSLogix 5000 and Studio 5000. Alternatively, if you know the IP address of the device, you can change your computer's IP to be on the same network and then connect to the EtherNet/IP device and change the IP address. The following screenshot shows the interface of the BOOTP/DHCP tool from Rockwell:

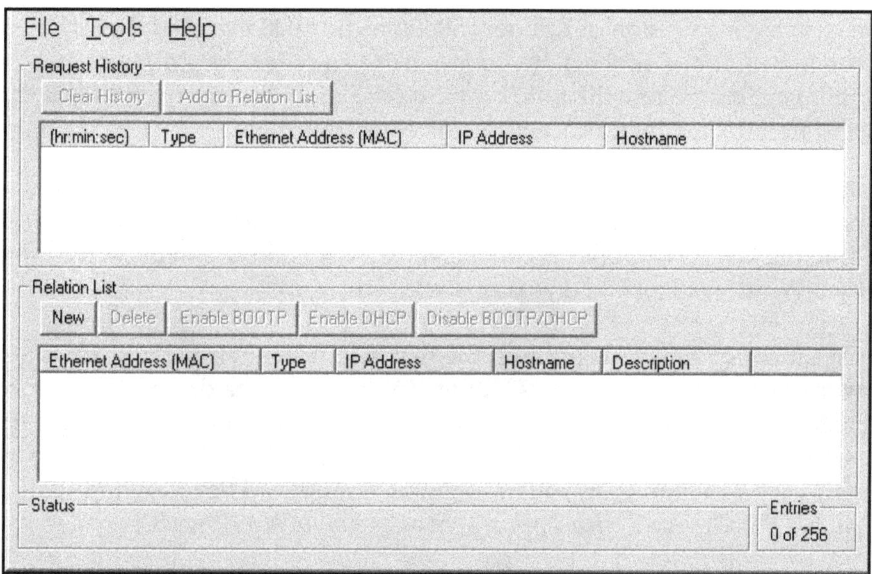

Once the BOOTP/DHCP tool is running and configured to connect to the same network that an EtherNet/IP device is on, you will begin to see pings from that device. You will see the number of pings, the device type, and the associated MAC address of the device. BOOTP is enabled for all new Rockwell devices. When BOOTP is enabled on a device, it will reset the IP address back to DHCP anytime a device power cycles. Therefore, it's important that you disable BOOTP once a static IP address is given to the device.

RSLinx communication using ControlLogix and a USB connection

In this exercise, we will connect to an L7x controller using RSLinx and the USB 2.0 connection on the front of the controller. Setting up communication to a device on the Logix platform requires three separate tools:

- **RSLinx**: This tool is used to configure the driver. The driver is a piece of software that allows you to communicate with hardware, such as a controller.
- **RSWho**: This tool is a component of RSLinx and is used to specify the driver and the path to the device.
- **RSLogix 5000/Logix Designer**: This tool communicates to the device using the path and the specified driver.

You will need to have a version of RSLogix 5000/Studio 5000 installed that supports the L7x platform (version 18.11 and higher). If you are using an older ControlLogix or a CompactLogix version, review the following exercise and then navigate to **RSLinx Help** | **Quick Start** to find the detailed procedures for your controller:

1. Before opening **RSLinx**, the first step is to connect your computer to your powered-on ControlLogix controller using a standard USB 2.0 cable. The first time the Logix controller is connected to your computer, you will be prompted by a **Windows Found New Hardware** setup.

   On older versions of Windows, the first step of the wizard will ask whether you want to connect to Windows Update to search for the driver. If the driver was installed automatically with RSLinx, select **No, not at this time**. Then, follow the wizard to complete the installation of the USB CIP device. The device setup form will vary depending on your version of Windows. The following screenshot shows the **Device Setup** popup that appears in Windows 8.1:

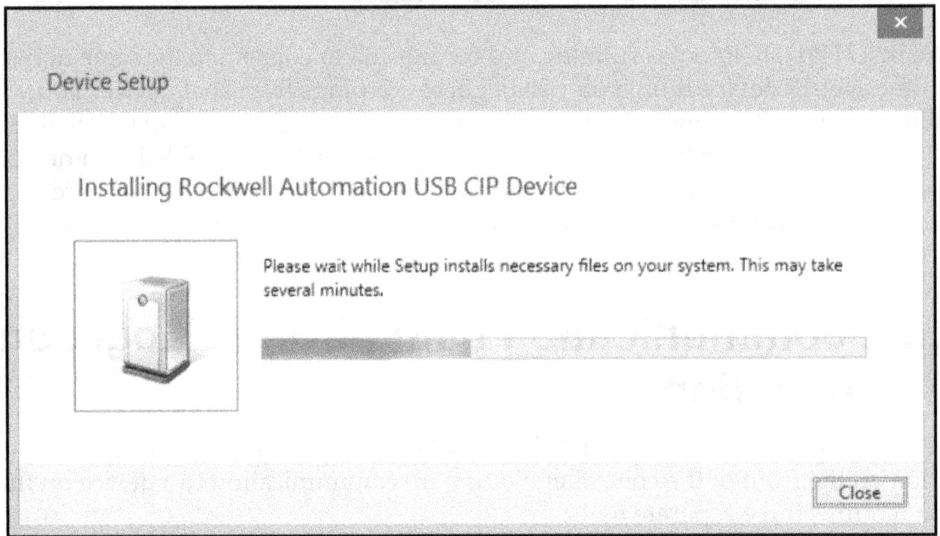

2. Next, open **RSLinx** and configure the driver to connect to the L7X controller. Open the **Configure Drivers** window by navigating to **Communications** | **Configure Drivers**. If everything is installed correctly with your USB connection, you should see a driver named **AB_VBP-1** with the **Status** column displaying **Running**:

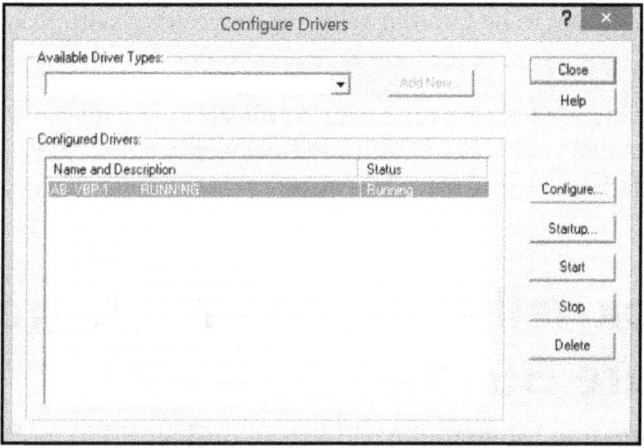

3. Next, let's open **RSWho** in RSLinx to verify that we can map a path to the device using the USB driver. Close the **Configure Drivers** window to return to RSLinx and open **RSWho** by selecting **Communications** | **RSWho**. You should be able to expand the **USB** tab on the left panel by clicking on the + symbol and selecting your controller:

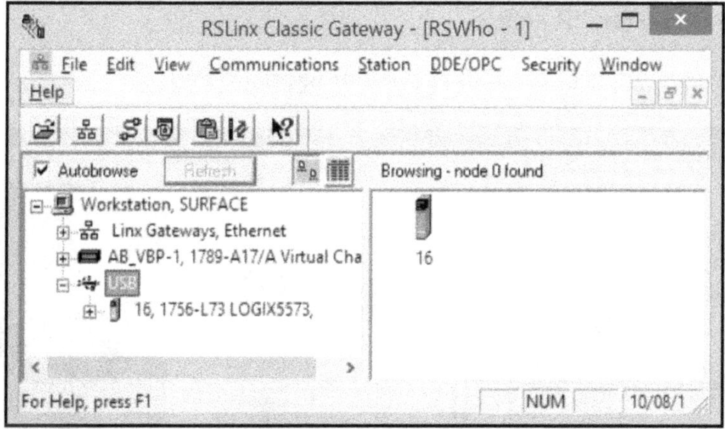

4. Now that we have established the driver and communication's path to our controller, we will be able to select it using RSLogix 5000 or Logix Designer and start uploading or downloading programs. We can also use RSLinx Classic as an **OLE for Process Control** (**OPC**) communications gateway by configuring the OPC topics. More information on RSLinx can be found in the appendix of this book or in Rockwell Automation Literature Library.

RSLinx is an important tool to be familiar with when working with Rockwell Automation-based networks.

In the following section, we will cover another application, which can assist with designing and scaling networks that incorporate multiple Rockwell technologies—the Rockwell Automation Integrated Architecture mobile app.

Using Rockwell Automation Integrate Architecture Builder

The **Rockwell Automation Integrated Architecture Builder** (**IAB**) mobile app provides an iPad-based tool for creating industrial control network designs. The IAB app allows you to architect a simple Logix network using all of Rockwell Automation's major hardware platforms and EtherNet/IP. Using the IAB app, you can drag and drop your Logix solution together, analyze the EtherNet/IP performance data, and generate a bill of materials and send it to the nearest distributor/sales office. In addition, you can export your IAB app network to the IAB desktop-application version for system validation. The IAB app is available for free on the Apple app store and appears to be a replacement for **Rockwell Automation Small System Sketcher**.

The following screenshot is of the IAB app running on an iPad:

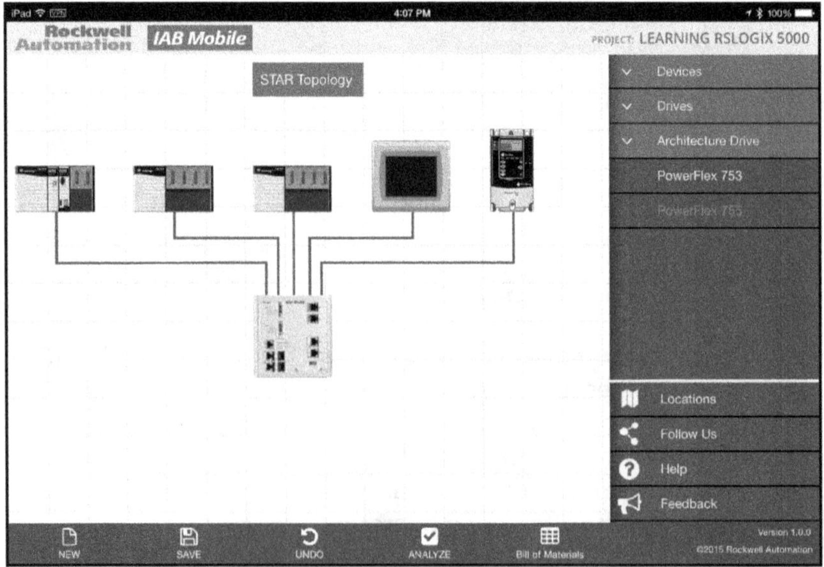

The IAB app allows users to drag and drop devices into a network and streamline the bill of materials and scaling of network resources.

Networking safety systems

Rockwell automation has a line of **Safety Instrumented Function** (**SIF**) controllers, I/O cards, and remote I/O modules that align with the international safety system application standards, as detailed in the following table:

Standard	Description
IEC 61508	Functional safety of electrical/electronic programmable safety-related systems
IEC 61511	**Safety Instrumented Systems** (**SIS**) for the process industry sector
IEC 62061	Electrical control systems implementation of on safety-related machinery
NFPA 85	Safety standards for boiler and combustion systems
NFPA 86	Safety standards for ovens and furnaces
EN54	Safety standards for fire alarm panels and control
EN298	Automatic gas burner control systems for gas burners and gas-burning appliances with or without fans
EN50156	Design and installation requirements for electrical equipment for furnaces and ancillary equipment
UL 508	Safety for industrial control equipment and covers industrial control and related devices rated 1,500 volts or less used for starting, stopping, controlling, regulating, or protecting industrial control equipment

Rockwell Automation's safety equipment is known as GuardLogix and can provide the redundancy and high availability required for most SIF applications. The most commonly used term when referencing an industrial safety system is the **Safety Integrity Level** (**SIL**). The SIL level is the relative level of risk reduction provided by a SIF. The required SIL level is identified and determined through engineering processes called a **Hazard and Operability Study** (**HAZOP**) and a **Layers of Protection Analysis** (**LOPA**). SIL applications usually require varying levels of redundancy. GuardLogix controller and remote I/O devices can provide redundancy at the following levels:

- Rack redundancy
- Network redundancy
- Controller redundancy
- I/O redundancy
- Remote I/O redundancy

Often, safety systems will require a different approach from a networking perspective, such as a ring topology or redundant networks. As such, it is important to keep these requirements in mind when you are designing your Rockwell control system.

Summary

In this chapter, we learned about the communication technologies that are available in the Logix controller family. We investigated the strengths and limitations of each communication method and took a deep dive into EtherNet/IP and EtherNet/IP Capacity Tool. We explored RSLinx and its place within Integrated Architecture as the communications gateway. We also established communication with a ControlLogix L7x using the USB cable. Finally, we introduced the easy-to-use IAB mobile app for designing your Logix networks.

In the next chapter, we will introduce the modules that are available on the Logix platform and demonstrate their configuration with RSLogix 5000/Logix Designer.

Questions

The following questions can be used to test your retention of the concepts introduced in this chapter. You can find the answers to these questions in the back of the book under *Assessments*:

- What is the term used for each device on a Rockwell network?
- What is a localized section of the network with bridges, routers, or switches?
- In a Rockwell ControlNet network, what is the small *T*-shaped device that connects a trunk-line cable (the top of the *T*) to a drop-line cable (the bottom of the *T*)?
- In a Rockwell ControlNet network, what is the name of the 75 Ohm resistor that can be connected to a trunk-line connection that absorbs energy and prevents electrical signal reflection?
- What is the name of the Rockwell protocol that is specifically designed to communicate with and provide power to the lowest-level field devices?
- What Rockwell protocol is based on an open standard for industrial network protocols known as Fieldbus, uses the CIP to provide its functionality, uses a Quad Shield RG6 coaxial cable as a networking media, is capable of full network redundancy, and acts as the I/O communication backbone for a control system?

- What Rockwell Network protocol is based on the IEEE 802 standard Ethernet technology stack, utilizes the CIP protocol, can communicate control, safety, synchronization, motion, configuration, and diagnostic information with devices from hundreds of different vendors, and can collect data using nondeterministic, event-based methods?
- What Rockwell protocol is a fiber-optic communication technology that is streamlined to provide high-speed drive and motion control?
- What organization maintains open industry standards, such as DeviceNet, ControlNet, and EtherNet/IP?

Further reading

For more information on Rockwell protocols, refer to the following Rockwell documents:

- DeviceNet network configuration: `https://literature.rockwellautomation.com/idc/groups/literature/documents/um/dnet-um004_-en-p.pdf`
- ControlNet network configuration: `https://literature.rockwellautomation.com/idc/groups/literature/documents/um/cnet-um001_-en-p.pdf`
- EtherNet/IP network configuration: `https://literature.rockwellautomation.com/idc/groups/literature/documents/um/enet-um001_-en-p.pdf`
- EtherNet/IP network devices: `https://literature.rockwellautomation.com/idc/groups/literature/documents/um/enet-um006_-en-p.pdf`
- Getting results with FactoryTalk Linx: `https://literature.rockwellautomation.com/idc/groups/literature/documents/gr/lnxent-gr001_-en-e.pdf`

7
Configuring Logix Modules

In this chapter, we will look at the available modules for the Logix platform, as well as how to configure and use them in a Logix project. We will also include methods for identifying module features by their Logix module and **catalog numbers**, and introduce the address tree that a typical I/O module creates. After completing this chapter, you will be able to select and add I/O modules to your projects, modify the module configurations, and reference their real-time values using the recommended best practices.

This chapter will cover the following aspects of Logix modules:

- Understanding the module terminology
- Learning about the module types
- Configuring a ControlLogix module
- Reading the Logix module catalog numbers
- Learning about the module special features
- Addressing I/O data
- Configuring remote racks with RSNetWorx

This chapter begins by explaining some of the basic Rockwell module terminology.

Technical requirements

To complete this chapter, you will need to create a Rockwell Automation support account by going to `https://www.rockwellautomation.com/account/create-account`.

Creating an account is free and the material we will review in this chapter is publicly available to anyone who has registered with Rockwell Automation.

You will also need a copy of RSLogix or Studio 5000 that has a license for Emulate 5000 to program your project. You can either purchase this from your local distributor or request a time-limited trial version. You can find a local distributor for Rockwell Automation products at `https://locator.rockwellautomation.com/`.

Understanding the module terminology

Modules provide the interface between a computer and the physical world. There are a wide variety of modules available that perform specific functions in an industrial process. Before we can learn how to use modules in our programs, we need to understand their different properties, functions, and capabilities.

Let's begin by taking a look at some of the common Logix module properties:

- **Voltage**: This attribute is the difference in electrical potential between two points, measured in **Voltage A/C** (**VAC**) or **Voltage D/C** (**VDC**). When visualizing voltage, I prefer the age-old super soaker (water gun) analogy, where voltage is the pressure (the number of times you have pumped the super soaker).
- **Current**: This attribute is the flow of electrical charge measured in **Amps** (**A**) and **Milliamps** (**mA**). In the super soaker analogy, this is the diameter of the water gun's nozzle.
- **Signal**: This attribute is the modulation in voltage or current, which relays the operational state of a device. A signal is representative of values such as pressure, temperature, and flow.
- **Input**: This module is wired to detect the values that are sent from the field to the controller. Input values are used to determine, for example, whether a motor is running and the speed of a motor's rotation.
- **Output**: This module is wired to transmit values that are sent from the controller out to the field. Output values are used, for example, to start a motor and tell a motor how fast it should run.
- **Rack**: This attribute is a chassis that contains the controller modules, and typically ranges in size from 4 to 17 module slots. ControlLogix also supports multiple racks that can be connected to each other using communications technology such as EtherNet/IP or ControlNet. Most CompactLogix controllers are mounted along a DIN rail and do not use a rack.
- **Slot**: This attribute refers to a module's position in a rack. The number of slots will vary by rack size and the Logix controller you are using.

- **Module**: This attribute is a modular card that mounts in a slot of a rack or along a DIN rail. This module is used to handle a wide variety of automation tasks and is available from a number of vendors. In this chapter, we will focus on the most common modules, which simply process the input or output signals.
- **Channel**: This attribute is the individual input or output circuit on a module that links one signal connection with a device in the field.
- **Address**: This attribute is the complete path from a Logix controller to a module channel, property, or configuration value.
- **Adapter**: This attribute is the communication module that mounts in a slot on a rack, which enables a controller to communicate with a remote rack over EtherNet/IP or ControlNet. The adapter name is the root of the path to any address for modules located in remote racks.

Now that we have covered the basic components and terminology of Rockwell modules, we will explore the broader module types available in the following section.

Learning about the module types

In general, modules are classified as analog, digital, communication, controller, and specialty. They differ by the number of channels, the ranges of input and output they are capable of handling, and by the special features that are optionally available. In this section, we will explore the base module types and explain the possible feature sets.

In the following sections, we will enumerate some of the most common module types in the ControlLogix and CompactLogix families of controllers. We will cover the basic categories of modules that are available for Rockwell controllers, which include analog modules, digital modules, communication modules, CPU modules, and motion control modules.

Analog modules

Analog modules process the input and output of signals that vary by current and voltage and translate to real-world values, such as pressure, temperature, and flow. Analog modules vary by the number of channels (4 to 16), the operating temperature range, the maximum isolation voltage they can handle, the range of the current (0 mA to 21 mA), and the range of voltage (+/- 25 VDC). There are even combination analog modules that house both input and output channels.

Each analog channel usually requires three wires in order to complete an analog circuit correctly. The way that the channel is wired changes depending on whether you are using voltage or current. Be sure to review the wiring diagrams for your module at the Rockwell Automation Literature Library document referenced in the *Further reading* section of this chapter.

One of the most common modules used within most control systems is a digital module. In the following section, we will introduce digital modules.

Digital modules

Digital modules process the input and output of signals that vary by current and voltage and translate to either `ON` or `OFF` values. Digital modules vary by the number of channels (8 to 32), the operating temperature range, the maximum isolation voltage they can handle, and a range of supported voltage (0 VDC to 146 VDC and 10 to 265 VAC). We will work directly with DC digital input and DC digital output ControlLogix modules in `Chapter 15`, *Building a Robot Bartender in Logix*. In the sample application, we will evaluate a number of different digital I/O cards that will work for our Robot Bartender application.

Now that we have covered both digital and analog module types, we will explore some of the other modules, starting with communication modules.

Communication modules

There is a wide range of communication modules available that allows remote rack communications, device communications, and motion control. There are communication modules by Rockwell and third-party vendors that allow the Logix controllers to communicate using the network technologies we talked about in `Chapter 6`, *Industrial Network Communications*, and many other non-Rockwell Automation protocols.

Communication modules must be associated with a processor module to interpret and process communication protocols. In the next section, we will briefly discuss the controller processor (or CPU) modules.

Controller processor modules

We covered controller modules in `Chapter 2`, *Understanding ControlLogix*, and `Chapter 3`, *Understanding CompactLogix*. It is important to remember that ControlLogix can support multiple controller modules in a single rack. Controller processor modules are the CPUs, or brains, of our Logix application and execute our programs to control our processes.

In the following section, we will introduce motion control modules, which are used to manage multi-axis motion devices.

Motion control modules

Motion control is a discipline of industrial automation that involves moving parts of machines in a controlled manner. Motion control is widely used in distribution centers, printing, electronics production, packaging, and assembly (such as an automotive assembly). Motion control is supported within the Logix architecture by a variety of methods. The following is a brief list of methods for interfacing with motion control devices:

- Integrated motion on the EtherNet/IP network (for Ethernet-based drives)
- Kinetix-integrated motion solutions (uses a **Serial Real-time Communications System** (**SERCOS**) or EtherNet/IP interface)
- Logix-integrated motion control (the analog family of servo modules for controlling drives/actuators)
- DeviceNet networked motion control

In the case of SERCOS, a dedicated SERCOS fiber-optic motion control module can be used for high-speed motion control applications. For more information on motion control modules, please take a look at the *1756 ControlLogix Integrated Motion module specifications* link in the *Further reading* section of this chapter.

In the next section, we will finish off our coverage of Rockwell modules by providing an overview of some of the specialty modules that are available.

Specialty modules

Specialty modules allow your automation project to perform the following specialized tasks:

- **High-speed counting**: Used to count changes of state within a process control network
- **Flowmeter measurement**: Used to interface with specialty flowmeter equipment and can provide flow and calibration information as Logix tags within a program
- **Limit switch monitoring**: Dedicated modules for monitoring limit switch activation
- **Hydraulics control**: Specialized modules for the control and monitoring of hydraulic systems

Now that we have covered all the various types of modules available within the ControlLogix and CompactLogix families of controllers, in the following section, we will explore some of the wiring solutions available for these modules.

Introducing Logix terminal blocks

In the Logix family, most modules do not come with built-in screw terminals, so **Removable Terminal Blocks** (**RTBs**) or Bulletin 1492 **Interface Modules** (**IFMs**) must be purchased separately. You should carefully review the wiring requirements for your module using the online Rockwell Automation Literature Library resource (relevant links can be found in the *Further reading* section of this chapter). We cover RTBs in more detail in `Chapter 15`, *Building a Robot Bartender in Logix*, of this book.

Now that we have covered the basic Rockwell module types, we will go through an exercise where we will configure one using RSLogix or Studio 5000.

Configuring a ControlLogix module

In this exercise, we will learn how to add a ControlLogix module to a Logix project and look at a typical module configuration by performing these steps:

1. First, we will need to open RSLogix 5000/Studio 5000 Logix Designer. Create a new project and select a ControlLogix controller (in my case, I selected **1756-L73** on **Slot #0**). This process varies between versions of Logix, so we will not show these steps in detail.

2. Next, we will add the module by right-clicking on the **Controller Organizer** pane's **IO Configuration** tree and selecting **New Module...**, as seen in the following screenshot:

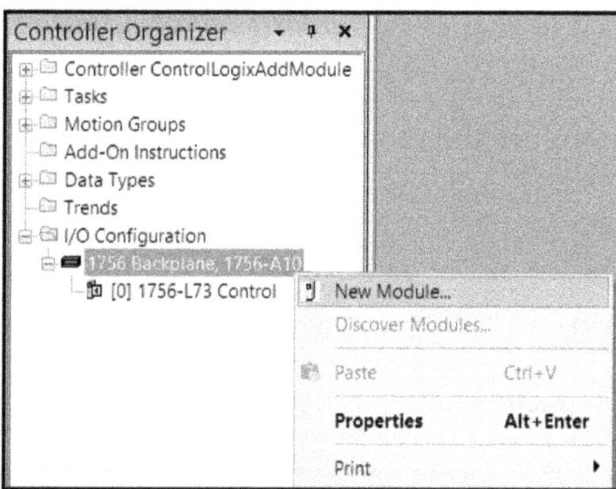

3. Now, we can select the module we wish to configure. For our example, it will be a digital input module, **1756-IB16D 16 Point 10V-30V DC Diagnostic Input**. The **Select Module Type** window varies from version to version of Logix, but regardless of the software, it is relatively easy to locate our module:

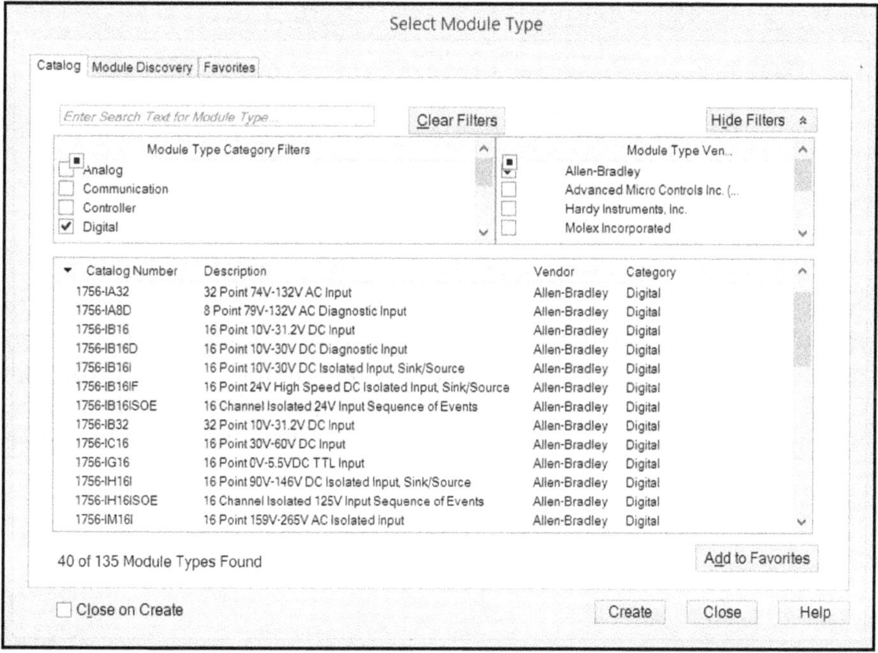

As you can see from the **Select Module Type** window, there is a wide range of modules that can be added to our rack. As a reminder, it is important to ensure the modules that are added are compatible with your processor and RSLogix or Studio 5000 version. You can always use the **Downloads and Compatibility** tool that we introduced in `Chapter 2`, *Understanding ControlLogix*, to verify compatibility.

4. Next, we will configure the module by providing these inputs (as shown in the following screenshot):
    - **Name**: `R01_S01`
    - **Slot**: `1`
    - **Description**: `DI Module`

The following screenshot shows the completed **New Module** form window:

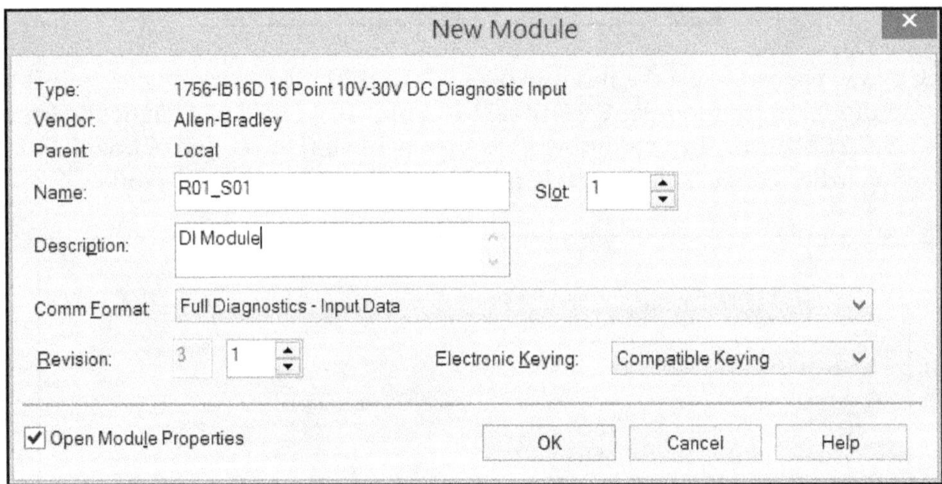

5. Next, we can configure the module properties and adjust the setup of the module. Each module in Logix has unique properties and configuration requirements, so it is imperative that you refer to the Rockwell Automation Literature Library document for any module you are configuring. Once you have reviewed the module properties, click on the **OK** button, as in this screenshot:

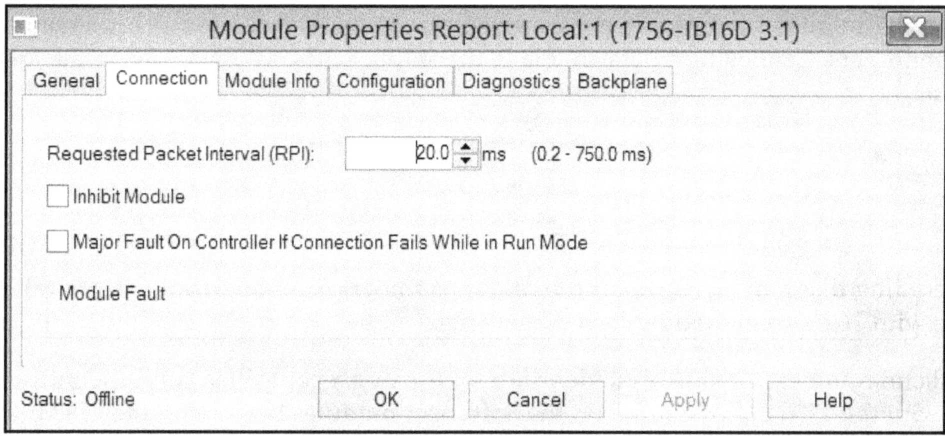

6. c has been configured and you can see it in the **Controller Organizer** pane in our rack:

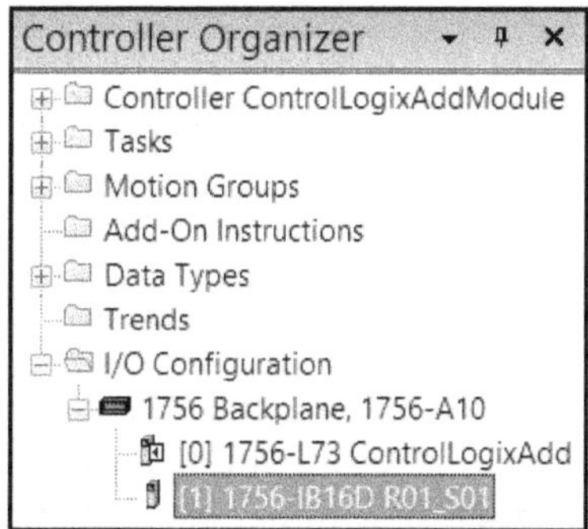

As we can see from our **I/O Configuration** setup, we have successfully added an I/O module to our project. In the next section, we will investigate the meaning of the various numbers and letters used in Rockwell product identifiers.

Reading Logix module catalog numbers

It is helpful to understand the features of a module at a glance simply by reading the device's catalog number. Rockwell has created a standard naming convention for their equipment, which we will explore in this section.

The modules in Integrated Architecture are referred to by their Rockwell Automation catalog numbers. Catalog numbers are made up of four parts, as illustrated in the following diagram:

The preceding diagram breaks apart the catalog numbers for a ControlLogix digital input module with 16 channels and built-in diagnostics.

The Bulletin number is a four-digit identifier for the Logix controller family. ControlLogix begins with the **1756** Bulletin number, the SoftLogix modules begin with the **1789** Bulletin number, and CompactLogix begins with the **1769** or **1768** Bulletin numbers.

The module type is the second part of the Rockwell Automation module catalog numbers. Types that begin with `I` are input cards and types that begin with `O` are output cards. Let's take a look at a few sample types for commonly used modules. Digital input types are usually `IQ` or `IG` for VDC and `IA` or `IM` for VAC. Analog inputs types are typically `IF`, `IR`, or `IT`; digital output types are typically `OB` for VDC or `OA` for VAC; and analog output types are typically `OF`.

Channels are the third part of catalog numbers. Channels represent the number of field signals that can be wired to and processed by the module.

The last part of catalog numbers indicates the special features of the module. The special features indicate any unique capabilities of the module. There are links to the **I/O analog** and **I/O digital** module reference materials in the *Further reading* section of this chapter. For more information about the module catalog numbers, please refer to the Rockwell documentation.

We have now learned how to decipher the Logix module catalog numbers. In the next section, we will briefly overview some of the special features you may find on different Logix modules.

Learning about the module special features

In this section, we will detail many of the ControlLogix module features that are available within the Rockwell product lines. It is important to be familiar with these terms as you will frequently encounter them when selecting ControlLogix modules or when reviewing Rockwell documentation on modules.

Special features provide additional support to the Logix modules and some of the following optional features:

- **HART**: This feature allows modules to read the transmitter status and health information or adjust the configuration and calibration of equipment through a Logix controller.
- **Diagnostic information**: This feature provides diagnostic information for each channel on the module. The following diagnostic information values are available in Logix:
    - **Field Power Loss Detection**: When the field power to the module is lost, it can cause values to be misrepresented. Field power loss detection will generate a point-level fault to the controller.
    - **Open Wire Detection**: This feature is used to verify that the field wiring is connected correctly by measuring the minimum leakage current. A leakage resistor must be connected across the contacts of the device in order to provide the minimum leakage current.
    - **No Load Detection**: This feature is a diagnostic feature of a module that detects a break in the field wiring by comparing it to a specified minimum load current (3 mA or 10 mA, depending on the module).
- **Output state verification**: This module confirms with the controller that it received a command and whether the field-side device connected to the module has executed the command.
- **Electronic fusing**: This feature is the internal electronic fusing that prevents over-current through the module.
- **Individually isolated channels**: This feature is the per-point isolation where each channel can be wired with its own individual power source.
- **Per-point timestamping**: This module can be configured to record or latch the time at which a state is changed from `ON` to `OFF`, `OFF` to `ON`, or both.
- **FIFO mode operation**: This feature stores 160 timestamps, event sequence numbers, status, and input point numbers on the module for recording high-speed events (for example, shutdowns).
- **Ultra-fast on/off times**: This feature is capable of switching within 15 uS.

Some examples of the Logix module catalog numbers are as follows:

- `1756-IA32`: ControlLogix Digital 74-132 VAC Input 32 Pts (36 pin)
- `1756-IA8D`: ControlLogix Digital 79-132 VAC Diagnostic Input 8 Pts (20 pin)
- `1756-IF16H`: ControlLogix Analog Input-16 Point HART

- `1769-IF8`: CompactLogix 8 channel analog current/voltage input module
- `1769-IQ16F`: CompactLogix 16 point high-speed 24 VDC input module

Although this is not an exhaustive list of all the special features found within Logix modules, it does cover many of the commonly used ones. In the next section, we will learn how to address the individual data points found on Logix modules within our RSLogix or Studio 5000 programs.

Addressing module I/O

As we learned earlier in this chapter, channels represent the field signals that can be wired to, and processed by, the module. But how do we reference these channels in our programs and read their values or write new values to field devices? In this section, we will learn the standard syntax for addressing I/O channels. Individual channels on a module can be referenced in your Logix Designer/RSLogix 5000 programs using its address. An address gives the controller directions to where it can find a particular piece of information about a channel on a module. The following diagram breaks down the syntax of a module value reference:

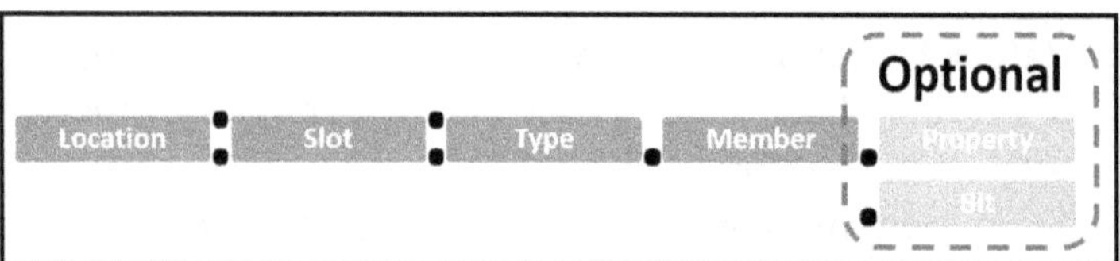

The first field of an address specifies the location of the channel (and is followed by a colon). The location can either be local to the controller or on a remote rack, which connects through a network adapter or bridge module. So, this field can be one of the following bridges:

- **LOCAL**: This module is on the same rack or DIN rail as the controller.
- **Adapter name**: This module is the name you have configured for the network adapter or bridge module, which connects to the remote rack where the module is located.

The second field of an address is the slot number of the I/O module in its rack or DIN rail (and is followed by a colon). The address-slot numbering starts at `0`. In the case of CompactLogix (where power supplies can be placed in the middle of the DIN rail), power supplies do not count as a slot position.

The third field of an address is a single letter that represents the type of data. These are the following four types that are specified in an address:

- **I**: Input
- **O**: Output
- **C**: Configuration
- **S**: Status

The fourth field of an address specifies the member data of the I/O module. Different modules store data of different types. For a digital module, a data member usually stores the input or output bit values. For an analog module, a channel member (`CH#`) usually stores the data for a channel.

The fifth field can be either a property or a bit of a member. A property provides specific data related to a member. A bit provides a specific point on a digital I/O module. The bit range will depend on the size of the I/O module and, like the slot position, it also starts at 0 (0 to 31 for a 32-point module).

Some examples of the Logix module addresses are as follows:

Logix module addresses	**Description**
`MyRack_3:11:O.Ch4Data`	Channel 4 of the analog output module on slot 11 of the `MyRack` adapter
`Local:3:I.Data.24`	Channel 24 of the digital input module on slot 3 in the local rack
`Local:3:I.Fault.24`	Fault status for channel 24 of the digital input module on slot 3 in the local rack
`Local:3:C.DiagCOSDisable`	Configuration Boolean value for disabling the **Change of State** (**COS**) diagnostic information for the digital input module on slot 3 in the local rack

In the following exercise, we will add a reference to a specific value of our I/O module within RSLogix or Studio 5000. Interfacing with I/O modules will allow us to activate pumps, read temperature values, and collect input from operator push buttons.

Exploring module addresses

Modules are the control system's interface to the physical world and they play a critical role in any industrial control system. In this section, we will learn how to read and write data to these critical industrial components.

In this exercise, we will explore the I/O module addresses for the digital module we added earlier in the chapter. Perform the following steps:

1. First, in the **Controller Organizer** pane, select and double-click on the **Controller Tags** option to open the **Controller Tags** panel, as in the following screenshot:

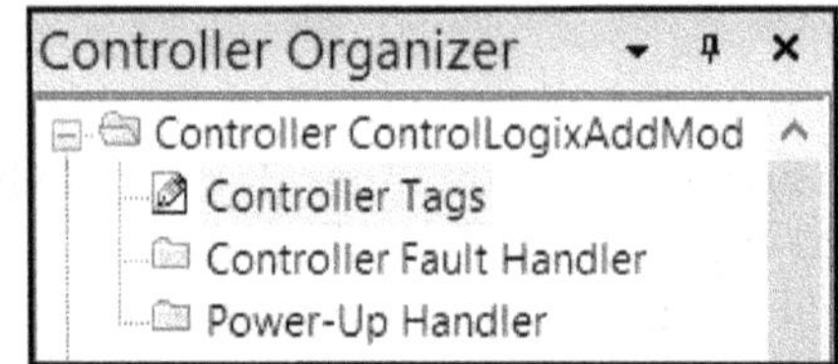

2. You will notice that because we added a diagnostic module, there are two address trees associated with the local slot. There is one address tree for the diagnostic configuration type data and another address for the input type data, `Local:1:C` and `Local:1:I`:

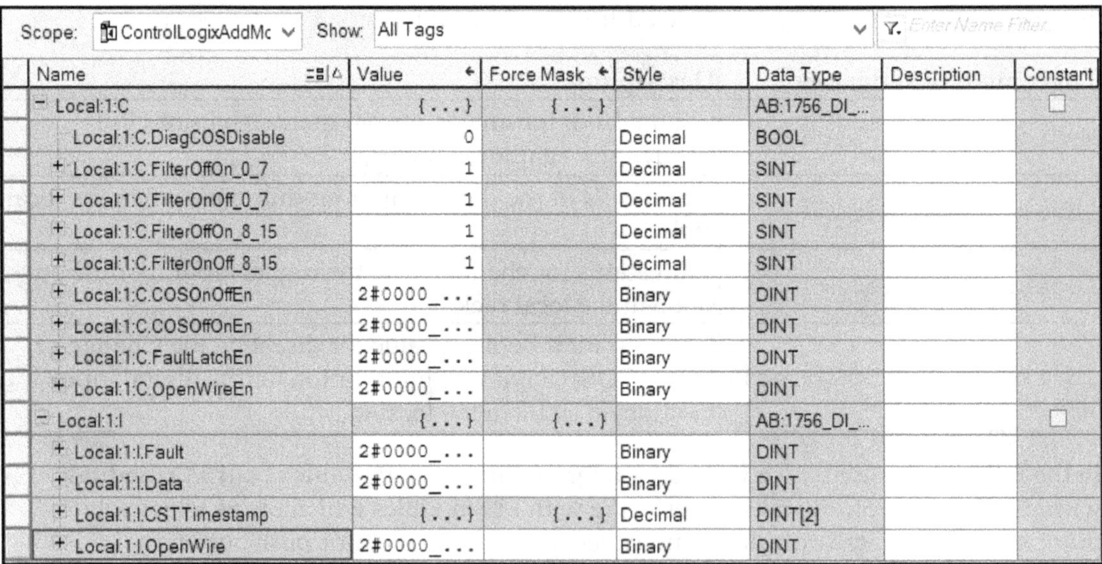

Name	Value	Force Mask	Style	Data Type	Description	Constant
- Local:1:C	{...}	{...}		AB:1756_DI_...		☐
Local:1:C.DiagCOSDisable	0		Decimal	BOOL		
+ Local:1:C.FilterOffOn_0_7	1		Decimal	SINT		
+ Local:1:C.FilterOnOff_0_7	1		Decimal	SINT		
+ Local:1:C.FilterOffOn_8_15	1		Decimal	SINT		
+ Local:1:C.FilterOnOff_8_15	1		Decimal	SINT		
+ Local:1:C.COSOnOffEn	2#0000_...		Binary	DINT		
+ Local:1:C.COSOffOnEn	2#0000_...		Binary	DINT		
+ Local:1:C.FaultLatchEn	2#0000_...		Binary	DINT		
+ Local:1:C.OpenWireEn	2#0000_...		Binary	DINT		
- Local:1:I	{...}	{...}		AB:1756_DI_...		☐
+ Local:1:I.Fault	2#0000_...		Binary	DINT		
+ Local:1:I.Data	2#0000_...		Binary	DINT		
+ Local:1:I.CSTTimestamp	{...}	{...}	Decimal	DINT[2]		
+ Local:1:I.OpenWire	2#0000_...		Binary	DINT		

3. After expanding the type address space, we can see the member data contained within the configuration and input types.

4. Under the configuration member addresses, we can view and adjust the configuration values for all the diagnostic features of our I/O module (recall `D` at the end of the Logix module catalog numbers of the I/O module we selected—`1756-IB16D`). We can see the configuration member data for COS, open wire, fault latching, and filtering. You can easily modify the configuration of these features by double-clicking on the **Value** field and entering a new value.
5. Under the input member address tree, we see the real-time values from our input module. In addition to the normal digital input values, our input module is armed with diagnostic information such as channel faults, channel open wire detection, and channel change of state timestamping. These addresses can be referenced in our program code (ladder logic, function block, structured text, sequential flow diagrams) and evaluated directly in our logic.

The recommended best practice is to buffer the module I/O data before evaluating it in logic. In the next section, we will introduce the concept of module I/O data buffering.

Buffering module I/O data

In `Chapter 1`,*The History of Rockwell Automation Technologies,* we briefly looked at the Logix operating cycle and the differences between asynchronous and synchronous execution. In the olden days of PLC-5s and SLC-500s, before we had access to high-performance asynchronous controllers such as the ControlLogix, SoftLogix, and CompactLogix families, program execution was synchronous and very predictable. In an asynchronous controller, there are many activities that appear to be happening at the same time. The input and output values can change in the middle of a program scan and put the program in an unpredictable state. Today, there is a rule, in most automation companies, that requires programmers to write code that buffers the I/O data to base tags that will not change during program execution. We will look at the buffering examples later in the book and also explore a new alternative to buffering I/O available in Logix Designer version 24 and higher using the program parameters.

In modern ControlLogix programs, it is best practice to always buffer your I/O module data. In the next section, we will learn how we can add remote racks using the RSNetWorx tool.

Configuring remote racks with RSNetWorx

RSNetWorx is a standalone application that is used to configure the Logix network topologies and export them to an **Electronic Data Sheet** (**EDS**) file, which we can import into our Logix application. Without an EDS file, we are unable to set up remote racks in an application.

EDS files are a plain text format based on the CAN open standard and used to specify various descriptive and communication data for hardware devices. EDS files are used by RSNetWorx and RSLinx to provide device information, configuration information, and an icon for that device. Device EDS files can be downloaded from the **Compatibility & Downloads** section of the Rockwell website, referenced in `Chapter 2`, *Understanding ControlLogix*

RSNetWorx is on the annual release of the Rockwell Automation toolkit. It can also be found on the Rockwell website as a free download for approved customers and system integrators. There are three versions of the product—one for each Logix network type (EtherNet/IP, ControlNet, and DeviceNet).

The following is a screenshot of the RSNetWorx for the EtherNet/IP software solution from Rockwell:

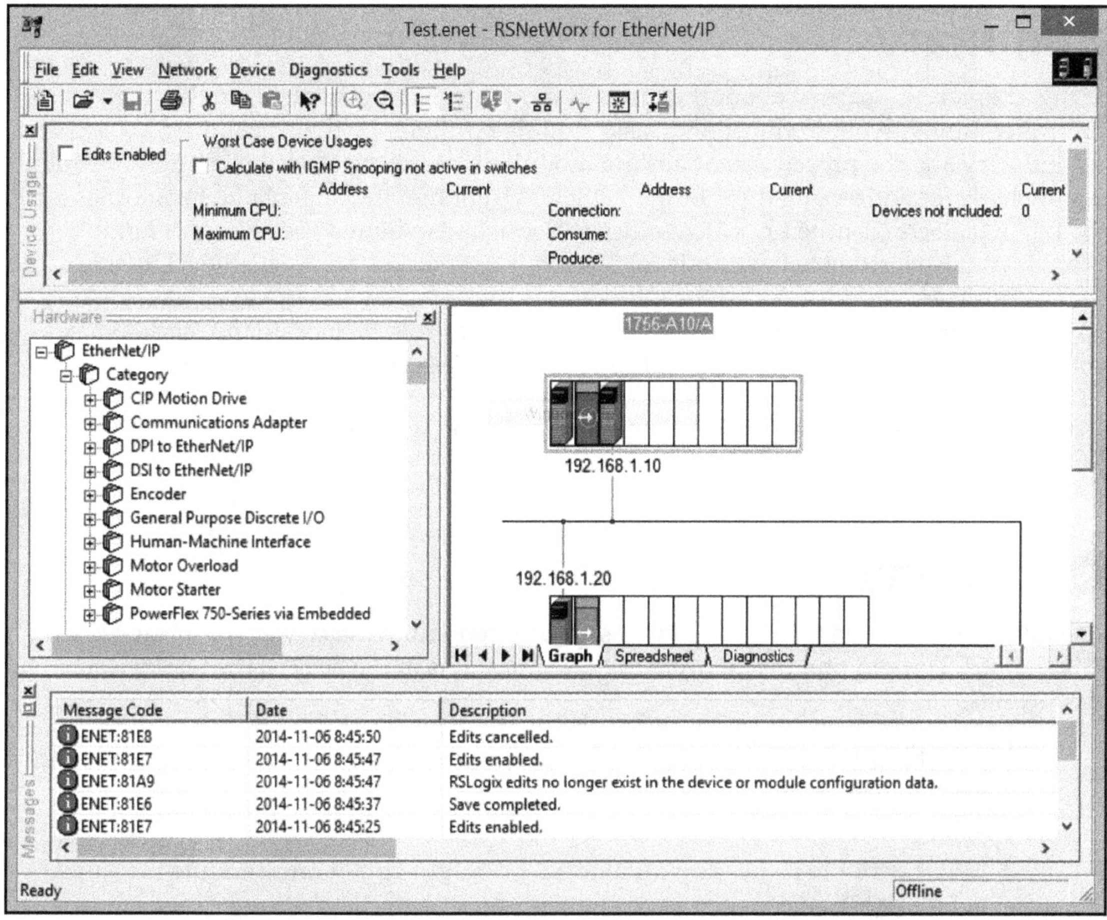

RSNetWorkx allows users to configure Rockwell device networks using multiple network technologies and network media. It is important to be aware that this tool is used to configure the communication modules that are added to your rack. Remote racks are an advanced topic in the Logix platform and we will not cover this in detail in this book. For more details on RSNetWorx, see *Getting results with RSNetWorx for DeviceNet* in the *Further reading* section of this chapter, which is a link to the Rockwell Automation Literature Library document.

Summary

In this chapter, we learned about the types of modules that are available in the Logix controller family. We introduced the basic module terminology that is commonly used in the industry and the procedure for adding modules to our project, as well as demonstrated the methods for addressing the module values. We enumerated the available modules for the Logix platform, learned how to configure them, and explored their use in a Logix project. We also introduced methods for identifying module features by their Logix module catalog numbers and introduced the address tree that a typical I/O module creates. You now know how to select and add I/O modules to your projects, modify the module configurations, and reference their real-time values using the recommended best practices.

In the next chapter, we will begin to work with RSLogix or Studio 5000 to write ladder logic.

Questions

The following questions can be used to test your retention of the concepts introduced in this chapter. You can find the answers to these questions in the back of the book under *Assessments*:

1. What is the term for a chassis that contains the controller modules and typically has a range of 4 to 17 module slots?
2. What attribute refers to a module's position in a rack?
3. What attribute is the individual input or output circuit on a module that links with one signal connection with the field?
4. What is the name of the attribute that is the complete path from a Logix controller to a module channel, property, or configuration value?
5. What module type processes the input and output of signals that vary by current and voltage and translate to real-world values such as pressure, temperature, and flow?
6. What module type processes the input and output of signals that vary by current and voltage and translate to either `ON` or `OFF` values?

Further reading

For more information about ControlLogix communication modules, refer to the following Rockwell documents:

- ControlLogix communication modules: `https://literature.rockwellautomation.com/idc/groups/literature/documents/td/1756-td003_-en-e.pdf`
- ControlLogix analog I/O modules: `https://literature.rockwellautomation.com/idc/groups/literature/documents/um/1756-um009_-en-p.pdf`
- ControlLogix digital I/O modules: `https://literature.rockwellautomation.com/idc/groups/literature/documents/um/1756-um058_-en-p.pdf`
- 1756 ControlLogix Integrated Motion module specifications: `https://literature.rockwellautomation.com/idc/groups/literature/documents/td/1756-td004_-en-e.pdf`
- Getting results with RSNetWorx for DeviceNet: `https://literature.rockwellautomation.com/idc/groups/literature/documents/gr/dnet-gr001_-en-e.pdf`
- Getting results with RSNetWorkx for EtherNet/IP: `https://literature.rockwellautomation.com/idc/groups/literature/documents/gr/enet-gr001_-en-e.pdf`

8
Writing Ladder Logic

In this chapter, we will look at the history of ladder logic and the development of the **International Electrotechnical Commission** (**IEC**) standard programming languages. Then, we will jump into the ladder logic programming by creating a simple pump control program. We will demonstrate how to buffer inputs and outputs in our ladder logic code and discuss the importance of this process. Finally, we will explore the new program parameter features in Logix Designer version 24 (and higher) and how they can be used to buffer values and significantly reduce the amount of ladder logic required for a program.

This chapter will cover the following aspects of ladder logic:

- Ladder Logic overview
- Understanding IEC 61131-3
- Understanding IEC programming logic
- Programming Ladder Logic
- Buffering module I/O data
- Buffering using program parameters.

We will begin this chapter by covering the genesis of Ladder Logic in the following section.

Technical requirements

To complete this chapter, you need to create a Rockwell Automation support account by going to `https://www.rockwellautomation.com/account/create-account`.

Creating an account is free, and the material we will refer to in this chapter is publicly available to anyone who has registered with Rockwell Automation.

You will also need a copy of RSLogix or Studio 5000 to program your project. You can either purchase this from your local distributor or request a time-limited trial version. You can find a local distributor for Rockwell Automation products at `https://locator.rockwellautomation.com/`.

Ladder Logic overview

Ladder Logic, also known as **Ladder Diagram** (**LD**), is one of five IEC standard 61131-3 languages, which include the following:

1. **LD**
2. **Functional Block Diagram** (**FBD**)
3. **Instruction List** (**IL**)
4. **Sequential Functional Charts** (**SFCs**)
5. **Structured Text** (**ST**)

Ladder Logic was originally a written method for capturing the wiring of relay circuits, also known as relay logic. The name *Ladder Logic* can be attributed to the diagrams it uses that resemble a ladder. Two vertical lines (often referred to as `L1` and `L2`) represent the voltage of the circuit and the horizontal lines and symbols represent the devices (buttons, motors, and breakers) connected to the circuit.

Each horizontal line in the circuit is known as a **rung**. Once microprocessors enabled programmable logic in control systems, Ladder Logic evolved into a programming language, rather than an engineering diagram.

The following diagram is an example of a single relay logic rung:

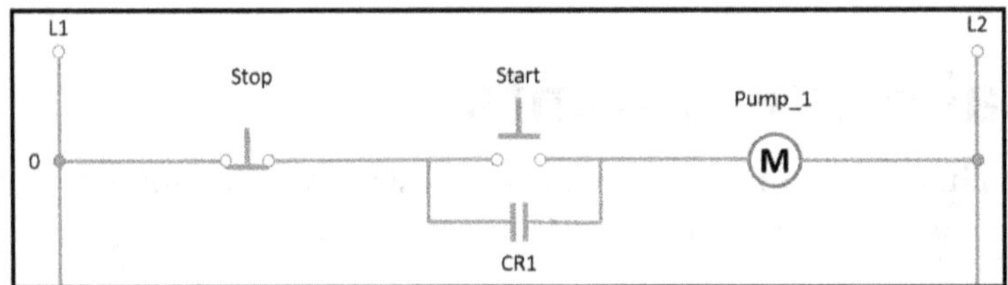

Ladder Logic is still the most popular industrial automation programming language of all the IEC 61131 languages. In the following section, we will talk about the other IEC 61131 languages and what these languages have in common.

Understanding IEC 61131-3

As mentioned in the previous section, Ladder Logic is one of the five IEC 61131-3-compliant languages available in Logix. IEC 61131-3 defines a standard set of real-time automation programming language structures, that are shared across multiple vendors' software products (most people refer to them as IEC languages).

In general, IEC languages share the following features:

- Naming conventions
- Data types
- Task structure, scheduling, and execution control
- Execution flow control
- Program execution
- Triggers
- Scheduling

IEC, which was first published in December 1993, enables you to transition between programming platforms designed by different vendors. Furthermore, it improves the safety and reliability of automation applications by making them easy to understand for a wider audience.

Each vendor's **Programmable Logic Controller** (**PLC**) programming environment and hardware has its own unique differences and challenges. In my own experience, the similarities between vendor programming environments end with the IEC programming language. As a control system integrator or PLC programmer, becoming proficient in a platform means that you must learn these nuances.

Now that we have introduced the IEC 61131 languages, in the next section, we will cover IEC programming logic.

Understanding IEC programming logic

All computer programming languages have logical expressions. A logical expression is typically an equation that evaluates to either `1` or `0`, which represents `true` or `false`. IEC programming languages are no different, and each type of IEC language has its own method of creating logical expressions.

Each rung of Ladder Logic is an equation solved by the controller's **Central Processing Unit** (**CPU**) as `True` (`1`) or `False` (`0`), also known as `Energized` (`1`) or `De-energized` (`0`). Ladders are executed one rung at a time from top to bottom, and each rung executes one instruction (also known as an **element** in Logix) at a time from left to right.

The following diagram details the anatomy and terminology of a simple Ladder Logic program:

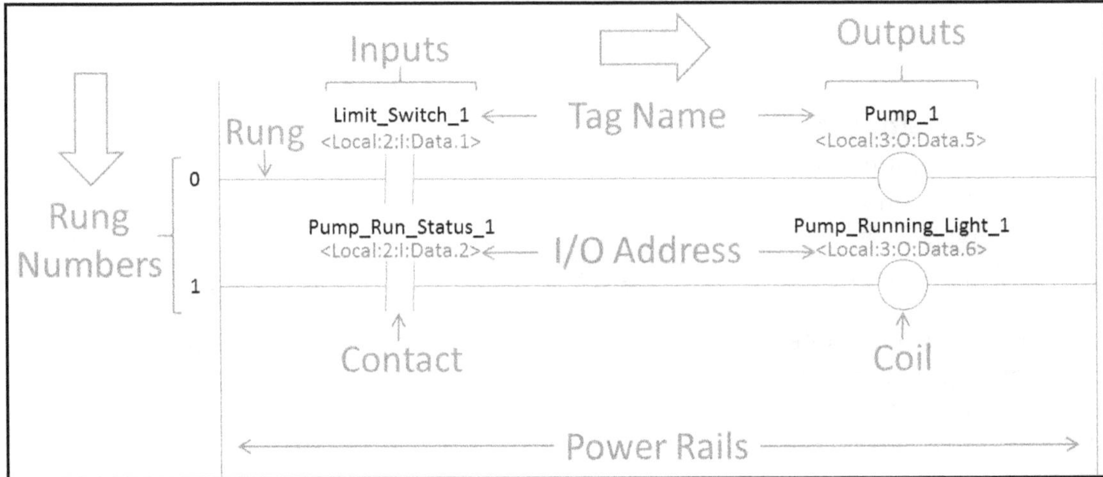

In the following sections, we will cover `AND` logic, `OR` logic, and `NOT` logic. As we will learn in the following sections, the `AND`, `OR`, and `NOT` logic instructions allow a programmer to change the flow of program execution depending on the current industrial process state.

AND logic in Ladder

When the Ladder Logic instructions are positioned side by side, known as `AND` logic, both instructions need to evaluate as true in order for the output (or coil) to energize.

The following diagram illustrates a simple example of `AND` logic:

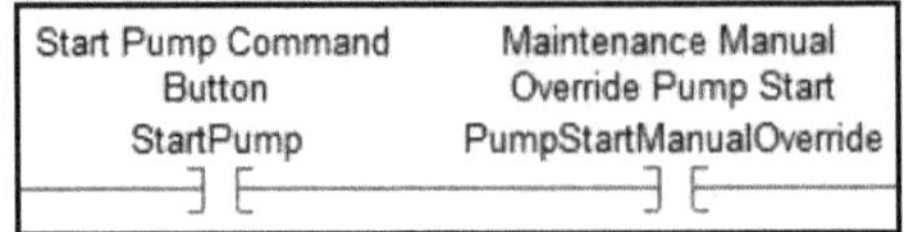

Next, we will cover how to create `OR` logic in Ladder.

OR logic in Ladder

When the Ladder Logic instructions are stacked on top of each other, known as `OR` logic, either of the instructions can evaluate as `True` in order to energize the output.

The following diagram demonstrates `OR` logic in a Ladder Logic rung:

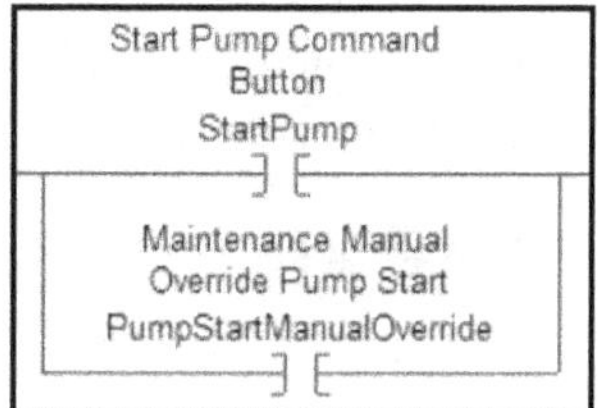

Next, we will cover `NOT` logic within Ladder Logic.

NOT logic in Ladder

When Ladder Logic contacts are energized, they evaluate as true. There is another form of Ladder Logic contact instruction that evaluates as false when energized and can be identified by the diagonal line that passes through it. These contacts evaluate as true when they are not energized. This is referred to as the `NOT` logic construct in Ladder Logic. The following diagram shows an example of `NOT` logic:

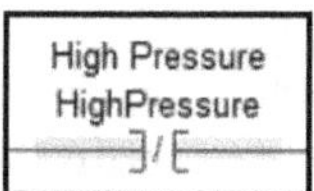

In the preceding example, when the `HighPressure` value is not energized, the contact will return a `True` value. In this case, we are looking to trigger an action when a high pressure reading is not present.

Now that we have covered the basics of `AND`, `OR`, and `NOT` logic, in the following section, we will start learning to write our own Ladder Logic.

Programming Ladder Logic

In this section, we will create a Ladder Logic program using Studio 5000's Logix Designer (previously known as RSLogix 5000). Using a Ladder Logic program is a way of organizing a collection of Ladder Logic rungs that work together to accomplish a single goal (ideally). Typically, a control system will read inputs from sensors and equipment, use the inputs in logic routines, then write to outputs. This activates the equipment to manipulate a process. To provide an example that aligns with a typical control system, we need to ensure that our project contains both a digital input module and a digital output module.

In order to complete this exercise, you will need to do the following:

1. Load the project created in `Chapter 3`, *Configuring Logix Modules*, or simply create a new project and add a controller and a 16-channel digital input module to it (1756-IB16D 16 points 10V-30V DC diagnostic input).
2. Then, add a digital output module (1756-OB16D 16 points 19.2V-30V DC diagnostic output module) by following the process we detailed in `Chapter 3`, *Configuring Logix Modules*:

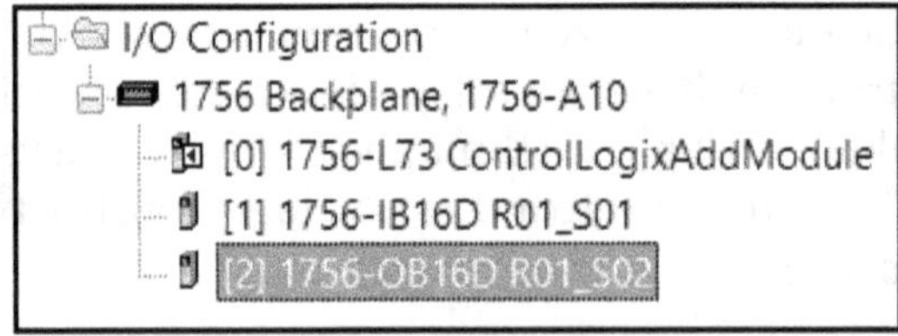

As discussed in the `Chapter 2`, *Understanding ControlLogix*, buffering I/O data is an important part of Logix program development. In the following sections, we will cover the module I/O buffering techniques.

Buffering module I/O data

One important issue we must address prior to starting the development of our program is the buffering of module I/O data. In `Chapter 2`, *Understanding ControlLogix*, we briefly looked at the Logix operating cycle and the differences between asynchronous and synchronous execution. Traditionally, PLCs have been synchronous, which means that everything happens in a predictable order every single time a program executes. Synchronous controllers read from inputs, process logic, and finally, write to outputs. In modern asynchronous operating cycles, there are many activities that appear to be happening at the same time. The input and output values could change in the middle of a program scan and put the program in an unpredictable state if the program was written with synchronous operation in mind.

Imagine a program starting a pump in one line of code, and then closing a valve directly in front of that pump in the next line of code because it detected a change in process conditions. To address this issue, we use a technique called **buffering**, and depending on the version of Logix you are developing on, there are a few different methods of achieving this. The two widely accepted methods of buffering are as follows:

- Buffering to base tags
- Program parameter buffering (only available on Logix version 24 and higher)

Buffering is a technique where the program code does not directly access the real input or output tags on the modules during the execution of a program. Instead, the input and output module tags are copied at the beginning of a program's scan to a set of base tags that will not change the state during the program's execution. Buffering these values is a means of simulating synchronous execution in an asynchronous controller. Think of buffering as taking a snapshot of the process conditions and making decisions on those static values, rather than on the live values that are fluctuating every millisecond.

Do not underestimate the importance of buffering a program's I/O. I worked on an expansion project for a process control system where the original programmers had failed to implement buffering. Once a month, the process would end up in a strange state that the program could not recover from. The operators had attributed problems to "gremlins" for years before identifying and correcting the issue.

In the following section, we will cover how to create and define the tags that will be used in our Logix program to hold and label data.

Defining tags

In Logix, a tag allows you to allocate and reference data stored in the controller. When working with legacy PLCs, programmers would often use registers to store data and reference them using their addresses in memory. Modern PACs, such as the Logix family, use name-based tags to store and manipulate data. Tags can be a simple, single element, an array, or a structure.

There are four types of tags in Logix:

- **Base**: These tags are the default variable tag type in Logix. Base tags allow you to specify a unique name-based tag to store and manipulate data in your program. For example, a digital input to start a pump might have a `Local:1:I.Data.0` base tag.
- **Alias**: These tags allow you to assign your own unique name to a module channel, an existing tag, or a structure tag member. When you create an alias tag, you also select what it is an alias for. They are most frequently assigned to module channels in order to improve code readability and ease of maintenance. For example, if you consistently refer to a digital input module's channel as an alias tag and the channel wiring changes to a new location, you can easily update your code by only changing the configuration of your single alias tag. For example, once you get tired of remembering the base tag location of the pump start button, you might assign an alias such as `PushButton_Pump_Start` to it.
- **Produced**: This tag allows you to pass a tag's value to a remote Logix controller at a predictable (real-time) frequency. A produced tag is always paired with a consumed tag on the controller that reads the tag's value.
- **Consumed**: This tag allows you to receive a tag's value from a remote Logix controller at a predictable (real-time) frequency. A consumed tag is paired with a produced tag on the controller that is sending the tag value.

Each tag that is created in Logix is also assigned a scope. The scope defines the area within our Logix project where the tag can be accessed. The scope can be configured as either of the following levels:

- **Controller level**: This level is globally accessible across all programs.
- **Program Level**: This level is accessible only within a single program. The program scope is selected during the tag configuration.

It is important to note that the tag scope cannot be easily changed once it is configured. So, care should be taken when selecting the tag's scope level. Now that we have a better understanding of how tags are scoped and used in our project, we will cover how to buffer base tags in the next section.

Buffering base tags

As we will learn later in `Chapter 12`, *Using Tasks and Programs for Project Organization*, Logic can be organized into manageable pieces and executed based on different intervals and conditions. The practice of buffering base tags takes advantage of Logix's ability to organize code into routines.

The default Ladder Logic routine that is created in every new Logix project is called `MainRoutine`. `MainRoutine` is the *only* routine that is called by default by `MainTask`,and so any other routines we want to execute will need to be called from `MainRoutine`. In the following exercise, we will edit the `MainRoutine` Ladder Logic program and add three routines that will be called by it:

- One for reading the input values
- One for executing logic
- One for writing the output values

Open the Logix project we created earlier in this chapter with the digital input and output modules. In the following steps, we will use these previously created modules to create and buffer our tags:

1. Using the **Controller Organizer** pane, open the `MainProgram` folder, which can be found by navigating to **Tasks** | **MainTask**:

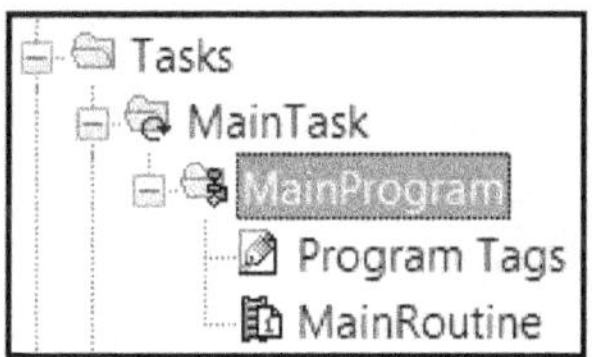

2. Right-click on **MainProgram** and select the **New Routine**... option.

3. In the **New Routine** window that appears, set the following field values:
    - **Name:** `BufferInputs`
    - **Description:** `Buffer input values prior to executing logic against them`
    - **Type: Ladder Diagram**
    - **In Program or Phase: MainProgram**
    - **Assignment: <none>**

The following screenshot shows the completed **New Routine** form:

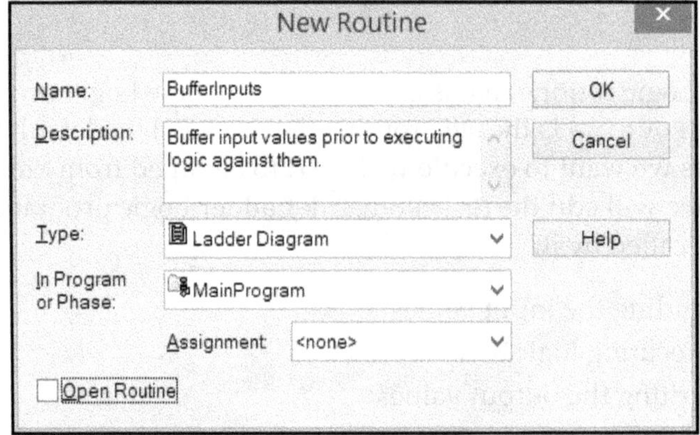

4. Create two more new routines. Use the following configurations for the first one:
    - **Name:** `PumpControl`
    - **Description:** `Pump control routine`
    - **Type: Ladder Diagram**
    - **In Program or Phase: MainProgram**
    - **Assignment: <none>**
5. Use the following configurations for the second one:
    - **Name:** `BufferOutputs`
    - **Description:** `Buffer write output values after executing logic`
    - **Type: Ladder Diagram**
    - **In Program or Phase: MainProgram**

6. Now, let's start some Ladder Logic programming! Open up the **BufferInputs** routine.

   Ladder Logic programs are primarily created through drag and drop (although if you prefer good old coding, you can always right-click on a rung and select **Edit Code** to type in the logic). Now, let's configure a contact from our digital input module to write a value (buffer it) to our coil base tag value. First, we will add a ladder rung for buffering a digital input module channel for a start pump button signal to a base tag.

7. Above our Ladder Logic routine, you will find the Ladder Logic element groups and elements. These can be dragged and dropped into our Ladder Logic routines. Under the **Bit** element group, you will see our contact element (known as **Examine On** in Logix) and our coil element (known as **Output Energize** in Logix). Drag the **Examine On** element to the left of our `BufferInputs` ladder rung `0`, as in the following screenshot:

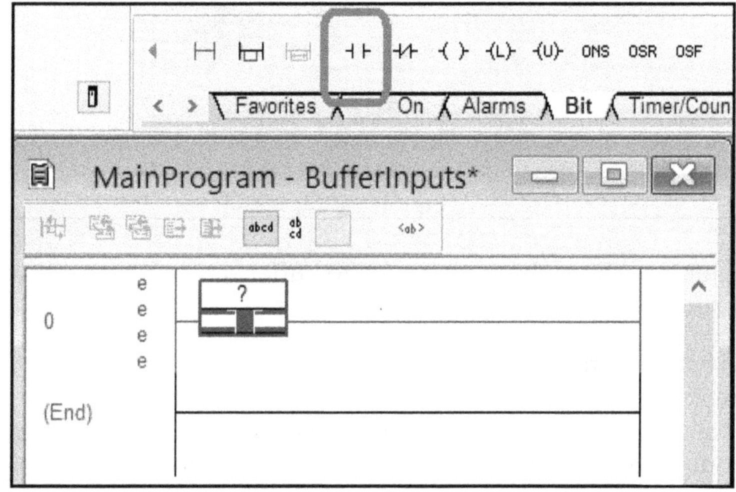

8. Now, we can assign the **Examine On** value to a channel of our digital input module. Double-click on the question mark above the **Examine On** element and select or type `Local:1:I.Data.0` in the module and channel, as in the following screenshot:

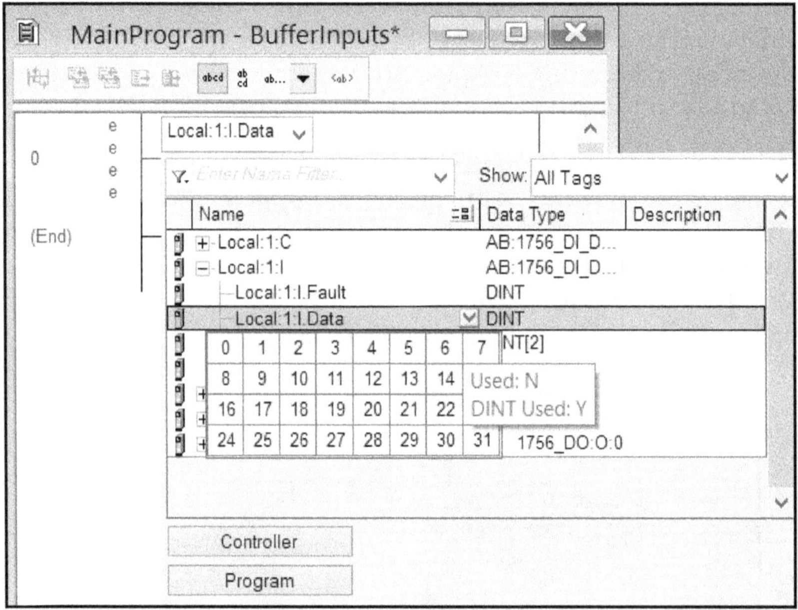

We should now have the tag we wish to buffer set as the contact within our ladder rung.

A common practice for handling the module inputs and outputs in a Logix program is to assign them to aliases and reference only the aliases throughout your program. This allows you to change the location of the module value easily in the future if required. However, as long as we only reference our module inputs and outputs in our buffering routines, we shouldn't clutter up our tag list with module alias tags.

9. Next, we will add the contact, known as **Output Energize** in Logix, to rung `0`. Find the **Output Energize** element in the **Bit** element group and drag and drop it to our rung:

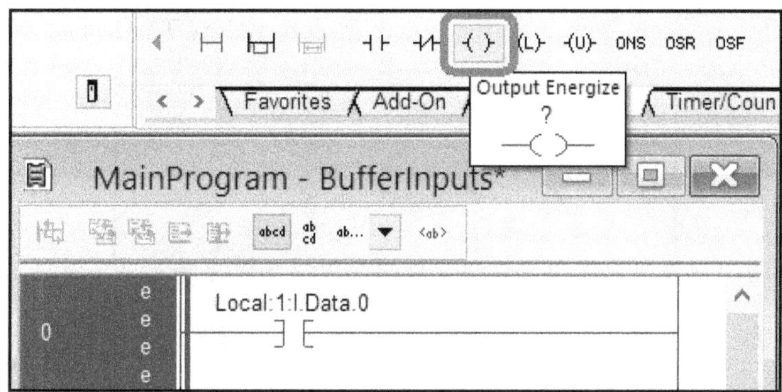

10. Now, we will assign the value of our input module channel `0` to a base variable using the **Output Energize** element (channel `0` is wired to start the push button and the input gets energized when the button is pressed). Right-click on the question mark above the **Output Energize** element and select **New Tag...**, as in the following screenshot:

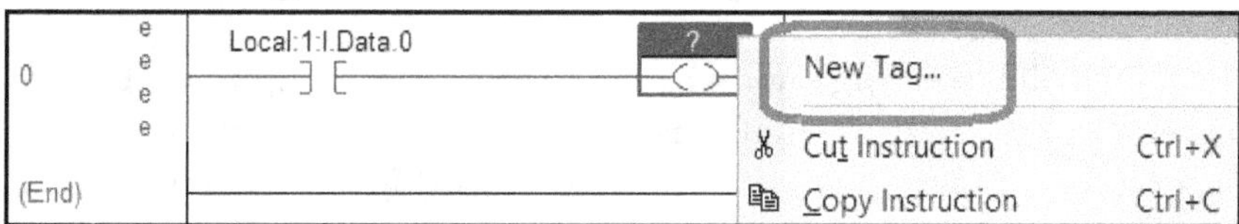

We should now have the target of our tag buffer as the coil of our Ladder Logic rung.

It is possible to interlace **Examine On** (input contacts) and **Output Energize** (coils) across a Ladder Logic rung. The **Output Energize** elements evaluate as the value that is being written to them in the logic. However, mixing coils and contacts in the middle of a rung can create Ladder Logic that is difficult to follow.

11. The **New Tag** window will appear and allow you to set the following parameters for a newly created tag:
    - **Name**: `StartPump`
    - **Description:** `Start Pump Command Button`
    - **Data Type**: **BOOL**
    - **Scope**: **MainProgram**
    - **External Access**: **Read/Write**
    - **Style**: **Decimal**

The following screenshot shows the completed **New Tag** form:

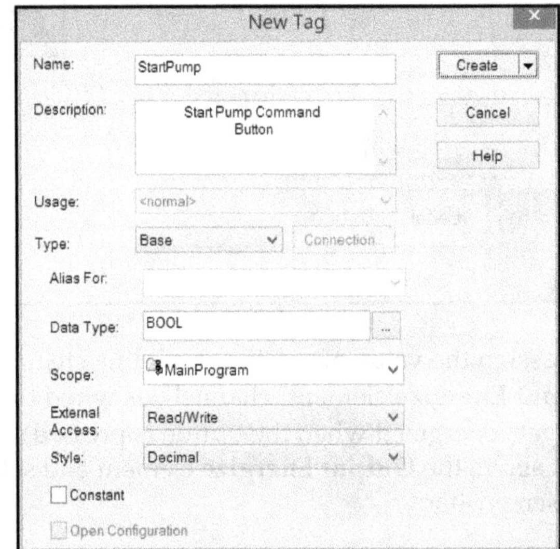

12. Next, we will be adding another rung to our `BufferInput` routine in order to buffer a `HighPressure` digital input module channel signal to a base tag. Right-click on the Ladder Logic rungs and select **Add Rung**, as in the following screenshot:

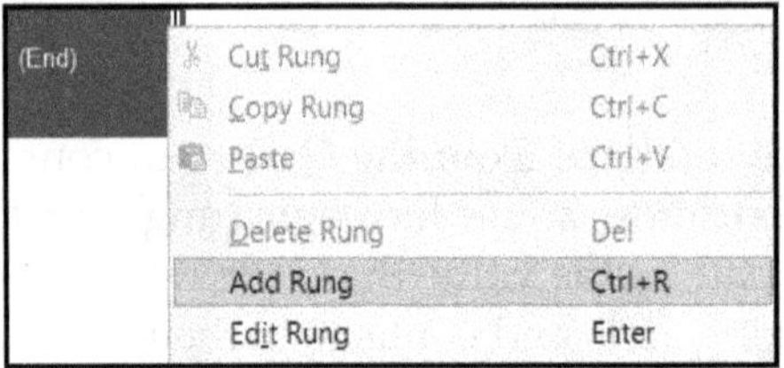

13. Drag an **Examine On** element to our newly added rung `1` and set the value to `Local:1:I.Data.1`.

14. Drag an **Output Energize** element to rung `1` and create a new base tag with the following parameters:
    - **Name**: `HighPressure`
    - **Description**: `High Pressure`
    - **Data Type**: **BOOL**
    - **Scope**: **MainProgram**
    - **External Access**: **Read/Write**
    - **Style**: **Decimal**

The following diagram demonstrates the completed **High Pressure** alarm input rung:

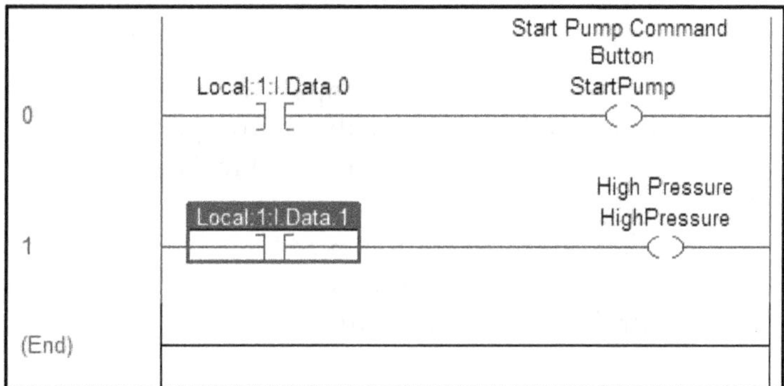

We will add one more Ladder Logic rung for `Maintenance Manual Override Pump Start`. Add a new ladder rung (rung `2`) and add `Local:1:I.Data.2` as the **Examine On** element. Then, add the **Output Energize** element and base tag with the following parameters:

- **Name**: `PumpStartManualOverride`
- **Description**: `Maintenance Manual Override Pump Start`
- **Data Type**: **BOOL**
- **Scope**: **MainProgram**
- **External Access**: **Read/Write**
- **Style**: **Decimal**

The following diagram demonstrates the completed **Pump Start Manual Override** Ladder Logic Rung:

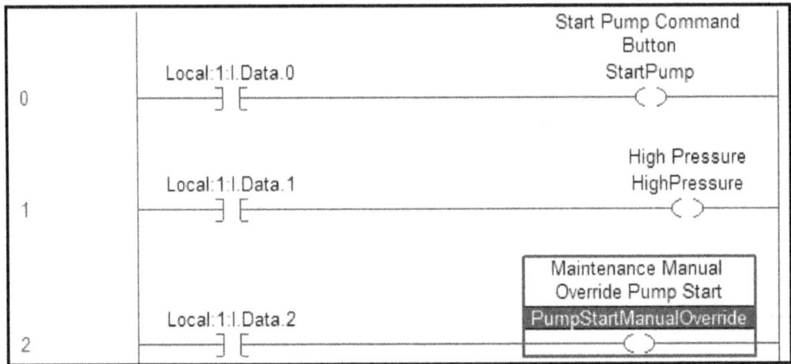

15. Now that we have buffered the digital inputs for our simple Ladder Logic program, we will now buffer the outputs. Our output will be `Run Pump Permissive from our program`. The pump will only run if the **Start** button is switched to `run` and the `HighPressure` value is not present. Open the `BufferOutputs` Ladder Logic routine we created earlier and drag an **Output Energize** element to rung `0`. Now, set the `Local:2:O.Data.0` output tag value to channel `0` of our digital output module:

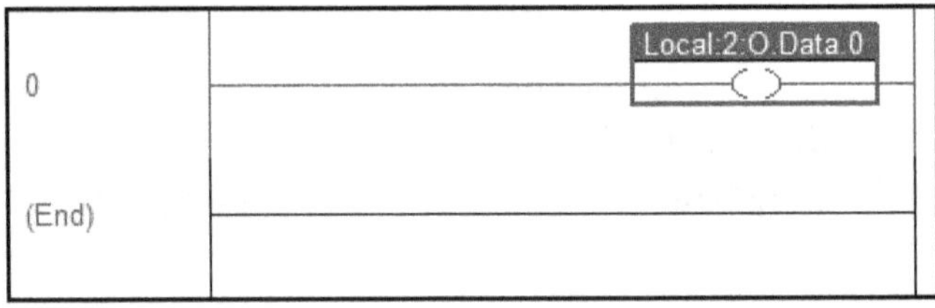

16. Next, we will add our **Examine On** element and create a new base tag with the following parameters:

    - **Name:** `RunPump`
    - **Description:** `Run Pump Permissive`
    - **Data Type: BOOL**
    - **Scope: MainProgram**
    - **External Access: Read/Write**
    - **Style: Decimal**

The following diagram demonstrates the completed rung of Ladder Logic:

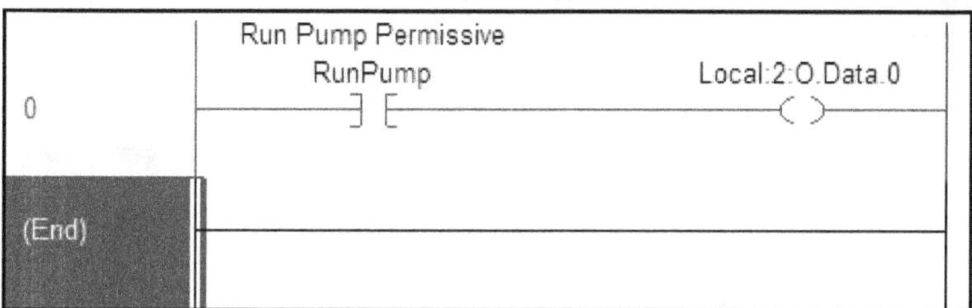

We have successfully buffered our tags and protected our programs from encountering a state change during the middle of execution. In the next section, we will continue with our Ladder Logic program to create the pump control logic for our control system.

Creating the pump control logic

We have now buffered our module inputs and module outputs to ensure they do not change in the middle of a program's execution and potentially put our process in an undesirable state.

In the following exercise, we will proceed with creating the pump start and stop logic:

1. We will use `AND` and `NOT` logic to control our pump using our buffered base tags. Open the `PumpControl` routine that we created.
2. Drag an **Examine On** element (contact) to ladder rung `0` in the `PumpControl` routine and assign the element to our `StartPump` base tag.
3. Drag an **Examine Off** element (looks similar to the **Examine On** element but with a line through it) to ladder rung `0`. You will notice that the **Examine Off** element appears beside the **Examine On** element, creating an `AND` logical expression. Assign the **Examine Off** element to the `HighPressure` base tag we created in our buffering routine. The `HighPressure` **Examine Off** element will protect our process from being over-pressurized by shutting down the pump if the pressure is too high.

4. We will complete our Ladder Logic rung by adding the **Output Energize** element to ladder rung `0` and assigning it to our buffered output base tag, `RunPump`:

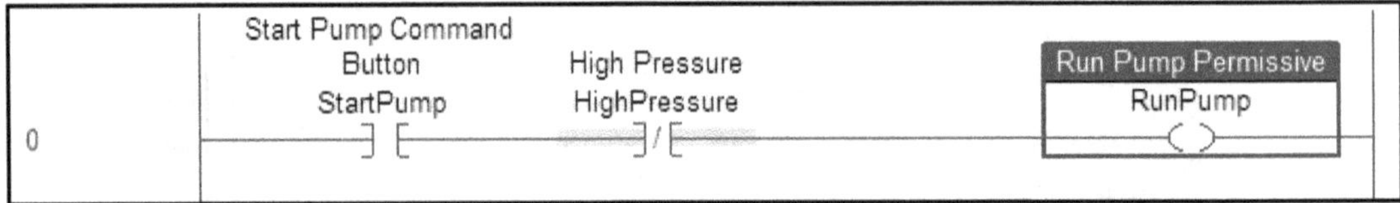

5. The `HighPressure` **Examine Off** element uses a `NOT` logic expression, which is illustrated by the slash across the element symbol. This element will evaluate as true when the `HighPressure` digital input reads `false`. With the two elements side by side, our Ladder Logic rung now utilizes the `AND` logic expression. Both `StartPump` and `HighPressure` must evaluate as true in order to energize the `RunPump` output coil.

We created the following logic expression using Ladder Logic in our rung, which will check to make sure we do not already have a high-pressure alarm before starting the pump:

```
IF StartPump = True AND HighPressure = False THEN RunPump
```

When creating logic expressions, truth tables can be a helpful tool in understanding all the possible input combinations and their outputs.

The following truth table shows all the input and output combinations of our Ladder Logic rung:

StartPump	HighPressure	RunPump
False (0)	False (0)	False (0)
True (1)	False (0)	True (1)
False (0)	True (1)	False (0)
True (1)	True (1)	False (0)

In the last exercise, we implemented the basic pump start logic. However, we still need to account for maintenance and start up scenarios where we want to override the pump condition and start it, regardless of the pressure sensor reading.

In the following exercise, we will implement a maintenance manual override mode.

Implementing maintenance manual override

We still need to add our `Maintenance Manual Override Pump Start` start element for our pump control logic. This feature will allow the operator to run the pump regardless of the process conditions.

In order to implement this feature, we will add a branch to our Ladder Logic rung, which evaluates as an **OR** logic expression, by performing the following steps:

1. The branch element is the second element in all of the element groups. Drag the branch element to rung `0`:

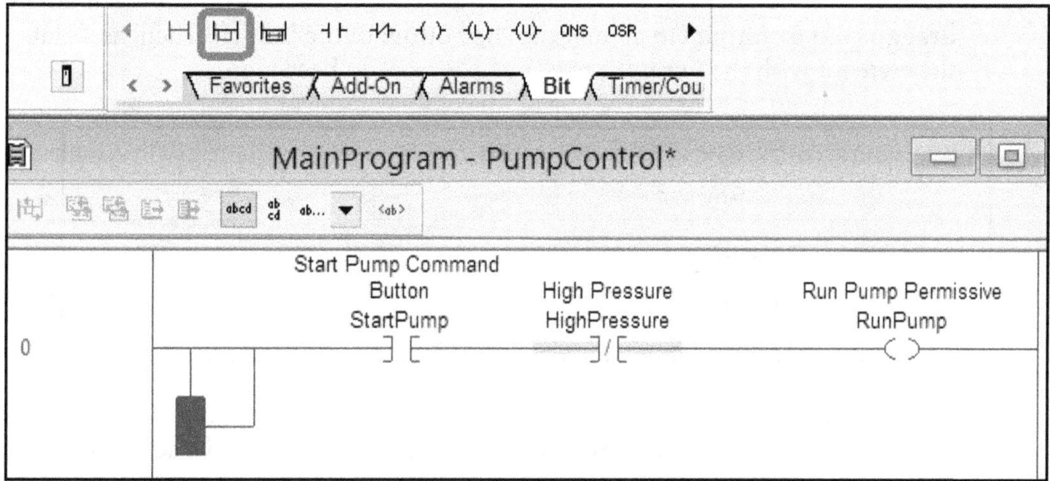

We have created an `OR` branch in our logic and can now add an alternate path for our maintenance mode to run in.

It is possible to nest multiple branch elements to create a very complex `OR` logic expression.

2. In order for the `OR` logic expression to override all of our other module inputs, we need to drag and drop the **StartPump** and **HighPressure** elements to the top line of the branch element:

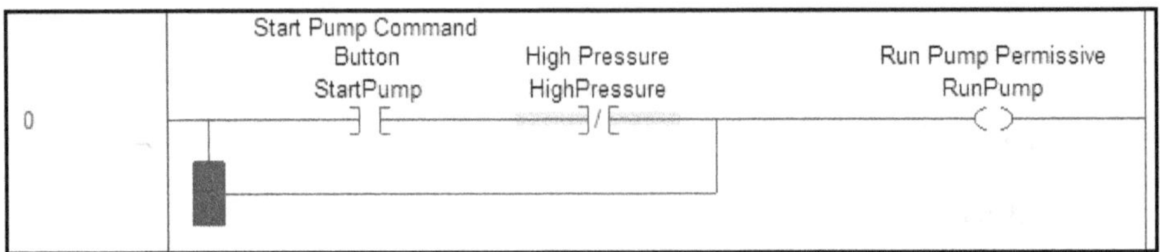

3. Adding `Maintenance Manual Override Pump Start` is now just a matter of dragging an **Examine On** element to the bottom of the branch. Then, associate the element with the `PumpStartManualOverride` base tag:

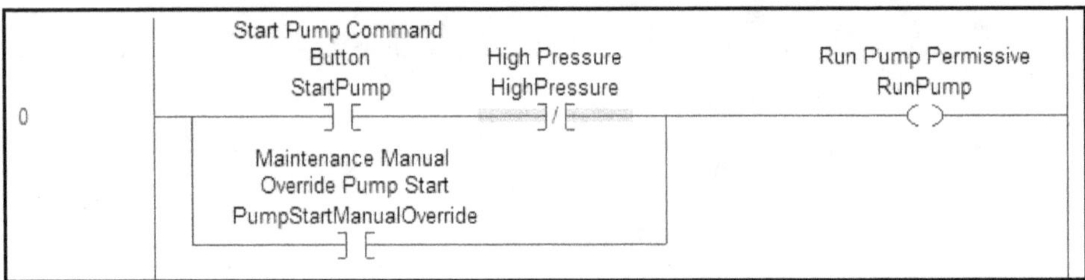

4. During maintenance periods or turnarounds, we want to be able to start and stop the pump, regardless of the current vessel pressure; so, we have added the `PumpStartManualOverride` tag to the expression to allow us to override the normal pump controls.

We have updated our rung to override the `StartPump` and `HighPressure` inputs with `Maintenance Manual Override Pump Start` and created the Ladder Logic that is equivalent to following logic expression:

```
IF (StartPump = True AND HighPressure = False)
 OR
 PumpStartManualOverride = True
 THEN RunPump
```

The following truth table shows all the input and output combinations of our updated Ladder Logic rung:

StartPump	HighPressure	PumpStartManualOverride	RunPump
False (0)	False (0)	False (0)	False (0)
True (1)	False (0)	False (0)	True (1)
False (0)	True (1)	False (0)	False (0)
False (0)	False (0)	True (1)	True (1)
True (1)	True (1)	False (0)	False (0)
False (0)	True (1)	True (1)	True (1)
True (1)	False (0)	True (1)	True (1)
True (1)	True (1)	True (1)	True (1)

Currently, our routine will not execute in the program on our Logix controller because `MainProgram` (which contains our Ladder Logic routines) is configured to *only* run the `MainRoutine` program. This is a common stumbling block for newcomers to ControlLogix and even catches experienced users by surprise from time to time.

In order for our routines to execute, we must reference them in the `MainRoutine` program:

1. The **Jump To Subroutine** (**JSR**) Ladder Logic element allows us to execute the routines we created from the **MainRoutine** program.
2. Open the **MainRoutine** program and find the **JSR** element in the **Program Control** element group and drag it to rung `0`:

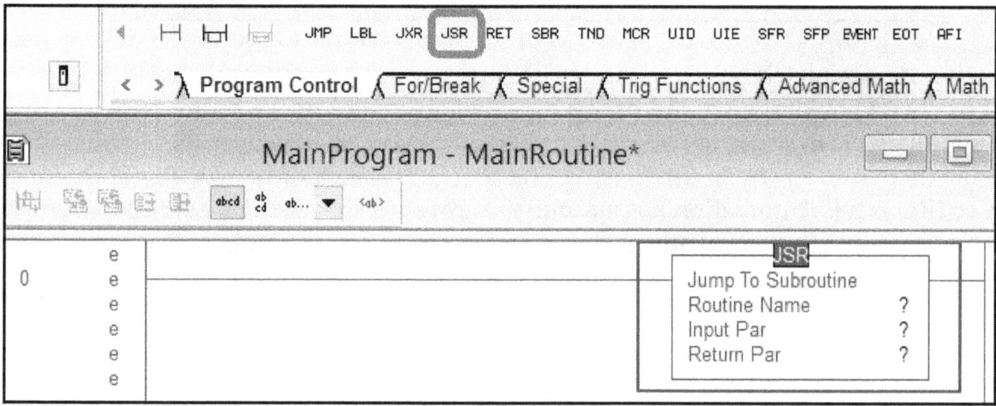

3. Now, we can associate the **JSR** element with our `BufferInputs` routine by setting the **Routine Name** parameter to `BufferInputs`.

4. We will need to remove the **Input Par** and **Return Par** parameters from the **JSR** element by right-clicking on the **JSR** routine and selecting **Remove Instruction Parameter** on both the **Input Par** and **Return Par** parameters.
5. In order to add the **JSR** elements for our other routines, we will need to add two more ladder rungs and add the **JSR** elements with the following parameters:
    - JSR rung `1`: `PumpControl`
    - JSR rung `2`: `BufferOutputs`

The following screenshot demonstrates how we should add JSR instructions to the Ladder Logic rungs:

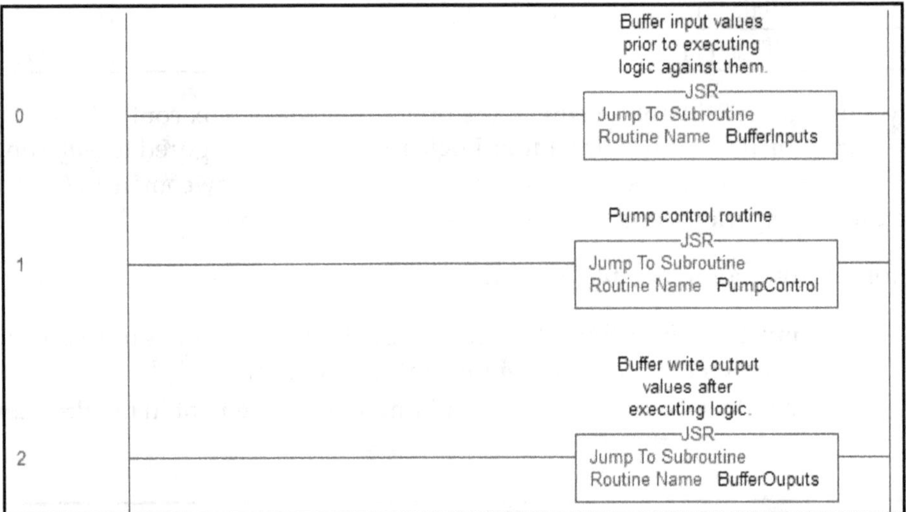

We have now completed our first Ladder Logic program. Ladder Logic can easily be created by dragging and dropping elements to a rung. There are far too many elements available in Logix to cover in this book, but you can discover them yourself by dragging them into a rung, right-clicking on them, and selecting **Instruction Help**. In addition, Rockwell Automation has a number of resources on Ladder Logic programming in their Literature Library Resources document (refer to the appendix of this book for some useful links).

We have completed our first Ladder Logic program in RSLogix. In the following section, we will cover an alternative method of buffering program tags using program parameters that is available in the later versions of Studio 5000.

Buffering using program parameters

Program parameters are a powerful new feature in Logix that allows the association of dynamic values with tags and programs as parameters. The importance of program parameters is clear by the way they permeate the user interface in newer versions of Logix Designer (version 24 and higher). Program parameters are extremely powerful, but the key benefit to us in using them is that they are automatically buffered. This means we can effectively create the same result in one Ladder Logic rung that we did with the eight we created in the previous section.

There are the following four types of program parameters:

- **Input**: This program parameter is automatically buffered and passed into a program on each scan cycle.
- **Output**: This program parameter is automatically updated at the end of a program (as a result of executing that program) on each scan cycle, similar to the way we buffered our output module value in the previous section.
- **InOut**: This program parameter is updated at the start and end of the program scan. It is also important to note that unlike the **Input** and **Output** parameters, the **InOut** parameter is passed as a pointer in memory. A pointer shares a piece of memory with other processes, rather than creating a copy of it. This means that it is possible for an **InOut** parameter to change its value in the middle of a program scan. This makes the **InOut** program parameters unsuitable for buffering when used on their own.
- **Public**: This program parameter behaves like a normal controller tag and can be connected to the **Input**, **Output**, and **InOut** parameters. Similar to the **InOut** parameter, **Public** parameters are updated globally as their values are changed. This makes the **Program** parameters unsuitable for buffering when used on their own. Primarily, the **Public** program parameters are used for passing large data structures between programs on a controller.

In Logix Designer version 24 and higher, a **Program** parameter can be associated with a local tag using **Parameters** and **Local Tags** in the **Control Organizer** pane (formally called program tags). The module input channel can be associated with a base tag within your program scope using the **Parameter Connections** option.

The following screenshot demonstrates how we can add the module input value as a parameter connection:

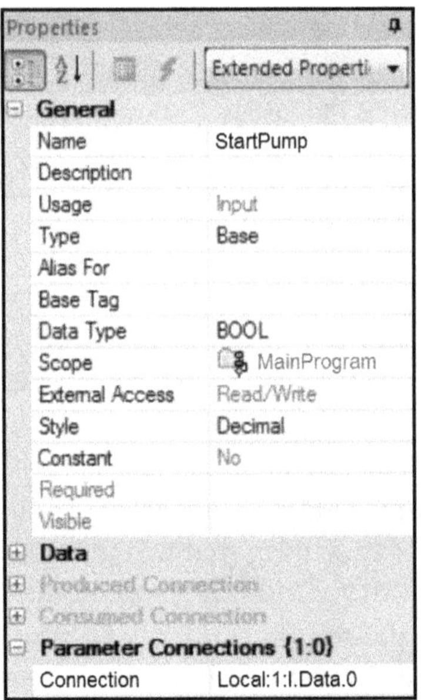

We have now demonstrated how we can associate the input module channel with our `StartPump` base tag using the parameter connection value. We have also covered the basics of Ladder Logic and how to buffer input values using program tags and program parameters.

Summary

In this chapter, we explored the genesis of Ladder Logic programming and the IEC programming language standards. We learned how to create Ladder Logic by dragging and dropping elements to a ladder rung in a routine. We also learned the importance of buffering inputs and outputs and some techniques for accomplishing this. We now understand how to read and write most Ladder Logic programs, and as it is based on the IEC standard, this knowledge can be applied to PLC programs from a myriad of vendors. At this point, it would not be too difficult for you to also write Ladder Logic for other vendors' PLCs.

In the next chapter, we will introduce another IEC language, FBD, and explore its use within the Logix family.

Questions

The following questions can be used to test your retention of the concepts introduced in this chapter. You can find the answers to these questions in the back of the book under *Assessments*:

1. What IEC language was originally a written method for capturing the wiring of relay circuits, also known as relay logic, and resembles a ladder?
2. What is the name of the standard set of real-time automation programming language structures that are shared across multiple vendors' software products?
3. Each rung of Ladder Logic is an equation solved by the controller's CPU and results in one of which two values?
4. When the Ladder Logic instructions are positioned side by side, both instructions need to evaluate as true in order for the output to energize. What is this logic statement known as?
5. When the Ladder Logic instructions are stacked on top of each other, either of the instructions can evaluate as true in order to energize the output. What is this logic statement known as?
6. The Ladder Logic contact instructions, by default, are normally considered open, and when closed, they evaluate as true. There is another form of Ladder Logic contact instruction that is normally closed and can be identified by the diagonal line that passes through it. What is the name of this logic statement in Ladder Logic?
7. What is the name of the tags that are the default variable tag type in Logix that allow you to specify a unique name-based tag to store and manipulate data in your program?
8. What tags allow you to assign your own unique name to a module channel, an existing tag, or a structure tag member?
9. What tag scope level is globally accessible across all routines?
10. What tag scope level is accessible only within a single program?
11. What is an alternative method of buffering tags (other than mapping tag values in ladder logic) that is available in later versions of Logix?

Further reading

For more information about writing Ladder Logic with Logix controllers, please refer to the *Logix 5000 Controllers Ladder Diagram* Rockwell document:

`https://literature.rockwellautomation.com/idc/groups/literature/documents/pm/1756-pm008_-en-p.pdf`

9
Writing Function Block

In this chapter, we will explore the merits of Function Block programming by building a small sample application. Furthermore, we will introduce the concept of language compilation in Logix, as well as instruction lists and bytecode. We will also provide instructions for modifying the Function Block properties and performing online edits.

The following Function Block topics will be covered in detail in this chapter:

- Understanding language compilation in Logix
- Writing Function Block
- Understanding Function Block logic
- Writing a Function Block program
- Online monitoring and editing

We will begin this chapter by discussing the **International Electrotechnical Commission (IEC)** language compilation within the RSLogix/Studio 5000 platform.

Technical requirements

To complete this chapter, you will need to create a Rockwell Automation support account by going to `https://www.rockwellautomation.com/account/create-account`.

Creating an account is free and the material we will be reviewing in this chapter is publicly available to anyone who is registered with Rockwell Automation.

You will also need a copy of RSLogix or Studio 5000 that has a license for Emulate 5000 to program your project. You can either purchase this from your local distributor or request a time-limited trial version. You can find a local distributor for Rockwell Automation products at `https://locator.rockwellautomation.com/`.

Understanding language compilation in Logix

Logix Designer, like most IEC 61131-3-compliant applications, takes any program you create in any IEC-compatible language, converts it into **Instruction List** (**IL**)—a low-level language that resembles assembly—and compiles it down to bytecode (the binary language used internally by the controller) in order for the controller to execute it.

The following diagram illustrates the ways that various languages are compiled down into the same bytecode language:

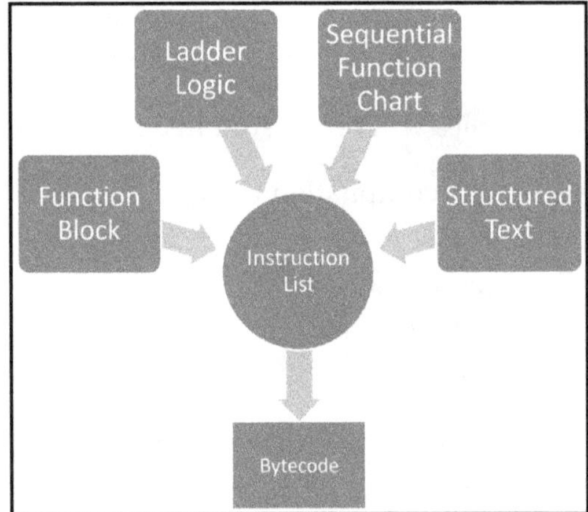

Ultimately, the controller is not aware of which language you created your program in (**Ladder Logic**, **Function Block**, or **Sequential Function Chart**); it always ends up as the same bytecode language that is executed on the controller. Within Logix Designer, you can create the exact same program using Ladder Logic that you would create using **Function Block Diagrams** (**FBDs**), and it would (in theory) translate down to the same **Structured Text** (**ST**) commands and compile down to the same bytecode for the controller. It is important to understand the direct relationship between Ladder Logic, Function Block, and other IEC languages.

In the following section, we will provide more details on Function Block programming prior to creating our Function Block program.

Introducing Function Block

The Function Block programming language is a graphical flow diagram language where program instructions appear as blocks (function blocks). Each function block has inputs and outputs that can be wired to other function blocks to create a visual representation of data flow. In the same way that Ladder Logic is based on relay logic engineering drawings, FBDs are also derived from engineering discipline standards. Before being used as a programming language, FBDs were used in system/software engineering to describe the interrelationships between electronic systems.

The following FBD is from NASA's Space Shuttle program and describes the electronic system relationships in an IBM AP-101S general-purpose computer:

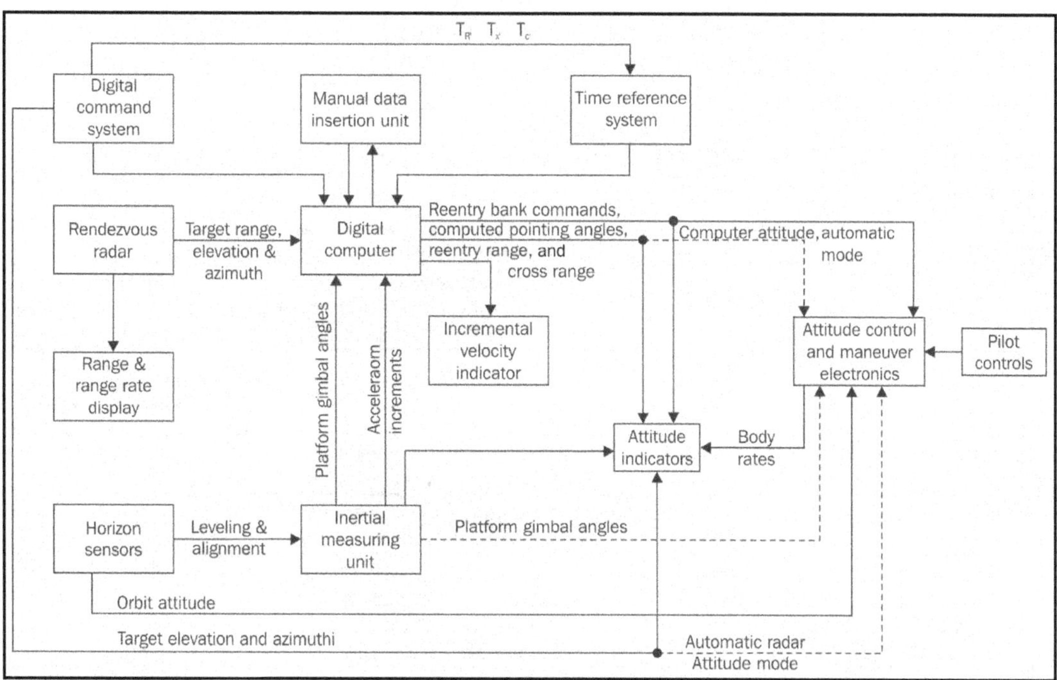

Within Logix, it is important to note that editing FBDs is not supported by all editions of the Logix programming software. Only the Professional, Full, and Lite editions allow you to write programs using Function Block; however, all the editions will allow you to upload and download the existing Function Block programs. It is important to understand the version and edition of Logix you are using and the capabilities that are enabled.

Now that we have introduced the concept of Function Block, let's compare it to what we learned in the previous chapter about Ladder Logic. In the following section, we will compare and contrast Function Block and Ladder Logic.

Function Block versus Ladder Logic

As mentioned earlier, both Function Block and Ladder Logic eventually compile down to the same controller bytecode language. The available functions and development interface in these two programming languages are vastly different and it is important to highlight these differences. Ladder Logic, as you will recall from the previous chapter, is executed from the top of the ladder to the bottom, and from the left-hand side of the rung to the right-hand side. Function Block also executes from left to right, so if you want a particular function block to execute before another, position it more to the left than the other blocks on the page. The inputs and outputs also help Logix to determine the order of execution for the function blocks on a sheet.

The following table lists some of the notable differences between Ladder Logic and Function Block:

Ladder Logic	**Function Block**
This language is executed from top to bottom and from left to right.	This language's execution order is determined by the input and output connections and the horizontal position on the sheet (left to right).
In this language, the input values can change during execution, so buffering the input data is recommended.	Here, input values are only read once at the start of the execution, so buffering the input values is not required.
This language uses normally open or normally closed contacts.	This language doesn't use normally open or normally closed contacts.
This language is organized by ladders, which execute in sequential order.	This language is organized by sheets. All the sheets execute at the same time.
This language is a low-level language. Ladder elements have very basic functionality and consume fewer processor cycles. It produces more code to maintain.	This language is a high-level language. Function Block elements have very powerful functionality and consume more processor cycles. This language produces less code to maintain more powerful functions.
This language uses the controller- and program-scoped tags.	This language uses the controller- and program-scoped tags.

Ultimately, when choosing whether to use Ladder Logic or Function Block to write a routine, it comes down to selecting the right tool for the job. Some problems are better suited to the powerful features of Function Block, and other problems would benefit from the low-level control provided by Ladder Logic.

When selecting a language to solve a problem, you should try to select the language that will allow you to strike a balance between the following:

- Ease of development
- Ease of maintenance
- Efficient use of processor cycles

Now that we have compared the Ladder Logic and Function Block programming languages, we can begin to explore the various components that make up a Function Block program in the next section.

Function Block sheets

Within a routine, FBDs are created in an area called a sheet, and the sizes of the sheets directly correspond to standard metric or English printer page sizes (we use ledger/11 x 17 inch in the following example—11 x 17 is the default page size as of version 31 of Studio 5000 Logix). This allows the sheets to be easily printed, presented, and even signed like a typical engineering drawing. It is helpful to think of each sheet as a drawing for a single device.

You can adjust the size of a sheet by right-clicking on an empty area of the Function Block routine and selecting **Properties**.

You can connect multiple sheets together using the input wire connectors and output wire connectors; we will discuss connectors in more detail later in this chapter. Each sheet has a sheet number and sheet name to identify it. A routine can contain an unlimited number of sheets, but it is important to understand that all the sheets are executed at the same time (not one sheet at a time).

Here is a diagram displaying two sheets, each containing a function block wired together using the input and output wire connectors:

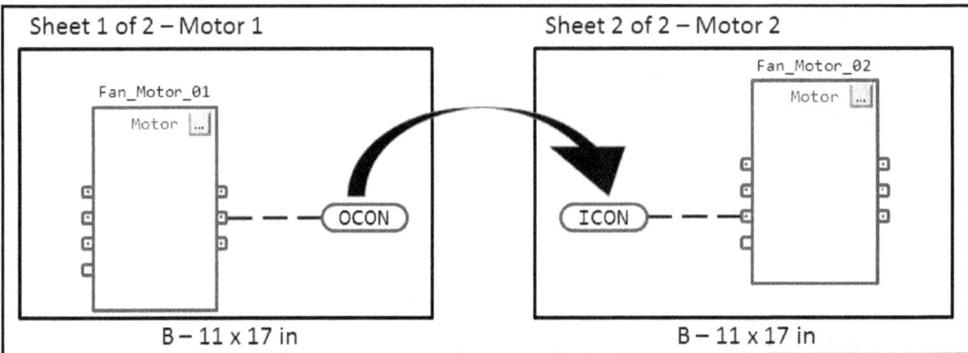

As depicted, sheets can be connected to create complex programs using Function Block that can still be printed off in standard 11 x 17 engineering drawings and stored in a binder.

In the following section, we will introduce more of the elements that make up the Function Block programming language.

Function Block elements

The following six elements are used within an FBD:

- **Input reference** (`IREF`): These elements are the input tag values that are read into a Function Block routine before it executes.
- **Output reference** (`OREF`): These elements are the output tag values that are written to once the Function Block routine completes its execution.
- **Input wire connector** (`ICON`): This element receives data from another function block that is on a different sheet within the same routine or far apart on the same sheet.
- **Output wire connector** (`OCON`): This element sends data to another function block that is on a different sheet within the same routine or far apart on the same sheet. A single output connector can be wired to multiple input connectors.
- **Function block** (`FB`): This element executes an operation based on the values of its input pins and then provides results to its output pins.
- **Textbox**: This element is used to provide the code comments to the Function Block routines.

The following Function Block routine identifies these six elements and how they are connected:

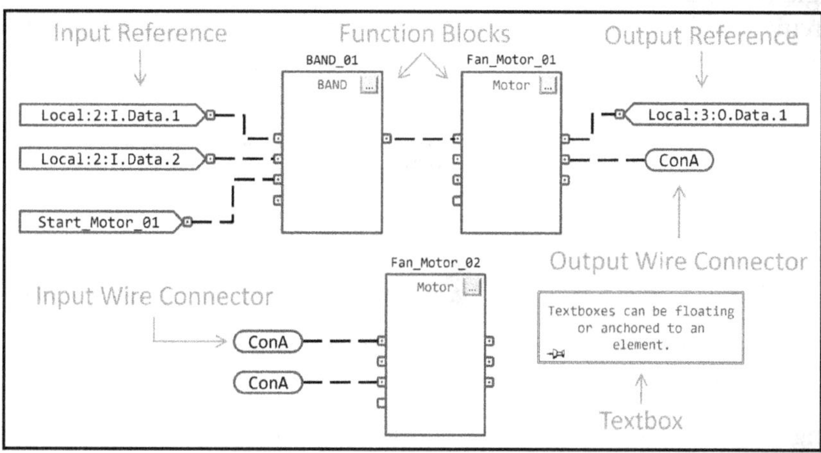

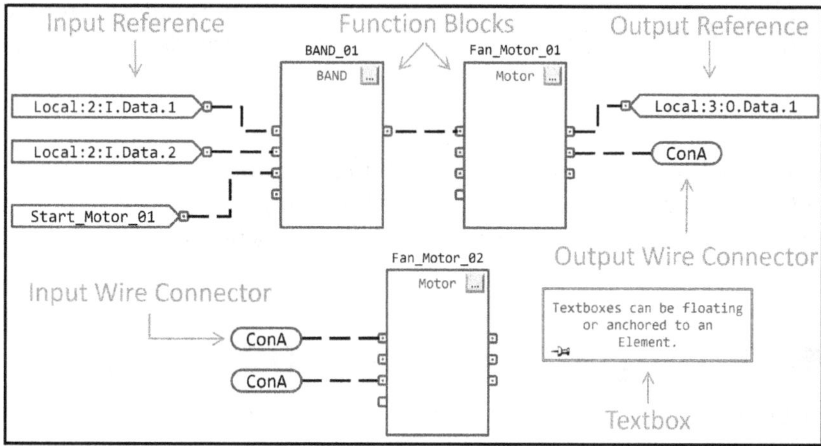

Although Function Block programming is made up of only six core programming elements, it is possible to create extremely complex programs capable of performing nearly any industrial process you can imagine.

In the following subsection, we will cover how these six core elements can be interconnected to create complex programs in more detail.

Function Block wiring

Within a single sheet, the function blocks are wired together in a similar fashion to an electronic circuit board. Wires are used to connect input tags to function blocks, function blocks to function blocks, and function blocks to output tags. Pins are used to connect wires to the Function Block elements:

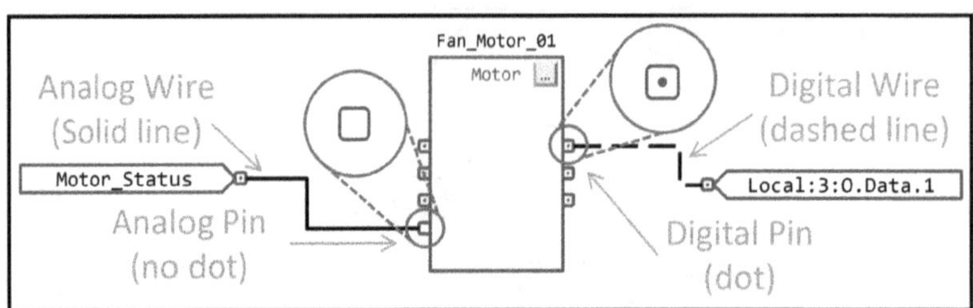

The preceding diagram demonstrates the use of wires and pins in a simple Function Block routine:

Note that there is a visible difference between the analog wires (solid lines), digital wires (dashed lines), analog pins (no dot in the center), and digital pins (dot in the center).

We have now covered the six basic elements of Function Block programming and how to connect them to create complex programs. In the following sections, we will cover the basic logical statements and how they are performed within Function Block.

Understanding Function Block logic

While Ladder Logic uses the element position on a rung to create logic expressions, Function Block logic expressions are handled by dedicated Function Block elements. In the next sections, we will explore some of the logical Function Block elements that are available and see how they are used.

AND logic in Function Block

Within a Function Block routine, you can evaluate an AND logical expression using the BAND function block. This block will evaluate an AND logical expression using all the input references passed into it and provide the solution to its output reference pin. The following diagram shows the same simple AND logical expression in Function Block:

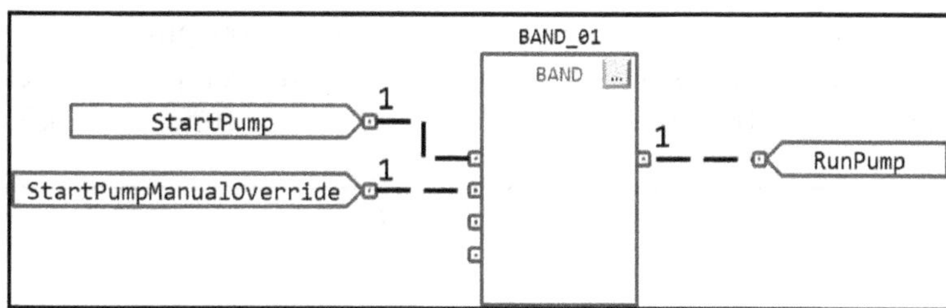

When the StartPump and StartPumpManualOverride input references are both true, the RunPump output reference will energize. Note that the input reference values to the right on the input reference pins indicate the current value of the references. Also, the output reference pin on the BAND function block displays the current value of the AND expression. Although we are only displaying four digital input references in this diagram, you can add up to eight digital input references to a BAND block.

Of course, we cannot talk about AND logic without covering its cousin, the OR logic expression. In the following section, we will detail how we can perform OR logic within FBD.

OR logic in Function Block

The BOR function block will accept and evaluate an OR logical expression against its input reference pins and provide output to its output reference pin:

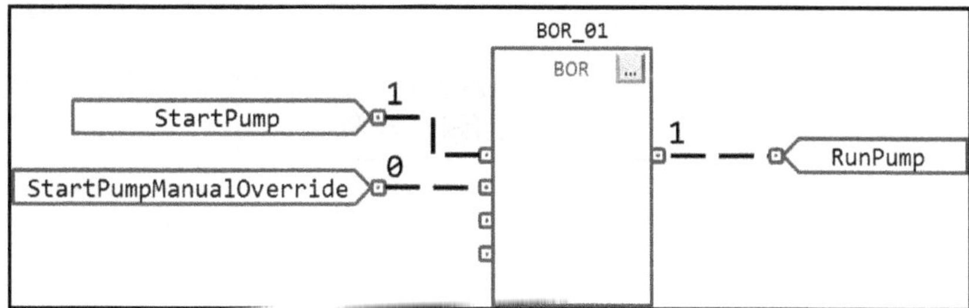

As depicted in the preceding diagram, we can see that the `OR` logic block is very similar to the `AND` logic block in form and function.

NOT logic in Function Block

The `BNOT` function block will invert the value of the input reference provided. Passing a `1` value to the input reference pin will result in a `0` value in the output reference pin, and passing `0` into the input reference pin will result in a `1` value in the output reference pin. The following diagram illustrates a simple example of a `BNOT` function block:

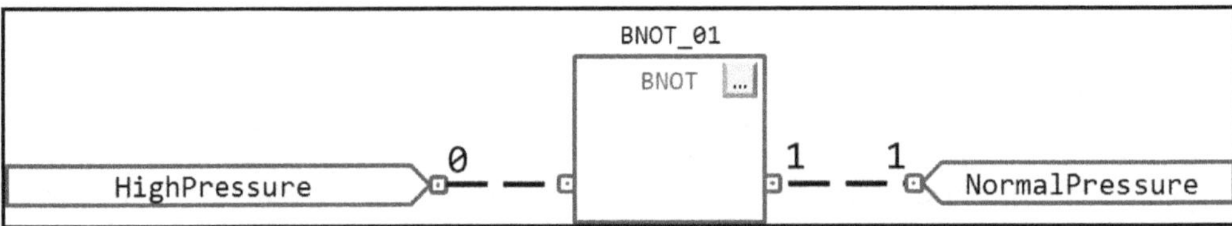

As we can see from the preceding diagram, the `NOT` function block works in a similar fashion to the `AND` and `OR` function blocks. In the next section, we will leverage what we have learned so far about function block programming to create our own simple program.

Creating a Function Block program

Now that we have covered the basic elements and logic functionality of FBDs, let's start to build our first Function Block routine. The following exercise will create a simple digital alarm routine using the **Alarm Digital** (`ALMD`) function block:

1. Open the **Controller Organizer** pane, expand the tree by navigating to **Tasks** | **Main Tasks** | **Main Program**, and then right-click and select **New Routine**:

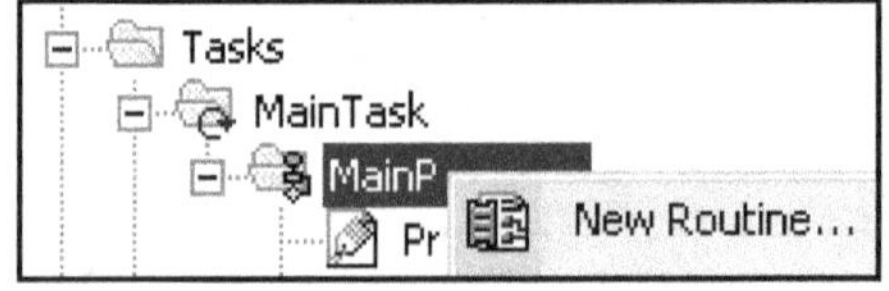

2. Configure a new functional block diagram routine by setting the following values:
    - **Name**: `DIGITAL_ALARMS`
    - **Description**: `Digital Alarms`
    - **Type**: **Function Block Diagram**

The following screenshot shows the **New Routine** form with the necessary fields completed:

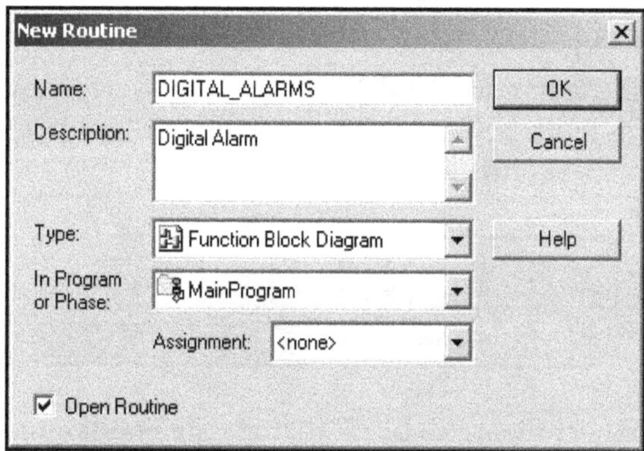

3. In order for our newly created routine to be executed with each scan of the Programmable Logic Controller (PLC), we need to add a reference to it in the `MainRoutine` program, which is executed with each scan of `MainTask`. Double-click on our **MainRoutine** program to display the **MainRoutine** ladder logic:

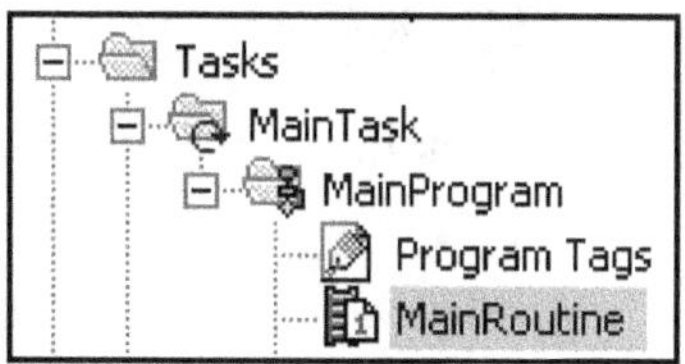

4. In the previous chapter, we added **JSR** for our Ladder Logic diagram. We can simply copy and paste this ladder rung and change the value to point at our routine, `DIGITAL_ALARMS`. Right-click on the left-hand side of the first ladder rung (where `0` is displayed) and select **Copy** (or press *Ctrl* + *C*).
5. Right-click below the first rung and select **Paste** (or press *Ctrl* + *V*).

6. Now, double-click on the **Routine Name** parameter of the JSR element and select our newly added **DIGITAL_ALARMS** routine:

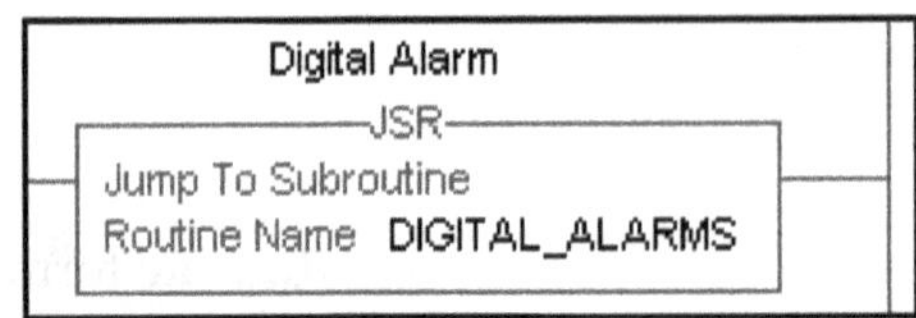

7. Now, we will return to our **DIGITAL_ALARMS** FBD by double-clicking on it in the **Controller Organizer** pane.
8. Next, we are going to add our digital alarm FBD, which we will use to manage our valve alarm fault. Select the **Alarms** element group just above the Function Block diagram sheet and click on **ALMD**:

9. We need to connect the `ALMD` block to our valve fault alarm using an input reference, so let's add one to our FBD. The input reference element looks like an arrow (with a square corner) that is pointing to the right. It can be found at the top-left part of the element group selector above the FBD. Click on the input reference object icon to add it to the diagram:

10. Right-click on the question mark in the input reference and select **New Tag**:

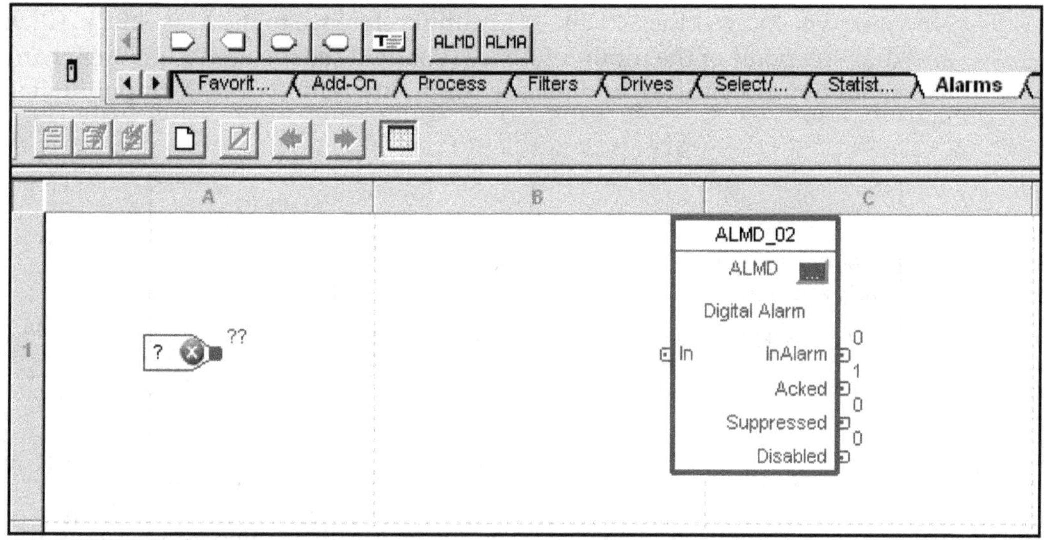

11. The **New Tag** window will appear and allow you to set the following parameters for a newly created tag:
    - Name: FC1001_FLT
    - Description: FLOW CONTROL VALVE 1001 POSITION FAULT
    - Data Type: BOOL
    - Scope: MainProgram
    - External Access: Read/Write
    - Style: Decimal

12. Now, our input reference is pointing to our fault base tag, `FC1001_FLT`:

13. Now, we need to reposition our blocks so that they fit properly on our FBD sheet. Click and drag the **ALMD** object a few inches to the right.

14. Now, we will connect the `FC1001_FLT` input reference to the `ALMD` block. Click and drag the point of the input reference (you will see the mouse pointer change to a connector mouse icon) and release the mouse button over the input digital pin:

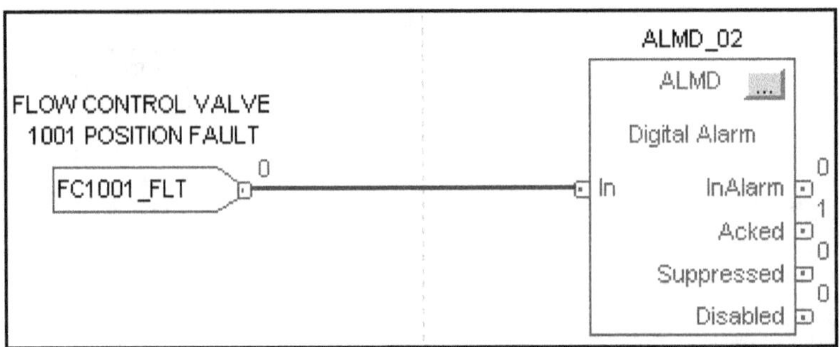

15. The `ALMD` function block we added was automatically created as a base type object in our program-scoped tag list (program tags). We will now change the name of the `ALMD` object to follow our existing tag naming convention. Right-click on the top title of the **ALMD** object and select the edited `ALMD_01` element.
16. Change the **Name** field of the element properties to `FC1001_FLT_ALM` and click on **OK**. The scope of our FBD base tag is set to the `MainProgram` scope automatically when we add it to our routine:

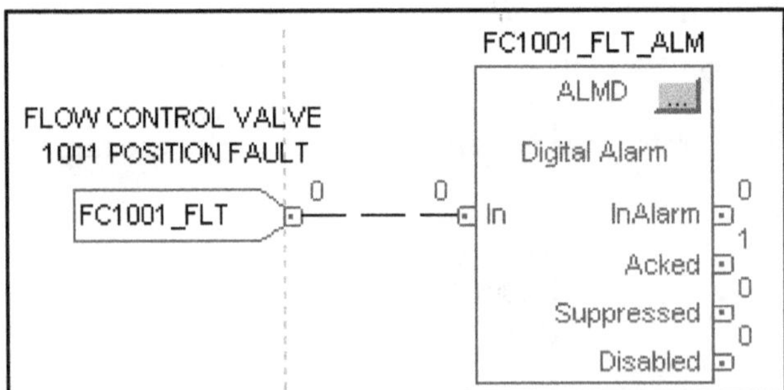

This exercise combined what we have learned in this chapter about Function Block into a simple Function Block program. In the next section, we will use this program to demonstrate how to make online edits using the Logix platform.

Online monitoring and editing

After completing a routine in any language, the next step in development is to test it thoroughly. Logix Designer incorporates powerful monitoring and debugging features, which can be used to test our routine.

Perform the following steps to go online with our FBD program and view the real-time values:

1. First, we need to ensure that the communication path to our controller (physical or virtual) has been established. Open **Who Active** by navigating to **Communications** | **Who Active** or by clicking on the **Who Active** icon:

2. The **Who Active** window allows us to browse to the controller that will run our program. Expand the RSLinx Driver tree and navigate to your virtual or physical controller. The following screenshot shows the Virtual RSLogix 5000 Emulator selection in the tree:

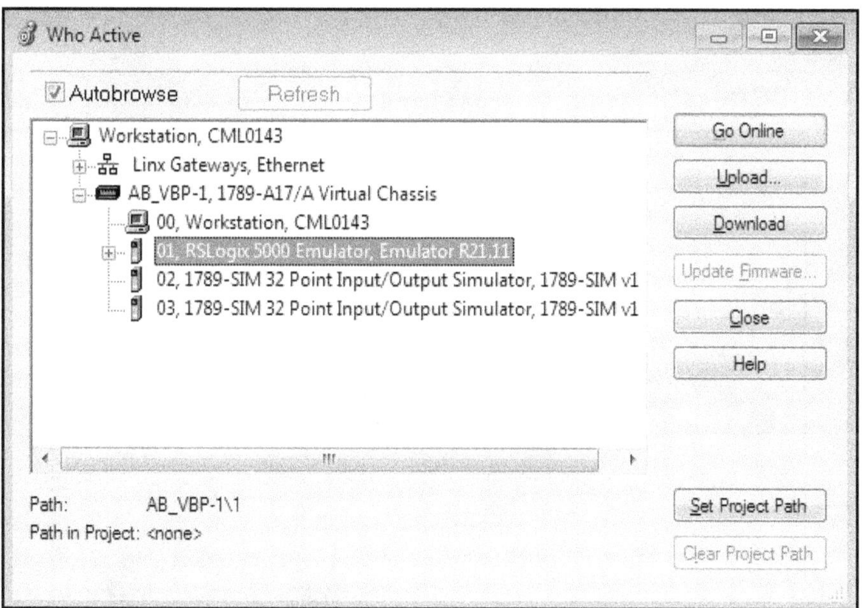

If you have any difficulties with finding your controller in the tree or the tree is empty, you may want to refer to the RSLink section in `Chapter 5`, *Industrial Network Communications*.

The following buttons appear on the right-hand side of the **Who Active** window:

- **Go Online**: This button will try to connect to the controller and start monitoring the execution of whichever program is currently running on it.
- **Upload**: This button will upload the program currently running on the controller to your local computer.
- **Download**: This button will download the current program you have open in Logix Designer to the controller.
- **Update Firmware**: This button will allow you to upgrade the firmware on your controller.
- **Set Project Path**: This button will update the path stored in your project file, which will automatically set this as the communication path the next time you open your project.

3. Click on the **Go Online** button. The **Connected To Go Online** window appears, providing the current status information of the controller and the **Download**, **Select File...**, and **Cancel** options.

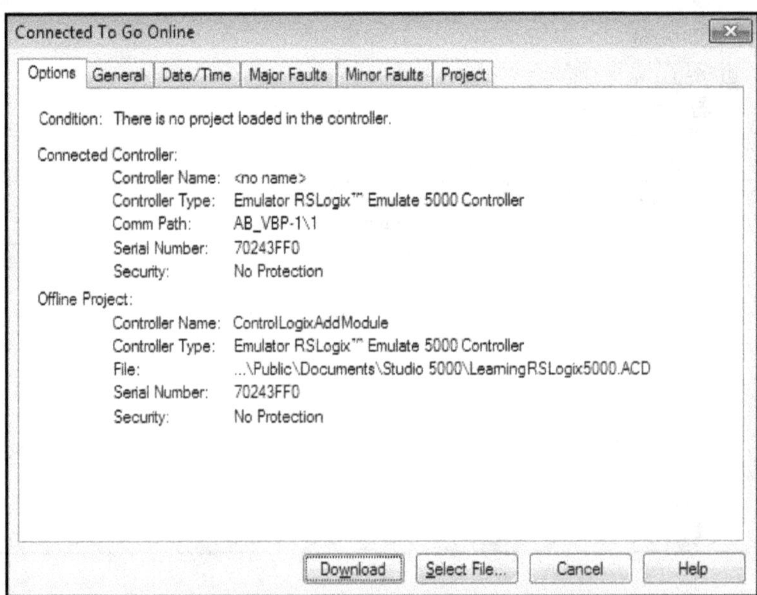

4. Click on the **Download** button. A **Download** window containing a safety message appears:

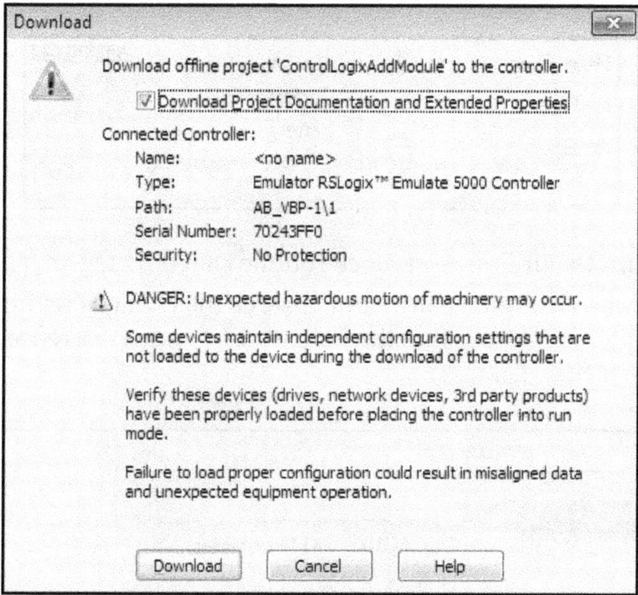

Next, we will start downloading our edits to the online controller.

Downloading a program to a controller can cause a process to lose its state or trip. Always take the proper safety measures to ensure that you will not put people or the facility at risk before working on operating equipment.

5. Click on the **Download** button in the preceding window to copy your program into the controller memory.
6. Once the download process is complete, you may see a dialog box asking whether you want to put the controller back to remote run. Click on **Yes**:

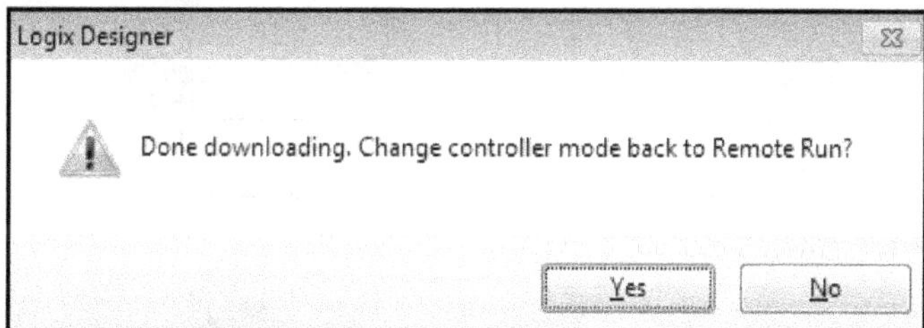

7. You will want to ensure that your controller is in **Run Mode** so that you can see live changes in your program. Now, we can start to monitor our tags and test our routines. Logix Designer should now show that we are in the **Rem Run** mode:

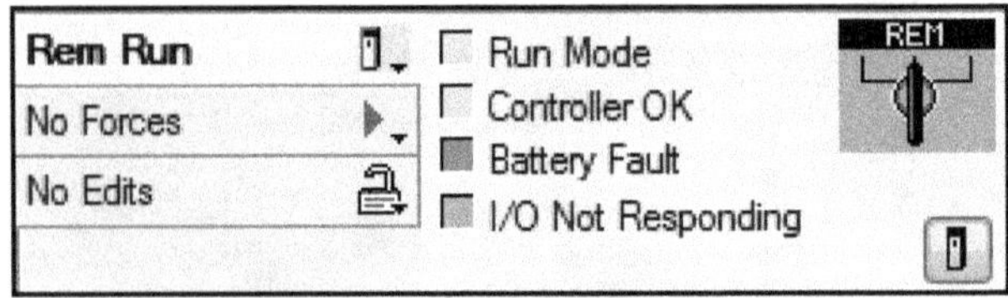

8. Now, return to our Function Block routine called `DIGITAL_ALARMS`.
9. Let's activate our digital alarm and observe the changes within our Function Block outputs. Right-click on the **FC1001_FLT** input reference and select `Monitor "FC1001_FLT"`:

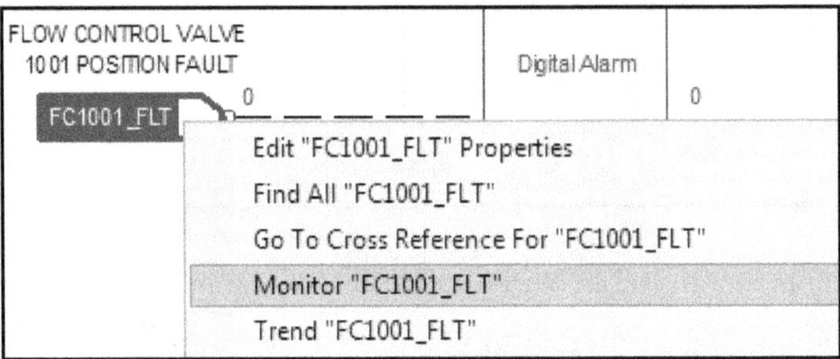

10. The **Monitor Tags** panel now appears in the foreground and provides us with a list of all the tags in the **MainProgram** scope. We can manually set the value of the `FC1001_FLT` tag to trigger our digital alarm function block. Enter `1` into the **Value** column of the `FC1001_FLT` tag and press **Enter**:

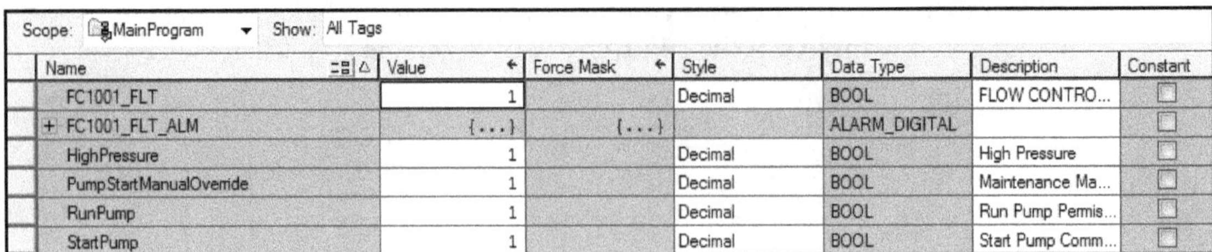

Scope: MainProgram Show: All Tags

Name	Value	Force Mask	Style	Data Type	Description	Constant
FC1001_FLT	1		Decimal	BOOL	FLOW CONTRO...	☐
+ FC1001_FLT_ALM	{...}	{...}		ALARM_DIGITAL		☐
HighPressure	1		Decimal	BOOL	High Pressure	☐
PumpStartManualOverride	1		Decimal	BOOL	Maintenance Ma...	☐
RunPump	1		Decimal	BOOL	Run Pump Permis...	☐
StartPump	1		Decimal	BOOL	Start Pump Comm...	☐

11. Alternatively, from the **DIGITAL_ALARMS** routine, you can open the **Watch** panel by navigating to **View** | **Watch**. The **Watch** panel will appear directly under your FBD sheet and displays a monitoring list of all the tags in the current routine:

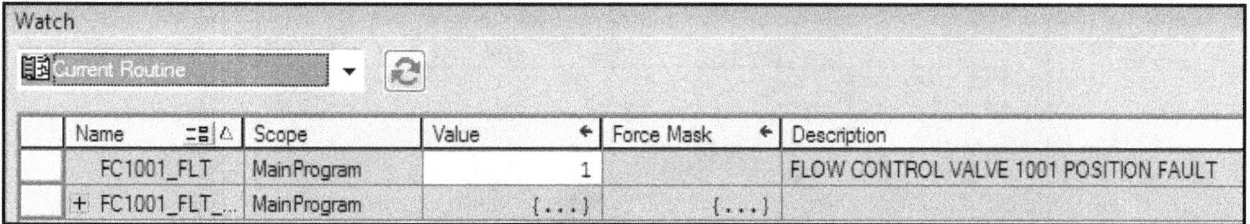

12. Return to the **DIGITAL_ALARMS** routine by navigating to **Window** | **MainProgram - DIGITAL_ALARMS**:

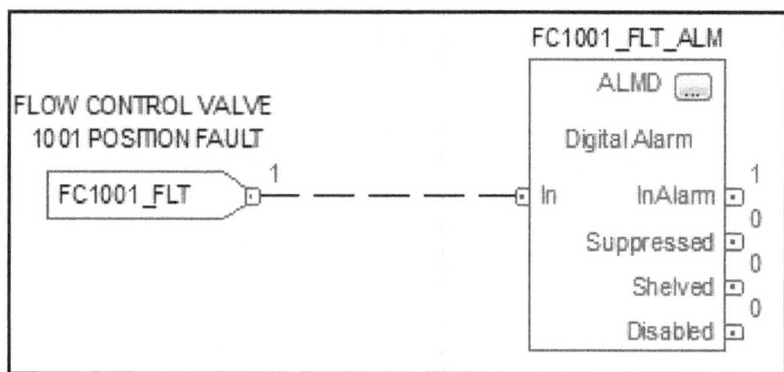

13. Now, we can see that the `InAlarm` output pin on `FC1001_FLT_ALM` has a value of `1`, indicating that the digital alarm function block is now in alarm. If you right-click on the digital alarm function block and select **Properties...**, you can see all the current **Parameter** values. These values can be referenced throughout your program in the various languages and also by the **Human Machine Interface** (**HMI**) / **Supervisory Control and Data Acquisition** (**SCADA**) system that is providing the graphical user interface for your program.

14. After selecting a valid controller, the buttons on the right-hand side (explained in the following list) will be enabled:

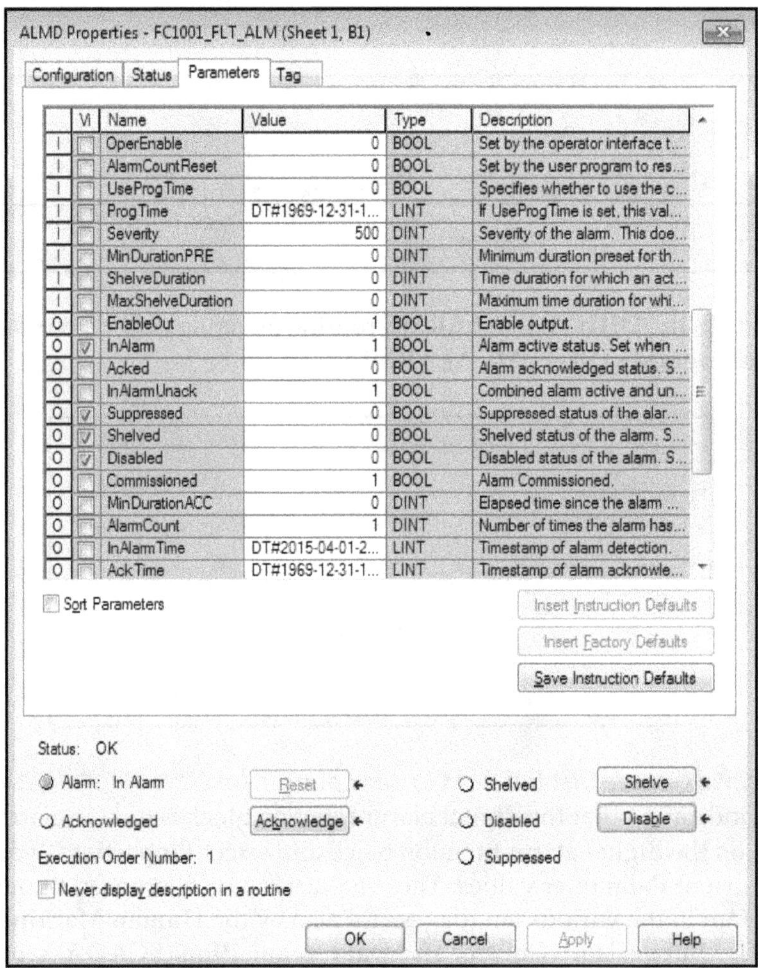

Function blocks provide high-level functionality and are relatively easy to configure and maintain. Function blocks work especially well with **Rockwell's FactoryTalk HMI** program. FactoryTalk provides graphical faceplates that align with the functionality of the Logix function blocks. Faceplates make it easy to provide a feature-rich control system user interface for operators.

In the next section, we will dig further into the FBD properties and how they can be used to customize function blocks.

The FBD properties

Double-clicking on an FBD block will open its properties. Each FBD block contains a unique set of properties, and detailed help documentation is provided (by pressing the *F1* key). Many of these properties allow you to integrate your PLC controller with your HMI computer more tightly.

Using FBD can allow you to configure many properties, such as alarm names, in the PLC rather than in the HMI. Many SCADA system vendors are moving to a more **Distributed Control System** (**DCS**) style, single database configuration. Rockwell Automation's PlantPAx automation system takes this type of DCS functionality to the next level, but that is a subject for another book.

The following screenshot depicts the **ALMD Properties** window:

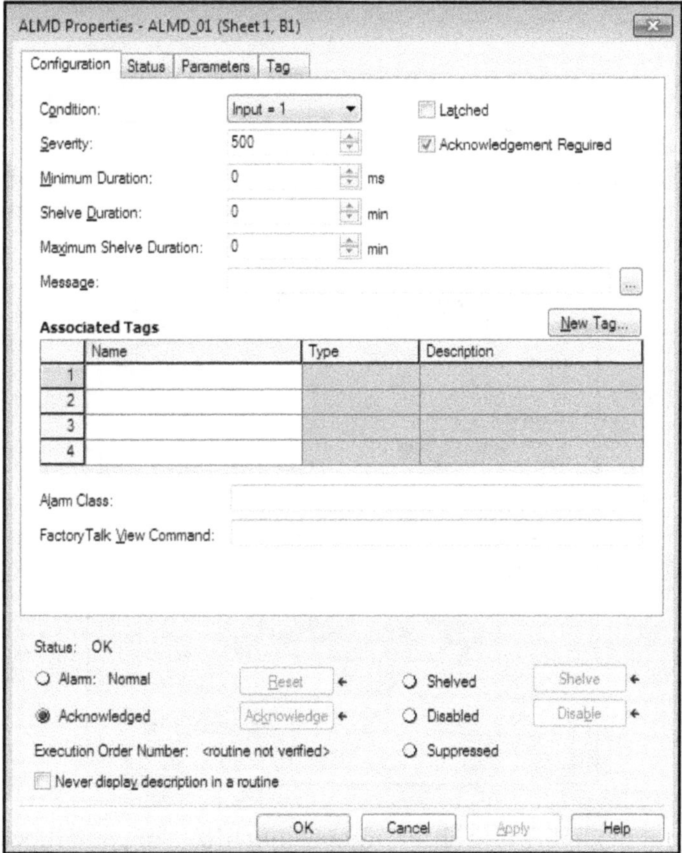

In the next section, we will cover the primary method for organizing our Function Block programs using sheets.

Adding and naming sheets to a routine

In the following exercise, we will add a new sheet to our FBD program:

1. You can add sheets to your FBD by clicking on the **New Sheet** icon above your FBD routine:

2. You can also provide a helpful name for each sheet by editing the **Sheet** text field:

3. The **Sheet size** and **Orientation** fields can also be modified (using standard English and metric page sizes) by right-clicking on the white space of a **Function Block** routine and selecting **Properties**:

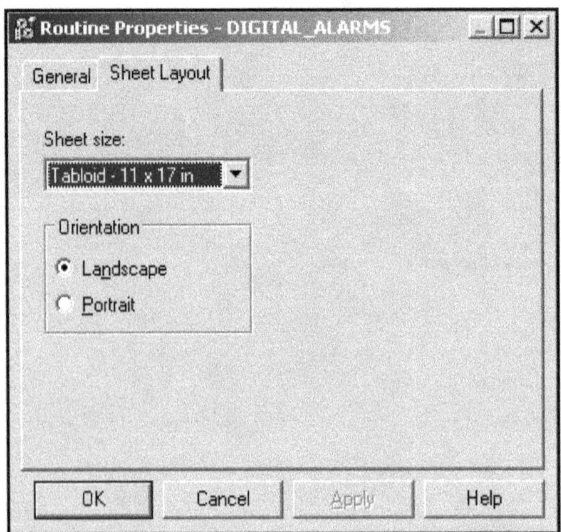

4. The layout flexibility and sheet organization that Function Block routines provide make them more suitable for printing than Ladder Logic.

In the next section, we will cover a method for improving the readability of our Function Block programs using textboxes.

Adding a textbox to a Function Block routine

Textboxes can be added to a Function Block routine to provide a floating box of documentation. Adding documentation to a Function Block routine can improve the readability of code and make it easier to maintain in the future. Just keep in mind that the textbox documentation will also need to be maintained and updated as the routine evolves, so keep the documentation clear and concise.

A textbox can be added to a Function Block routine by dragging the textbox icon from the language element toolbar to the target routine:

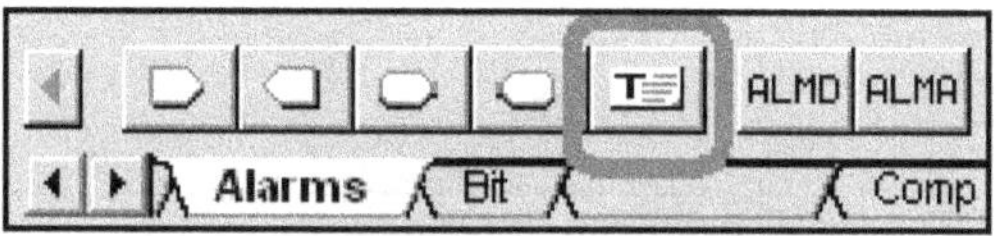

You can double-click on the textbox and enter your code notes, and press *Ctrl* + *Enter* when finished. The textbox can be attached to a Function Block element by clicking on the pin symbol on the textbox and clicking on the Function Block element you want to attach it to. Once the textbox is linked with a function block, it will move with the function block when it is moved around the sheet:

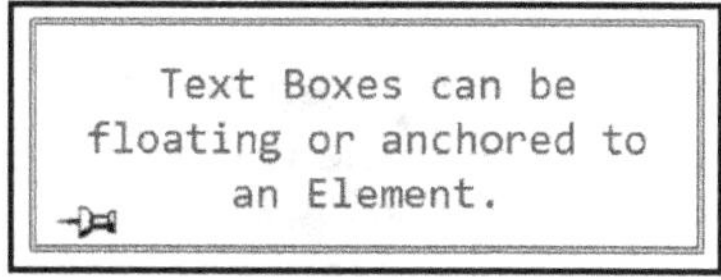

In the next section, we will cover how we can hide and remove pins of our function blocks to improve the aesthetic.

Hiding and showing function block pins

Function blocks often have some of their input or output pins hidden from view. You can view the available pins of a function block by clicking on the **Function Block Properties** box or by right-clicking on the function block and selecting **Properties**. The available input and output pins are listed under the **Parameters** tab. You can control the visibility by checking or unchecking the checkboxes under the **Vis** column.

In the next section, we will learn how to add a constant value to a function block. This is often a requirement for hardcoding alarm levels and within formulas.

Assigning a constant value to a function block

Rather than assigning a tag to an input reference of a function block, you can assign a hardcoded value. You can specify a constant value by double-clicking on the input reference element and entering the desired value:

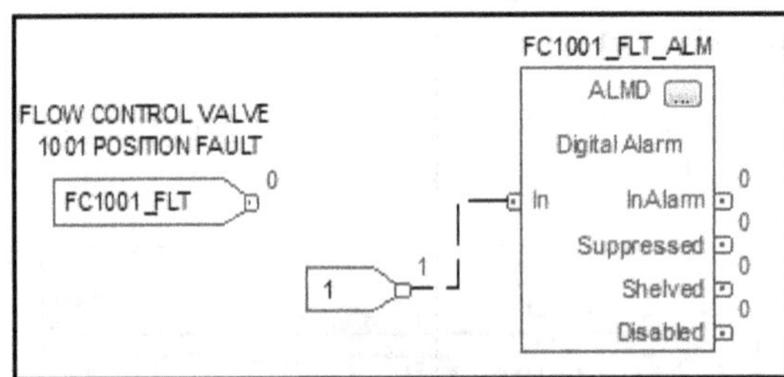

As you can see, it is fairly easy to add constant values to function blocks. This concludes our coverage of the basics of Function Block programming.

Summary

In this chapter, we explored the FBD origins in systems engineering and introduced the basic concepts of IEC FBD programming. We learned how to create FBDs by dragging and dropping elements into a sheet in a routine. The way Logix compiles IEC languages down to bytecode was also explored in this chapter.

We also learned how to wire input and output references to function block pins and how to identify digital and analog connections and monitor their values online. We now understand how to read and write Function Block, and we can apply this knowledge to Rockwell products or products from other industrial automation vendors who follow the IEC standards.

In the next chapter, we will introduce another IEC language, called Structured Text Programming, and its use in the Logix family.

Questions

The following questions can be used to test your retention of the concepts introduced in this chapter. You can find the answers to these questions in the back of the book under *Assessments*:

1. Ultimately, the controller is not aware of which language you created your program in (that is, Ladder Logic, Function Block, or Sequential Function Chart); it always ends up as the same language that is executed on the controller. What is the name of the language that it ends up as?
2. What is the name of the IEC graphical flow diagram programming language where program instructions appear as blocks?
3. What is the name of the Function Block program organizer that typically directly corresponds to standard metric or English printer page sizes (we used ledger/11 x 17 inches in our following example)?
4. In Function Block code, what type of connection does a solid line depict?
5. In Function Block code, what type of connection does a dashed line represent?
6. What can be added to an FBD to provide documentation?

Further reading

For more information about Function Block programming within the Logix platform, please take a look at the *Logix 5000 Controllers Function Block Diagram* Rockwell document at `https://literature.rockwellautomation.com/idc/groups/literature/documents/pm/1756-pm009_-en-p.pdf`.

10
Writing Structured Text

In this chapter, we will explore the strengths and weaknesses of **Structured Text** (**ST**) programming by examining the typical uses of this language and building several small sample applications. As you will soon learn, there are some instances where writing ST programming can have many advantages over Ladder Logic and Function Block, such as real-time mathematical calculations.

This chapter will cover the following ST topics:

- Applying ST programming
- Writing structured routines
- Using ST operators
- Using expressions
- Understanding instructions
- Using the OSRI instruction
- Understanding the ST constructs

In the first section of this chapter, we will provide a brief overview of ST programming.

Technical requirements

To complete this chapter, you need to create a Rockwell Automation support account by visiting `https://www.rockwellautomation.com/account/create-account`.

Creating an account is free, and the material we will be reviewing in this chapter is publicly available to anyone who is registered with Rockwell Automation.

You will also need a copy of RSLogix or Studio 5000 that has a license for Emulate 5000 to program your project. You can either purchase this from your local distributor or request a time-limited trial version. You can find a local distributor for Rockwell Automation products at `https://locator.rockwellautomation.com/`.

Applying ST programming

ST is another **International Electrotechnical Commission** (**IEC**) **61131-3** language (one of the five open international standards for programmable logic controllers) that can be used in your Logix applications. As the name implies, ST is a text-based programming language with a syntax that resembles Pascal (which it is based on) or **Visual Basic for Applications** (**VBA**). Like the other IEC 61131-3-based languages, it shares IEC common elements and reference tags, as well as objects created in other languages with your Logix program.

Before we begin writing our own ST programs, we will explore the typical uses and the editing environment in the following subsections. Let's first learn about the typical uses of ST.

Typical uses of ST

ST is extremely robust and is capable of matching the functionality of any other IEC-based language. However, you will find that ST is used sparingly in most automation projects. I have seen automation projects built entirely in ST code and they work fine. However, the practice of developing entirely in ST is frowned upon by most automation professionals. Often, you will see this done by an engineer who is fresh out of school and is accustomed to modern, text-based programming languages.

Since its inception in 1968, Ladder Logic has been—and continues to be—the primary automation programming language. Selecting an IEC language for your routine requires selecting the right tool for the job. Ladder Logic is a powerful language for simple sequential process control problems; it is easy to write and easy for other automation professionals to understand. Function Block provides a high-level, object-based language that can create powerful routines with minimal effort that are easy to maintain. ST is a relatively low-level language that excels at complex algorithms, complex decisions (logical statements), and text manipulation.

Let's take a look at some of the ST editing tools and features that are available to us in the following subsection. The first thing that we will cover is the ST editor.

Exploring the ST editor

The ST editor appears in the routine window of Logix Designer and is the development environment for writing ST code. The ST editor window allows you to type in ST code or drag and drop code elements from the ST element toolbar.

The following is a screenshot of the ST editing environment in RSLogix:

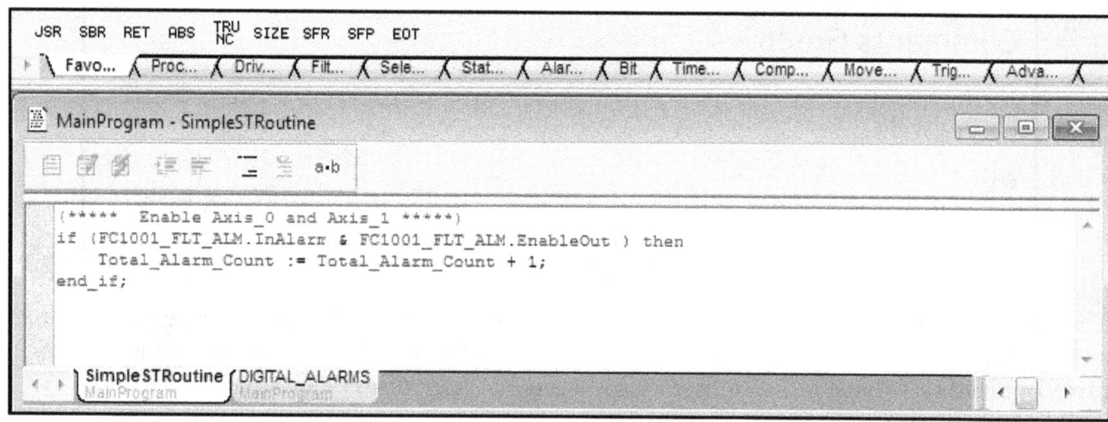

The ST editor features a toolbar that allows you to do the following:

- Toggle the code view between original and pending edits and test edits when making online changes to your ST code
- Increase and decrease the indent of a selected piece of ST code (this can also be accomplished using the *Tab* hotkey to increase the indent and the *Shift* + *Tab* hotkeys to decrease the indent)
- Comment and uncomment out a selected piece of ST code
- Show and hide the whitespace and tab characters

The following diagram describes the tool icons on the ST editors toolbar:

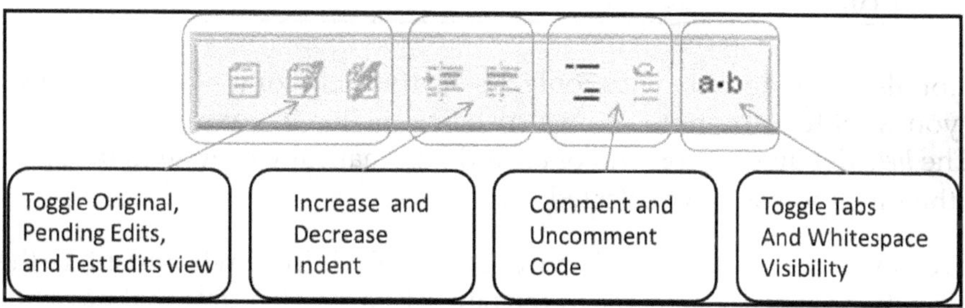

The code area of the ST editor provides context-sensitive code coloring to improve the readability of the code. Color is used to signify that a word is recognized by the ST editor and helps to ensure that syntax is valid at a glance. The code colors can be adjusted from the **Tools** | **Options...** drop-down menu.

The following diagram describes the color schema used by the ST editor in RSLogix:

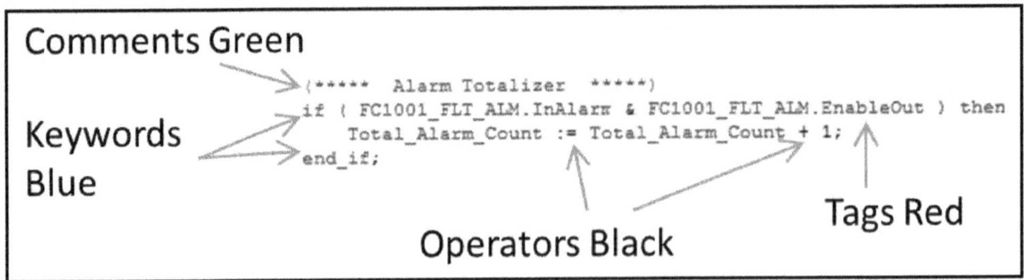

The ST editor also provides a syntax checker function as you edit. Any unrecognized words are indicated by a red, wavy underscore line beneath the word. Any syntax that is unrecognized or unverified is marked with a green, wavy underscore line beneath the word.

The following diagram demonstrates syntax errors highlighted using colored squiggly underlines. You will notice that the formatting is similar to the way Microsoft Word highlights spelling errors:

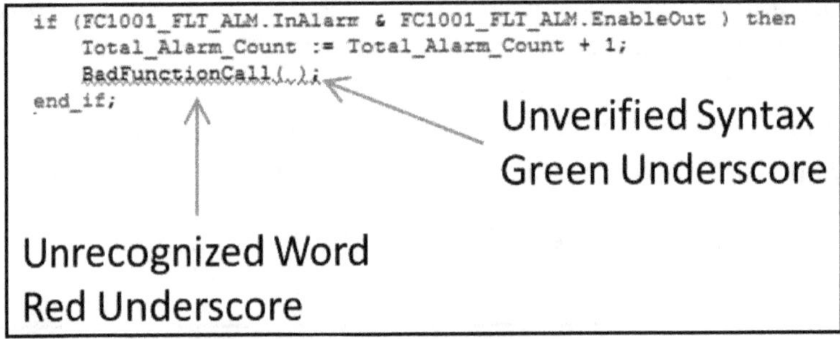

The ST editor also provides you with context-sensitive help for the functions in your routine. If you want to learn more about a specific function in your routine, select it and press `F1`. The *help* documentation will open and automatically browse to the specific chapter of the function you have selected.

Now that we have covered the basic features of the ST editing environment, in the following section, we will detail some of the new ST editing features that have been added to version 31 of Studio 5000.

New features in Studio 5000 version 31

With the release of Studio 5000 version 31, Rockwell has worked to modernize the ST editing environment. They have integrated many of the features a programmer would expect to see in a full-blown **Integrated Development Environment** (**IDE**), such as Microsoft's Visual Studio.

These features are designed to improve productivity and code-editing efficiency. Some of these modern features include the following:

- **Line numbers and bookmarks**: Enables ease of access and navigation within a code base
- **Descriptive tool tips and syntax highlighting**: To support method syntax lookups
- **Collapsible code segments**: Allows you to hide and show segments of code for ease of code readability
- **Inline value monitoring**: Shows the current values of variables to ease online debugging
- **Code snippets**: Allows you to create reusable chunks of code
- **Smart indent capabilities**: Helps to keep your code aligned and easy to read

These features can be turned on and off by opening the **Workstation Options** window and expanding the **Structured Text Editor** tree. Now that we have explored the feature set of the ST editing environment, let's begin to learn how to write ST in the following sections.

Writing structured routines

It is time to jump into the ST editing environment we have talked about. To get started with ST, we will write a simple routine and break down the components. In the next few sections, you will see how ST programming can be useful for handling certain tasks, such as formulas, looping logic, and carrying out complex branching logic that Ladder Logic is not well suited for.

In the following exercise, we will use a basic ST syntax to keep track of the number of times a specific alarm is tripped. This control system construct is typically referred to as a totalizer.

We will begin the next section by creating a simple ST routine to count every time an alarm is activated in our control system.

A simple ST routine

We have briefly looked at the ST editor, so now we will write a simple ST routine to introduce some of the syntax and conventions. Our first ST routine will provide an alarm count totalizer. It will also provide an opportunity to test some of our troubleshooting skills.

We will begin by creating our totalizer routine and then attaching it to `MainProgam`, as we have done in past exercises, so that the logic will be executed by our controller:

1. Open **Controller Organizer** and expand the **Tasks** | **MainTask** | **MainProgram** tree, then right-click and select **New Routine...**, as shown in the following screenshot:

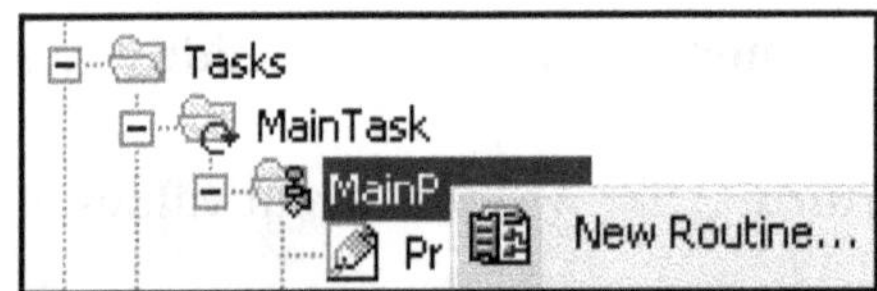

2. Configure a new ST routine by setting the following values:
    - **Name**: `AlarmTotalizer`
    - **Description**: `Digital Alarms`
    - **Type**: **Structured Text**

   The following screenshot shows the completed **New Routine** form:

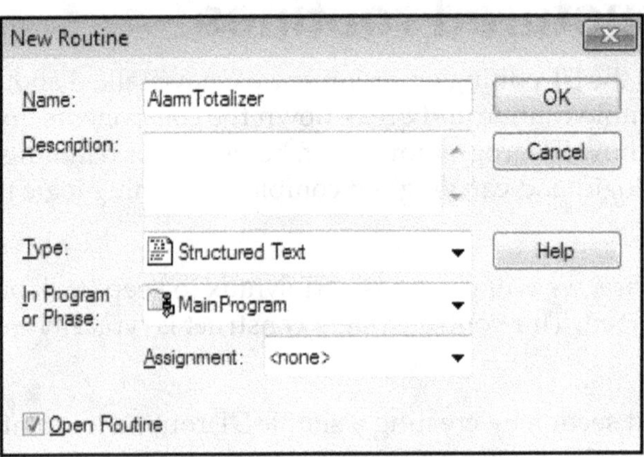

3. In the ST editor, enter the following code:

```
(*****  Alarm Totalizer  *****)
if ( FC1001_FLT_ALM.InAlarm AND NOT FC1001_FLT_ALM.Disabled ) then
      Total_Alarm _Count := Total_Alarm_Count + 1;
end_if;
```

4. Next, we will ensure that we have not made any syntax errors in our code by running a **Verify** routine.
5. Open the **Logic** | **Verify** | **Routine** drop-down menu.

   The following screenshot demonstrates the **Verify** | **Routine** selection that you will need to click in order to ensure that your ST code is free from errors:

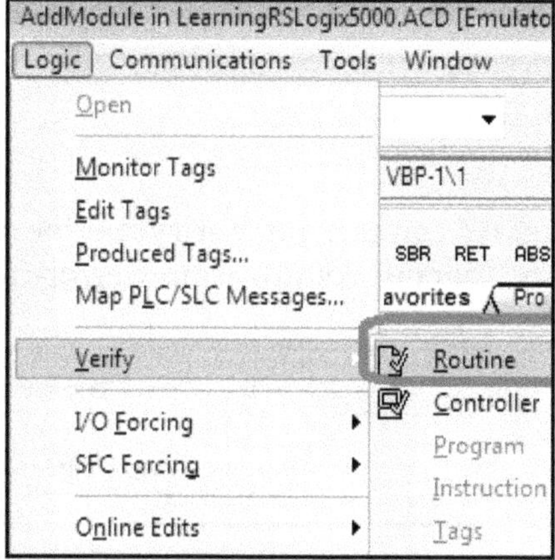

6. The **Verfiy** routine determines whether there are any errors or warnings in our code. An error is any problem in your routine that will prevent it from running on the controller. A warning is an issue that will still allow the routine to run on the controller. If you have made any syntax errors, you will see them listed in the **Errors** panel at the bottom of the screen. If you have entered the text correctly, you should see two errors, which are shown in the following screenshot:

```
DIGITAL_ALARMS  AlarmTotalizer
MainProgram     MainProgram
Errors
Verifying routine: MainProgram - AlarmTotalizer...
Error: Line 3, 'Total_Alarm_Count': Referenced tag is undefined.
Error: Line 3, 'Total_Alarm_Count': Referenced tag is undefined.
Complete - 2 error(s), 0 warning(s)
```

7. The errors identified by the **Verify** routine are due to a tag we referenced in our structured text that has not been declared. You can see that the ST editor also highlights this for us using a red, wavy underlined line. To resolve this error, you can simply right-click on the **Total_Alarm_Count** tag and select **New Tag "Total_Alarm_Count"...**, as in the following screenshot:

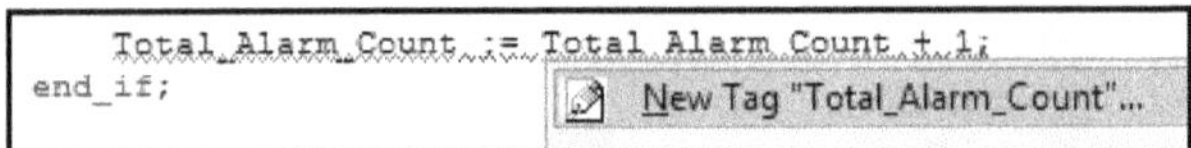

8. Use the **New Tag** form to create a new `Total_Alarm_Count` DINT tag:
    - **Name**: `Total_Alarm_Count`
    - **Description**: `Total Alarm Count of Process`
    - **Data Type**: `DINT`
    - **Scope**: `MainProgram`
    - **External Access**: `Read/Write`
    - **Style**: `Decimal`
9. After adding the tag, we can run our **Verify** routine again, and we can see, in the following screenshot, that our routine is now error-free:

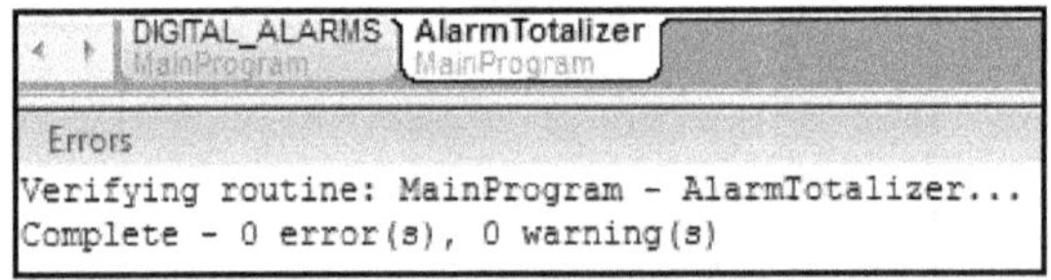

10. Finally, we cannot forget to add the `AlarmTotalizer` routine to `MainRoutine`. Otherwise, it will never get executed. We can simply copy and paste one of the ladder rungs in `MainRoutine` and change the value to point at our `AlarmTotalizer` routine. Right-click the left side of the first ladder rung (where `0` is displayed) and select **Copy** (or press *Ctrl* + *C*).
11. Right-click below the first rung and select **Paste** (or press *Ctrl* + *V*).
12. Now, double-click the **Routine | Name** parameter of the **JSR** element and select our newly added `AlarmTotalizer` routine, as in the following screenshot:

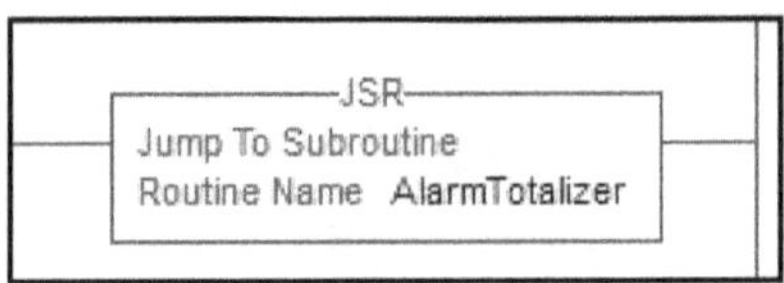

Now that we have the `AlarmTotalizer` ST routine created and linked into `MainRoutine`, we will review each line of our routine in detail in the following section.

Breaking down the simple ST routine

Now that we have created a simple ST routine, let's use it to break down some of the components of ST.

Our simple ST routine begins with a comment:

```
(*****  Alarm Totalizer  *****)
```

Comments are ignored by the compiler and are used to provide documentation within your structured text.

The second line of our ST routine is a construct, which is a conditional statement used to trigger other code statements. In our code, we use an `IF` construct to determine whether our logical expression is true. If the expression is true, we will increase our total alarm count:

```
if ( FC1001_FLT_ALM .InAlarm AND NOT FC1001_FLT_ALM.Disabled ) then
```

Within the conditional statement is the `AND` (`&`) logical operator, which we use to evaluate whether the fault alarm is in alarm and whether it is enabled.

The third line increments out total alarm count by `1`:

```
Total_Alarm_Count := Total_Alarm_Count + 1;
```

The := assignment operator is used to assign the new value of the alarm count to the old value of the alarm count plus `1`.

Finally, to close out the `IF` construct, we added the `END_IF` statement to line two:

```
END_IF;
```

The `END_IF` statement tells our program where to stop executing code related to our original `IF` statement.

If we were to run and test our program, we would immediately see an issue with our alarm totalizer counter. Once the digital alarm is triggered, the `Total _Alarm_Count` value continuously increases with each scan cycle. Certainly, this was not the intent of our alarm counter routine. Later in this chapter, in the *Using the OSRI instruction* section, we will investigate the helpful **One-Shot Rising with Input** (**OSRI**) instruction to develop a solution to the bug in our routine.

Now, we will explore the IEC standard syntax of ST operators in the following section.

Using ST operators

ST is not case sensitive, so uppercase and lowercase letters are considered the same character by the compiler. There are best practices for using upper and lowercase letters, which we will demonstrate in our routines. Also, the ST compiler ignores *whitespace*, which is any space or tab character. This allows you to space out your code in order to make it easier to read.

Now that you have seen some structured text in action, let's take a look at the available operators in ST.

The assignment operator

The assignment operator changes a value stored in a tag. An assignment operation is comprised of four parts:

- The tag
- The operator (:=)
- The expression
- A semicolon at the end

The tag maintains the assigned value until it is changed by another assignment value. Even after a power cycle, the value is retained. In this respect, the non-retentive assignment operator is similar to an output latch in Ladder Logic.

The following code snippet provides some simple assignment operator examples:

```
// Assignment Operator Examples
tag := expression;
PumpSpeed := 100;
ValvePosition := OpenPosition;
FourValue := 2 + 2;
```

The previous example demonstrates how the assignment operator can be used to assign the following:

- A variable tag to another variable tag
- A variable tag to a numeric value
- A variable tag to a formula

These values remain the same after a **Power Cycle** (**PC**), as they are retentive.

In the next section, we will explore an important variation of the assignment operator—the non-retentive assignment operator.

The non-retentive assignment operator

The non-retentive assignment operator changes a value stored in a tag. A non-retentive assignment operation is comprised of four parts:

- The tag
- The operator (`[:=]`)
- The expression
- A semicolon at the end

The tag maintains the assigned value until it is changed by another assignment value. Non-retentive assignment operations differ from an assignment operation. In assignment operation, its value is reset after a power cycle of the controller or when the controller is switched back to run mode. In this respect, the non-retentive assignment operator is similar to an `Output Energize` element in Ladder Logic. An `Output Energize` Ladder Logic element does not retain its last value after a PLC power cycle.

The following code snippet provides some simple assignment operator examples:

```
// Non-retentive Assignment Operator Examples
tag [:=] expression;
PumpSpeed [:=] 100;
ValvePosition [:=] OpenPosition;
FourValue [:=] 2 + 2;
```

The previous example demonstrates how the non-retentive assignment operator can be used to assign the following:

- A variable tag to another variable tag
- A variable tag to a numeric value
- A variable tag to a formula

These values are reset back to `0` (or their default values) after a PLC power cycle.

Now that we have reviewed non-retentive assignment operators, it is time to compare it more closely to its cousin—the retentive assignment operator—in the following section.

Retentive versus non-retentive assignment operators

When developing an industrial automation program, it is essential to consider how the program will recover from a sudden loss of power or when the controller is switched to run mode. After a power cycle or change to run mode, you may want some values to reset to `0` and others to maintain their last known value. For example, you may not want the speed and run condition of a **Variable Frequency Drive** (**VFD**) to assume the last known value after a process comes back online. Following a power failure or a process upset, you may want to manually start up your VFD from your **Human Machine Interfaces** (**HMI**). Veteran automation professionals will always consider the values that should be retentive (or latched) and the values that should be non-retentive (or energized) in their program:

Operator type	Operator	Maintains the last assigned value after a power loss
Retentive	`:=`	True
Non-retentive	`[:=]`	False

In the following section, we will discuss how ST can also be used to solve the asynchronous controller buffering issue.

Buffering ST I/O module values

Just like Ladder Logic, ST I/O module values should be buffered at the beginning of a routine or before executing a routine to prevent the values from changing mid-execution and putting the process into a state you could not have predicted.

The following is an example of the Ladder Logic buffering routine we wrote for `Chapter 8`, *Writing Ladder Logic*. This time, the routine has been rewritten in ST and uses the non-retentive assignment operator:

```
(*
I/O Buffering in Structured Text
Input Buffering
*)
StartPump [:=] Local:2:I.Data[0].0;
HighPressure [:=] Local:2:I.Data[0].1;
PumpStartManualOverride [:=] Local:2:I.Data[0].2;
(*
I/O Buffering in Structured Text
Output Buffering
*)
Local:3:O.Data[0].0 [:=] RunPump;
```

The preceding code will buffer `StartPump`, `HighPressure`, and `PumpStartManualOverride` by pulling the current values from the digital input cards and storing them in a variable. It will also write the present value of the `RunPump` variable to a digital output channel, connected to a pump.
In the next section, we will introduce relational operators, which are used to compare values.

Relational operators

Relational operators compare two (typically numeric) values and provide a Boolean (`BOOL`) value (which can be true or false) in return.

The following table lists the available relational operators in ST:

Relational type	**Operator**
Equal	=
Less than	<
Greater than	>
Less than or equal to	<=
Greater than or equal to	>=
Not equal	<>

Relational operators are typically used in a construct, such as the following motor control ST:

```
(* Relational Operator Example *)
if ( TankLevel >= 100 AND MotorRunStatus = 0) then
 StartMotor [:=] 1;
end_if;
```

In the previous example, if `TankLevel` is greater than or equal to `100` and the `MotorRunStatus` value is good (that is, it equals `0`), then the motor will automatically start to lower the tank level.

In the following section, we will cover logical operators in ST, which are used to compare logical statements.

Logical operators

We have looked at logical operators for the Ladder Logic and Function Block programming languages in this book already. ST has the same capabilities for logical statements as the other IEC languages. Logical operators compare Boolean values and always evaluate an expression to either true (`1`) or false (`0`):

Logical type	Operator
And	`&` or `AND`
Or	`OR`
Not	`NOT`
Exclusive Or	`XOR`

Logical operators are typically used in a construct, such as the `IF` statement we used in our previous simple example:

```
(* Logical OR Operator Example *)
if ( Tank1Level >= 100 OR Tank2Level >= 100) then
   StartMotor [:=] 1;
end_if;
(* Logical AND Operator Example *)
if ( TankLevel >= 100 AND MotorRunStatus = 0) then
   StartMotor [:=] 1;
end_if;
(* Logical NOT Operator Example *)
if ( NOT MotorRunPermissive) then
   StartMotor [:=] 0;
end_if;
```

In the next section, we will introduce arithmetic operators, which are used to perform mathematical functions for formulas and other industrial process calculations.

Arithmetic operators

The final—and yet extremely important—set of ST operators we will explore are arithmetic operators. Arithmetic operators are used in calculations, which is the real strength of ST when compared to other IEC languages.

The following is a table of the available arithmetic operators:

Calculation type	Operator
Add	+
Subtract/negate	-
Multiply	*
Exponent	**
Divide	/
Modulus (division remainder)	MOD

Arithmetic operators are used for calculations and formulas within industrial control processes. It is essential to understand that arithmetic operators in IEC languages do not behave in the same way as a typical calculator. For example, when rounding a value on a calculator, we would typically round `2.5` up to the next whole number, `3`. In IEC languages, rounding operations round down to the last whole number. For example, IEC arithmetic operations round `2.2`, `2.5`, and even `2.9` down to `2`.

The following is a list of examples of ST arithmetic operators:

```
(* Arithmetic Operator Addition Example *)
total_volume := tank_01_volume + tank_03_volume + tank_02_volume;

(* Arithmetic Operator Subtraction Example *)
speed := speed - 15;

(* Arithmetic Operators Multiply Example *)
tank_01_volume := 3.14159265359 * (tank_radius * tank_radius) *
tank_level;

(* Arithmetic Operators Exponent Example *)
tank_radius_squared := tank_radius ** 2;

(* Arithmetic Operators Division Example *)
```

```
position := ( adjustment / adjustment_ratio ) + ABS((sensor1 + sensor2)
/ 2);

(* Arithmetic Operators Modulus Example *)
remainder := adjustment mod adjustment_ratio;
```

Logical operators are typically used in an expression, which we will detail in the next section.

Using expressions

Expressions are a combination of values, constants, tags, operators, and functions that are interpreted according to the particular rules of precedence and produce a value. Expressions in Logix either evaluate to a number (numerical expression) or a true or false state (`BOOL` expression). Parentheses, `()`, can be used to control the order of operation, just as they would in any mathematical equation.

The following table lists the order of operation in Logix:

Operation	**Order**
Parentheses—`()`	1
Instructions—`function(...)`	2
`**`	3
Negate—-	4
`NOT`	5
`*`, `/` , and `MOD`	6
+ and subtract—-	7
<, <=, >, and >=	8
= and <>	9
`&` or `AND`	10
`XOR`	11
`OR`	12

In the following example, we will utilize these expressions to check the tank level and stop a motor, as well as to perform a calculation to determine the current tank volume:

```
(* Expression Example *)
if ( (Tank1Level + Tank2Level) * 10 >= 1000) then
 StopMotor [:=] 1;
```

```
end_if;
(* Numeric Algorithm Example *)
TankVolume = 3.14*(TankRadius**)*TankLength
```

We have now covered the core set of ST operators that are defined by the IEC standard and are used within the Logix platform. In the following section, we will introduce a few instructions used in ST to perform specific functions.

Understanding instructions

Instructions are the built-in functions that make up the building blocks of most ST routines. Logix Designer provides a rich set of instructions to utilize within a structured text. All the available ST instructions are listed in the element groups, described in the previous section, in the ST editor and can be dragged into your routine. Alternatively, you can right-click in the ST editor and select **Add ST Element...** (or press *Alt* + *Ins*), and select them from the **Add Structured Text Element** pop-up window that appears.

The instructions in ST are equivalent to the Ladder element instructions in Ladder Logic and the Function Block element instructions in Function Block diagrams. However, each language executes IEC instructions slightly differently. The execution of Function Block instructions is triggered using the `EnableIn` pin. ST instructions execute as if `EnableIn` is always energized. Ladder Logic element instructions use energized rungs to trigger the execution of an instruction, while structured text will execute each time it is scanned unless you put a conditional construct around it (such as an `IF` statement).

The first set of instructions that we will cover are arithmetic instructions, which can be used in formulas and calculations.

Arithmetic instructions

There are many sets of instructions available in ST in the element groups. One of the most foundational instruction sets for ST is arithmetic instructions. A arithmetic instructions assist with any complex calculations you are embedding into your ST routine.

The following table details the arithmetic instructions available in the Logix platform, as defined by the IEC standard:

Calculation type	Instruction syntax
Absolute value	ABS (numeric expression)
Arc cosine	ACOS (numeric expression)
Arc sine	ASIN (numeric expression)
Arc tangent	ATAN (numeric expression)
Cosine	COS (numeric expression)
Radians to degrees	DEG (numeric expression)
Natural log	LN (numeric expression)
Log base 10	LOG (numeric expression)
Degrees to radians	RAD (numeric expression)
Sine	SIN (numeric expression)
Square root	SQRT (numeric expression)
Tangent	TAN (numeric expression)
Truncate	TRUNC (numeric expression)

In the following ST code example, we will use arithmetic instructions to perform speed and area calculations:

```
(* Arithmetic Instructions Example *)
DriveSpeed [:=] ABS((FrequencyValue + Offset)/2);
PolygonArea [:=] 0.5*SideCount*SIN(360/SideCount)*Length**;
```

We have now covered much of the basic syntax of ST programming. In the following section, we will return to our previous example and utilize the OSRI instruction to resolve the continuous addition error.

Using the OSRI instruction

In the simple ST sample we created in the previous exercise, we encountered an issue where our alarm total count continued to increment with each scan cycle while the digital alarm was active. In order to adjust our code to count only new alarms, as we initially intended, we would need to only count a new alarm in the event of a change of alarm state from `off` to `on`. This is known as detecting the rising edge of the signal. We can accomplish this in ST using the OSRI instruction.

In the following exercise, we will add the OSRI instruction to the routine we started earlier in this chapter to resolve our alarm counting issue:

1. Open up the ST routine we created earlier, called `AlarmTotalizer`, as in the following screenshot:

```
(*****  Alarm Totalizer  *****)
if (FC1001_FLT_ALM.InAlarm AND NOT FC1001_FLT_ALM.Disabled) then
    Total_Alarm_Count := Total_Alarm_Count + 1;
end_if;
```

The previous screenshot should match the code in your ST routine. We need to rewrite this code using the OSRI instruction to resolve the continuous addition problem.

2. Add in the following ST code after the comment and change the `IF` construct value:

```
(*****  Alarm Totalizer  *****)
OSRI_01.InputBit := FC1001_FLT_ALM.InAlarm;
OSRI(OSRI_01);
if (OSRI_01.OutputBit AND NOT FC1001_FLT_ALM.Disabled) then
   Total_Alarm_Count := Total_Alarm_Count + 1;
end_if;
```

3. Now, highlight the OSRI instruction in the ST editor and press *F1* to take a closer look at the way it is used within ST. From the *help* documentation, we can see that the OSRI instruction is passed an `FBD_ONESHOT` data type.
4. So, we will need to add our `OSRI_01` missing data type value to our program tags by right-clicking on the missing tag and selecting **New Tag "OSRIP _01"...**:

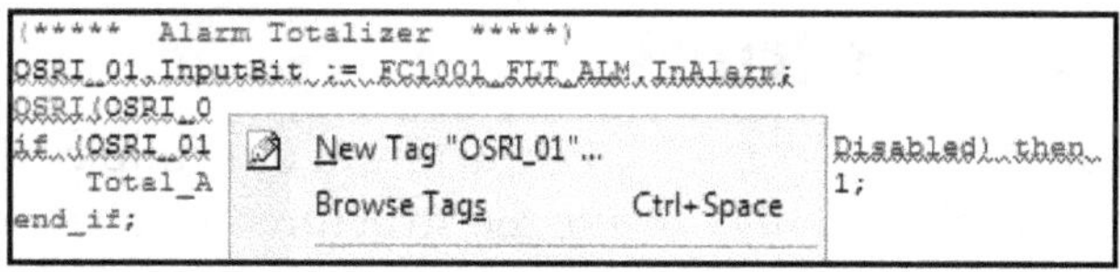

5. By selecting the **New Tag** option, the **New Tag** window will appear and allow us to add the missing tag.

6. We will need to add the `OSRI_01` tag as a `FBD_ONESHOT` data type in order to support the `.InputBit` and `.OutputBit` properties and pass them to the OSRI instruction.

7. Use the **New Tag** form to create a new `OSRI_01 FBD_ONESHOT` tag:
    - **Name:** `OSRI_01`
    - **Description:** `One Shot for Catching Rising Edge of Digital Alarm`
    - **Type:** `Base`
    - **Data Type:** `FBD_ONESHOT`
    - **Scope:** `MainProgram`
    - **External Access:** `Read/Write`

8. Now, if we compile, download, and test our routine, we will see that the digital alarm is now incrementing correctly—only once per new alarm.

Now we have successfully updated our code to properly track the number of times that our digital alarm goes into an alarm state. In the next section, we will introduce some additional ST logical functions and syntax.

Understanding the ST constructs

When writing a program, we need to be able to alter the way that a program is executed depending on the input values or context. Constructs control the flow of our ST routine and allow us to create decision statements, state machines, and loops.

In the following sections, we will explore the various types of constructs available in ST programming.

The IF_THEN construct

We are already familiar with the `IF_THEN` construct from our simple ST exercise earlier in this chapter. An `IF` construct will only execute the structured text between `IF` and `END_IF` when its expression evaluates as true (`1`).

`IF` statements can be nested using the `ELSE...IF` statement and the `ELSE` statement can be added to execute when all other statements do not.

In the following example, the `IF` and `ELSE...IF` statements are used to check the tank level and pump permissive before starting a pump:

```
(* IF THEN ELSEIF ELSE Example *)
if (TankLevel >= 50) then
 Pump1Permissive [:=] 1;
elseif (TankLevel >= 100) then
 Pump1Permissive [:=] 1;
Pump2Permissive [:=] 1;
else
 Pump1Permissive [:=] 0;
Pump2Permissive [:=] 0;
end_if
```

Next, we will explore another branching logic structure, called the `CASE_OF` construct.

The CASE_OF construct

A `CASE_OF` statement can be used to execute statements based on a numeric value. The following ST example evaluates the current numeric value of the `sequence_number` variable and triggers the start of different pieces of equipment depending on its value:

```
(* CASE Example *)
case sequence_number of
   1: StartPump [:=] 1;
      OpenValve [:=] 1;
   2: StartBlower [:=] 1;
   3,4: StartMixer [:=] 1;
   4..10: StartAuger [:=] 1;
else
   StartPump [:=] 0;
end_case;
```

Next, we will introduce loops with the `FOR_DO` construct.

The FOR_DO construct

The `FOR_DO` construct loops a specific number of times before continuing to execute the routine. Loops are quite useful when working with arrays of values.

The following code shows the typical syntax for a loop using pseudocode:

```
FOR count := initial_value=
TO final_value
    { BY increment If you don't specify an increment, the loop
increments by 1. - Optional }
DO
```

The following FOR_DO loop example iterates over an array of 10 alarms and sets all of their values to 0:

```
For LoopCount := 1 TO 10 By 1
      ALARMS[LoopCount] = 0;
DO
```

In the next section, we will introduce another loop-type construct, known as WHILE_DO.

The WHILE_DO construct

The WHILE_DO loop construct continues to perform an action while certain expressions evaluate as true:

```
WHILE <expression - continues to run loop while true> DO
    <Statements to repeat>;
END_WHILE;
```

The following example iterates over 10 loops, stores each value in an array, and calculates the sum of all the numbers in the loop:

```
LoopCount := 0;
Sum := 0;
WHILE LoopCount < 10 DO
 Sum := Sum + Values[ LoopCount ];
 LoopCount := LoopCount + 1;
END_WHILE;
```

In the next section, we will introduce another loop type construct, known as REPEAT_UNTIL.

The REPEAT_UNTIL construct

The REPEAT_UNTIL loop can be used to continue performing an action until conditions are evaluated as true.

The following is an example of the `REPEAT_UNTIL` loop in action:

```
REPEAT
    <Statements to repeat>;
    <More code to execute - use the EXIT statement to leave the loop
early>
UNTIL <expression - when this evaluates as true, the loop stops>;
END_REPEAT;
```

The following example iterates over 10 loops, stores each value in an array, and calculates the sum of all the numbers in the loop:

```
LoopCount := 0;
Sum := 0;
REPEAT
    Sum := Sum + Values[ LoopCount ];
    LoopCount := LoopCount + 1;
UNTIL LoopCount >= 10 END_REPEAT;
```

We have now finished covering all of the ST statements used as part of IEC.

Summary

In this chapter, we introduced ST and the best uses for it within an automation solution. We started by exploring the ST editing environment and introduced some of the new editing features available in Studio 5000 version 31 and higher. We created a simple ST routine and learned about the powerful syntax of ST code. Then, we explored the full range of operators, expressions, instructions, and constructs available in the ST language.

We now have a solid foundation, which we can use to read and write ST code within Logix and within other products that implement the IEC standard ST language.

In the next chapter, we will introduce the final Logix IEC language, called Sequential Function Chart Programming.

Questions

The following questions can be used to test your retention of the concepts introduced in this chapter. You can find the answers to these questions in the back of the book under *Assessments*:

1. What type of assignment operator sets a value that will not be restored after a power cycle of the controller or when the controller is switched back to run mode?
2. What set of operators always evaluates an expression to either `true` (`1`) or `false` (`0`) and is typically used in a construct such as the `IF` statement?
3. What is the name of the set of ST operators that are used in calculations (which is the real strength of ST compared to other IEC languages)?
4. What is the ST term for a combination of values, constants, tags, operators, and functions that are interpreted according to particular rules of precedence and produce a value?
5. What set of instructions aids with complex calculations in an ST routine?
6. What ST instruction can be used to only trigger the rising edge of a signal?
7. What construct only executes a block of structured text when its expression evaluates as `true` (`1`)?
8. What ST statement can be used to execute different statements based on a numeric value?
9. What ST construct loops a specific number of times before continuing to execute the routine (which is quite useful when working with arrays of values)?

Further reading

For more information about the ST programming within the Logix platform, please take a look at the *Logix 5000 Controllers Structured Text* Rockwell document at `https://literature.rockwellautomation.com/idc/groups/literature/documents/pm/1756-pm007_-en-p.pdf`.

11
Building Sequential Function Charts

In this chapter, we will implement a **Sequential Function Chart** (**SFC**) routine and break down the steps, actions, transitions, and branches that are used to construct it. We will also work with the online editing capabilities of SFC routines. Just as we have seen with the other IEC languages, SFC shares many of the common elements of other languages, but allows us to structure our programs in a different way. SFC programs are very well suited to running batches and cycles that follow a sequential step process or decision tree.

In this chapter, we will cover the following topics:

- Introducing SFCs
- Applying SFCs
- Using the SFC editor
- Building a backwash SFC routine

We will start this chapter with an overview of SFCs and their typical use within an industrial control system solution.

Technical requirements

To complete this chapter, you will need to create a Rockwell automation support account by going to `https://www.rockwellautomation.com/account/create-account`.

The account is free and the material we will be reviewing in this chapter is publicly available to anyone who is registered with Rockwell Automation.

You will also need a copy of RSLogix or Studio 5000 that has a license for Emulate 5000 to program your project. You can either purchase this from your local distributor or request a time-limited trial version. You can find a local distributor for Rockwell Automation products at `https://locator.rockwellautomation.com/`.

Introducing SFCs

SFC is another IEC 61131-3 language that allows you to program visually using a flowchart construct. The IEC SFC language is based on the GRAFCET language, which was the original industrial automation flowchart programming language. In some regions and within some companies, you will find that the terms *SFC* and *GRAFCET* are used interchangeably. Like other IEC-based languages, it can share common IEC elements and reference tags, as well as objects created in other languages, with your Logix program. SFC is a powerful, high-level language, similar to Function Block Diagram. Often, you can create the equivalent functionality of 40 Ladder Logic rungs in a few SFC steps. An SFC routine (again like Function Block) will typically have more computational overhead than the same routine developed using low-level languages such as ladder logic or structured text. SFC routines are very easy to debug and maintain because of their compact visual design. SFC has its strengths and weaknesses, like other IEC languages. An automation professional will select the correct language to meet the particular challenges of the process they face. It is not uncommon for automation professionals to realize that they have selected the wrong language for a particular task and rewrite the routine in a different IEC language.

In the next section, we will jump right into the typical use cases for SFC before we start to explore the features of the SFC editing environment.

Applying SFCs

As the name implies, SFC is well-suited for sequential step processes. You will also find that SFC is popular within batch processes as it closely aligns with the step-by-step requirements of batching. It is particularly useful when paired with other IEC languages. Within SFC routines, you use structured text for any logical expressions, assignments, or other constructs. By using the structured text function—JSR—(or similar functions), you can reference ladder logic, Function Block, structured text, or even other SFC routines. SFC can be used as a high-level program flow controller (business logic), and the detailed step logic can be created in separate routines. Structuring a program in this way will make it easy to follow, troubleshoot, and modify in the future.

Now that we understand when it is best to use SFC programming, we will discuss the SFC editing environment in the next section.

Using the SFC editor

The SFC editor appears in the **Routine** window of Logix Designer and is the development environment for writing SFC routines. Within an SFC routine, the SFC elements are created in an area called a sheet, and the sizes of the sheets directly correspond with the standard metric or English printer page sizes (similar to the Function Block diagram sheets). This allows the sheets to be easily printed, presented, and even signed like a typical engineering drawing. It is helpful to think of each sheet as a drawing paper for a single device. Unlike Function Block diagram sheets, you cannot divide your SFC into multiple named sheets. However, the SFC routine is not limited in size as a Function Block routine is. You can expand the size of the SFC routine to have up to 175 x 175 cross-reference grid blocks. An SFC routine can span multiple sheets horizontally and vertically. The specified sheet size makes it easier to organize the way the SFC routine appears when printed. You can see the sheet size divisions as solid gray lines on your SFC routine. The SFC editor window allows you to add the SFC elements from the SFC element group, drag them around the sheet, and connect the flow of the SFC elements using wires. The following screenshot shows an SFC routine window in RSLogix 5000:

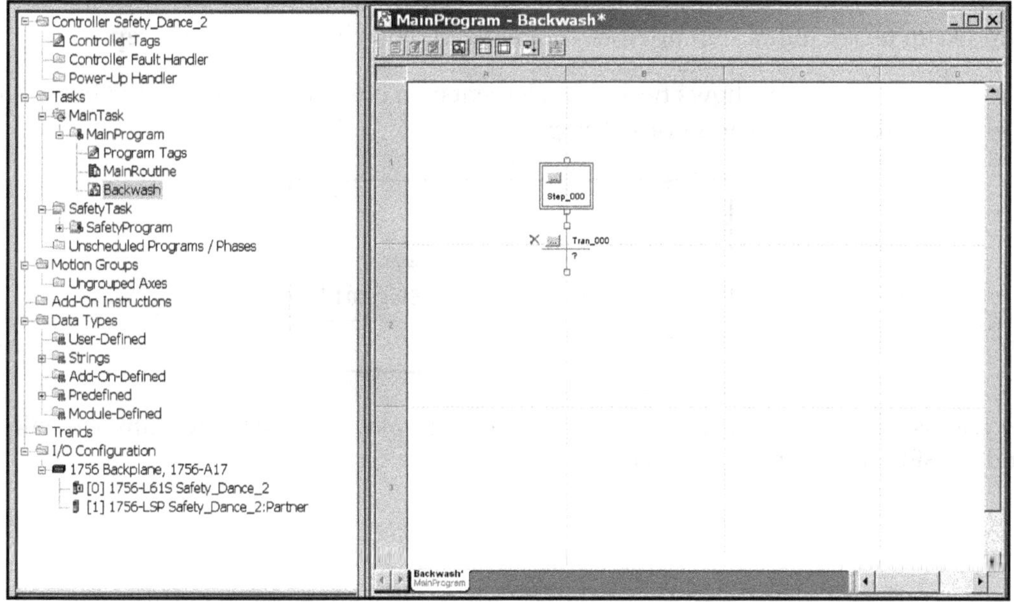

In the following section, we will describe the use of SFC steps within the SFC editor to create our program flow diagrams.

Defining the SFC steps

Steps are the main building blocks of SFC routines. A step is associated with the logic to be executed at a specific point in your process. A step is represented by a rectangle shape in an SFC routine with a pin at the top and bottom. Steps can be referenced just like Function Block elements and contain a number of properties, as follows:

- `.T`: This property is the length of time that the step has been active for.
- `.PRE`: This property is the preset amount of time to run a step for.
- `.DN`: This property is the Boolean flag that triggers `high` once the timer reaches the preset amount of time.
- `.X`: This is a bit that is ON the entire time that the step is executing.

There are also a number of alarm properties that can be configured and triggered if a step runs too long or not long enough. The complete list of step properties can be found in the *Help* documentation by selecting a step element and pressing *F1* on the keyboard.

All SFC routines must have an initial step defined in order to run. The initial step is indicated with a double line around its rectangle shape. You can specify which step you would like to be the initial step by right-clicking on it and checking **Initial Step**.

The following screenshot shows two `Step` elements; on the left-hand side is the initial step, and on the right-hand side is a normal step:

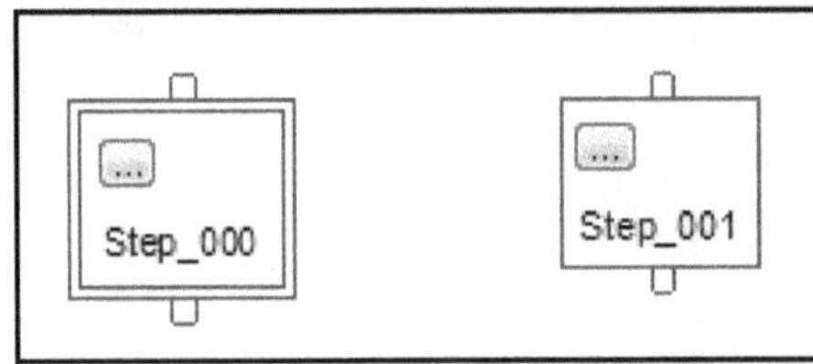

Now that we understand the important role that steps play in an SFC program, we will introduce SFC actions in the following section.

Defining the SFC actions

Actions are associated with a step and contain the structure text code used to perform functions such as starting a pump. You can associate multiple actions with a single step. There are two types of actions:

- **Non-Boolean**: These actions allow you to execute the structured text code or reference other routines using the JSR function.
- **Boolean**: These actions set a Boolean tag value to `true` when it is ON. This action will require other logic to monitor this tag value in order to execute.

The following diagram shows a non-Boolean action on the left-hand side and a Boolean action on the right:

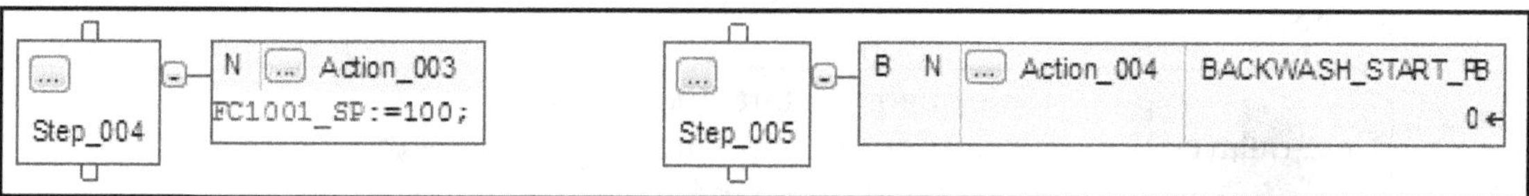

Each action element and its properties can be referenced and monitored. Action elements have the following properties:

- `.A`: This property means that the Boolean property is ON when the action is active.
- `.T`: This property is the length of time that the action has been active for.
- `.PRE`: This property is the preset amount of time to run an action.
- `.Count`: This property is the number of times the action has been active.

There are also a number of other properties that can be monitored on actions. The complete list of action properties can be found in the *Help* documentation by selecting an action element and pressing *F1* on the keyboard.

Actions also use qualifiers to determine when they should start and stop. By default, each action is set to non-stored qualifiers, which means it will execute when the step is associated with its execution.

The following qualifiers are available for actions:

Symbol	Name	Description
`N`	Non-stored	This qualifier starts when the step is activated and stops when the step is deactivated.
`P1`	Pulse (rising edge)	This qualifier starts when the step is activated and executes only once.
`L`	Time-limited	This qualifier starts when the step is activated and stops when the timer runs out or when it is deactivated.
`S`	Stored	This qualifier starts when the step is activated and stays active until a reset action property is triggered.
`SL`	Stored and time-limited	This qualifier starts when the step is activated and stays active until a reset action property is triggered or the timer runs out. It does not deactivate when the step is deactivated.
`D`	Time-delayed	This qualifier starts the action for a predefined amount of time after the step is active and while the step is still active. It stops when the step is deactivated.
`DS`	Delayed and stored	This qualifier starts the action for a predefined amount of time after the step is active and while the step is still active. It stays active until an action reset property is triggered.
`SD`	Stored and time-delayed	This qualifier starts when a specific amount of time has passed after the step is activated, even if the step is deactivated before this action. It stays active until an action reset property is triggered.
`P`	Pulse	This qualifier executes the action once when the step is activated and again when the step is deactivated.
`P0`	Pulse (falling edge)	This qualifier starts when the step is deactivated and executes only once.
`R`	Reset	This qualifier resets (turns off) an action and can be used to reset some of the other action qualifiers.

We are now familiar with SFC steps and actions. In the following section, we will introduce two more important SFC elements: transitions and branches.

Defining SFC transitions and branches

Transitions are used to bind steps to other steps and specify a structured text logical condition (which could also include a jump to a subroutine function) that must be `true` in order to proceed. A branch is a wire that connects to multiple transitions or steps. Branches and transitions work together to control the flow of an SFC sequence. There are three types of transitions/branches:

- **Sequence transition**: This transition provides a logical expression between each step.
- **Selection branch transition**: This transition provides a logical expression that will direct the step flow to one of many steps (similar to an `OR` expression). Additional steps can be added to a selection branch by right-clicking on it and selecting **Extend Branch**.
- **Simultaneous branch step**: This transition executes two or more steps at the same time (similar to an `AND` expression). Additional steps can be added to a simultaneous branch by right-clicking on it and selecting **Extend Branch**.

The following diagram illustrates the visual style of each transition and branch type:

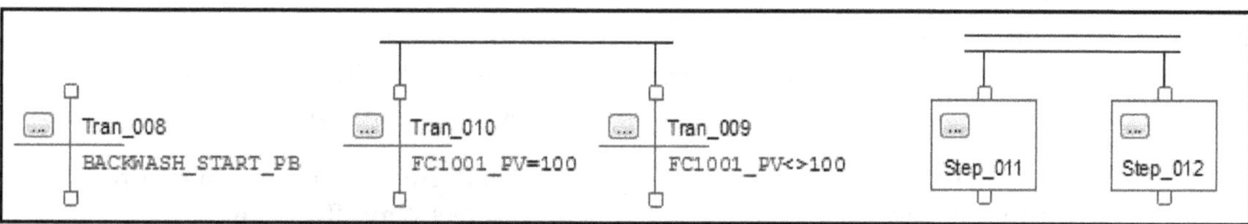

In the next section, we will discuss the final element of an SFC program, the `Stop` element, which ends the execution of our program flow.

Defining the SFC Stop element

The SFC `Stop` element stops the execution of an entire SFC routine or a particular branch of an SFC routine and waits for a restart to be triggered.

The following diagram demonstrates the use of a `Stop` element in an SFC routine:

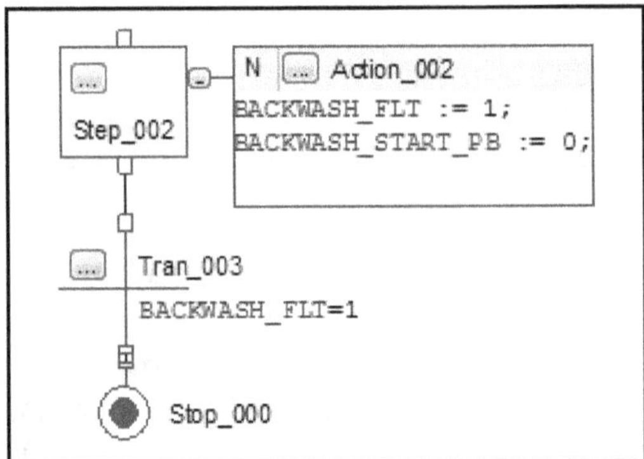

Now that we have covered all the basic elements of the SFC programming language, we will create our own SFC backwash routine in the following exercise.

Building a backwash SFC routine

In this section, we will demonstrate the use of an SFC by building a backwash process using a step-by-step guide. The backwash process will be run to flush out the filters used in our process once they become too dirty. Let's follow these steps to do so:

1. First, we will need to declare our new routine. Right-click on the **MainProgram** scope in the **Controller Organizer** pane and select **New Routine**:

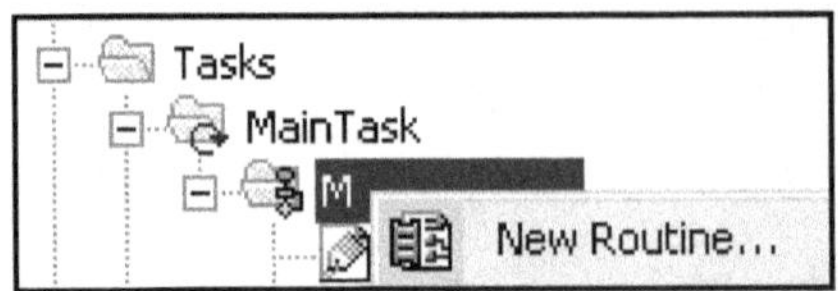

2. In the **New Routine** form that appears, enter or select the following values:
    - **Name**: `BACKWASH`
    - **Description**: `Backwash Sequence`
    - **Type**: `Sequential Function Chart`

   Then, click on **OK**:

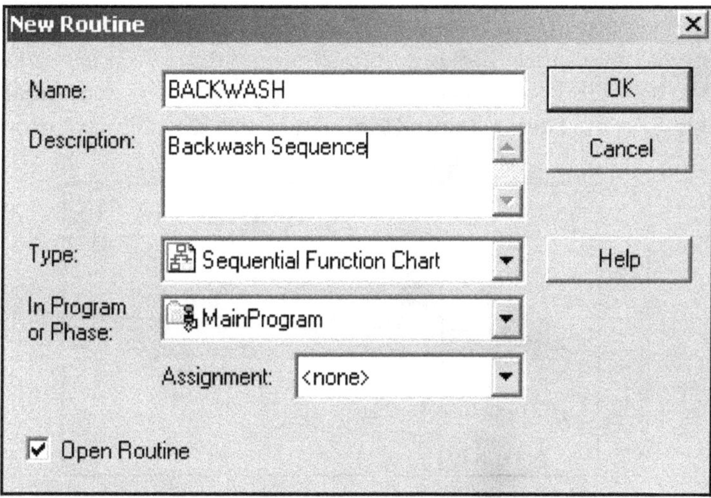

3. In order for our newly created routine to be executed with each scan of the controller, we will need to add a reference to it in the `MainRoutine` program, which is executed with each scan of `MainTask`.
4. Double-click on our `MainRoutine` program to display the `MainRoutine` ladder logic.
5. Now, we can simply copy and paste one of the JSR ladder rungs we created earlier and change the value to point at our `BACKWASH` SFC routine.
6. Right-click on the left-hand side of the last ladder rung (where the rung number is displayed) and select **Copy** (or press *Ctrl* + *C*). Right-click below the last rung and select **Paste** (or press *Ctrl* + *V*).
7. Now, double-click on the **Routine Name** parameter of the JSR element and select our newly added `BACKWASH` routine:

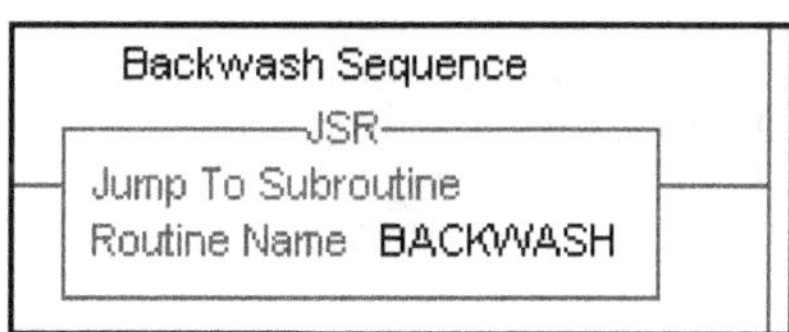

8. Now, we will return to our `BACKWASH` SFC by double-clicking on it in the **Controller Organizer** pane.

9. As we have learned, the base unit of any SFC routine is a step. Certainly, we are planning to have more than one step in our routine, so it is wise to add a transition as well. We can add our first SFC step and transition at the same time by clicking on the **Step + Transition** icon in the SFC element group:

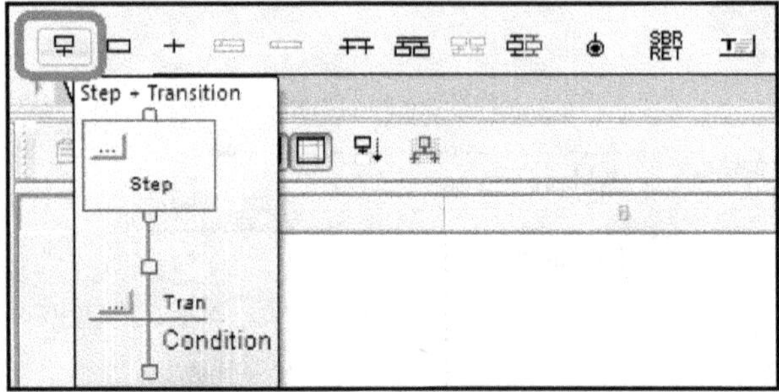

10. You will see `Step_000` and `Tran_000` appear in the SFC editor window:

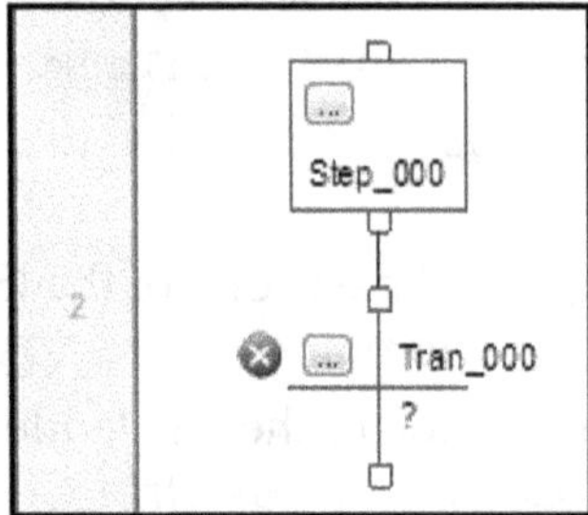

11. Add an action to `Step_000`. Right-click on **Step_000** and select **Add Action** (alternatively, you can select the **Action** element from the SFC element group toolbar above our routine):

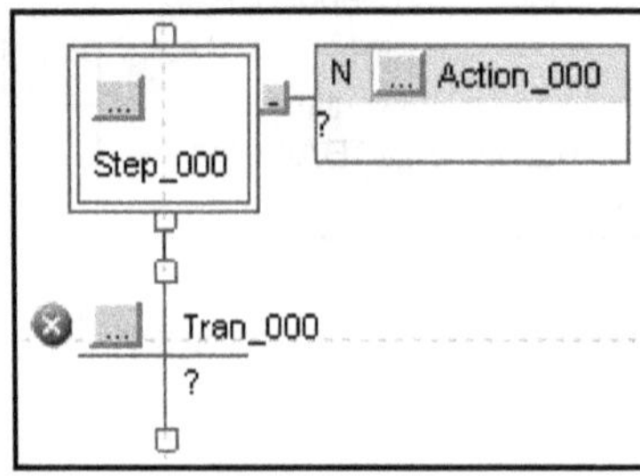

12. Now, we will add the initialization values for our SFC routine using the structured text syntax. Double-click on the box with the **?** symbol at the bottom of `Action_000` and enter the following structured text:

```
BACKWASH_START_PB:=0;
BACKWASH_FLT:=0;
```

The following screenshot shows the values of `BACKWASH_START_PB` (a push button for testing the backwash process) and `BACKWASH_FLT` (a variable that holds the fault condition for the backwash process) as `0` in `Step_000`:

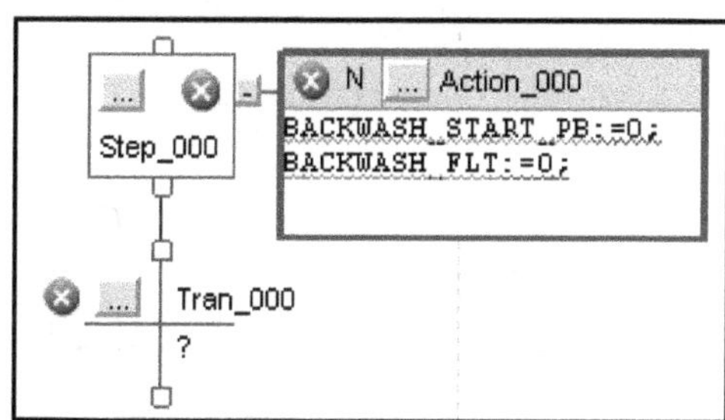

13. A red icon with an **X** symbol will appear to the side of **Action_000** to indicate that there is an error with the structured text we have added. The error is due to the `BACKWASH_START` and `BACKWASH_FLT` tags not yet being declared in our routine. We can easily add these tags by right-clicking on the `BACKWASH_START_PB` tag in the **Action_000** box and selecting the **New Tag "BACKWASH_START_PB"** option.
14. The **New Tag** form will appear, which will allow us to create our new tag, as follows:
    - **Name:** `BACKWASH_START_PB`
    - **Description:** `START BACKWASH PUSH BUTTON`
    - **Type:** `BOOL`
    - **Scope:** `MainProgram`
15. Repeat the same process for the second new tag by right-clicking on the `BACKWASH_FLT` tag and clicking on the **New Tag** form. Enter the following properties:
    - **Name:** `BACKWASH_FLT`
    - **Description:** `BACKWASH SEQUENCE FAULT`
    - **Type:** `BOOL`
    - **Scope:** `MainProgram`

16. Next, we will add the transition conditional value, which will start our backwash sequence. Double-click on the **Tran_000** question mark and enter the following structured text logical statement (which is equivalent to `BACKWASH_START_PB=1`):

```
BACKWASH_START_PB
```

The following screenshot shows the addition of the transition action to the SFC logic:

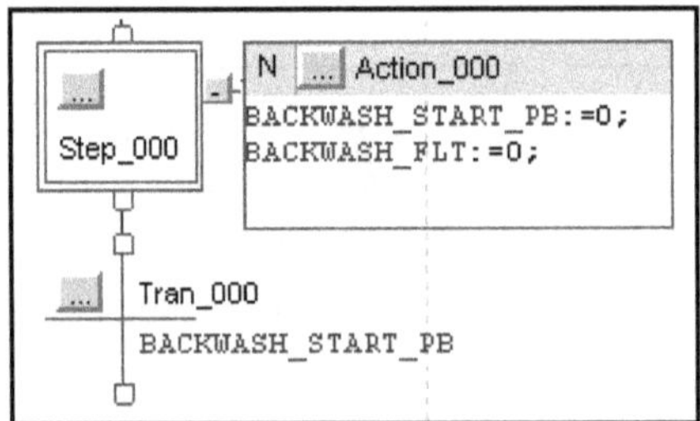

17. Next, we can add an action to `Step_001` that will represent our backwash process.

At this stage, we can easily add a structured-text JSR function to call a separate ladder logic, Function Block, structured text, or even another SFC routine. By combining SFC and the JSR function, we can control the flow of our program from SFC. This technique is very helpful when developing and debugging complex batching or sequencing programs.

18. Right-click on **Step_001** and select **Add Action**:

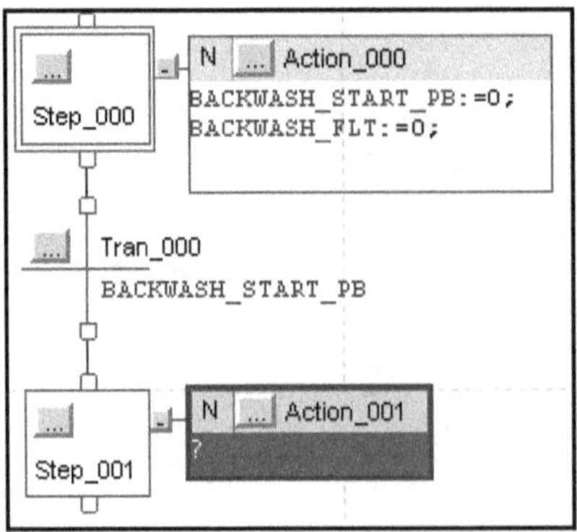

19. Now, we will add our action element's structured text code by double-clicking on the **?** symbol in **Action_001** and entering the following structured text code:

```
FC1001_SP:=100;
```

20. We will also need to add the new `FC1001_SP` tag by right-clicking on it and selecting the **New Tag** option.
21. Configure the new tag with the following properties:
    - **Name**: `FC1001_SP`
    - **Description**: `FLOW CONTROLLER 1001 SETPOINT`
    - **Type**: `DINT`
    - **Scope**: `MainProgram`

The following diagram shows the completed SFC with the newly added `FC1001_SP` tag:

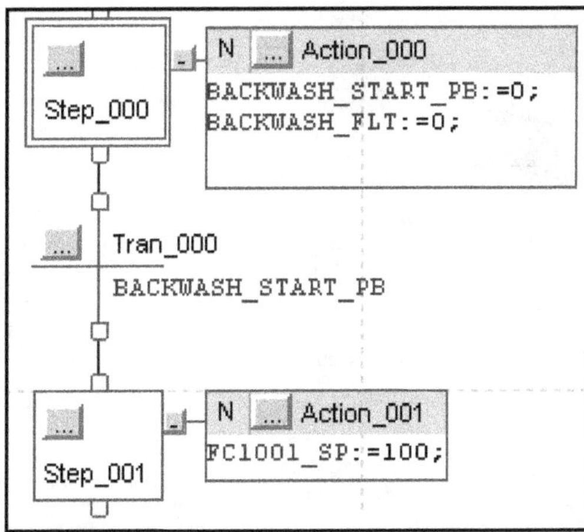

22. Let's add a delay to our `Step_001` box in order to give our backwash time to complete. Right-click on **Step_001** and select the **Step Properties** menu option. In the **Step Properties** form, set the **Preset** field to `30000ms` (30 seconds) and click on **OK**:

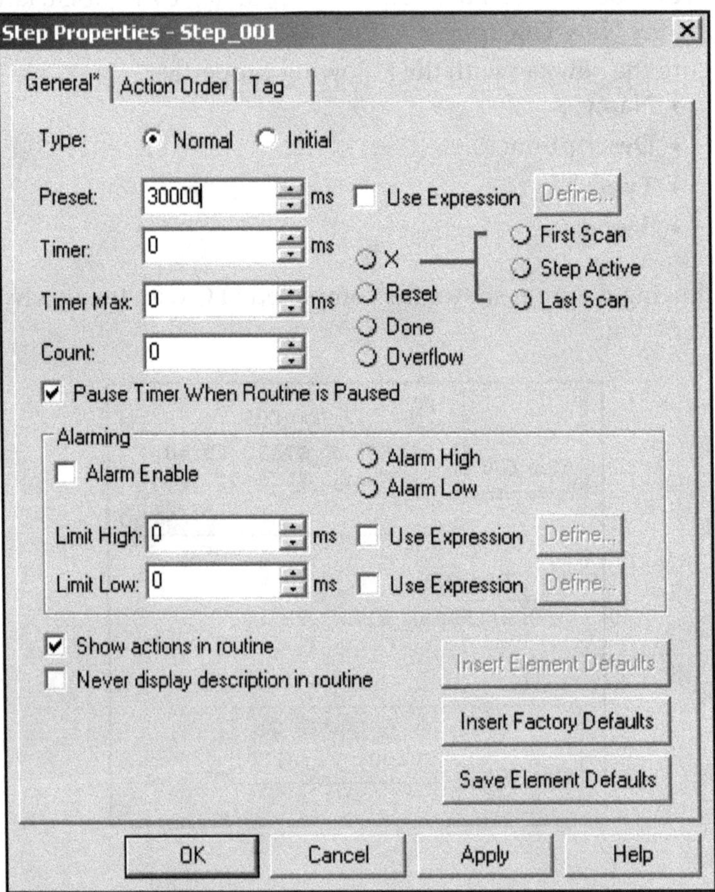

23. Next, we will add a selection branch diverge in order to reset our sequence or trigger a fault if there is a problem. Select **Step_001**, and then click on the selection branch diverge element icon ( ) just above our sequence chart. A selection branch diverge executes one sequence or another sequence (`OR`), while a simultaneous branch diverge will execute two sequences in parallel (`AND`):

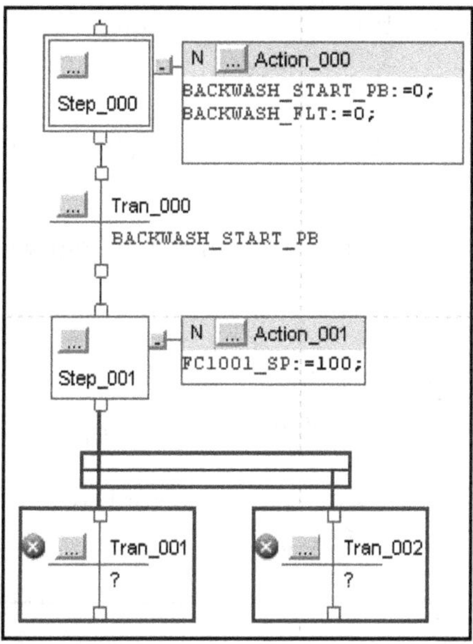

24. The next piece of development work is to add our backwash sequence steps. Select the **Tran_000** transition box, and then click on the `Step` element icon in the SFC element group above our SFC routine. The **Step_001** step box will be added and automatically connected to **Tran_000** (because we selected the transition before adding our new step):

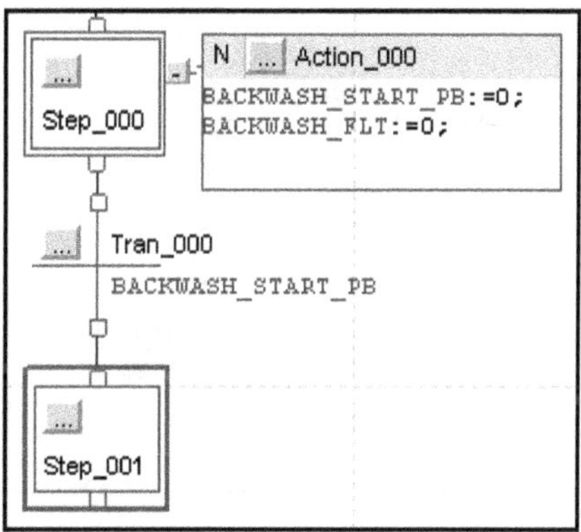

25. Our sequence will automatically reset and await another backwash if the flow controller valve position (`FC1001_PV`) has been 100 percent opened. Select **Tran_001** and click on the **?** icon to set the logical statement, which will execute this selection branch.

Type the following structured text logical statement:

```
FC1001_PV=100
```

We will also need to add the `FC1001_PV` tag to our program by right- clicking on it and selecting **New Tag**

26. In the **New Tag** window, enter the following field values:
    - **Name**: `FC1001_PV`
    - **Description**: `FLOW CONTROLLER 1001 VALVE POSITION VALUE`
    - **Scope**: `MainProgram`
27. We want our sequence to reset after it has completed the backwash, so we will connect a wire from our transition, `Tran_001`, to the top SFC element in our sequence, `Step_000`. Click on the connector box under **Trans_001** and drag it to the connector box on top of **Step_000**:

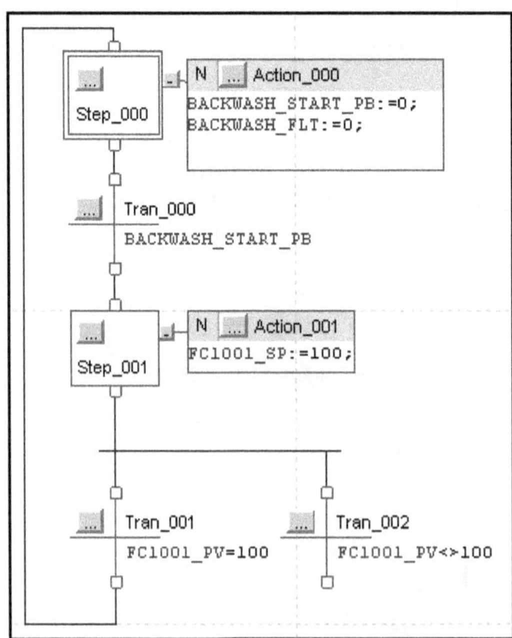

28. If our valve fails to open, we want to raise a fault before resetting our sequence. Select **Tran_002**, click on the question mark, and enter the following structured text logical statement:

```
FC1001_PV<>100
```

29. In order to raise a fault, we need to add a step. Select **Tran_002** and click on the `Step` element icon.
30. Add an action to our newly created step, `Step_002`, by right-clicking on it and selecting **Add Action**.
31. Double click on the **?** icon of our newly added action and add the following structured text code:

```
BACKWASH_FLT:=1; BACKWASH_START_PB:=0;
```

The following screenshot shows the completed action code added to the SFC step:

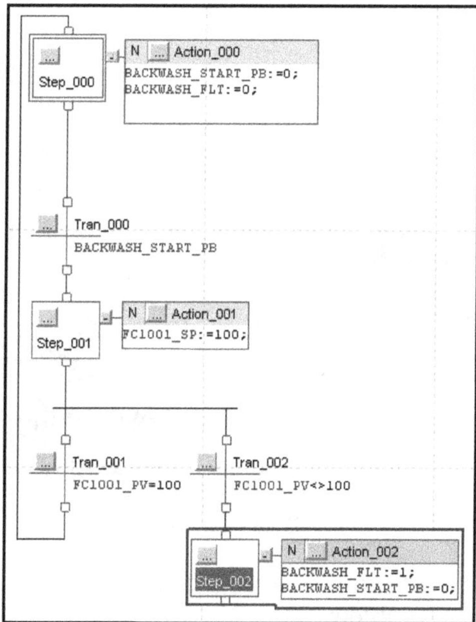

The fault bit will prevent the backwash sequence from running again until the problem is investigated and the fault bit is reset.

32. Finally, in order to make our sequence easy to understand, let's add a textbox comment. Click on the **Text Box** element in the SFC element group toolbar to add it to the sequence diagram and drag it to the right of the sequence. Enter the following comment.

```
Backwash fault triggered if valve FC1001 fails to open.
```

The following screenshot shows the textbox comment added to our SFC program:

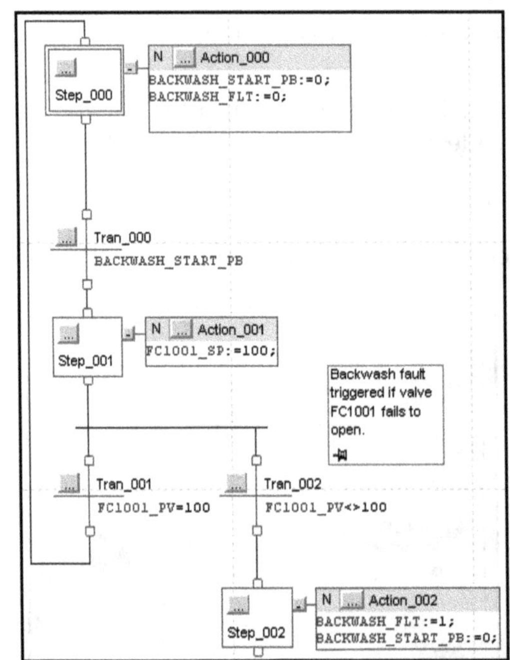

In the **Errors** panel, you should see the following output:

```
Verifying Routine: MainProgram - BACKWASH...

Complete - 0 error(s), 0 warning(s)
```

If you do encounter an error, double-click on the error message to be taken to the exact location of the problem.

In the last exercise, we kept the default names for our steps, actions, and transitions. It is easy to rename the SFC elements to make the sequence easier to read and maintain. You can double-click on the existing name of a step, action, or transition and type in a new name to rename it.

33. The complete SFC routine should be verified to ensure that there are no errors or warnings. From the drop-down menu, navigate to **Logic** | **Verify** | **Routine**.

We have now completed our first SFC routine to support a simple backwash operation. The previous exercise covered SFC steps, actions, transitions, and the stop element in a single program.

Summary

In this chapter, we explored SFCs and their typical uses within an automation project. We looked at the few core elements that make up an SFC and created a simple backwash process routine. The use of SFCs varies from industry to industry; however, there are certain cases where leveraging the IEC SFC construct can greatly simplify the creation and debugging of a program.

As with the previous IEC languages that we have covered in this book, selecting the appropriate language for your application is like selecting the correct tool to solve the problem you are facing. Although some programmers will only ever write in ladder logic, there are many advantages to using the full range of IEC languages where appropriate.

In the next chapter, we will identify ways to organize and control the scan frequency of a routine using tasks and programs.

Questions

The following questions can be used to test your retention of the concepts introduced in this chapter. You can find the answers to these questions in the back of the book under *Assessments*:

1. What is the name of the IEC language that allows you to program visually using a flowchart construct and is based on the GRAFCET language?
2. What SFC element is considered to be the main building block of SFC routines, is associated with the logic to be executed at a specific point in the process, and is represented by a rectangle shape with a pin at the top and bottom?
3. What SFC element is associated with a step and contains the structure text code used to perform functions such as starting a pump?
4. What SFC element is used to bind steps to other steps and specify a structured text logical condition that must be `true` in order to proceed?
5. What SFC element is a wire that connects to multiple transitions or steps?
6. What SFC element stops the execution of an entire SFC routine (or a particular branch of an SFC routine) and waits for a restart to be triggered?

Further reading

For more information about SFC programming within the Logix platform, please take a look at the Logix *5000 Controllers Sequential Function Charts Rockwell* document at `https://literature.rockwellautomation.com/idc/groups/literature/documents/pm/1756-pm006_-en-p.pdf`.

3

Section 3: Advanced Logix Programming

In this section, you will learn about a few more advanced topics, such as managing tasks and troubleshooting faults. You will also learn the best practices for deploying a Logix solution. We will also introduce some of the cybersecurity and code-protection features available on the Logix platform. Finally, you will create a sample application from scratch that combines the various techniques and skills learned throughout this book.

This section comprises the following chapters:

- `Chapter 12`, *Using Tasks and Programs for Project Organization*
- `Chapter 13`, *Faults and Troubleshooting in Logix*
- `Chapter 14`, *Understanding Cybersecurity Practices in Logix*
- `Chapter 15`, *Building a Robot Bartender in Logix*

12
Using Tasks and Programs for Project Organization

In this chapter, we will look at how to structure a Logix project using the basic organizational units that we have discussed throughout this book—tasks, programs, and routines. As we will learn in this chapter, project organization makes it easier to maintain and troubleshoot your code base. By dividing code into separate tasks and routines, you can inhibit and prioritize different parts of your program, which can support debugging and program optimization. We will also look at how task scheduling and prioritization can be used to balance the processing time of a controller.

This chapter will cover the following topics in detail:

- Introducing project organization in Logix
- Understanding the organizational units in Logix
- Learning about the controller task types
- Applying the best practices of Logix task usage
- Creating a task
- Inhibiting programs and tasks
- Setting task priorities
- Tuning a Logix controller

We will begin this chapter by covering the basic organization units available within RSLogix/Studio 5000.

Technical requirements

To complete this chapter, you will need to create a Rockwell Automation support account by going to `https://www.rockwellautomation.com/account/create-account`.

Creating an account is free, and the material we will be reviewing in this chapter is publicly available to anyone who is registered with Rockwell Automation.

You will also need a copy of RSLogix or Studio 5000 that has a license for Emulate 5000 to program your project. You can either purchase this from your local distributor or request a time-limited trial version. You can find a local distributor for Rockwell Automation products at `https://locator.rockwellautomation.com/`.

Introducing project organization in Logix

As we have already seen, a Logix project is organized into tasks, programs, and routines. When a new project is created, Logix automatically adds one of the following basic organizational units to the project:

- A task
- A program
- A routine

We have seen these units used many times in our controller organizer. The following screenshot shows the breakdown of tasks, programs, and routines in the controller organizer:

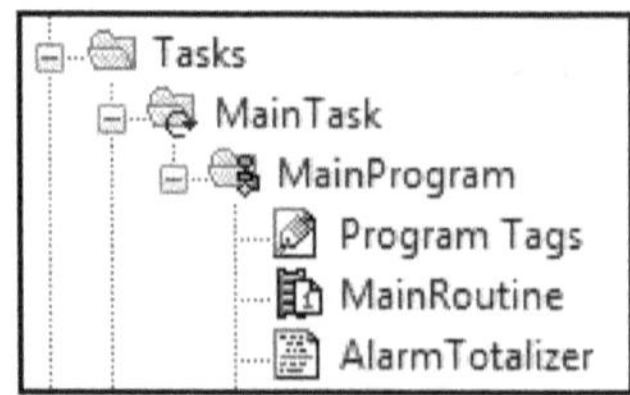

These units also allow us to select how often and at what priority programs and routines are run. Project organization also allows us to control and optimize the way our projects run to reduce the processing load on a controller.

In the next section, we will take a look at each organizational unit in more detail.

Understanding the organizational units in Logix

As stated in the previous section, the organizational units in Logix are tasks, programs, and routines. The following diagram illustrates the one-to-many relationships within a Logix project organization:

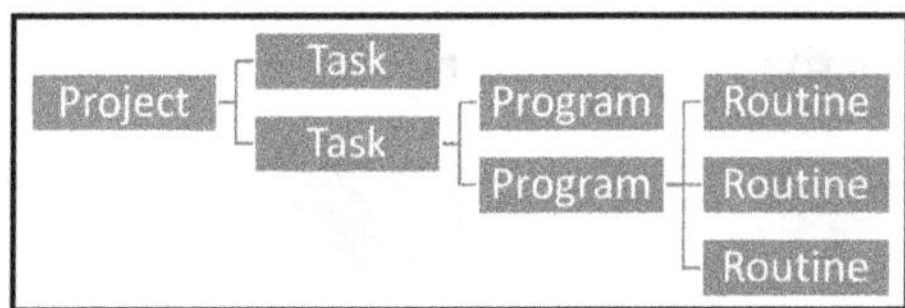

As the preceding diagram illustrates, Logix Designer is only capable of opening a single project at a time. A project can contain multiple tasks, a task can contain multiple programs, and programs can contain multiple routines.

In the following section, we will introduce our first organizational unit type—controller tasks.

Learning about controller tasks

A task is the most foundational and powerful organizational unit in the Logix platform. When we create a new project in Logix, we are provided with a single task that runs all of our logic. Also, up to this point, we have only used a single task to develop our application. It is possible to add multiple tasks to your project that can schedule and prioritize programs. However, it should be noted that there is a small controller-performance hit when switching between tasks (around 1 ms). With that said, it is wise to limit the number of tasks in your program to less than a handful.

We will discuss the program organizational-unit type and typical project task configuration in the next section.

Learning about controller programs

Controller programs are associated with tasks and they can be assigned to controller events (such as a controller startup or fault). Programs are a collection of related routines and tags executed by a task. Multiple programs can be scheduled to run within a task, and the order in which they execute can be adjusted.

Tags can be declared within a program and their scope is limited to a single program. This allows you to use the same tag names across multiple programs. Programs can also be inhibited, moved between tasks, and monitored for performance (execution time).

The following screenshot shows the **New Program** dialog in Studio 5000 Logix Designer and the configuration options that are available:

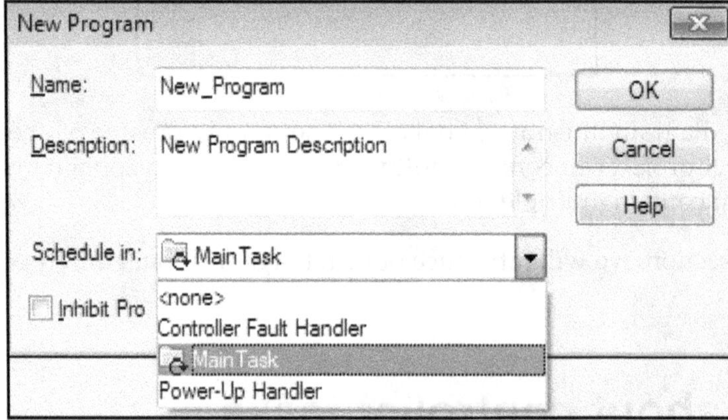

Programs can be scheduled to execute in a variety of ways within a project, as follows:

- Equipment phases
- Unscheduled programs
- Controller-fault handler programs
- Power-up handler programs

In the next section, we will introduce our final organizational unit in Logix—the controller routine.

Learning about controller routines

Routines contain the code that is executed by the controller. They are at the lowest level of the organizational unit tree that we saw earlier in this chapter, but they are the unit that actually executes the code on the controller. A program can contain multiple routines of mixed **International Electrotechnical Commission** (**IEC**) languages. Each program is assigned a main routine to be executed. Only the routines that are called by the main routine are executed within a program.

In previous chapters, we used the **Jump to Subroutine** (**JSR**) element to connect routines to the main routine, as in the following screenshot:

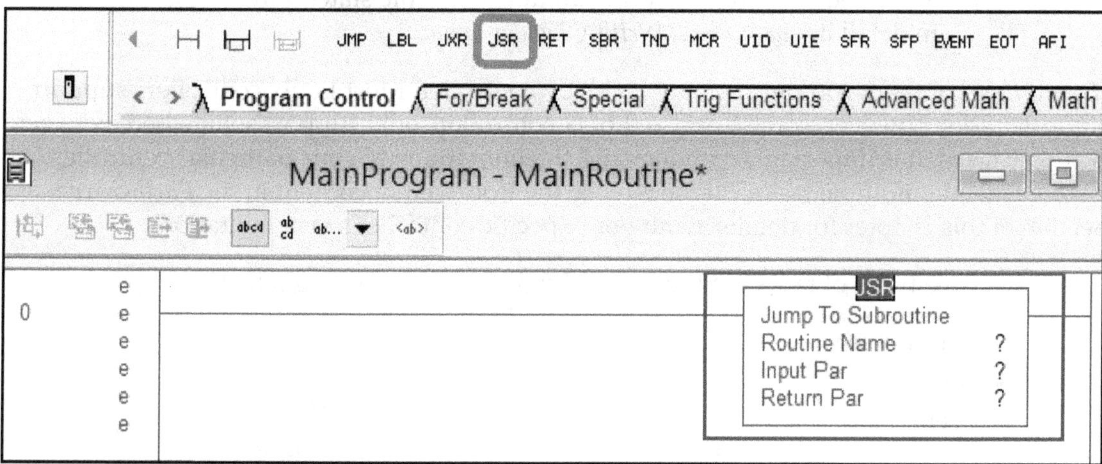

We have now covered each of the main types of project organizational units within RSLogix/Studio 5000. You will find that your programs are much easier to develop and maintain when they are divided into logical groupings. This is particularly the case as projects become larger and multiple people are involved in their development. There is no real limit to the number of programs or routines that you can use within RSLogix and Studio 5000 to organize your project.

In the following section, we will dive deeper into tasks, which allow parts of your solution to run independently of other parts. Unlike the basic organizational units (programs and routines), the number of tasks that can be run is limited to a set number, depending on the controller you are using.

Learning about the controller task types

Tasks are the most configurable organizational unit and are at the core of a Logix project. They provide a means of optimizing the execution of our project. It is crucial to remember that Logix controllers are only capable of running one task at a time. However, tasks can interrupt the execution of other tasks if they are triggered and have a higher priority value. Tasks that are interrupted will start again from where they left off in the execution of their code.

It is important to keep in mind that other tasks can change the data that your routine's code is executing on. Care should be taken to buffer tags to avoid the code from entering an unpredictable state. Buffering is covered in detail in `Chapter 8`, *Writing Ladder Logic*.

The number of tasks you can support varies by controller. Most Logix controllers support up to 32 tasks; however, some CompactLogix controllers only support somewhere between 3 and 16 tasks. It is important to understand the limitations of your particular controller before creating multiple tasks. Please refer to the Rockwell document in the *Further reading* section of this chapter for details about your specific controller's task limitations.

There are three types of tasks in Studio 5000 Logix Designer (RSLogix 5000):

- Continuous
- Periodic
- Event

In the following subsection, we will cover our first task type and the task type we have used in all of our programs so far—the continuous task.

Learning about continuous tasks

Continuous tasks execute as quickly as they can and always run on the controller when other tasks aren't doing so. After a continuous task has completed its execution, it immediately starts running again. Only one continuous task is allowed to be declared per project. The main task, which is added by default when you create a new project, is automatically set up as a continuous task. A continuous task is typically used as the program flow controller in a project. Using a continuous task is not mandatory, but only one can be used in a project.

In the next section, we will introduce our second task type—the periodic task.

Learning about periodic tasks

Periodic tasks run at an interval that you can specify in milliseconds (with a default value of 10 ms). Periodic tasks are typically used in projects for values that must be updated at a specific interval. In the exercise that we will try out later in this chapter, we will create a periodic task that runs every 250 milliseconds to check for a specific alarm condition.

In the next section, we will discuss our final task type—the event task.

Learning about event tasks

Event tasks run when a condition triggers it. The condition that triggers an event task can be as follows:

- A change of digital input
- A new sample of analog data
- Motion operations, such as axis watch and axis registration
- A consumed tag
- An event instruction
- Microsoft Windows events (SoftLogix only)

We have now covered the three task types. It is important to remember that the number of tasks is limited (typically to 32), depending on which controller your project is running.

The capabilities of your controller may limit the event triggers that are available for your project.

Now that we have an understanding of the various tasks types, we will cover how a typical RSLogix/Studio 5000 solution leverages tasks in the following section.

Applying the best practices of Logix task usage

During runtime, there is a small performance hit on the Logix controller when switching between tasks. You should avoid using tasks to organize a project's structure and instead rely more on programs and tasks to create a logical structure that resembles the process being automated. If numerous tasks are running on a controller, this increases the risk of some tasks not having the time to complete their program execution before they are triggered again and reset. Often, we hear of programmers who are new to the Logix platform who create dozens of tasks in a project (for example, one per process cell). An experienced automation professional will limit the use of tasks to less than a handful (however, certainly, there are exceptions). A typical Logix application will have one continuous task to handle the main program execution and perhaps one or two event tasks to handle special cases.

Now that we have covered the best ways to use tasks within our project, as well as some of the other basic program organizational units, lets put them to use in an exercise. The following exercise will create a task for monitoring alarm conditions in our industrial control system.

Creating a task

As we have learned so far in this chapter, organizational units within RSLogix and Studio 5000 provide a much-needed logical structure to our projects. They also allow us to prioritize critical tasks within our project.

In the following exercise, we will create a task that periodically monitors an important alarm condition within our application:

1. In the **Controller Organizer** pane, right-click on the **Tasks** icon, and then click on **New Task...**:

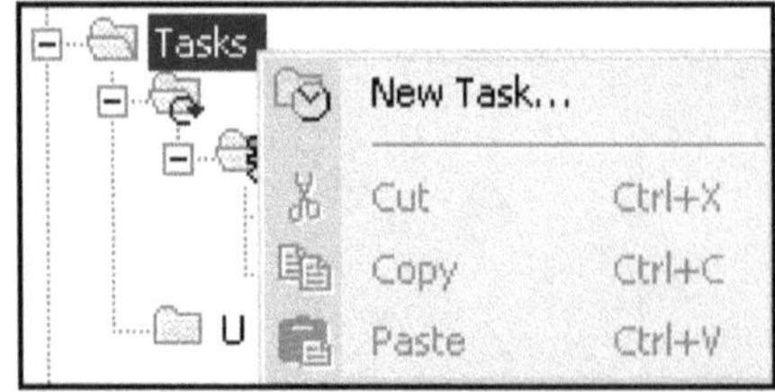

In our project, there is no need to check for non-critical alarms by the default periodic task time of every 10 ms. We will create a new periodic task for processing alarms every 250 ms and give it low priority in order to reduce the load on our processor.

2. In the **New Task** form that appears, enter the following values:
    - **Name**: `AlarmTask`
    - **Description**: `Task for calculating alarm conditions`
    - **Type**: `Periodic`
    - **Period**: `250.000 ms`
    - **Priority**: `11`
    - **Watch Dog**: `500.000 ms`

The following screenshot shows the **New Task** window filled in with the preceding form values:

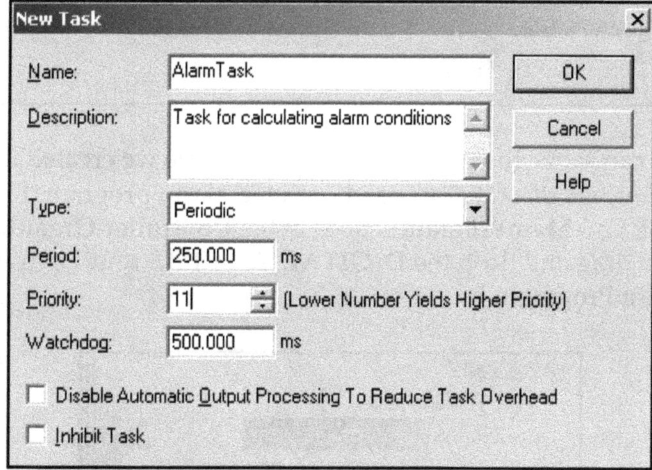

3. Next, we will add our program, which will contain our alarm function and handle the alarm processing for our project. Right-click on our newly created alarm task, and then click on the **New Program...** option:

4. In the New Program form that appears, enter the following values:
   - **Name**: `MainAlarmProgram`
   - **Description**: `Program for processing Alarms`
   - **Schedule In:** `AlarmTask`

   The following screenshot displays the **New Program** window form elements filled in with the correct field values:

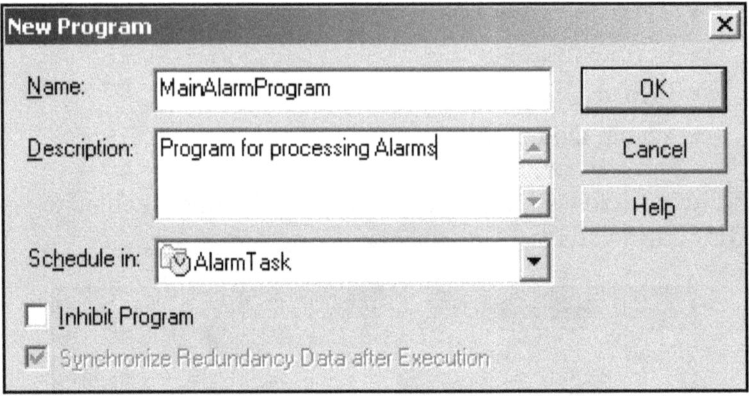

5. Now, we can move the `DIGITAL_ALARMS` routine we created in `Chapter 6`, *Writing Function Block*, to our newly created alarm program. Expand the **MainTask** and **MainProgram** scopes in the **Controller Organizer** pane's **Tasks** scope and drag and drop the **DIGITAL_ALARMS** routine from **MainProgram** to **MainAlarmProgram:**

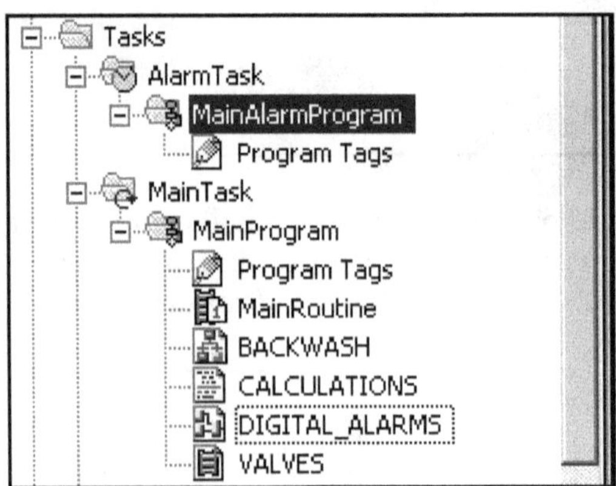

6. We will now set the `DIGITAL_ALARMS` routine to be the main routine of `MainAlarmProgram`. Right-click on **MainAlarmProgram** and select **Properties** (or *press Alt + Enter*). In the **Program Properties** form that appears, select the **Configuration** tab, and under the **Assign Routines** header, select `DIGITAL_ALARM` from the main drop-down box:

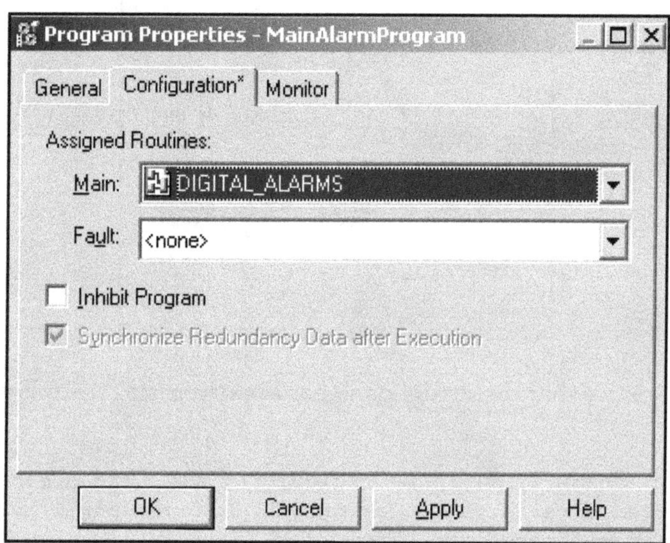

7. You will notice that after assigning the `DIGITAL_ALARM` routine as the main routine for `MainAlarmProgram`, the `DIGITAL_ALARM` icon changes to display a small **1** icon, which indicates that it is the main routine for the program:

8. Next, we will check to see whether we have introduced any errors to our controller with our latest changes. From the drop-down menu at the top of RSLogix 5000, navigate to **Logic** | **Verify** | **Controller**:

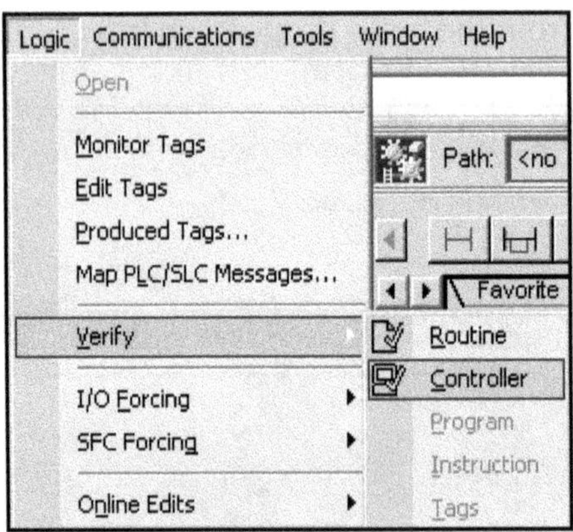

9. You will notice that the **Errors** pane has appeared and the following errors are listed:

```
Error: Sheet 1, B1, ALMD, FC1001_FLT_ALM: Tag doesn't
 reference valid object or target. Error: Rung 1, JSR, Operand 0:
Invalid reference to unknown
 routine.
```

10. Clicking on the first error message will take you directly to the `DIGITAL_ALARMS` function block and highlights the `FC1001_FLT_ALM ALMD` element.
11. The red **X** mark on the function block element indicates that there is a problem with the block's configuration. The error has occurred because the original `FC1001_FLT_ALM` element was created with a scope of `MainProgram` and it cannot be accessed from `MainAlarmProgram`. The function block tags are automatically created with the scope of the current program you are working under when they are added to a routine. In order to declare a function block at the controller-scope (global-scope) level, you will need to create it manually using the **New Tag** form.
12. In order to fix this problem, we need to create the `ALMD` tag again at a more global scope level. Right-click on the `FC1001_FLT_ALM` tag and select the new `FC1001_FLT_ALM` menu option (or press *Ctrl* + *W*).

13. The **New Tag** form will appear; ensure that the **Scope** field is set to `FirstController` and click on **OK**:

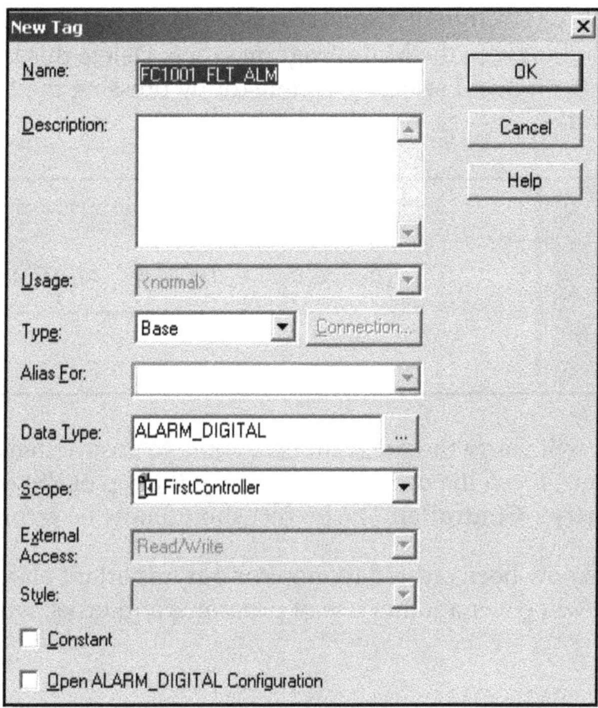

14. Next, we should remove the duplicate `FC1001_FLT_ALM` tag that exists in the **MainProgram** scope. Under the **MainTask** and **MainProgram** folders in the **Controller Organizer** pane, right-click on the **Program Tags** icon and select **Edit Tags**:
15. The **Edit Tags** table will appear. Select the `FC1001_FLT_ALM` tag, right-click on the box to the left of the name, and select the **Delete** menu option (or press the *Delete* key).

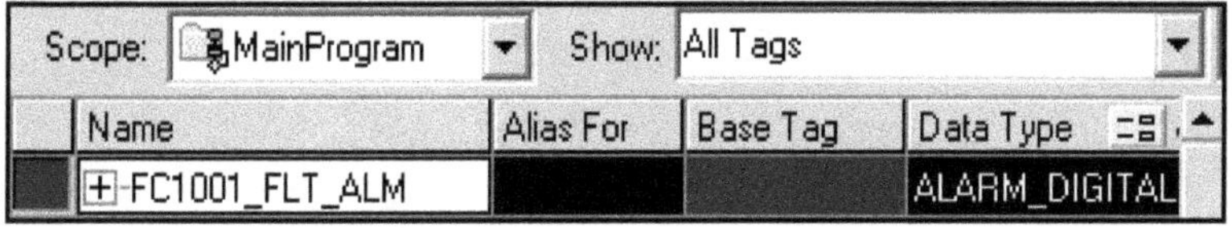

16. We have fixed the first error message; now let's resolve the second. Clicking on the second error message in the **Errors** pane will take you directly to the JSR reference within our **MainProgram** scope's `MainRoutine` routine to the `DIGITAL_ALARM` routine. The error is displayed because the `DIGITAL_ALARM` routine is no longer in the **MainProgram** scope. Delete this ladder logic rung by right-clicking on it and selecting **Delete** (or by pressing the *Delete* key with the rung selected):

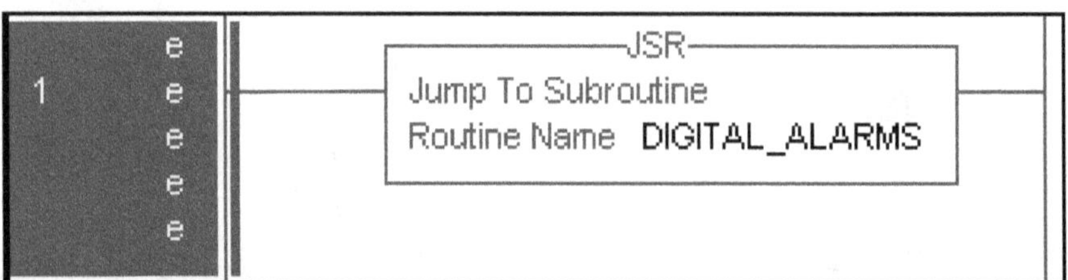

17. Finally, we will verify the program once more to ensure that we no longer have any problems. From the drop-down menu at the top of RSLogix 5000, navigate to **Logic** | **Verify** | **Controller**. The project should now be error-free.

Our first new task has now been created to monitor our important alarm condition. In the following section, we will cover another use of programs and tasks, which is the inhibit feature.

Inhibiting programs and tasks

One advantage of dividing your project into tasks and programs is that you can inhibit them individually if needed and prevent them from executing. To inhibit a task or program, right-click on it and open its properties. The **Inhibit Program** option is found in the **Configuration** tab of the **Program Properties** window:

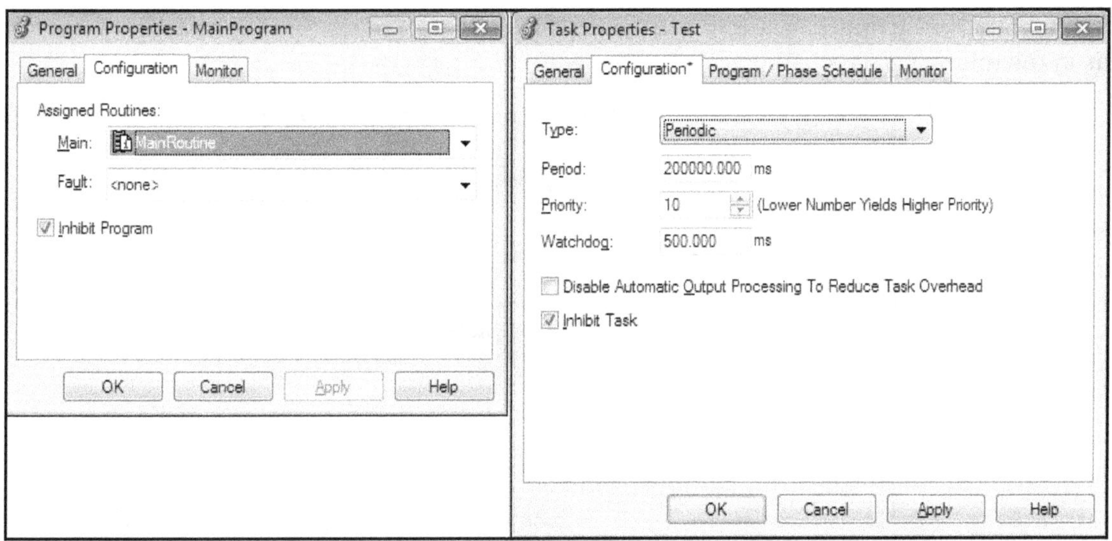

There are numerous use cases for inhibiting programs and tasks, such as debugging, troubleshooting, and temporary programs.

In the next section, we will cover the basics of task prioritization within RSLogix/Studio 5000.

Setting task priorities

Task priorities allow control over the order that a task runs on a controller. A Logix controller is only capable of running a single task a time. When multiple tasks happen to occur at the same time, a task's priority setting will allow the controller to select which task it should run first. Within Logix controllers, there are 15 priority levels (except for SoftLogix, which only has 3). The lower the priority number, the higher the priority of the task. So, a task with a priority of `1` will have the highest priority, and a task with a priority of `15` will have the lowest priority.

The task's priority option is found in the **Configuration** tab of the **Task Properties** window, as in the following screenshot:

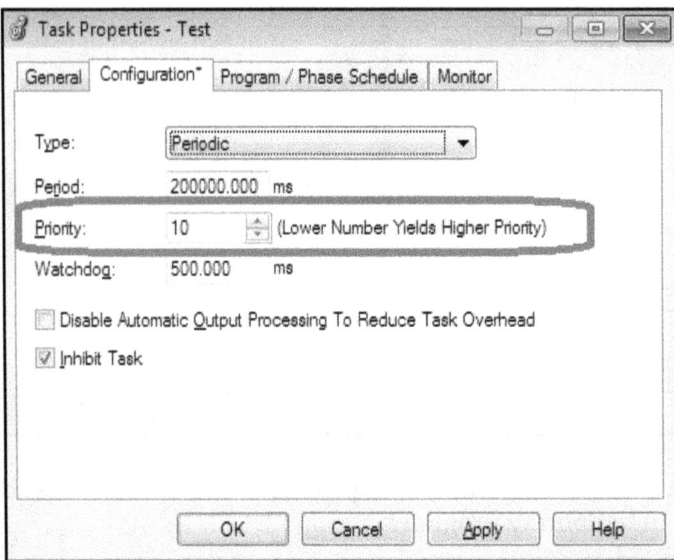

Now that we have covered the prioritization of tasks within RSLogix/Studio 5000, we are starting to understand the ways in which Rockwell controllers execute our code.

In the following sections, we will dive deeper into controller optimization and introduce tools to help us monitor the performance of our solutions.

Tuning a Logix controller

Overloading a Rockwell controller with too many tasks and programs, or running tasks too quickly, can have disastrous consequences. In the worst cases, the controller can completely trip and shut down our process unexpectedly. In best-case scenarios, our tasks will not run as frequently as we would expect them to, which can lead to unexpected results and process conditions. Fortunately, RSLogix/Studio 5000 provides methods for monitoring and tuning the performance of the projects running on a controller.

In the next few sections, we will explore some of the available options for project optimization. Let's start with system overhead time slice.

System overhead time slice

System overhead time slice is a controller setting that allows the specification of the percentage of time dedicated to ongoing background tasks. These ongoing background tasks are also referred to as unscheduled communications and will always require a percentage of the controller's processing power.

Logix unscheduled communications include the following features:

- Programming and device monitoring communication with Logix Designer/RSLogix
- Service communication
- Communication with the HMI devices
- Controller-to-controller communication
- Redundant controller synchronization
- I/O connection health monitoring and connection re-establishment

System overhead time slice only has an impact when a continuous task is configured in a project. When no continuous task is present, the background tasks take up any extra controller cycles that are available (effectively 100 percent).

A balance must be found between the overhead time slice and the task execution time. When the overhead time slice value is set too low, you may encounter the following issues:

- The HMIs take a long time to re-establish communications with the controller. With only a short amount of time dedicated to background tasks, it can take the HMI and controller a long time to build the list of tags and initialize communications.
- The HMI values are not updated regularly or stale values are displayed.
- The HMI appears slow to respond to commands and may take longer to switch between page views.
- Logix takes a long time to download or upload a project from a controller.
- Logix takes a long time to connect to the controller or has difficulty connecting.

When the overhead time slice percentage is set too high, you may encounter a different set of problems:

- Programs are not able to complete their execution before they are scheduled to run again (known as overlap).
- The controller CPU utilization is very high.

Finding the optimum overhead time slice value can be a challenge, particularly on complex programs with resource-constrained controllers. Fortunately, there are tools and techniques provided by Rockwell Automation that give you insights into striking a balance.

In the next exercise, we will modify the system overhead time slice percentage on our controller within RSLogix/Studio 5000.

Setting the system overhead time slice

In the following exercise, we will configure the overhead time slice on the controller of our project by following these steps:

1. In the **Controller Organizer** panel, scroll down to the **I/O Configuration** folder and expand the backplane that we have configured. Right-click on the controller you have configured and select **Properties**.
2. In the **Controller Properties** dialog box, click on the **Advanced** tab.
3. In the **System Overhead Time Slice** box, raise the overhead time slice to `30%`, and then click on **OK**:

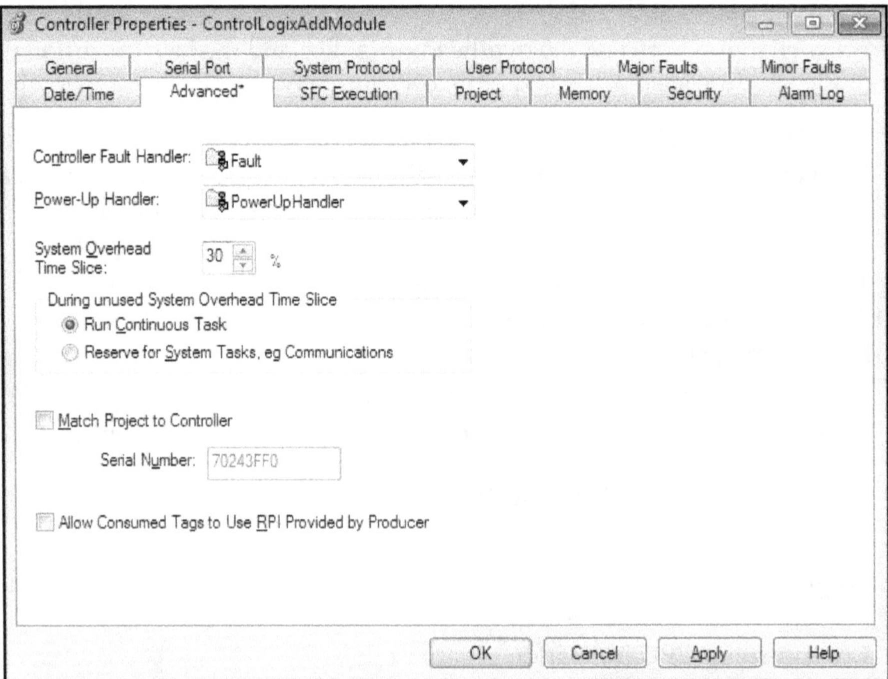

4. There is also a radio button in the **During unused System Overhead Time Slice** group box that allows us to select **Run Continuous Task** (default) or **Reserve for System Tasks**.
5. When the **Run Continuous Task** radio button is selected, the controller immediately returns to executing the continuous task once all the unscheduled communications are complete (normal behavior).
6. When the **Reserve for System Task** radio button is selected, the controller will always allocate 1 ms to unscheduled communications before returning to the continuous task. This setting is useful for simulating a communication load on the controller (for testing purposes only).

In the next exercise, we will learn how to monitor task performance and check for overlaps (which can occur when a routine does not have enough time to execute all of its code).

Monitoring task execution time and overlap

Overlap is when a task is unable to complete the execution of its programs and routines before it is scheduled to run again. Overlaps cause the execution of code to stop and start again from the beginning of the task. They should not occur on a running system and should always be investigated and resolved when reported. In the following exercise, we will learn how to monitor the task execution time and check for the overlap errors by performing these steps:

1. Go online with your program by navigating to **Communications** | **Go Online**. If prompted, download your project to the controller.
2. Put the controller in run mode by navigating to **Communications** | **Run Mode**.
3. Right-click on the **MainTask** scope in the **Controller Organizer** pane, open **Properties**, and select the **Monitor** tab.

4. When Logix is online with the controller, you will see live scan times (the time required to execute the task), as well as the **Interval Times** and **Task Overlap Count** information. If the **Task Overlap Count** value is ever greater than `0`, you should investigate the cause and work to optimize the execution of your project:

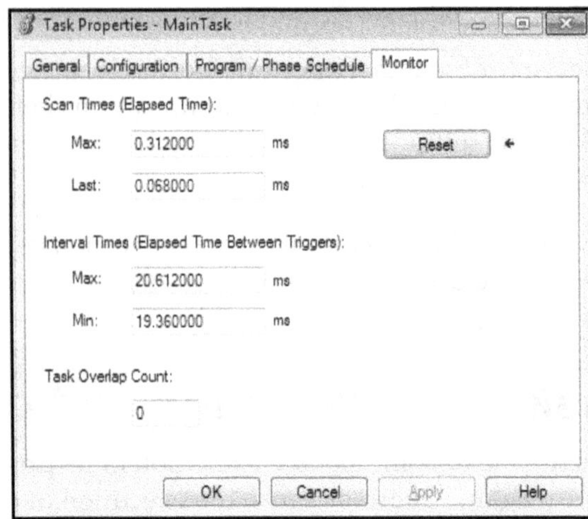

5. Right-click on the **MainProgram** scope in the **Controller Organizer** pane, open **Properties**, and select the **Monitor** tab. Here, you will see the **Max** and **Last** scan-time fields (the time required to execute `MainProgram`):

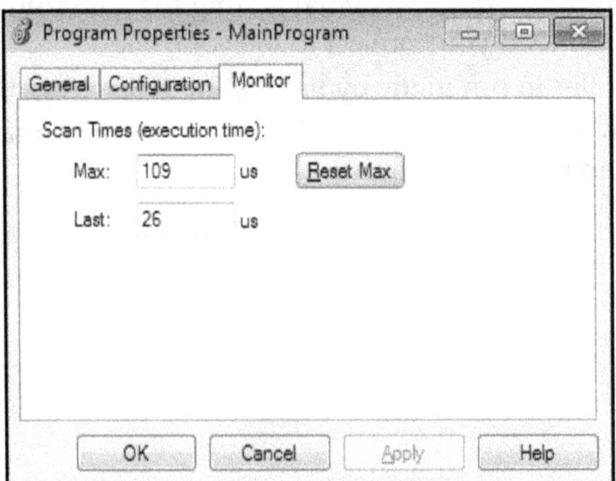

In the next section, we will learn how to set the watchdog time, which can be used to trigger a major fault when a task takes too long to execute.

Task watchdog time

Tasks also allow you to specify a watchdog time, which will trigger a major fault if the task runs for too long. The default watchdog time for a task is 500 ms, and the watchdog time includes interruptions by other higher-priority tasks. A watchdog time can range from 1 to 2,000,000 ms (2,000 seconds). Depending on how your project's fault handler is configured, the watchdog time may cause your controller to stop executing, so use this feature with caution.

The following screenshot demonstrates where the **Watchdog** value can be set from within the **Task Properties** window:

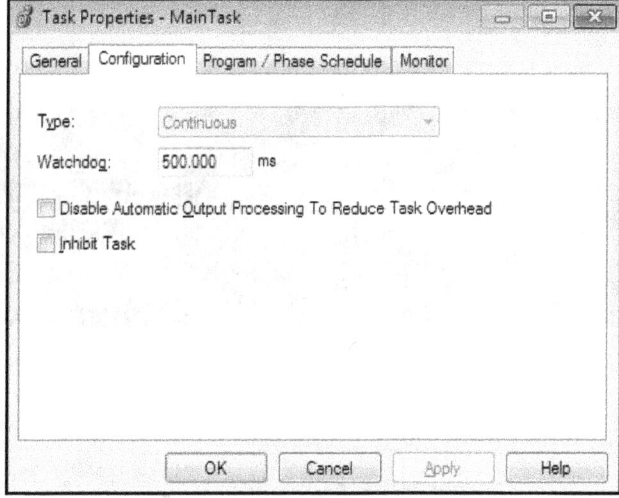

In the next section, we will introduce the Logix5000 **Task Monitor** tool, which can provide insights into the performance of a running controller.

The Logix5000 Task Monitor tool

The Logix5000 **Task Monitor** tool shows the current load of the Logix CPU. It provides insights into the current tasks that are running on the controller, active connections, and memory usage. This tool can be downloaded from the Rockwell Automation website or found on the Rockwell Automation distribution CD or hard disk drive. This tool can provide insights into the way your controller's CPU is being used. You can tune your Logix application by optimizing code, adjusting the task configurations, and modifying the overhead time slice percentage.

The following screenshot demonstrates how we can monitor the CPU and memory usage within a running controller using the Logix5000 **Task Monitor** tool:

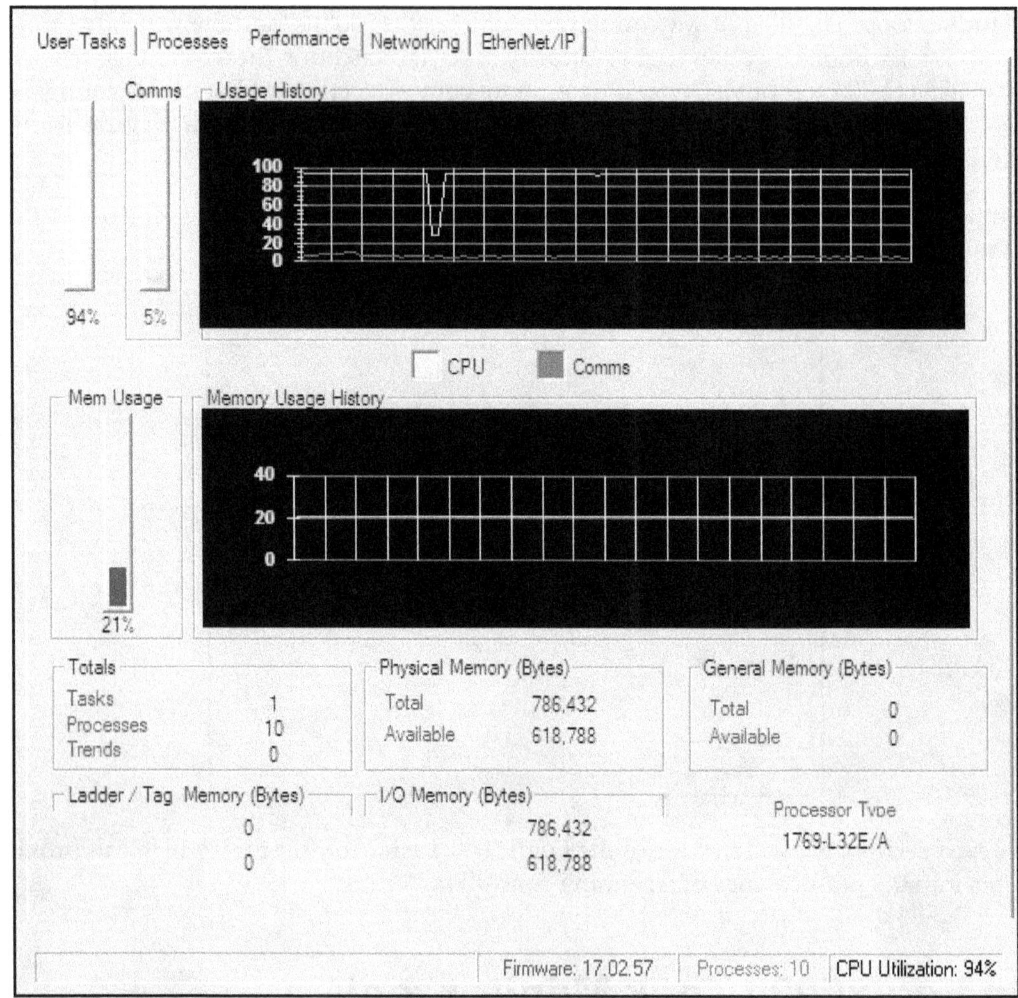

The Logix5000 **Task Monitor** tool is an extremely helpful tool when troubleshooting performance or capacity issues in an RSLogix/Studio 5000 solution.

Summary

In this chapter, we further investigated the project organizational units we have been using throughout this book. We detailed the way that a Logix controller executes tasks and how the CPU divides its time based on priority. We introduced the overhead time slice feature and emphasized its importance when optimizing a Logix application. Finally, we investigated methods within the Logix platform to monitor and troubleshoot performance issues. We can now troubleshoot and optimize Logix project performance on larger solutions.

In the next chapter, we will dig deeper into troubleshooting controller issues and faults.

Questions

The following questions can be used to test your retention of the concepts introduced in this chapter. You can find the answers to these questions in the back of the book under *Assessments*:

1. What is the most foundational and powerful organizational unit in the Logix platform?
2. What organizational unit is associated with tasks and can also be assigned to controller events (such as a controller startup or fault)?
3. What organizational unit contains the code that is executed by the controller and can use a mixture of different IEC languages?
4. What task type executes as quickly as it can and always runs on the controller when other tasks are not running?
5. What task type runs at an interval that you can specify in milliseconds (with a default value of 10 ms)?
6. What task type runs when a predetermined condition triggers it?
7. What can be configured on a task to trigger a major fault if a task runs for too long?
8. What is the controller setting that allows the specification of the percentage of time dedicated to ongoing background tasks?
9. What is the term used when a task is unable to complete the execution of its programs and routines before it is scheduled to run again?
10. What tool shows the current load of the Logix CPU and provides insights into the current tasks that are running on the controller, the active connections, and memory usage?

Further reading

For more information about project organization within RSLogix and Studio 5000, please refer to the *Logix 5000 Controllers Tasks, Programs, and Routines* Rockwell Automation programming manual at `https://literature.rockwellautomation.com/idc/groups/literature/documents/pm/1756-pm005_-en-p.pdf`.

13
Faults and Troubleshooting in Logix

In this chapter, we will learn how to identify and troubleshoot faults in a Logix controller. We will also detail a list of the fault codes that provide insights into the problems encountered by the platform. Then, we will introduce the process of fault recovery, which allows a program to resume its execution after encountering a specific fault type. After that, we will look at the troubleshooting applications available for your iOS and Android devices. The following topics will be covered in this chapter:

- Troubleshooting Logix solutions
- Troubleshooting Logix faults
- Clearing a fault
- Fault handling and recovery
- The Get system value and Set system value instructions
- Learning about user-defined data types
- Understanding FactoryTalk TeamONE

In the first section of this chapter, we will cover the myriad of resources that Rockwell provides for technical support and troubleshooting issues.

Technical requirements

To complete this chapter, you will need to create a Rockwell Automation support account by visiting `https://www.rockwellautomation.com/account/create-account.`

Creating an account is free, and the material we will be reviewing in this chapter is publicly available to anyone who is registered with Rockwell Automation.

You will also need a copy of RSLogix or Studio 5000 that has a license for Emulate 5000 to program your project. You can either purchase this from your local distributor or request a time-limited trial version. You can find a local distributor for Rockwell Automation products at `https://locator.rockwellautomation.com/`.

Troubleshooting Logix solutions

Automation problems have an odd way of occurring at the most inconvenient time, such as on Christmas Eve or on your partner's birthday. Regardless of the timing, you will always need to quickly resolve problems as they often translate to lost production time and lost revenue for the company.

Here are a few best practices to troubleshoot in the Logix platform:

- **Familiarize yourself with the Rockwell Automation knowledgebase**: The issue you encounter has most likely been encountered by someone else too. Knowledgebase is a great first line of defense for solving a problem. If you don't have an account set up, you should create one before you need it by going to `http://www.rockwellautomation.com/services/online-phone/techconnect.page`.
- **Verify that you have an active Rockwell Automation support contract and keep your Rockwell Automation technical support information and authorization number handy**: Rockwell Automation provides world-class support, so make sure you understand how to access this support before you need it. It also provides a handy wallet-sized cutout of your technical support information and it is a good idea to carry this around with you as you never know when you are going to get a call from your workplace asking for help.
- **Get to know your local Rockwell Automation sales representative**: They can also help you to quickly escalate support cases if required. Buy them coffee or lunch (or let them buy *you* coffee or lunch) and foster a relationship. Remember that they want to help and see you succeed.
- **Get involved with the Rockwell Automation community**: Sign up to their terrific (and free) TechConnect Education webinars and Genius webinars and attend local "lunch and learns" or conferences. There is no substitute for in-depth knowledge of the Logix platform when troubleshooting problems.

Now that we have covered some of the resources that are available to us, let's learn about some of the specific practices for identifying and troubleshooting faults in the following sections.

Troubleshooting Logix faults

A fault is an error state in your controller that prevents it from executing normally. It must be resolved in order for the controller to resume its normal execution. There are a few ways of confirming that a controller fault is the cause of a process upset:

- An operator may notice that a controller fault is indicated on a **Human Machine Interface** (**HMI**) display.
- The fault light is lit up on your controller, or a fault code is listed on the scrolling status display on the controller.
- You can see a fault indicated when you go online with your controller from RSLogix5000/Logix Designer.

The following screenshot demonstrates a major fault from the **Controller Properties** window:

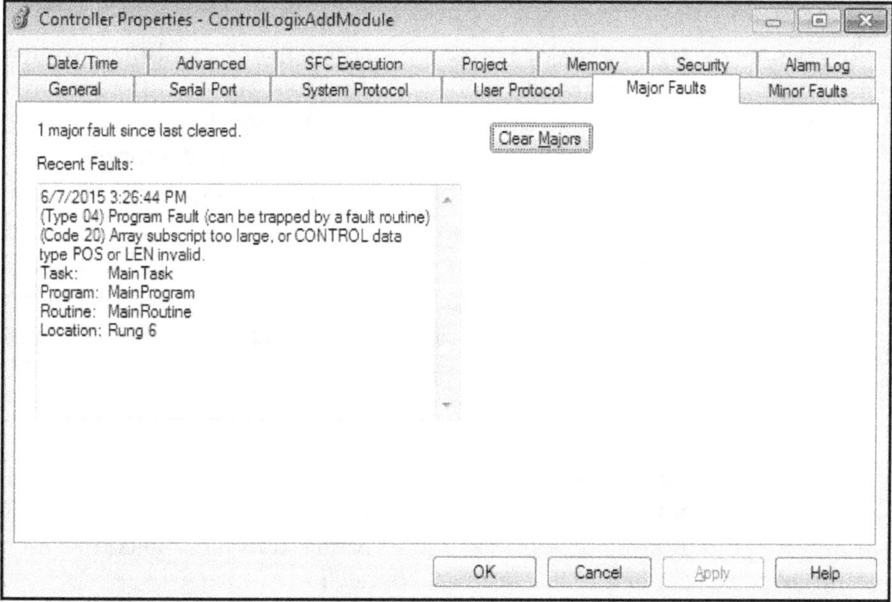

Troubleshooting faults in Logix is the process of locating and resolving problems encountered during the execution of a project on a controller. Access to **Piping and Instrumentation Diagram** (**P&ID**) drawings, cause-and-effect diagrams, wiring drawings, and junction box drawings will certainly help you with this. However, there is no substitute for working knowledge of a control system.

Troubleshooting is the analytical process of elimination to narrow down and permanently fix a problem. Faults are a mechanism used in Logix controllers (and by other **Programmable Logic Controller** (**PLC**) / **Programmable Automation Controller** (**PAC**) vendors) to stop the execution of a process when a problem is detected. Capturing and handling faults is the first step to take when determining the root cause of a serious control system problem.

In the next few sections, we will investigate faults and how to handle them in a project.

Understanding the fault categories

In this section, we will cover the various fault categories within Logix.

The following is a list of the three categories of faults within the Logix platform:

- **Major**: This is a fault where the Logix controller stops executing routines. An I/O module will allow you to configure the program to enter either a fault mode or program mode when a major fault occurs. Also, the I/O module outputs are set to their configured values for the faulted mode. There are 77 different types of major faults listed in the *Logix5000 Controllers, Major, Minor, and I/O Faults* Rockwell Automation Literature Library document—for example, when the controller detects a problem with the chassis, a major fault is triggered.
- **Minor**: This fault will trigger a bit to go high in the `MinorFaultBits` system status class object, but the controller will continue to run without interruption. There are 31 different types of minor faults listed in the faults document—for example, low battery or energy storage status. When a problem is detected with the L6 battery or the L7 Energy Storage Module (ESM), the `MinorFaultBits` bit 10 will be high. Also, the battery light on the front panel of the L6 controller will be lit when this bit is high.
- **I/O**: This fault is due to a problem with an I/O module, which, by default, will not cause the Logix controller to stop executing routines. However, on the individual I/O module properties, in the **Connection** tab, the controller can be configured to trigger a major fault on connection failure.

The following screenshot displays the I/O module's properties with the major fault on the I/O connection failure option checked and an active I/O fault code:

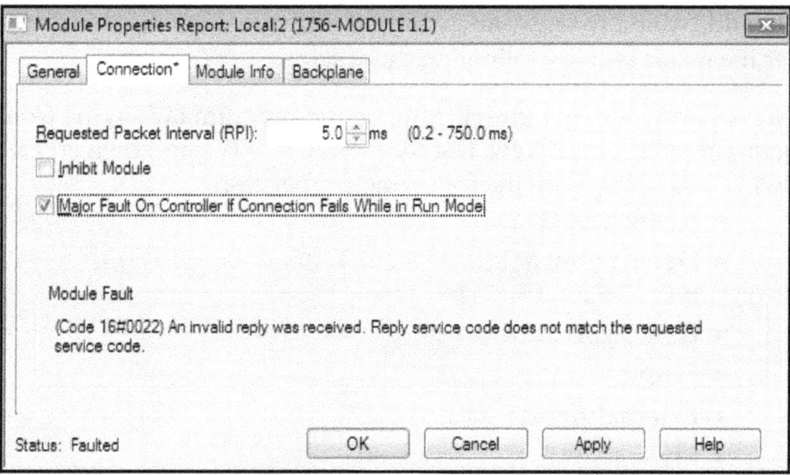

There are 95 different types of I/O faults listed in the previously mentioned document. The following bullet points detail the different user-defined fault types that can be utilized on the RSLogix/Studio 5000 platform:

- **User-defined major**: This is a custom fault that can be triggered based on any automation condition using a **Jump to Subroutine** (**JSR**) instruction to the fault handler routine (more on that later) and by passing a numeric parameter of 990 to 999 (the reserved range for user-defined fault codes). A user-defined major fault is handled by the controller just like any other major fault, stopping the execution of routines and setting the output I/O modules to their fault values.
- There are 10 different types of user-defined faults available in the same document, such as `type 4 code 990` and `type 4 code 999`.

We have learned that faults can fall under different built-in and user-defined categories. In the next exercise, we will learn how we can clear a fault after it has been triggered in our controller.

Clearing a fault

Once a controller encounters a major fault, not much can be done with it until the fault has been cleared. You will be unable to download an updated program to your controller until you clear all the major faults. In the following exercise, we will trigger a major fault and then learn how to view and manually clear it. We will trigger a programmatic major fault (type 4) by referencing a value outside of an array's configured range.

We will need to add two more tags—an array and array position tag—to our project in order to trigger the major fault by following these steps:

1. Create an array tag by right-clicking on the program tags in the **Controller Organizer** pane, select **New Tag** (or press *Ctrl* + *W*), and then create an array called `SmallArray` with the following properties:
    - **Name**: `SmallArray`
    - **Description**: `A Small Array Used to Trigger a Programmatic Major Fault (Type 4)`
    - **Data Type**: `DINT[10]`
    - **Scope**: `MainProgram`
    - **External Access**: `Read/Write`
    - **Style**: `Decimal`

    The following screenshot depicts the **New Tag** and **Select Data Type** windows:

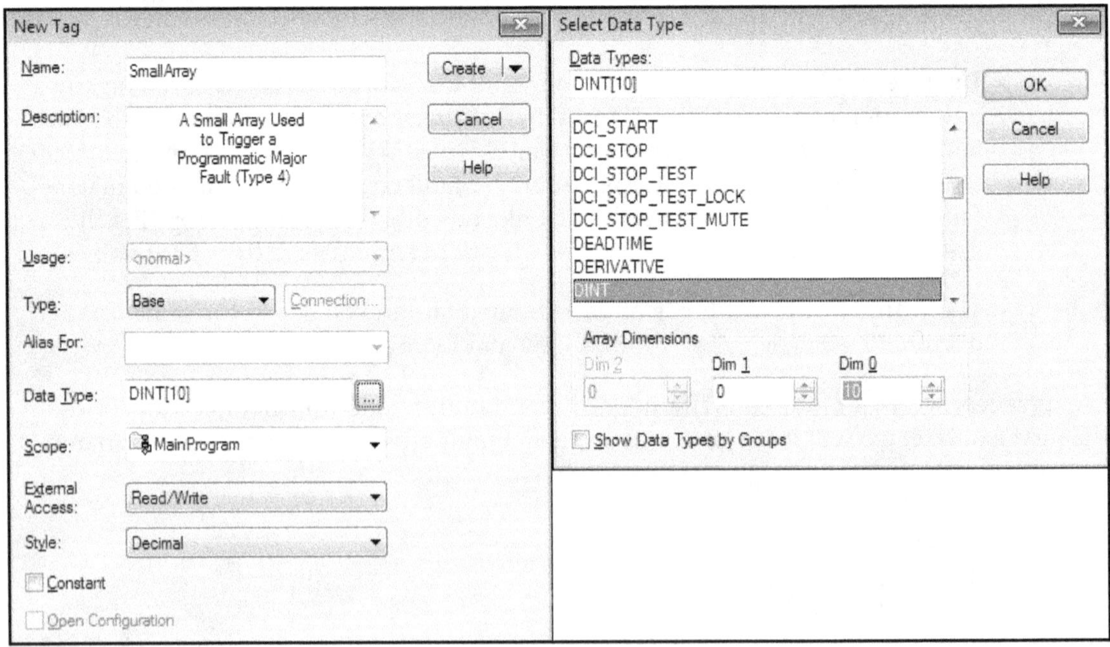

2. Next, create a `DINT` tag with the following parameters:
    - **Name**: `SmallArrayPos`
    - **Description**: `The Position to Update in the Small Array to Trigger a Major Fault.`
    - **Data Type**: `DINT`
    - **Scope**: `MainProgram`
    - **External Access**: `Read/Write`
    - **Style**: `Decimal`

   The following screenshot demonstrates the completed **New Tag** window form after *step 2*:

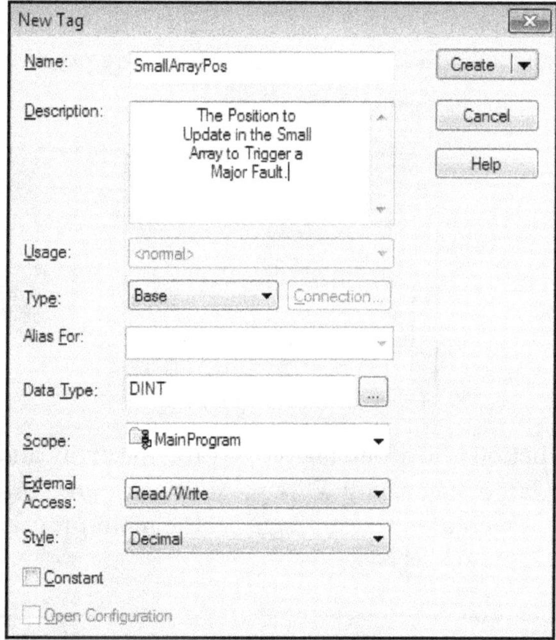

3. Next, we will add a ladder rung to the `MainRoutine` program, which we can use to trigger the major fault. Open the **MainRoutine** program from the `Controller Organizer` pane and add a new rung to the end of the routine by right-clicking on the last rung (**End**) and selecting **Add Ladder Element...** (or by pressing *Alt* + *Insert*).

4. On the newly created routine, add an `MOV` instruction by navigating to the **Move/Logical** element group and clicking on the **MOV** element:

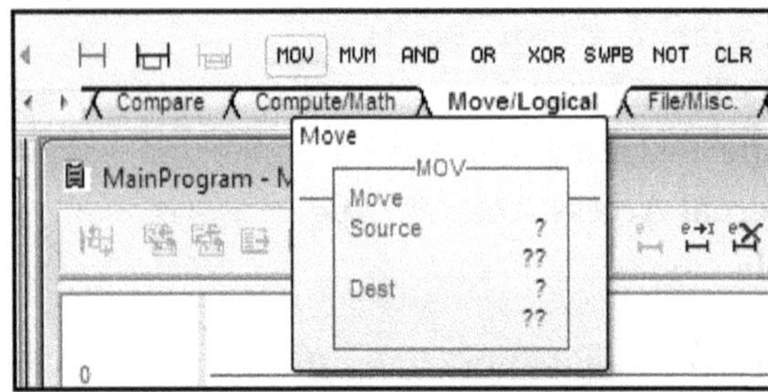

5. Next, set the **Source** measure of the `MOV` instruction to a literal value of `1`, and then set the **Dest** value of the `MOV` instruction to the newly created `SmallArray` tag and `SmallArrayPos` as the array position value, `SmallArray[SmallArrayPos]`:

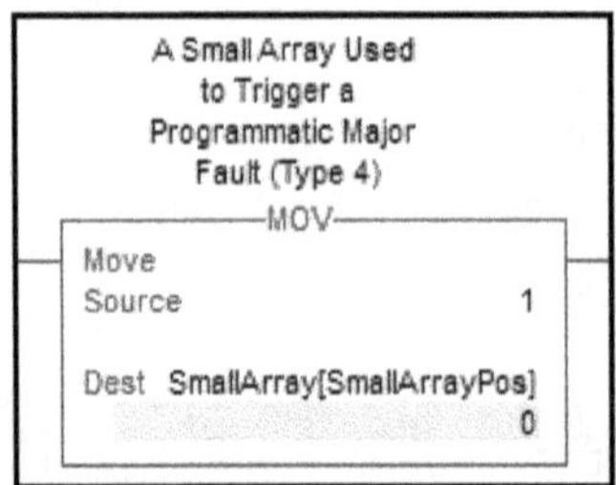

6. The `MOV` instruction will allow us to overflow the array and trigger an array subscript to a large major fault. Download the updated project to the controller and go online. Open the program tags for the main program and update the value of `SmallArrayPos` to `11`:

+	SmallArray	{...}	DINT[10]	A Small Array Used to Trigger a Programmatic Major Faul...
+	SmallArrayPos	11	DINT	The Position to Update in the Small Array to Trigger a Maj...

7. Overflowing the array triggers a major fault in the controller. The controller status now displays as **Faulted**:

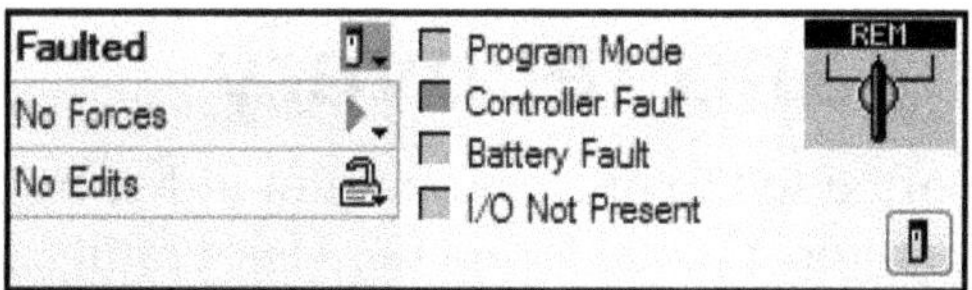

8. The major fault can be viewed by navigating to **Next Communications** | **Go To Faults**. Click on the **Clear Majors** button to clear the fault:

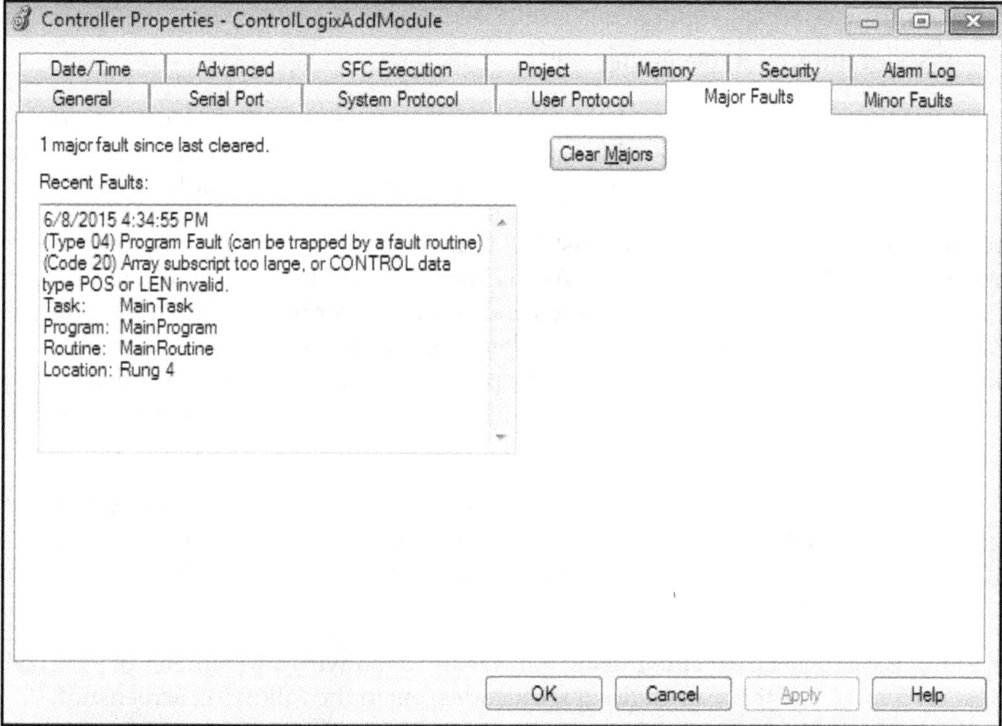

9. In order to clear the fault condition and continue the normal operation of the controller, we will adjust the `SmallArrayPos` value back to `1`.
10. Finally, change the controller back to run mode by navigating to **Communications** | **Run Mode**.

We have now learned the steps required to reset a fault and return our process back to normal. In the next section, we will learn about other methods of fault handling and recovery.

Fault handling and recovery

Minor faults should be reported to the process operator either by updating a bit for the HMI or by illuminating a light on a panel faceplate. Major faults, however, should be trapped and automatically recovered where possible.

Some major faults cannot be recovered, which further divides major faults into two categories:

- Major recoverable faults
- Major unrecoverable faults

Logix allows the user to create a fault routine, which can trap a fault and attempt to recover and continue running the process where possible. When a Logix controller encounters a major fault, it executes the program assigned to the controller fault handler.

It is recommended best practice to at least log all the faults that occur in the controller before programmatically clearing them. As discussed earlier, faults play an important role in troubleshooting problems with a process and should never be ignored. If a fault is still present after the controller fault handler has been executed, the controller will stop running. Fault routines can be declared at the program scope or at the controller scope (for capturing faults during tag assignment, start up pre-scan, and **Sequential Function Chart** (**SFC**) post-scan).

When a major fault occurs during the execution of a logic instruction, such as in the preceding exercise, the controller does not actually execute that instruction. The controller will simply move down to the next instruction in the routine.

Fault routines can also be executed using a JSR instruction with a parameter of 990 to 999 (the reserved range for the user-defined fault codes), as in the following screenshot:

In the next section, we will introduce the instructions used to check and reset the major and minor fault information from the controller system values.

Programmatically clearing faults

Legacy Rockwell PLCs (PLC-5 and SLC-500) had a dedicated status file (S2) that was continuously updated by the controller with system values. The ControlLogix platform has removed this dedicated status file in order to reduce the controller processing load. In place of the dedicated status file, ControlLogix has provided two self-serve instructions that allow direct control over the system value access and are neatly organized into class objects.

The **Get System Value** (**GSV**) instruction retrieves a system value status from the controller and updates a specified destination tag with that value. The **Set System Value** (**SSV**) instruction updates a controller system value status from a specified source tag.

The following screenshot demonstrates the **Get System Value** and **Set System Value** elements within a Ladder Logic rung:

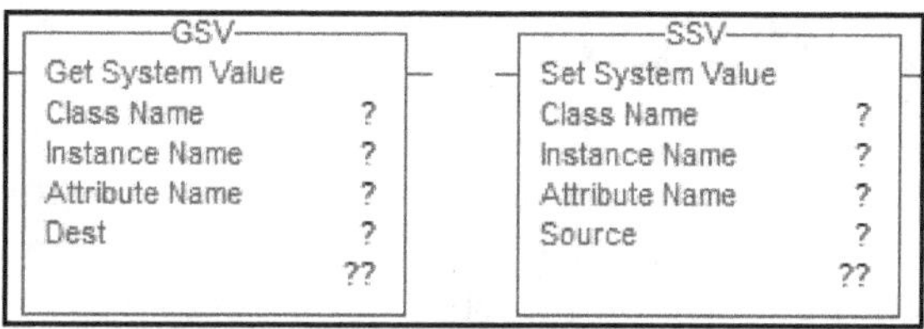

In the next section, we will dig deeper into the GSC and SSV instructions and how they can be used to reset a fault before causing the controller to stop.

The GSV and SSV instructions

The GSV and SSV instructions can be accessed from Ladder Logic and Structured Text, but are not directly available in Function Block. Typically, you will see these values scheduled periodically (for example, with a `TON` instruction), so as not to burden the controller's processor.

The GSV and SSV instructions play an important role in retrieving fault information and resetting the fault before causing the controller to stop:

- The `FaultLog` class name and `MinorFaultBits` attribute name system value can be used to check for any minor faults present in the controller
- The `MajorFaultRecord` system value attribute can be used to check for the presence of a major fault and collect its details

The following screenshot demonstrates the use of a **Timer** (`TON`) instruction executing a GSV to collect `MinorFaultBits`:

Minor_Fault_Check_Timer.DN

GSV
Get System Value
Class Name FaultLog
Instance Name
Attribute Name MinorFaultBits
Dest Minor_Fault_Bits
0

In the next section, we will introduce the **User-Defined Data Type** (**UDT**) element in Logix and create a simple example program that will use a UDT to capture a major fault.

Learning about UDTs

UDTs are object-based constructs that allow you to create custom structures containing a number of different data types. UDTs are used to organize data into objects that align with the properties of physical-world equipment. In the case of fault trapping, we will be using a UDT to capture the details of a major fault, which is covered in the next section.

Trapping a fault

In the following exercise, we will trap a major fault and clear it before the controller stops the previously mentioned steps:

1. In order to trap a major fault, we must create a `User-Defined` data type to store the fault information.

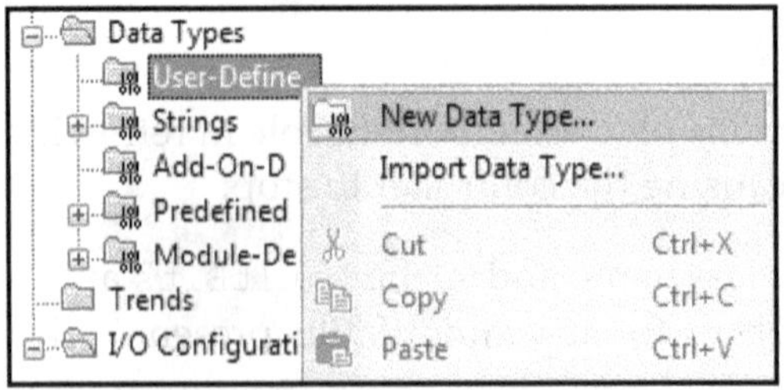

2. In the **Data Type** window that appears, creates the following `FAULTRECORD` UDT:

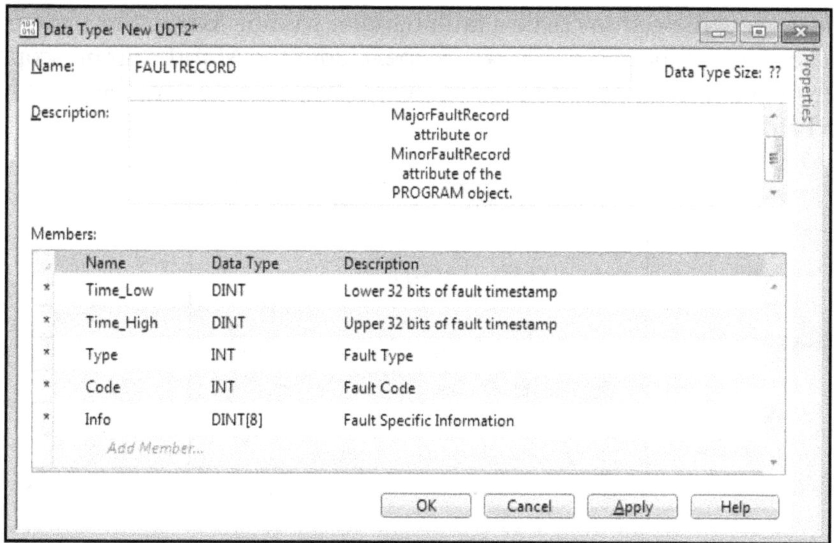

3. We will need to add an instance of our newly created `FAULTRECORD` UDT to our project at the **MainProgram** scope level:

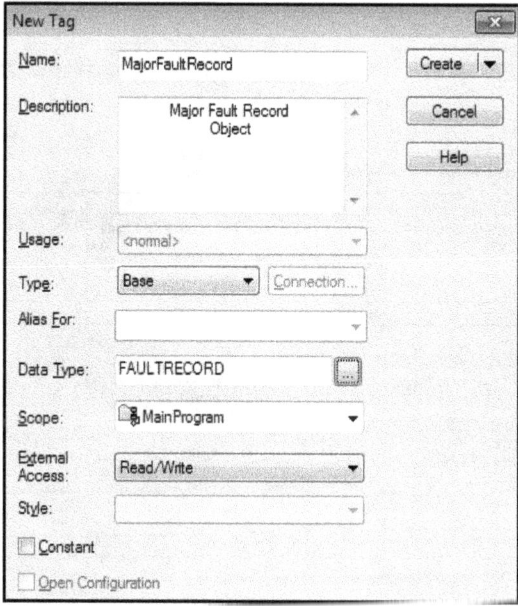

4. Next, we will need to create a fault handler routine to trap the array-overflow major fault in the **MainProgram** scope. Under the **MainProgram** scope, create a new Ladder Logic routine named `Fault_Routine` and set the **Assignment** value to **Fault**:

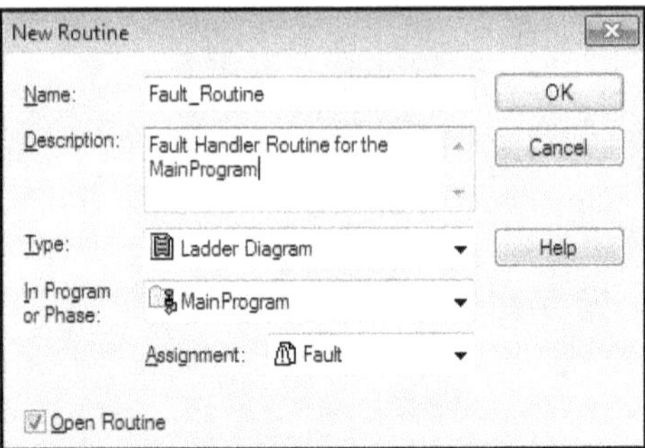

5. Add the following Ladder Logic instructions to check for our fault type and fault code and clear the major fault and the condition causing it:

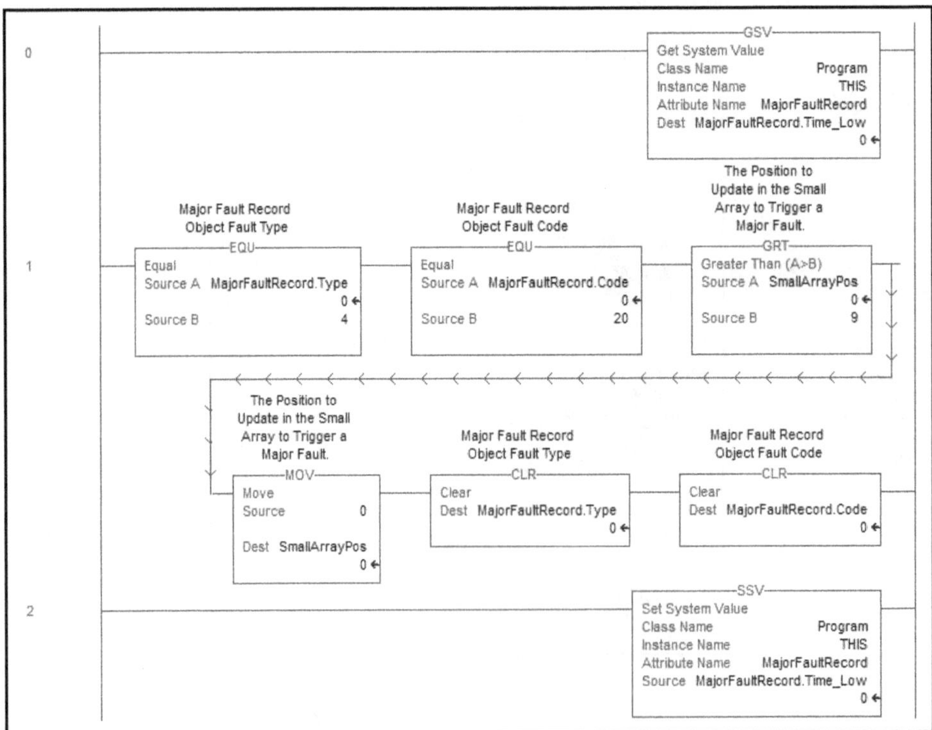

6. Download and run the project on your controller. You will find that when you try to trigger a major fault using the `SmallArrayPos` value, as we did in the previous exercise, the `SmallArrayPos` value will reset to `0` and the controller will no longer trigger a major fault.

In this section, we learned about the numerous ways of capturing faults and troubleshooting controller issues. In the final section of this chapter, we will introduce a handy tool that Rockwell has released to support the troubleshooting of ControlLogix products.

Understanding FactoryTalk TeamONE

In 2017, Rockwell Automation created a powerful app that runs on iOS and Android devices to provide real-time system health and maintenance support of Logix-based solutions. **TeamONE** can be configured as a collaborative team-based tool for tracking maintenance and health issues in an operating plant. It is capable of syncing data to the cloud and running without internet access.

TeamONE can offer troubleshooting guidance and support as faults or issues are identified. The app allows you to look up information on the fault codes and guides you through the process of troubleshooting the issue to resolution. The app includes a ton of embedded resources, which can be extremely valuable when troubleshooting an issue at a remote site. FactoryTalk TeamONE allows plant operators to walk around the plant network and monitor devices from their mobile phones or tablets without even having to open up a control cabinet.

Summary

In this chapter, we provided recommendations for improving your troubleshooting capabilities on the Logix platform. We also learned how to identify and troubleshoot the various types of faults that can occur on a Logix controller. We used Ladder Logic to trigger a major fault, and then we learned how to trap the major fault and prevent the controller from stopping when it occurs. Finally, we introduced the FactoryTalk TeamONE app, provided by Rockwell Automation for troubleshooting Logix issues while in the field from a mobile device.

In the next chapter, we will cover some of the security features that are available within RSLogix/Studio 5000.

Questions

The following questions can be used to test your retention of the concepts introduced in this chapter. You can find the answers to these questions in the back of the book under *Assessments*:

1. What is the term used to describe an error state in a controller that prevents it from executing normally?
2. What is the term used to describe an error state in a controller that still allows the controller to run without interruption?
3. What is the term used to describe an error state in a controller that has arisen due to a problem with an I/O module, which, by default, will not cause the Logix controller to stop executing routines?
4. What is the instruction that retrieves a system value status from the controller and can update a specified destination tag with that value?
5. What is the instruction that updates a controller system value status from a specified source tag?
6. What object-based construct allows you to create custom structures containing a number of different data types to organize data into objects that align with the properties of physical-world equipment?
7. What is the name of the Rockwell Automation app that runs on iOS and Android devices to provide real-time system health and maintenance support of Logix-based solutions?

Further reading

For more information on faults and troubleshooting ControlLogix, refer to *Logix 5000 Controllers Major, Minor, and I/O Faults* at `https://literature.rockwellautomation.com/idc/groups/literature/documents/pm/1756-pm014_-en-p.pdf`.

14
Understanding Cybersecurity Practices in Logix

In this chapter, we'll introduce cybersecurity resources and best practices when working with the ControlLogix platform. Cybersecurity is a vast topic and requires the coordination of multiple teams, technologies, and processes. Rockwell Automation has been working for many years to support ICS cybersecurity through consulting and numerous product features that support ICS cybersecurity. Analyzing all aspects of ICS security and all of Rockwell's ICS cybersecurity offerings is well outside the scope of this book. However, we will detail the best practices and cybersecurity tools as they specifically pertain to Logix control systems. We will also demonstrate where we can find Rockwell product critical updates and security patch information, as well as the security features that are available in the Logix platform.

The following topics will be covered in this chapter:

- The Rockwell Industrial Security Advisory Index
- Introducing RSLogix security features
- Source Key protection or License protection
- The Logix CPU Security Tool
- FactoryTalk AssetCentre
- Understanding Converged Plantwide Ethernet architectures
- Introducing Common Industrial Protocol (CIP) Security for EtherNET/IP
- Implementing CIP Security

We will begin this chapter by introducing the Industrial Security Advisory Index, where you can find the latest Rockwell product security vulnerability reports.

Technical requirements

To complete this chapter, you will need to create a Rockwell Automation support account by visiting the following URL: `https://www.rockwellautomation.com/account/create-account`

The account is free and the material we will be reviewing in this chapter is publicly available to anyone who has registered with Rockwell Automation.

The Rockwell Industrial Security Advisory Index

As cyber threat activity groups and cybersecurity researchers focus more on enumerating and attacking industrial control systems, vendors have been challenged with how best to communicate vulnerabilities in their products to their customer base. Rockwell Automation has demonstrated its commitment to a transparent and supportive dialogue with the vulnerability research and disclosure community.

Rockwell Automation has formed a **Product Security Incident Response Team** (**RA PSIRT**) that initiates its vulnerability management process. Rockwell is one of the first **Industrial Control System** (**ICS**) vendors to align their Vulnerability Handling and Disclosure processes with IEC standards (IEC 29147 and 30111).

Rockwell also works closely with national response organizations, such as the American **Industrial Control System Computer Emergency Response Team** (**ICS-CERT**), to broadcast vulnerabilities to a larger audience.

ICS-CERT has traditionally been the primary source of information for ICS-related vulnerabilities: `https://www.us-cert.gov/ics/alerts`

In 2008, Rockwell first dedicated an area of their online knowledge base to cybersecurity alerts called the **Industrial Security Advisory Index**. The Industrial Security Advisory Index was created to do the following:

- Share newly disclosed vulnerabilities
- Share updates on previously disclosed vulnerabilities
- Share details on firmware and software updates as and when they are made available
- Share security advisories
- Share security recommendations

The Industrial Security Advisory Index provides a running list of Rockwell product vulnerabilities and allows you to subscribe as new alerts come out. The Rockwell Automation Industrial Security Advisory Index can be found at the following URL: `https://rockwellautomation.custhelp.com/app/answers/detail/a_id/54102`

You will need to create a Rockwell Automation support account to access the Industrial Security Advisory Index. You can do this at `https://www.rockwellautomation.com/account/create-account`.

Reviewing the Industrial Security Advisory Index

In the following exercise, we will be using the Rockwell Industrial Security Advisory Index to view the latest Rockwell security advisories. Let's get started:

1. First, you will need to log in to the Rockwell knowledgebase by visiting the following URL and entering your Rockwell support username and password: `https://rockwellautomation.custhelp.com/app/answers/detail/a_id/54102`
2. Once you have logged in to the Rockwell knowledgebase and accessed the Industrial Security Advisory Index, you will see an overview of the advisory's purpose.

The following screenshot shows the screen you'll see when you first open the Industrial Security Advisory Index page. To see the latest security advisories, you need to scroll down the page:

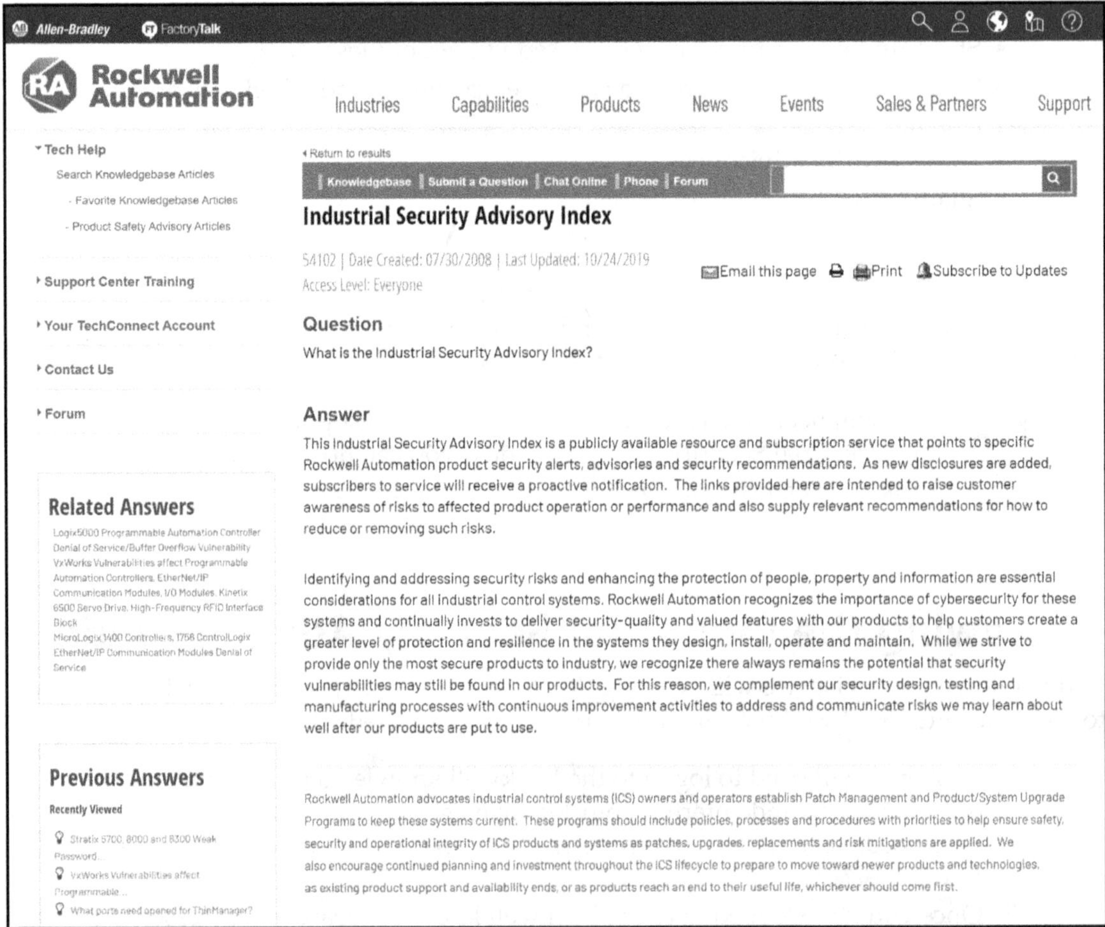

3. As we mentioned earlier, you will need to scroll down the page to see the list of recent advisories. The following screenshot shows what the latest advisories actually look like:

Rockwell Automation Security Notices & Alerts:

- 1088800 - Multiple Vulnerabilities in Arena Simulation Software (UPDATED 19-SEP-2019)
- 1088561 - VxWorks Vulnerabilities affect Programmable Automation Controllers, EtherNet/IP Communication Modules, I/O Modules, Kinetix Servo Drive, High-Frequency RFID Interface Block (UPDATED 09-OCT-2019)
- 1088080 - Ability to gain root-user level access to PanelView 5510 Graphic Terminals (UPDATED 02-AUG-2019)
- 1087194 - Notice Regarding BlueKeep: Windows Security Vulnerability (CVE-2019-0708) (UPDATED 15-AUG-2019)
- 1086288 - Open Redirect Vulnerability MicroLogix, CompactLogix 5370 Controllers
- 1085038 - RSLinx Classic Denial of Service Remote Code Execution Vulnerability
- 1084790 - Vulnerabilities Discovered in PowerMonitor 1000 Monitor (UPDATED 26-AUG-2019)
- 1084268 - EtherNetIP Web Server Module SNMP Service Denial of Service
- 1082688 - Stratix 5950 Denial of Service Vulnerability
- 1082687 - Stratix 54005410570080008300 Denial of Service Vulnerabilities
- 1082686 - Stratix 540054105700 Device Reload Vulnerability
- 1082684 - PowerFlex 525 AC Drives with Embedded EtherNetIP Port Communication Denial of Service (UPDATED 29-MAR-2019)
- 1081928 - MicroLogix 1400 Controllers, 1756 ControlLogix EtherNetIP Communication Modules Denial of Service
- 1075979 - CompactLogix 5370 Programmable Automation Controllers Denial of Service Vulnerabilities
- 1075747 - RSLinx Classic Heap and Buffer Overflow Vulnerabilities
- 1074747 - FactoryTalk Services Platform Denial of Service
- 1073860 - Stratix 5950 Client Certificate Bypass and Denial of Service Vulnerabilities (UPDATED 9-JUL-2018)
- 1073800 - RSLinx Classic and FactoryTalk Linx Gateway Privilege Escalation through Unquoted Service Path
- 1073708 - CompactLogix Compact GuardLogix 5370 Denial of Service (UPDATED 12-JUL-2018)
- 1073588 - Arena Simulation Software Denial of Service
- 1073315 - Stratix 8300 Denial of Service and Remote Code Execution Vulnerabilities
- 1073313 - Stratix 5900 Denial of Service and Remote Code Execution Vulnerabilities (UPDATED 29-MAY-2018)
- 1073268 - Stratix 5400541057008000 Denial of Service and Remote Code Execution Vulnerabilities

4. You can access details on a particular vulnerability or advisory by clicking on the links. Rockwell also provides details about when the articles have been updated, and so always highlights articles that you might need to revisit.

Beyond the disclosure of security vulnerabilities and advisories, Rockwell has created several security features and products, all of which will be detailed in the following sections.

Introducing RSLogix security features

This section introduces several of the security features that are built into the Logix platform. The RSLogix security features are primarily focused around four primary technologies:

- **FactoryTalk Security system**: Creating role-based access for editing projects.
- **Source Key protection or License protection**: Protecting the code stored in the Routines and **Add-On Instructions** (**AOIs**) (intellectual property) of the system integrator or **original equipment manufacturer** (**OEM**).
- **Logix CPU Security Tool**: Protecting a ControlLogix CPU from unauthorized changes.
- **FactoryTalk AssetCentre:** Source code control for Rockwell controllers and human machine interfaces (HMIs)

This solution is already mentioned above, so this sentence is superfluous and should be deleted.. Although not specifically a security product, AssetCentre does provide version control, which can be used to validate a Logix program's integrity.

In the following sections, we will discuss the software tools used to manage security within RSLogix.

FactoryTalk Security system

Within a large-scale automation project, there is often a requirement to segment access permissions. For example, some users would only need write access to edit the **Human Machine Interface** (**HMI**) screens and might have read-only access to the **Programmable Logic Controller** (**PLC**) logic. After all, when working on a distributed automation project, you would not want an HMI designer to accidentally modify logic as they reference code to create user interface elements.

The Rockwell FactoryTalk Security system is used to control access to the logic in your projects with centrally managed, role-based policy enforcement. The Rockwell FactoryTalk Security system relies upon the FactoryTalk Directory database to manage permissions across multiple development tools.

The **FactoryTalk Directory** (**FTD**) is a Rockwell solution for the central management of users, groups, tags, and other resources across an industrial control system solution that is shared between PLC programming software, HMI programming software, and other Rockwell software suites. FTD accounts and user group accounts can be associated with Windows Domain users and groups for ease of management.

FactoryTalk Directory is often compared to Microsoft's Active Directory. Both FactoryTalk Directory and Active Directory centrally manage users, groups, and resources.

Enabling FactoryTalk security involves connecting the Logix software to a FactoryTalk Directory and then enabling security within a Logix project on specific objects and features. FactoryTalk Security integrates a common security model across multiple products within Rockwell's Integrated Architecture ecosystem.

Detailing the role-based permissions and FactoryTalk Security configuration could easily be an entire book. If you have a requirement for fine-grained role-based permissions, I would highly recommend that you refer to the *FactoryTalk Security System Configuration Guide,* which can be found in the *Further reading* section of this chapter.

Source Key protection or License protection

ControlLogix solutions come in a myriad of form factors, and Logix developers can work on a variety of end use cases. At the end of the day, a control system created using Rockwell Integrated Architecture tools is a piece of software and a form of intellectual property. Some control system developers (much like traditional software developers) may wish to protect their intellectual property. For example, a manufacturer of an industry-specific and specialized pump control system might sell a packaged solution that contains the pump and control system in one unit (also known as an **Original Electronic Manufacturer** (**OEM**) solution). The purchaser of an OEM pump solution probably doesn't care too much about the underlying control logic that manages the pump, as long as it works.

The pump manufacturer also might not want its competitors to learn how their control scheme works or for a third party to be able to easily replicate their solutions. For such situations, Rockwell provides Source Key protection and License protection, which requires a specific key or license file to edit, access, or even run Logix programs.

Routines and add-on instructions can be **locked** using License Source Protection. Once a routine has been **locked**, its code is compiled to bytecode and then encrypted. The code is unencrypted by the controller at execution time using a license key that has been inserted into the controller.

The specific details of setting up source code protection are outside the scope of this book, but if you are interested in learning more, I would recommend that you read *Logix 5000 Controllers Security*, which can be found in the *Further reading* section of this chapter.

The Logix CPU Security Tool

The Logix CPU Security Tool allows the user to lock the controller so that the program cannot be modified. It has been replaced in newer versions of the product with Source Key protection, but it is important to still cover this topic as it is still common to encounter this feature in operating plants.

The Logix CPU Security Tool is a legacy solution and supported only in Logix Designer application versions 17, 18, and 19. It is not supported in versions 20 and later.

In the older version of Logix Designer, it was possible to password protect the program running on the controller and prevent unauthorized access or modification. Once a controller has been secured with the Logix CPU Security Tool, you will not be permitted to go online with the controller until the security is removed.

Adding and removing the CPU security requires you to enter a password into the Logix CPU Security Tool. The Logix CPU Security Tool is not installed by default but can be found on legacy installation CDs of RSLogix (versions 17–19) under tools: `Tools\LogixCPUSecurityTool\RSLogix CPU Security Tool Installer.msi`

FactoryTalk AssetCentre

FactoryTalk AssetCentre is a centralized source code repository for automation projects. It provides a mechanism for storing, versioning, tracking, and reporting on the software and configuration of PLCs, HMIs, network equipment, and other assets. It allows you to track what has changed between updates of a PLC program and whether rollback changes are required. From a cybersecurity perspective, it could help in situations where unauthorized changes were made to a PLC program.

AssetCentre will allow you to perform a *diff* (difference) on two versions of the same program to determine what has changed. AssetCentre can also provide support in disaster recovery situations where PLC programs are being reloaded, so you need to ensure you are loading the latest version of the PLC program. AssetCentre is also capable of performing automated backups of the programs that are actively running on the controllers, which can also support disaster recovery situations.

The FactoryTalk AssetCentre is a solution for versioning, securing, managing, tracking, and reporting automation-related asset information across an entire facility. FactoryTalk AssetCentre can be added to an industrial operations workflow without additional management oversight or work from employees. The customers I have worked with who have implemented this solution absolutely love it.

In the next section, we will introduce the Converged Plantwide Ethernet architectures that have been created by Rockwell and its partners to support best practices and secure ICS network architectures.

Understanding Converged Plantwide Ethernet architectures

Rockwell has worked closely with Cisco and Panduit to develop **Converged Plantwide Ethernet** (**CPwE**) architectures. These CPwEs are reference architectures and implementation guides that have been developed and tested by the expertise of Rockwell Automation, Panduit, and Cisco. Rockwell has also created a customized version of Cisco-managed switches and industrial firewalls under the Rockwell Stratix product line. The Stratix brand is designed to integrate with Rockwell products and protocols.

Rockwell has worked to create a **graphical user interface** (**GUI**) for the majority of the common configuration settings required for Stratix switches and firewalls. Purchasing normal Cisco equipment (non-Stratix branded equipment) will require programming using the Cisco **command-line interface** (**CLI**) rather than the Stratix Device Manager GUI or Studio 5000 Logix Designer. When designing a large-scale control network, it is beneficial to have these detailed reference architectures to follow. Addressing industrial cybersecurity risk requires a holistic approach to incorporating people, processes, and technology.

By following the architectures recommended in the CPwEs, the network architecture of your ICS solution will be well-positioned to reduce industrial cyber risk. I would highly recommend that you check out the Industrial Network Design guides on the Rockwell Automation website, *Industrial Network Design Guides*: `https://www.rockwellautomation.com/en_NA/capabilities/industrial-networks/technical-data/overview.page`

In the next section, we will introduce another important cybersecurity development from Rockwell Automation called **Common Industrial Protocol** (**CIP**) Security for EtherNet/IP. CIP Security provides protocol-level security for Logix-based industrial solutions.

Introducing Common Industrial Protocol (CIP) Security for EtherNet/IP

Within industrial control networks, there has traditionally been an inherent level of trust between devices in the network. Devices on the control network were able to freely exchange data and send commands to each other without any authentication, authorization, or encryption. However, since threat actors have increased their focus on ICS networks over the past few decades, there is a growing concern around the lack of security of ICS network protocols.

Today, there are even tools such as EtherSploit-IP (`https://github.com/thiagoralves/EtherSploit-IP`) that can be easily leveraged by an attacker to create havoc within an ICS network without the need for understanding the industrial control systems protocols or software. So, how do we defend against tools such as EtherSploit-IP, which take advantage of the insure-by-design nature of ICS networks? We could start by implementing secure protocols that implement authentication and integrity checks. The **Open DeviceNet Vendor Association** (**ODVA**), the organization responsible for writing the Common Industrial Protocol standard, first published their specification for a secure version of CIP in 2015.

This security specification is called **CIP Security**, and it added the following features to the EtherNet/IP transport layer:

- Endpoint authentication using trusted X.509 certificates or pre-shared keys.
- Integrity and authentication of messages to ensure messages have not been tampered with during transport.
- The optional encryption of messages to prevent unauthorized listeners from reading the content CIP messages.

In April 2019, the ODVA published an update to the *CIP Security* standard that further enhanced the capabilities of devices to *pull* their own security certificates, which reduces the overhead of updating and maintaining the security layer. ODVA is actively working toward their next *CIP Security* publication, which will add support for non-repudiation (the assurance that someone cannot deny the validity of a message) and device authorization (only allowing authorized devices to communicate on the EtherNet/IP network).

The ultimate vision of *CIP Security* is for the EtherNet/IP devices to self-manage security and effectively secure themselves from an attack in a manner that is mostly transparent to the programmer. These enhancements are based on the IT industry's protocol security best practices and are compatible with the Rockwell Stratix (CISCO) networking equipment. Proper implementation of CIP Security in your control network would prevent an attacker from connecting to the network and leveraging a malicious tool such as EtherSploit-IP.

In the next section, we will discuss the requirements for implementing a CIP Security solution in a ControlLogix network.

Implementing CIP Security

In this section, we will discuss the devices that natively support the new CIP Security protocol. CIP Security is still a relatively new part of the CIP protocol. Only the latest ControlLogix EtherNet/IP cards and Controllers (L8) support the creation of a *CIP Security Zone.*

The following EtherNetIP card models support CIP Security:

- 1756-EN4TR
- 1756-EN4TRK
- 1756-/EN2TRXT
- 1756-EN4TRXT

The following ControlLogix Controllers (5580 and firmware version 32+) support CIP Security:

- 1756-L81E
- 1756-L82E
- 1756-L83E
- 1756-L84E
- 1756-L85E
- Kinetix 5700 drive

Using CIP Security supported devices, the FactoryTalk Policy Manager software and FactoryTalk System Services allow CIP Security to be implemented in your ICS network. Implementing the CIP Security protocol requires interaction from a number of different Rockwell software products and is outside the scope of this book.

For more information on how to implement a *CIP Security* solution, please refer to the *Further reading* section of this chapter, where you can find a link to the document named *CIP Security with Rockwell Automation Products*.

Summary

In this chapter, we reviewed some of the ICS cybersecurity resources that have been provided by Rockwell Automation and the tools that can be used to prevent unauthorized project views or edits. Rockwell has invested heavily in its cybersecurity practices over the past decade and has come to the table with numerous products, services, and guidance to help protect their customers from cyber threats.

In the next chapter, *Building a Robot Bartender in Logix*, we will put all the pieces we have learned throughout this book together and use them to build a sample application. We will be working through the steps to create an operational robot bartender.

Questions

The following questions can be used to test your retention of the concepts introduced in this chapter. You can find the answers to these questions in the back of the book, under *Assessments*:

1. What mechanisms can be used to lock Routines and AOIs with Source Protection?
2. What Rockwell Automation tool allows the user to lock the controller so that the program cannot be modified?
3. What is the Rockwell centralized source code repository for automation projects that provides a mechanism for storing, versioning, tracking, and reporting on the software and configuration of PLCs, HMIs, network equipment, and other assets?
4. What is the name of the reference architectures and implementation guides that have been developed and tested by the expertise of Rockwell Automation, Panduit, and Cisco?
5. What is the name of the ODVA standard for EtherNet/IP devices to self-manage security in a manner that is mostly transparent to the programmer?

Further reading

Cybersecurity is a complex subject within industrial control networks. Fortunately, Rockwell has provided a number of guides that can help us with configuring the security features within the Logix platform:

- *FactoryTalk Security System Configuration Guide*: `https://literature.rockwellautomation.com/idc/groups/literature/documents/qs/ftsec-qs001_-en-e.pdf`
- *Logix 5000 Controllers Security*: `https://literature.rockwellautomation.com/idc/groups/literature/documents/pm/1756-pm016_-en-p.pdf`
- *Configuring System Security Features*: `https://literature.rockwellautomation.com/idc/groups/literature/documents/um/secure-um001_-en-p.pdf`
- *EtherNet/IP Secure Communications*: `https://literature.rockwellautomation.com/idc/groups/literature/documents/um/enet-um003_-en-p.pdf`
- *CIP Security with Rockwell Automation Products*: `https://literature.rockwellautomation.com/idc/groups/literature/documents/at/secure-at001_-en-p.pdf`
- *1756 ControlLogix Communication Module Specifications*: `https://literature.rockwellautomation.com/idc/groups/literature/documents/td/1756-td003_-en-e.pdf`

15
Building a Robot Bartender in Logix

In this chapter, we will build our very own control system from scratch. We will start by acquiring the required equipment and the software, and then move on to the project ladder logic and electrical wiring to create our very own robotic bartender. The robot bartender will allow patrons to press an industrial push button to select from a menu of beverages.

After a drink is selected, the robot bartender will use peristaltic dosing pumps to dispense the appropriate amount of liquid through food-grade silicone tubes into a glass. If you realize that you have selected the wrong beverage, you can always hit the emergency stop button to shut down the current beverage that is being dispensed. It is a very simple and yet extremely rewarding project.

In the first section of this chapter, we will review the technical requirements for building our robot bartender.

Technical requirements

To complete this chapter, you will need to create a Rockwell Support account by visiting `https://www.rockwellautomation.com/account/create-account`.

Creating an account is free, and the material we will be reviewing in this chapter is publicly available to anyone who is registered with Rockwell Automation.

You will also need a copy of RSLogix or Studio 5000 to program your project. You can either purchase this from your local distributor or request a time-limited trial version. You can find a local distributor for Rockwell products at `https://locator.rockwellautomation.com/`.

To complete the robot bartender build in this chapter, you will also need to have several tools and purchase some Rockwell Automation equipment. The required tools for this chapter can be found in the *Tools you will need for this project* section of this chapter. The *ControlLogix equipment budget* section in this chapter will give you a good idea of the ControlLogix parts required and their cost.

Building and housing a robot bartender

In this section, we will cover the ControlLogix parts, process control parts list, and tools required to build this project. We will also cover an estimated budget of what you can expect to pay for all these parts. eBay is a great source for decommissioned **Programmable Logic Controller** (**PLC**) equipment. Many plants and factories will rip out automation equipment that is still fully functional during upgrades and modernization efforts. There are many resellers who go through the process of properly testing the equipment and ensuring it works properly before shipping it off. Many of the tools and other pieces of equipment can be purchased on Amazon.

The following is a picture of a drink selector I have created for this build:

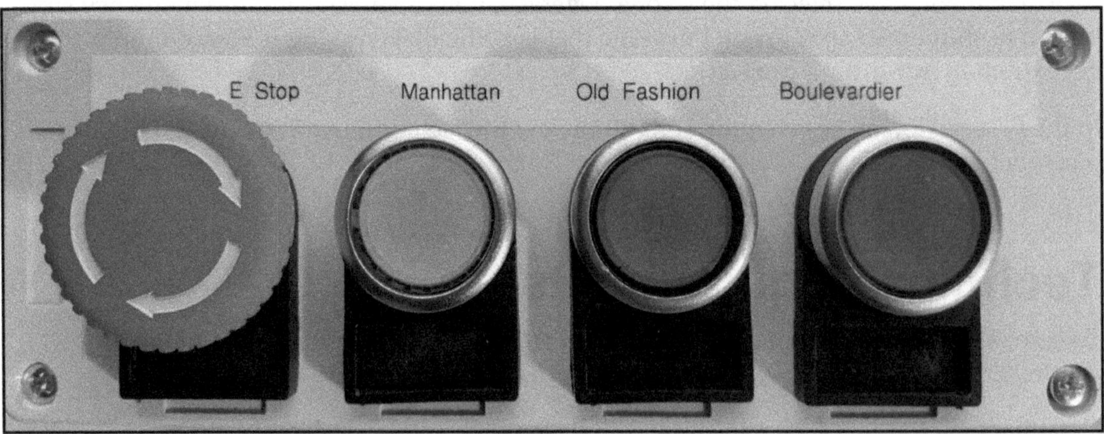

In the next section, we will detail the tools you will need for this project.

Tools you will need for this project

To build our robot bartender, we are going to need several tools. Many of the tools used in this project are commonly found in your home toolkit, but there are a few other tools that are not so common. Although it is not a requirement to have all of the tools on this list, I am sure you will find that they will make the build process go much smoother. Often, having the right tool for the job can save you a considerable amount of time and reduce the risk of damaging your equipment.

Here is a list of tools you will need during the robot bartender build process:

- Electrical tape
- Wire-strippers
- A flat-head screwdriver – 3.2 mm (1/8 in)
- A Phillips-head screwdriver – 8 mm (5/16 in)
- A Phillips-head screwdriver – 3.2 mm (1/8 in)
- Scissors
- An Ethernet cable
- A terminal wire ratchet crimping tool (for creating clean connector wires that can be used to connect to the PLC)
- Insulated terminal wire connectors
- A terminal wire ratchet crimping tool for spade connectors (for creating clean connectors for the 12 V dosing motors)
- A terminal wire spade connector
- A drill
- Hole saw drill bits

I was able to acquire all of these tools on Amazon within a few days of ordering them. In the next section, I will discuss how to approach mounting the robot bartender's equipment.

Housing the bartender

In this section, I will briefly touch on some options you might want to consider for mounting your robot bartender. I have used metal project boxes in the past with success.

The following is a picture of one of my earlier robot bartender builds mounted in a project box:

Bookshelves are also a great option as you can easily mount the PLC and dosing pumps to the back-side of the bookshelf. The following is a picture of a 50-pump robot bartender I created and mounted inside a bookshelf. I'm also working on a new version of the robot bartender that is entirely mounted inside a standing refrigerator:

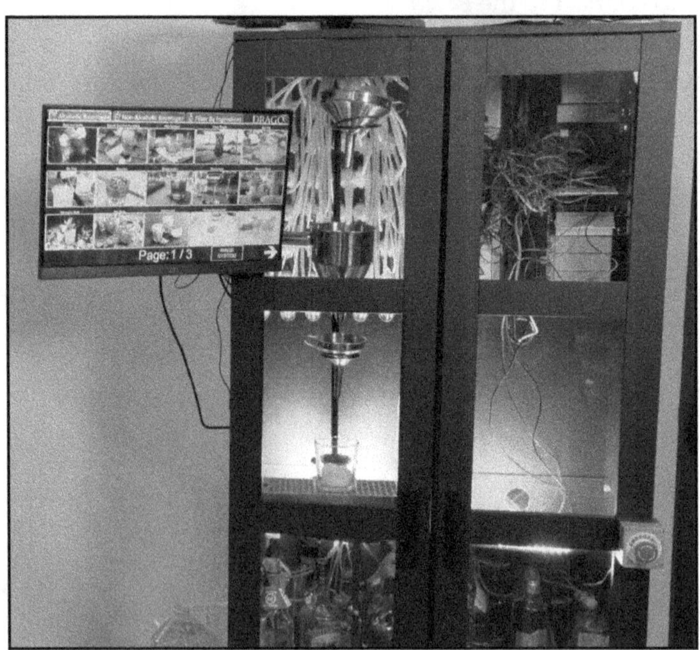

The preceding bartenders use a **Human Machine Interface** (**HMI**) touchscreen, rather than a push-button selector. A sturdy, industrial push-button selector will work fine for our purposes.

In the next section, we will discuss the ControlLogix PLC parts that we will need to build our project, as well as how to acquire them and what you can expect to pay for them.

Acquiring ControlLogix parts for this project

You will need to purchase several ControlLogix PLC components to create the robot bartender. As this project isn't meant for industrial use, it's fine to use lower-cost, used components. I have always had great luck purchasing used equipment off eBay. Rockwell equipment is quite rugged and meant to run for years. I have never purchased a used PLC part that was dead on arrival from the internet, but perhaps I have just been lucky. Damage to industrial control equipment happens after it reaches my lab.

I usually try to buy an entire rack that has been pulled from a control system. Sometimes, you can find Rockwell racks that are loaded with CPUs, Ethernet cards, and many modules for a reasonable price. Often, in these packages, I find cards I am familiar with, which gives me the opportunity to play around with them. If that strategy fails, it is perfectly fine to purchase each required component separately.

The following sections detail the bare-minimum PLC components you will need to build the robot bartender.

Purchasing a ControlLogix 1756-PA75 rack power supply

The 1756-PA75 chassis power supply provides a clean and stable power source to the chassis and cards of our ControlLogix control system.

The following is a photo of a 1756-PA75 power supply that has been removed from a rack:

The 1756-PA75 power supply attaches to the left side of the ControlLogix rack and provides power to the CPU and control modules. For our project, it will still be necessary to purchase dedicated power supplies to run our bartender pumps as this power supply only provides power to the backplane and any cards attached to it. It is common to purchase a power supply already attached to a rack, which is perfectly fine for our purposes. Now that we have the power supply, we will need a rack to attach it to and power.

In the next section, we will discuss some of the various rack sizes available and make a selection for our project.

Selecting a ControlLogix chassis

The ControlLogix chassis is where we mount the processor and cards for our industrial-grade robot bartender.

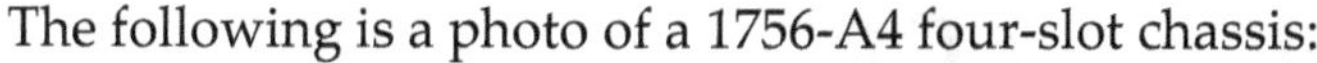

The following is a photo of a 1756-A4 four-slot chassis:

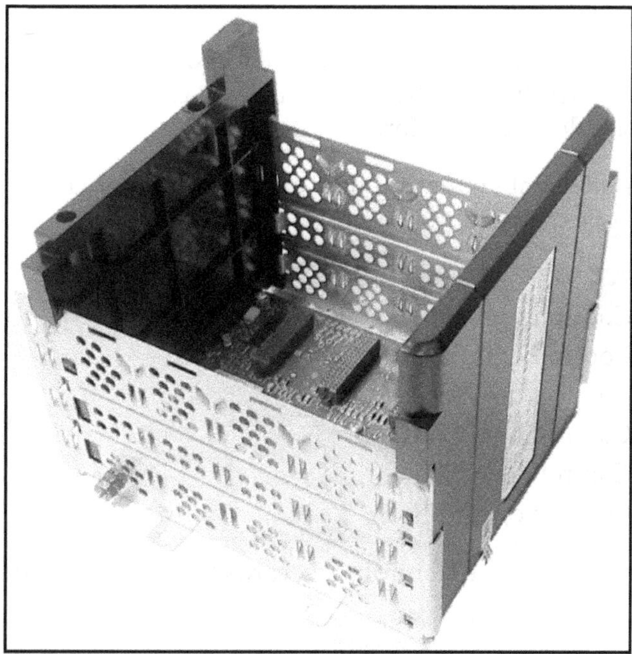

A four-slot chassis (also referred to as a rack) is the smallest size that is sold as part of the ControlLogix platform. To create our robot bartender, we will use all four slots. However, any size rack will work for our purposes. For a test lab setup such as this, the larger the rack you can get, the better. However, if you plan to mount the rack inside a cabinet, you need to ensure it is of an appropriate size for the installation you have in mind.

The following chassis backplane sizes are available in the ControlLogix standard family:

- 1756-A4 four-slot rack
- 1756-A7 seven-slot rack
- 1756-A10 10-slot rack
- 1756-A13 13-slot rack
- 1756-A17 17-slot rack

Now that we have our rack and power supply picked out, we can focus on acquiring the brains of our bartender—the ControlLogix CPU—in the next section.

Selecting a ControlLogix CPU

We will also require a ControlLogix CPU for our robot bartender project. It doesn't really matter which one you use as this will be a very small project that will not push the limits of any ControlLogix CPU. The best ControlLogix CPU you can acquire for the least amount of money is what you should be aiming for.

The following is a list of suitable ControlLogix CPUs that can be easily found on eBay (from least expensive to most expensive):

- 1756-L55/A
- 1756-L61 ControlLogix 5561
- 1756-L62 ControlLogix 5562
- 1756-L63 ControlLogix 5563
- 1756-L71 ControlLogix 5571
- 1756-L72 ControlLogix 5571
- 1756-L73 ControlLogix 5571

I will be using the least-expensive ControlLogix cards for the robot bartender—the 1756-L55/A:

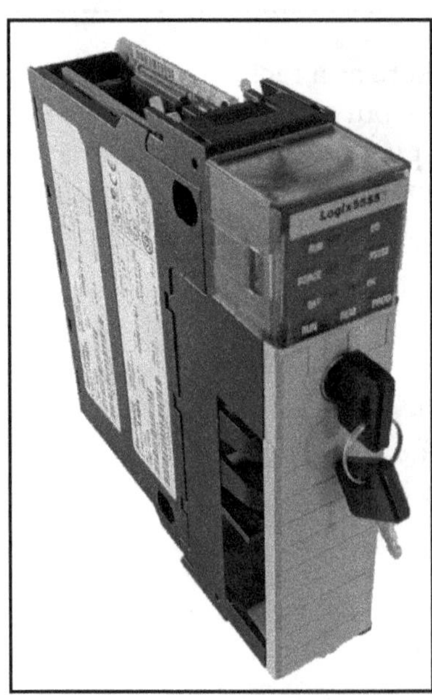

We now have a power supply, a rack, and a CPU for our robot bartender project. However, we want to be able to program it and connect to it using an EtherNet/IP card. Of course, it is possible to build and program this project using the serial connection on the CPU module; an EtherNet/IP card opens up lots of opportunities for future additions of things similar to HMIs, such as FactoryTalk ME or FactoryTalk SE.

In the next section, we will look at an EtherNet/IP card for our solution. As we learned in `Chapter 6`, *Industrial Network Communications*, there are many different communication mediums and protocols used within the Rockwell ecosystem. The EtherNet/IP card will allow our robot bartender to communicate over a traditional IP-based network.

Selecting a ControlLogix EtherNet/IP card

As mentioned in the last section, we could program and manage our ControlLogix program using a serial cable connection; however, having an IP-based connection is much more practical. In most cases, a ControlLogix EtherNet/IP card is required for us to connect to our controller using an Ethernet connection. Although it is possible to purchase L8 CPUs that have an integrated Ethernet connection, it is much cheaper to purchase a used CPU and an EtherNet/IP card separately. With that being said, when you are buying a new ControlLogix CPU, it is cheaper to buy the L8 than an L7 and an EtherNet/IP card separately.

The following is a photo of the EtherNet/IP card that I will be using for the Robot Bartender project:

I will be using the 1756-ENBT/EtherNet/IP module, although any 1756 Ethernet communication modules will suffice. Now that we have our power supply, rack, CPU, and network connectivity sorted out, we can focus on the parts of the solution that interact with our bartender equipment.

In the next section, we will discuss the options available to us for ControlLogix digital output modules.

Selecting a ControlLogix digital output module

A digital output module will be used in this project to run the pumps used by the robot bartender. Each pump will be connected to a digital output channel and a 12 V **Direct Current** (**DC**) power supply that will energize it. There is a wide variety of Allen-Bradley digital output cards available, and it is important that we select the right one for our project. When it comes to digital output cards (and digital input cards), there are two main categories within ControlLogix:

- **Alternating Current** (**AC**) digital output cards: Always begin with 1756-OA
- **DC** digital output cards: Always begin with 1756-OB or 1756-OV

Because we will be using 12 V DC low-voltage (and low-cost) pumps for our project, we need to select a digital output card that supports a voltage range from 10 V DC to 3O V DC. You must be careful when purchasing a DC output card for this project as many will not support our low-voltage requirements as most systems typically use 24 V DC.

The following is a list of digital output cards that are well suited for our purposes:

- The 1756-OB8 8-output DC (10 V – 30 V) output module
- The 1756-OB8EI 8-output DC (10 V – 30 V) electronically fused isolated output module
- The 1756-OB8I 8-output DC (10 V – 30 V) isolated output module
- The 1756-OB16E and 1756-OB16EK 16-output DC (10 V – 31.2 V) electronically fused output modules
- The 1756-OB16IEF and 1756-OB16IEFK 16-output DC (10 V – 30 V) electronically protected, sinking, or sourcing, isolated fast output modules
- The 1756-OB16IEFS 16-output DC (10 V –30 V) scheduled electronically protected, sinking, or sourcing, isolated fast output module

- The 1756-OV16E 16-output DC (10 V – 30 V) electronically fused sinking output module
- The 1756-OB32 and 1756-OB32K 32-output DC (10 V – 31.2 V) output modules
- The 1756-OV32E 32-output DC (10 V – 30 V) electronically fused sinking output module

If you are able to acquire one of these cards, you should also ensure that the module includes a **Removable Terminal Block** (**RTB**). Otherwise, you will need to source a removable terminal block that allows you to connect wires to the card. RTBs will be covered later in this chapter in the *Using RTBs* section.

In the preceding list of digital output cards, there are several card features that we have yet to discuss in detail. In the following section, we will break down these features for your reference as many of them will impact you as you build your robot bartender.

Understanding the ControlLogix digital output module features

There is a myriad of ControlLogix card features that changes the letter designation at the end of the product catalog number. In the following sections, we will explore the subset of specific features commonly found in ControlLogix digital output modules. By the end of this section, you will be able to identify the features included in a ControlLogix digital output module by merely looking at its model number.

I will detail these features in the following sections. Let's start with electronically fused digital outputs.

Working with electronically fused digital outputs

Electronically fused outputs (denoted by an *E* in the product catalog identifier) are a desirable feature to have in a digital output card as they protect the card's outputs from getting "blown" by using a fuse that can be reset in RSLogix. In a lab environment, when you are experimenting with different wiring and design ideas, it is pretty easy to accidentally short a connection and blow one of your digital outputs. I have personally blown a bunch of digital outputs using my multimeter, so be careful.

If you are not using an electronically fused card, those blown outputs are dead and can never come back. If your card has electronically fused outputs and you short the outputs, causing the fuse to trip, you can reset it from the card properties in RSLogix. If you find that your electronically fused digital output card is no longer working properly, you should first try resetting the fuses.

As the following screenshot demonstrates, you can find the **Reset** button for the fuses under the **Diagnostics** tab of the digital output module properties:

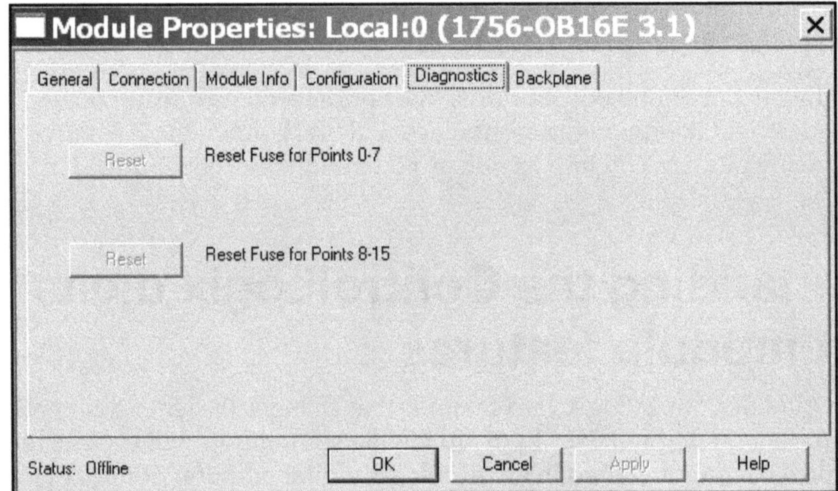

Warning: Resetting the fuse while your equipment is running can cause an unexpected operation. When an electronic fuse is reset, the outputs will often energize right away.

In the following section, we will introduce isolated output modules and detail their features and letter designation.

Isolated output modules

Isolated output modules (denoted by an *I* in the product catalog identifier) allow you to wire in a separate power source for each channel on the card. This differs from a normal (non-isolated output) module, which has one or more shared power sources for all the channels on the card. It is important to note that the wiring for an isolated card will differ from the non-isolated card.

In the next section, we will discuss the differences between sinking and sourcing modules.

Sinking versus sourcing modules

A basic digital output module **sources**, which means it provides a common (or shared) source for power to the individual digital outputs. The alternative to sourcing is **sinking**, which provides a common negative terminal, rather than a source for power. Selecting a sinking or sourcing module will impact the types of equipment that you can attach to it.

Fast output modules

Fast output modules (denoted by an *F* in the product catalog identifier) can trigger an on-and-off output faster than a normal output module.

The following table details the typical difference in the response time of a fast output module versus a normal output module:

	Normal Output Delay Time	Fast Output Delay Time
Off to on	60 μs nom/1 ms max	14 μs nom/23 μs max
On to off	200 μs nom/1 ms max	14 μs nom/23 μs max

As the table illustrates, a fast module can be anywhere from 5 to 100 times faster than a normal module. We also detailed some of the output modules features that are available and their letter designations.

In the next section, we will cover digital input modules.

Selecting a ControlLogix digital input module

The digital input module will be used in this project to execute different recipes in place of an HMI. Each recipe will be associated with a push button that will trigger the digital output cards to run a recipe. To avoid the cost of adding a second power supply, we will select a digital input module that also supports 12 V DC.

The following is a list of digital input cards that are well suited for our robot bartender project:

- The 1756-IB16 and 1756-IB16K 16-input DC (10 V – 31.2 V) input modules
- The 1756-IB16D and 1756-IB16DK 16-input DC (10 V – 30 V) diagnostic input modules
- The 1756-IB16I and 1756-IB16IK 16-input DC (10 V – 30 V) isolated input modules
- The 1756-IB16IF and 1756-IB16IFK 16-input DC (10 V – 30 V) sinking or sourcing isolated fast input modules
- The 1756-IV16 and 1756-IV16K 16-input DC (10 V – 30 V) sourcing input modules
- The 1756-IB32 and 1756-IB32K 32-input DC (10 V – 31.2 V) input modules
- The 1756-IV32 and 1756-IV32K 32-input DC (10 V – 31.2 V) sourcing input modules

Many of the features in the preceding list of digital input cards have been covered already. In the following section, we will break down the features that have not previously been covered and anything that is unique to digital input cards that we should understand prior to constructing our robot bartender.

Understanding the ControlLogix digital input module features

ControlLogix digital input modules share many of the same features and functions as their digital output siblings. There is, however, one difference—the diagnostic input module, which will be detailed in the following section.

Diagnostic input modules

A diagnostic input module (denoted by a *D* in the product catalog identifier) provides troubleshooting functionality that can detect when a wire is disconnected and can latch the value when an error occurs (used to diagnose intermittent issues). The diagnostic options are visible in the digital input module properties. The following screenshot illustrates the differences between a normal digital input module (on the left) and a diagnostic input module (on the right):

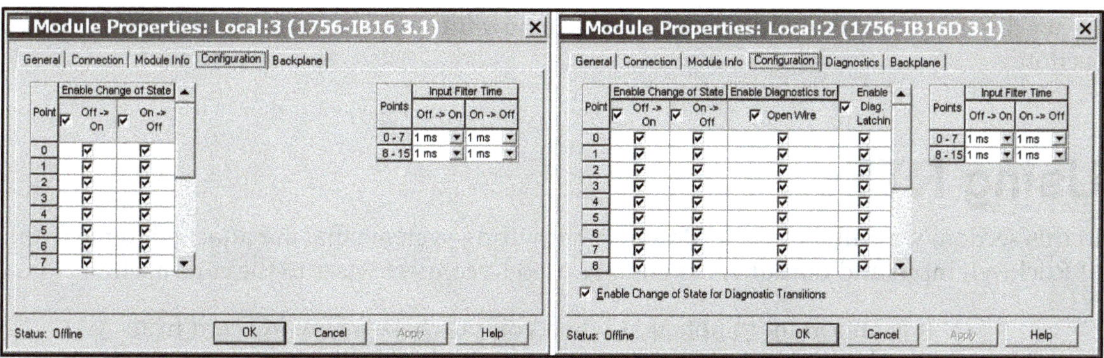

The following screenshot shows the contents of the additional **Diagnostics** tab that appears and allows the user to reset any latched diagnostic inputs:

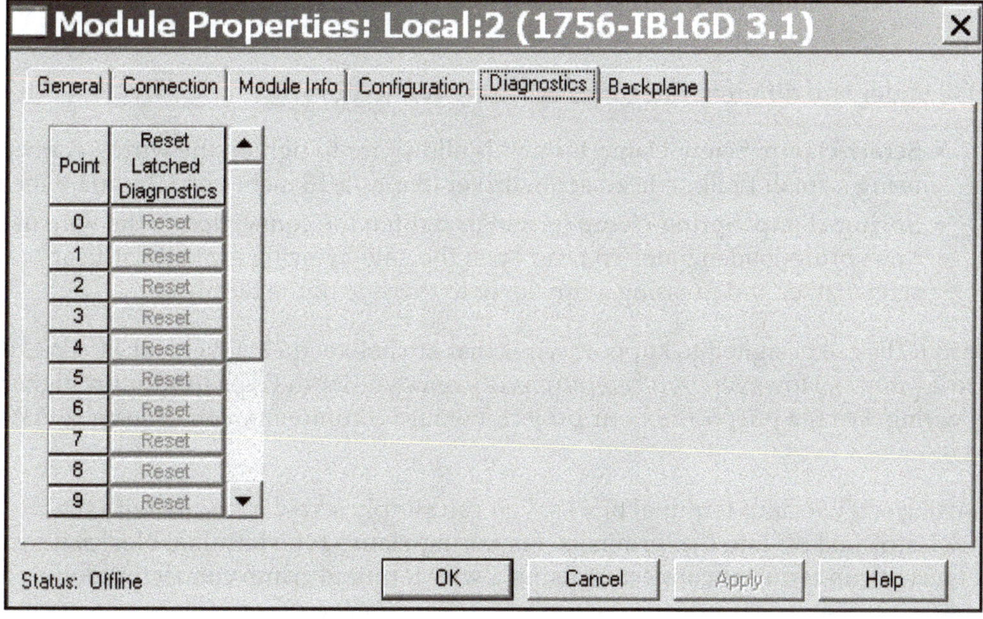

We now have the power supply, rack, CPU, digital output, and digital input cards selected for our robot bartender. The next step is to wire our digital input and digital output cards to the dosing pumps and push buttons to run our robot bartender process. To connect devices to our input and output cards, we will need to use ControlLogix RTBs, which provide the mechanism for attaching wires to our ControlLogix cards.

As we discussed earlier in this chapter, we will now introduce RTBs in the following section.

Using RTBs

In this section, we will discuss RTBs and other wiring systems that are attached to the front of Rockwell input and output cards and are used to connect wires to the card itself.

It is important to note that when you purchase a new I/O card from Rockwell, it will not necessarily come with an RTB. You will need to select and purchase an appropriate terminal block faceplate for each card. However, when you purchase a used I/O card, it will often come with the RTB installed (and quite often, with the wires still attached). You should try and note the particular RTB that you are purchasing as it may change how you wire your card.

RTBs fall under two different categories of wiring connection:

- **Screw-clamp**: Screw-clamp terminals allow you to tighten the wiring connection using a small Phillips-head screwdriver (8 mm/5/16 inches or 3.2mm/1/8 inches).
- **Spring-clamp**: Spring-clamp terminals tighten the connection to the wire using a tiny spring-loaded gate. You can open the gate by using a small flat-head screwdriver and pressing a tiny lever to the side of the terminal.

Standard RTBs are designed to support wires that are between 22 AWG and 14 AWG (0.3 mm2 to 2.1 mm2). However, you can purchase extended-depth RTBs to support higher-gauge wiring. For the purposes of our project, I would recommend you acquire 18 AWG wiring.

When using screw-clamp terminal blocks, you can simply screw in a wire with the insulation stripped off into the terminals. For spring-clamp-type terminal blocks, it's easier if you create clean terminal connectors using a wire terminal crimp connector tool.

In the following section, we will detail the most commonly used RTBs and briefly detail their characteristics.

Commonly used RTBs

In this section, we will detail the various form-factors for RTBs. The following table details the four most commonly used Rockwell RTBs for digital input and digital output cards:

	Terminal Count	Clamp Style	Screw Driver Required
1756-TBNH	20 (suitable for 8 or 16 terminal input/output cards)	Screw-clamp	Phillips-head 8 mm (5/16 in)
1756-TBSH	20 (suitable for 8 or 16 terminal input/output cards)	Spring-clamp	Flat-head 3.2 mm (1/8 in)
1756-TBCH	36 (suitable for 32 terminal input/output cards)	Screw-clamp	Phillips-head 3.2 mm (1/8 in)
1756-TBS6H	36 (suitable for 32 terminal input/output cards)	Spring-clamp	Flat-head 3.2 mm (1/8 in)

The 1756-TBE RTB provides an extended-depth terminal block housing for higher-gauge wiring.

It is often difficult to work with the 36 terminal RTBs in practice. Accessing all of the terminal inputs can become very difficult after adding all 32+ wires to the cards. If you are planning to use a 32 input card, you should consider using a Bulletin 1492 in-panel I/O wiring system module or cable, which we will discuss in the next section.

In-panel I/O wiring system modules and cables

Rockwell also sells Bulletin 1492 in-panel I/O wiring system modules and cables, which are pre-wired RTBs that are connected via a cable to an external wiring block.

The following is a photo of the 1492 cable and the 1492-IFM40F 40-point digital **Interface Module** (**IFM**):

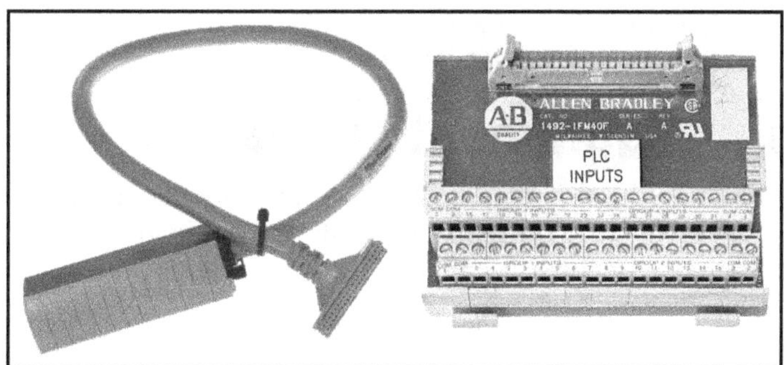

Rather than wiring a 32-input RTB directly on the card, you can leverage a pre-wired cable system, such as the preceding, to move the wiring to larger terminals on a DIN rail-mounted module. This alone can save many hours of wiring and is well worth the extra cost, especially when you consider troubleshooting and testing time.

If you are planning to use a 32-input digital input or output card, using a pre-wired cable system is a tremendous benefit. When selecting your pre-wired cable and IFMs, you must ensure that the number of inputs/outputs match the cable and IFM.

Here, we learned about the various options available for wiring modules within ControlLogix. We have now completed a review of the different ControlLogix hardware devices we will be using in our project. In the next section, we will list the required parts and estimate the total cost of the parts required for this project.

Estimating a robot bartender project budget

This section will detail what you can expect to pay for each component and we will come up with an estimated project budget. Many of the Rockwell components can be acquired on eBay for a fraction of their original cost. As we are building our control system for learning purposes only, there is no need to buy brand-new equipment. Of course, when building a real-world control system, you would want to purchase new original equipment from Rockwell and not use parts from unknown or untrusted sources such as eBay. I will be using the prices of components on eBay at the time that this book was written to estimate the cost of components.

As mentioned earlier in this chapter, if you are buying used components, you can either try to purchase the components separately or try to purchase an entire used rack that has all the I/O cards and components already included.

The following section will detail the minimum ControlLogix specific components you will require.

ControlLogix equipment budget

In this section, we will detail the ControlLogix PLC components you will require to build the robot bartender. Feel free to acquire the alternative components that were listed earlier in this chapter.

The items listed here represent the bare-minimum required components. All prices in the following table are in US dollars:

Component	Description	Cost
1756-PA75	ControlLogix rack power supply	$250.00
1756-A4	ControlLogix four-slot rack (feel free to purchase a larger one)	$250.00
1756-ENBT/A	ControlLogix EtherNet/IP module	$250.00
1756-OB16E	ControlLogix electronically fused digital output module with 16 outputs DC (10 V – 31.2 V)	$50.00
1756-IB16	ControlLogix digital input module with 16 inputs DC (10 V – 31.2 V)	$150.00
1756-L55/A	ControlLogix processor (CPU)	$250.00
1756-TBSH	ControlLogix spring-clamp RTBs and digital input card	$50.00
1756-TBSH	ControlLogix spring-clamp RTBs and digital output card	$50.00

The total cost of this ControlLogix equipment is US$1300.00.

As we are using only 16 inputs for both our digital input and digital output cards. There is no need to purchase a pre-wired cable and interface module. However, if you would like to go down this route, it will likely cost an additional US$300.00.

In the next section, we will detail the other required to make the robot bartender.

Robot bartender process equipment

Next, we will detail the components that will make up the robot bartender's process equipment. These will manage the pumping of liquids, the wiring, the tubing, and the process control buttons.

The following table details the other components needed to build the industrial robot bartender, their quantity, and their estimated cost:

Component	Description	Quantity	Cost
Dosing pumps	INTLLAB 12 V DC peristaltic pump 170~460 mL/min (6.4 mm ID x 9.6 mm OD)	6	$180.00
Silicone tubes	Food-grade silicone tubing 5mm ID X 7 mm OD 9.84 ft	6	$60
Bus bar	12-position dual-row 600 V 15 A screw terminal strip blocks	2	$10.00
Push buttons	LA38-11 heavy-duty panel-mount momentary push-button switches (22 mm)	5	$35.00
ESD button	Panel-mount emergency stop push switch (22 mm)	1	$10.00
Switch box	Six-hole push-button switch box with screws (22 mm holes)	1	$15.00

12 V power supply	LETOUR power supplies DC 12 V converter output 30 A 360 W	1	$25.00
18 AWG wire	40 ft 18-gauge 2-pin 2-color red-black cable	1	$20.00
Power cables	Typical (grounded) three-prong desktop computer cable	2	$15.00

These parts all come to US$370.00. You could purchase slower dosing pumps that are about half the price, but it does take about 60 seconds for those slower dosing pumps to move 1 oz of liquid. You will be far better off using the higher-speed pumps I have listed in the preceding table. Also, the food-grade silicone tubing is slightly smaller than the dosing pump's inner diameter; however, this has not caused any issues for me.

If you purchased pre-wired cables and an interface module, you will also need to purchase a DIN rail to mount it on. We now have all the items listed and their costs required to build the industrial robot bartender.

In the next section, we will detail the drinks that the robot bartender will be making.

Selecting the robot bartender bottles and recipes

To keep things fairly simple, the target bottle count for our robot bartender will be six. This means we will have six bottles of alcohol and mixers to combine in various ways to create our favorite drinks. Your robot bartender can make any drink that you desire. However, there is a bit of a balancing act in optimizing the bottle and drink combinations.

Based on my own personal experience of building a large-scale (50-bottle/45-recipe) version of this robot bartender and working with multiple professional bartenders on the recipes, I have prepared a list of five bourbon-based drinks. During an event at Dragos, where our robot bartender was unleashed on 300 guests, we found that we ran out of bourbon faster than any other alcohol. The bourbon-based cocktails were the most popular by far.

The following is a list of the six bottles required for our bourbon-based robot bartender recipes:

- Maker's Mark bourbon
- Angostura bitters
- Campari
- Lemon juice
- Simple syrup
- Sweet vermouth

You will also need the following garnish ingredients to put the finishing touches on the recipes:

- Ice cubes
- Orange slices and orange peels
- Maraschino cherries
- Mint leaves

To properly contain these beverages, you will need whiskey glasses and martini glasses.

Using these six ingredients, you can create the following cocktail recipes:

Recipe Name	Ingredients	Directions
Old Fashioned	2 oz bourbon 0.25 oz bitters 0.5 oz simple syrup	Fill a whiskey glass so that it is 3/4 full with ice cubes. Add the Old Fashioned robot bartender recipe ingredients to the glass. Stir, garnish with the orange slice and maraschino cherry, and serve.
Boulevardier	1 1/4 oz bourbon 1 oz Campari 1 oz sweet vermouth	Fill a whiskey glass so that it is 3/4 full with ice cubes. Add the Boulevardier robot bartender recipe ingredients to the glass. Stir and garnish with an orange slice.
Manhattan	1 1/2 oz bourbon 0.5 oz sweet vermouth 0.25 oz bitters	Fill a whiskey glass so that it is 3/4 full with ice cubes. Add the Manhattan robot bartender recipe ingredients to the glass of ice and stir. Strain the liquid into a martini glass. Rub the oil from an orange peel around the rim of the martini glass. Garnish with an orange peel and serve.
Whiskey sour	2 oz bourbon 1 oz lemon juice 3/4 oz simple syrup 0.25 oz bitters	Fill a whiskey glass so that it is 3/4 full with ice cubes. Add the whiskey sour Robot Bartender recipe ingredients to the glass of ice and stir. Strain the liquid into a whiskey glass. Stir, garnish with the orange slice and maraschino cherry, and serve. A real whiskey sour also contains an egg white (as fresh as possible) that has been dry-shaken with ice to create a layer of foam at the top. You can choose to add this extra step after the robot bartender dispenses the ingredients.
Mint julep	2.5 oz bourbon 1 oz simple syrup 0.5 oz lemon juice	Place the mint leaves on the bottom of a whiskey glass and mix them until the leaves begin to break down. Fill the glass so that it is 3/4 full with crushed ice and garnish with a sprig of mint. Add the mint julep robot bartender recipe ingredients, stir, and serve.

These recipes will be programmed into our robot bartender ladder logic. However, do feel free to experiment with your own recipes. All control systems require some level of "field tuning" and the robot bartender is no different. We will be using timer blocks to the correct proportions of each ingredient are added.

We have our recipe list sorted out, so now it is time to start assembling our industrial robot bartender. In the following sections, we will begin to detail the construction and wiring of the robot bartender's cards, pumps, and push buttons.

Building a ControlLogix rack

Once you have all the components for your ControlLogix rack, you will need to attach the 1756-PA75 power supply to the 1756-A4 rack. The 1756-PA75 slides right on to the left side of the 1756-A4 rack and can be tightened using the two black screws found inside the swing door of the 1756-PA75 power supply.

The I/O cards will slide and click into place easily. You should mount the cards in the positions referenced in the following table:

Card	Slot Number
1756-L55/A ControlLogix processor (CPU)	0
1756-ENBT/A ControlLogix EtherNet/IP module	1
1756-OB16E ControlLogix digital output module	2
1756-IB16 ControlLogix digital input module	3

Now that we have mounted all our cards, we will be powering up our ControlLogix rack in the next section.

Powering up your ControlLogix rack

Once you receive your ControLogix rack, the first thing you will want to do is test it out. In order to test out your rack, you will need to power it on. Most of the time, the PLC you receive will not come with a power cable. You will need to create your own power cable for the 1756-PA75 power supply by cutting the end off a typical desktop three-prong computer cable (grounded).

The following is a photo of a typical three-pronged computer power cable:

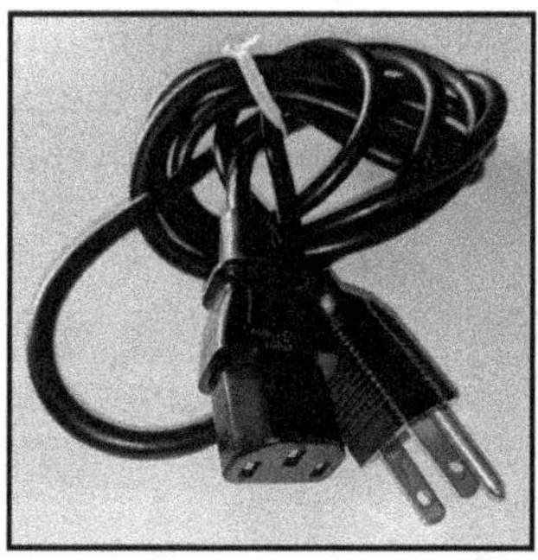

In the next section, we will share an exercise on how to create the power cable for our 1756-PA75 power supply.

Creating a power cable for the 1756-PA75 power supply

The following exercise will take us through the steps involved in creating a power cable for our ControlLogix 1756-PA75 power supply. It is rare for a power supply to come with its own cable, so it is important to understand how to create and wire a cable yourself.

Never cut or touch the ends of cable that is plugged into an outlet. Be sure to disconnect the power from the wire before cutting it and do not attempt to wire the A/C power while the power cord is plugged in.

The following steps will guide us through the safe creation of the power cable for our 1756-PA75 power supply:

1. First, we will need to cut off the end of a computer cable that you would normally plug into the back of a desktop computer. Next, we will carefully strip off about 2 inches of the black outer protective cable to reveal the three inner wires. Within most computer power cables, you will find three wires with the following colors:

    - Black – hot
    - White – neutral
    - Green – protective ground

2. Next, you will need to use wire strippers to strip off about a half-inch off the three inner wires. The ControLogix rack has an integrated power supply that has its own door on the left side of the rack. If you open the door, you can see the terminal block where you need to connect the power cable wires. The following is a photo of the power supply module with the front door open and the power wire connected:

You will notice that there is a power switch right above the connectors for the A/C power cord. You need to be sure to flip it to the on position when you are ready to test the chassis.

Please make sure your power cable is NOT plugged into the outlet before performing the next step.

3. The three power cable wires need to be connected to the following terminal blocks using your Phillips-head screwdriver. Open up all the terminal blocks by unscrewing the terminal block screws as high as they can go. Next, connect the wires to the following terminal blocks:

    - Black (hot) – L1
    - White (neutral) – L2/N
    - Green (ground) – ground

Wire the stripped power cable into the terminal blocks of the power supply. The following photo shows the three wires from the power cable connected to the power supply:

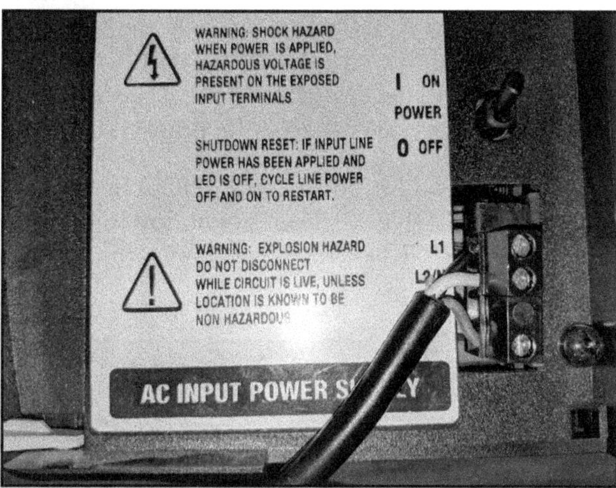

4. Once you have the wires inserted into the terminal block, tighten up the screws using your Phillips-head screwdriver, plug in the power cord, and flip on the power switch (pictured in the preceding photo) to the **ON** position. If everything is working properly, you should see your rack power up and lots of lights begin to flash on your controllers and cards. You should also see the **OK** light glow green for each of your cards.

Make sure that none of the cables or strands of copper are touching. Allowing the lines to touch can cause sparks and potentially create a fire.

We have now created a power cable and verified that our rack works and our cards are operational.

In the following exercise, we will test communications with our rack and ensure we can see it on our network so that we can begin programming it with our robot bartender ladder logic.

Testing communications with your rack

Now that your rack is powered on, you will need to test your ability to communicate with and interrogate the rack using RSWho. The EtherNet/IP card (1756-ENBT) you have purchased likely already has an IP address associated with it. If you look at the four-character display on the faceplate of the EtherNet/IP card, it lists the IP address that it is currently configured to use. You will need to change the IP address of your own computer or virtual machine to be on the same network that the EtherNet/IP card is configured to.

If no IP address is configured, you will need to use the BOOTP/DHCP tool to assign an address of your choosing to the EtherNet/IP card. The following screenshot shows what a typical rack will look like in RSLinx Classic RSWho when communications are working correctly:

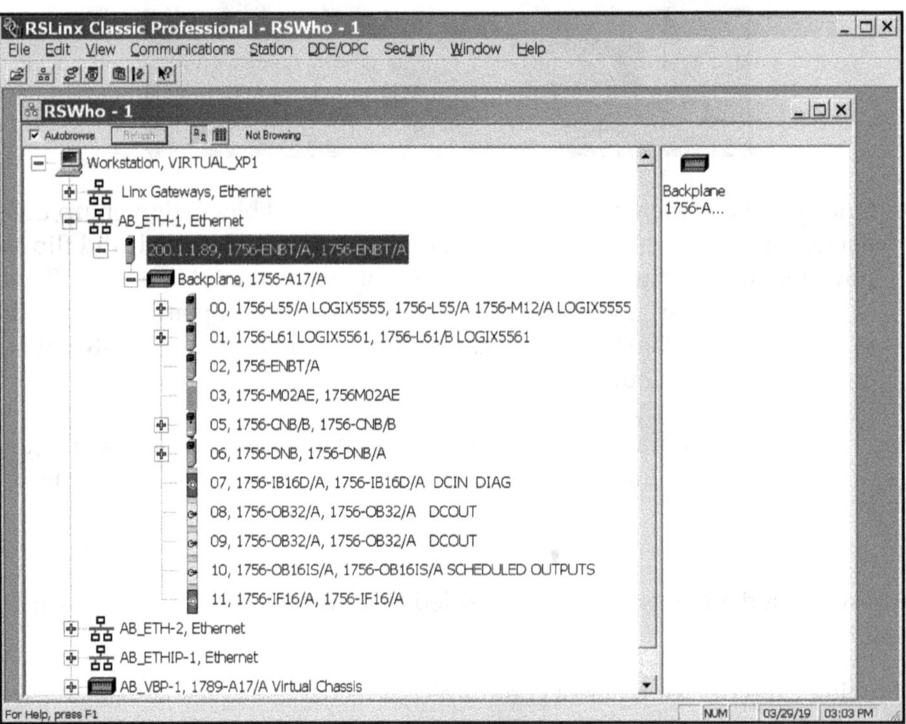

In the following section, we will create our new robot bartender RSLogix project and configure the Ethernet and I/O cards we have acquired.

Starting your RSLogix project

In this exercise, we will create our project in RSLogix and configure the cards on our rack. This project will first be used to test and validate the wiring we will carry out later for our pumps and buttons. Then, finally, we will configure our robot bartender recipes in the project's ladder logic.

In the following steps, we will be creating a new project and configuring the modules for our robot bartender:

1. To get started, we need to open up RSLogix and create a new project by going to **File** | **New**. Select the controller you are using under the **Type** field, set the **Slot** number to `0`, and specify a name and description for your project:

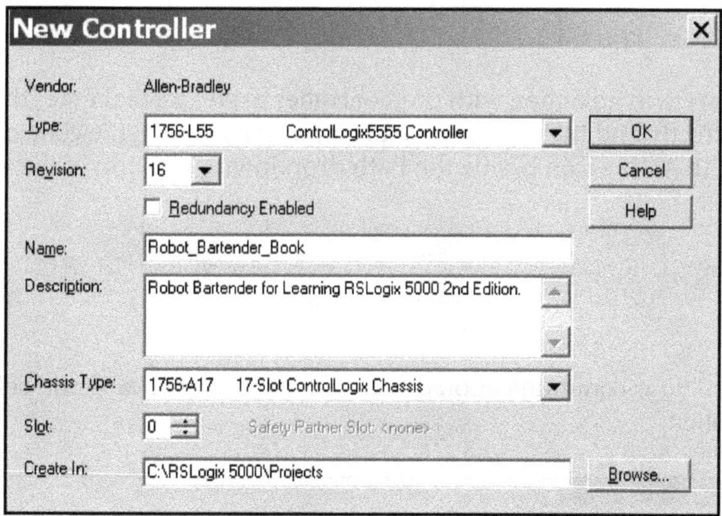

2. Next, add the cards to the project's rack by right-clicking on **1756 Backplane** in the **Controller Organizer** pane and selecting **Add Module...**.

RSWho can be a helpful tool for referencing the exact cards and module versions you have in your rack when adding them to your project. We can see from RSWho that the digital out module is in slot 2 and the revision is 2.4, so we enter that information into the dialog window.

3. We will be adding three cards to our project in a similar manner to how we added them back in `Chapter 7`, Configuring Logix Modules, earlier in this book:

    - Slot 1: The 1756-ENBT/A ControlLogix EtherNet/IP module
    - Slot 2: The 1756-OB16E ControlLogix digital output module
    - Slot 3: The 1756-IB16 ControlLogix digital input module

4. The end result should look similar to the following screenshot:

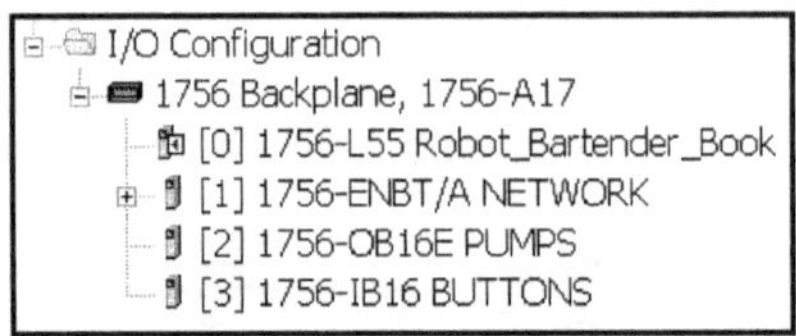

5. Now, we will go online with our controller to ensure that everything has been set up correctly and that we are able to communicate with the controller. Click on the **Who Active** icon beside the **Path** dropdown at the top of the window:

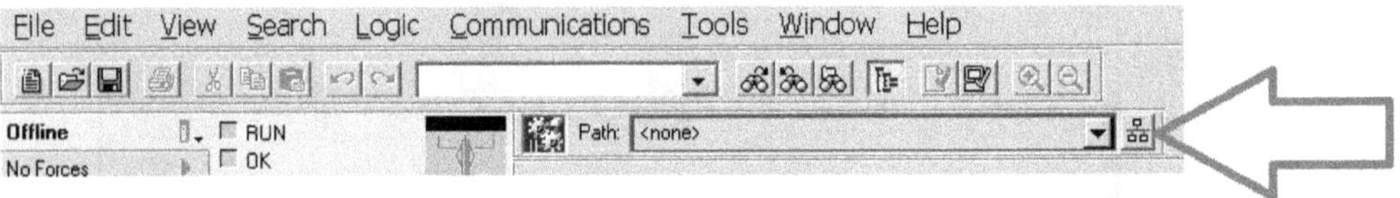

6. Expand your communication driver and the Ethernet card and select your rack's controller:

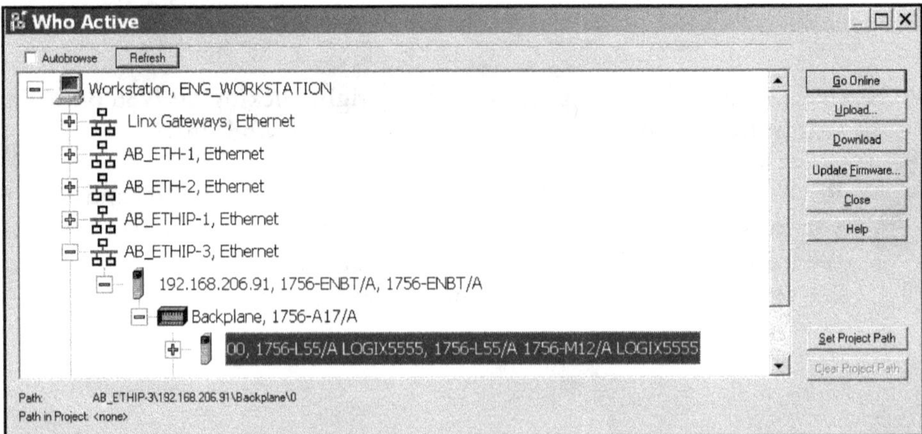

7. Click the **Download** button on the **Connected to Go Online** dialog box that appears.

You may be prompted to upgrade or downgrade the controller firmware version when you connect to the controller. We will touch on that briefly in the next section.

Firmware versions matter in the world of Rockwell Automation and the chances of the firmware version installed on the controller you purchased on eBay matching the firmware version of RSLogix/Studio 5000 you have installed is very slim. You will need to upgrade the firmware the controller to match the version of the software you are using.

8. If you are able to go online successfully, you are ready to start wiring up the pumps and buttons.

Now, our project has been created in RSLogix and we have configured communications and our I/O cards. In the next section, it is time to start wiring up our dosing pumps to the digital outputs on the 1756-OB16E cards (or whichever digital output card you selected). A document containing the Rockwell wiring diagrams for all ControlLogix cards can be found in the *Further reading* section of this chapter.

In the following section, we will be wiring our digital output cards to our 12 V power supply and dosing pumps. This will allow our ControlLogix program to run the dosing pumps based on our preset time values and execute our drink recipes.

Wiring the ControlLogix digital output cards

The Rockwell ControlLogix 1756-OB16E digital output card provides a shared power (+) source and a shared power sink (-), which are used to power our dosing pumps. Before wiring up our pumps, we will need to connect our power supply to the cards' shared source and sink and our bus bars' shared sink (negative).

In the following exercise, we will create the power cord for our 12 V power supply module.

Creating a power cable for the 12 V power supply

The following exercise is very similar to the exercise carried out in the *Creating a power cable for the 1756-PA75 power supply* section, where we created a power cable for the 1756-PA75.

Never cut or touch the ends of cable that is plugged into an outlet. Be sure to disconnect the power from the wire before cutting it and do not attempt to wire the A/C power while the power cord is plugged in.

The following steps will create an AC wiring harness for our 12 V power supply:

1. Cut off the end of a cable that would normally connect to a desktop computer or LCD screen. Now, remove about 1 inch of the black insulation off the cable to expose the three interior wires. There should be green, white, and black wires.
2. Using your wire strippers, strip off a quarter-inch of the insulation off the green, black, and white wires.
3. Connect the black wire to the AC input terminal with **L** above it.
4. Connect the white wire to the AC input terminal with **N** above it.
5. Connect the green wire to the AC input terminal with the ground symbol above it.

The power supply should now be wired up and should resemble the following photo:

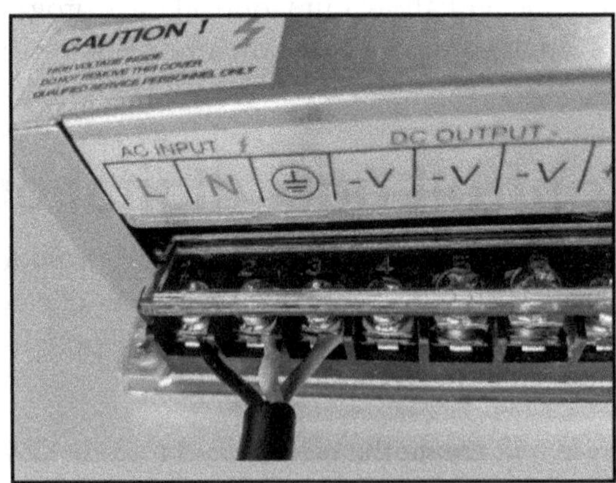

You can carefully test your power supply wiring by plugging it in. You should see the fan start up and a green light appear to show that the power supply is on.

In the following section, we will connect the 12 V power supply to our ControlLogix digital output card.

Connecting the power supply to the ControlLogix power supply

In this exercise, we will start wiring up our first I/O card, the 1756-OB16E digital output card (or whatever digital output card you were able to acquire). If your card differs from the 1756-OB16E, you can search for your card in the Rockwell Digital I/O module wiring documentation link found in the *Further reading* section of this chapter.

The terminals on our digital output card are labeled `1` to `20`. There are two shared sources and two shared sinks on the card. The shared sources are at terminal `10` and terminal `20` and the shared sinks are at terminal `9` and terminal `19`. Terminals `9` and `10` support group `0`, which is the `1` to `8` outputs. Terminals `19` and `20` support group `1`, which is terminals `11` to `18`. This allows us to support two different voltages on our digital output card. For example, group `0` could be running 12 V DC and group `1` could be running 24 V DC, each being supplied power from a different power supply. In the following exercise, we will wire up the 12 V power supply to the 1756-OB16E digital output card and the common sink bus (negative bus).

The following diagram shows the end result of this exercise, where we have our 12 V power supply connected to both our 1756-OB16E digital output card and the shared sink bus (negative power bus).:

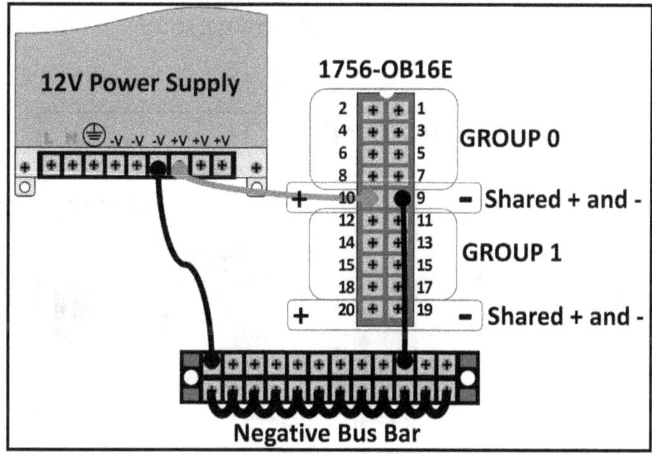

The following steps will create the same wiring as in the preceding diagram:

1. Attach the terminal barrier strips to one side of the negative bus bar so that all the terminals are connected. This will serve as a common sink (or common negative connection) for our dosing pumps.

2. Connect one wire from the 12 V power supply V+ terminal to terminal `10` of the 1756-OB16E. (Create a terminal connector using a crimping tool if you have a spring-clamp-type RTB.)
3. Connect one wire from terminal `9` of the 1756-OB16E to the negative bus bar. (Create a terminal connector using a crimping tool if you have a spring-clamp-type RTB.)
4. Connect one wire from the negative bus car to a V- terminal of the 12 V power supply.

The digital output card now has the power that it can provide to the six 12 V dosing pumps we will connect in our next exercise.

Wiring the 12 V dosing pumps to the digital output card

Now, we will attach our first 12 V dosing pump to the 1756-OB16E digital output card and test it out to ensure everything is wired up properly. Unlike some pump types, dosing pumps can be run dry without damaging them.

In this exercise, we will be hooking up our first pump to match the following diagram. Now that we have attached the power supply and negative bus bar, we simply need to wire the positive terminal of each dosing pump to their own group `1` terminal and the dosing pump to the negative bus bar:

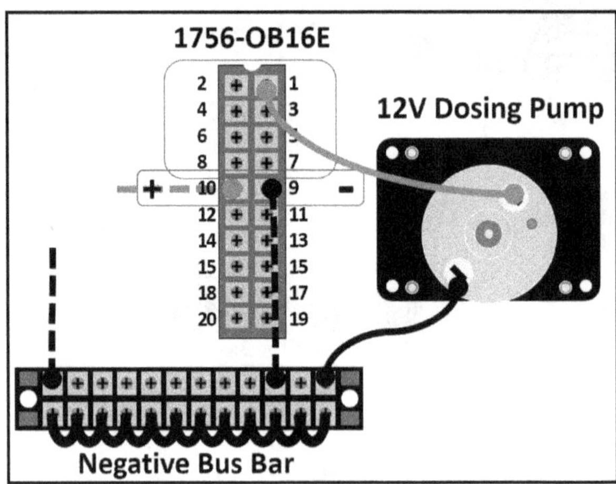

The following steps will create the same dosing pump wiring as in the preceding diagram:

1. Connect one wire from terminal `1` of the 1756-OB16E to the positive terminal of the dosing pump. It is best to use some crimping tools to create a nice, clean terminal connector to insert into the digital output card and spade terminal connector for the dosing pump. However, you can always just solder the wire tips if you don't have any wire crimping tools available.
2. Connect another wire from the negative terminal of the dosing pump to the negative bus bar. Ideally, you would create a spade terminal wire to connect to the pump terminal.

We have wired up our first dosing pump to our digital output. Now is a good time to test it out to ensure everything is working properly.

In the following exercise, we will use RSLogix 5000 to ensure we can control the dosing pump using our Logix controller.

Testing the digital outputs

In this exercise, we will force the digital output that we have connected to our dosing pump using RSLogix:

1. First, go online in RSLogix and force the digital output to test that our wiring is set up correctly.
   Open the robot bartender project in RSLogix and go online.
2. Set the controller to run mode (otherwise, the outputs will not activate).
3. Double-click on the controller tags under the **Controller Organizer** pane.
4. Expand the **Tag: Local:2:O.Data.0** controller.
5. Set the force value to `1`.

You should hear the pump running and your controller tags should look as in the following screenshot:

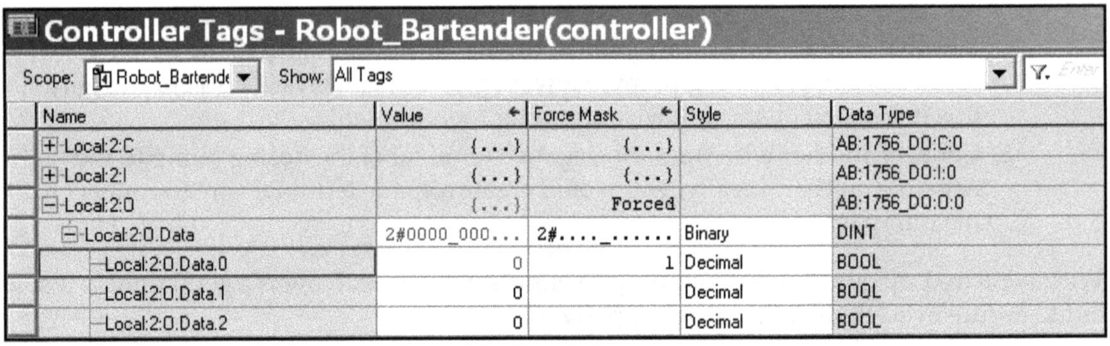

Controller Tags - Robot_Bartender(controller)

Scope: Robot_Bartende Show: All Tags

Name	Value	Force Mask	Style	Data Type
⊞-Local:2:C	{...}	{...}		AB:1756_DO:C:0
⊞-Local:2:I	{...}	{...}		AB:1756_DO:I:0
⊟-Local:2:O	{...}	Forced		AB:1756_DO:O:0
⊟-Local:2:O.Data	2#0000_000...	2#...._......	Binary	DINT
Local:2:O.Data.0	0	1	Decimal	BOOL
Local:2:O.Data.1	0		Decimal	BOOL
Local:2:O.Data.2	0		Decimal	BOOL

Now that we have the first pump working, we will need to repeat the same process with the other five pumps. Once you are finished, you will have connected the positive terminals of the dosing pumps to terminals `1` through `6` of the 1765-OB16E digital output card. You also need to test each of these outputs after wiring them to validate that everything is working properly.

If none of the pumps are working when you force the value, check to make sure your ControlLogix PLC is set to run mode. You may need to switch the key on the CPU to **RUN**, or if the key position is in REM, you should be able to set the program to **RUN** mode from RSLogix. If that does not work, double-check the 12 V power supply wiring and ensure that it is plugged in and running. If only one of the pumps doesn't work, double-check the wiring of the pump. Loose connections can be difficult to troubleshoot, but try wiggling the wires around when the pump is forced on. Finally, if none of those options work, you might be dealing with a dead output terminal or an electronic fuse that needs to be reset. Try resetting the fuse in ControlLogix under the card properties or by moving the pump output wire to a different terminal in the digital output card.

In the next exercise, we will connect our digital input card to our drink-selection momentary push buttons and the emergency stop button.

Wiring ControlLogix digital input cards

The robot bartender users will need buttons to be able to select their drinks, as well as an emergency stop button to hit if they select the wrong beverage. In the following exercise, we will wire up the momentary push buttons into our ControlLogix 1756-IB16 digital input module.

If your card differs from 1756-IB16, you can search for your card in the Rockwell Digital I/O module wiring documentation link found in the *Further reading* section of this chapter.

The following exercise will connect our momentary push buttons to the digital input card. The following diagram details how we will wire our digital input cards, push buttons, and power supply:

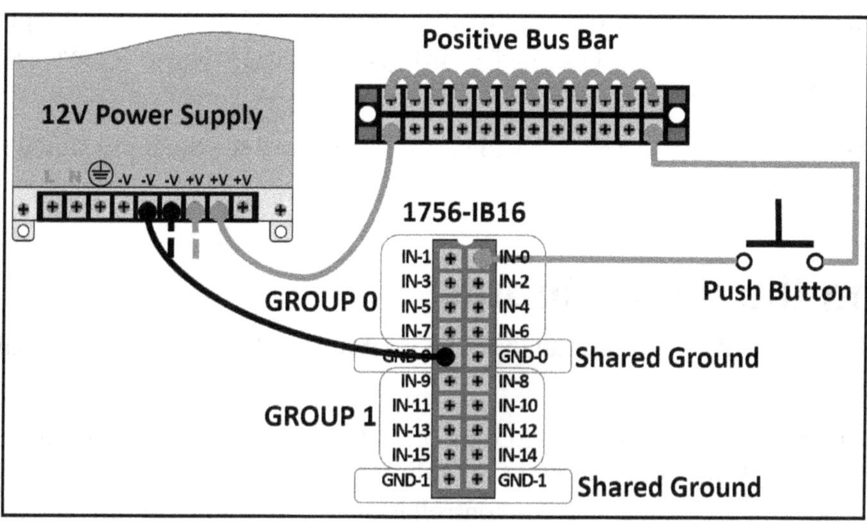

Our digital input card has a shared ground at terminals `9` and `10` (**GND-0** in the preceding diagram) and at terminals `19` and `20` (**GND-1**). Our digital input card wiring uses a shared positive bus bar for all six push buttons. Digital input cards detect voltage from a closed circuit. When our push button is depressed, it will momentarily close the circuit and trigger one of our digital inputs. However, the ESD button will typically work in the opposite manner. The ESD button circuit is opened when the button is pressed and is normally closed. So, the ESD button will also provide an `ON` digital signal until it is pressed, where it will provide an `OFF` signal to the digital input card.

Now, let's wire up our first push button by following these steps:

1. First, we will create our positive bus bar. Attach the red terminal barrier strips to one side of the positive bus bar so that all the terminals are connected. This will serve as a common source (or common positive connection) for our push buttons.
2. Next, we will create a wire to connect one of the positive terminals from the 12 V power supply (+V) to a terminal of the positive bus bar.

3. We will also need to connect the negative terminal (-V) of the 12 V power supply to terminal `10` of the 1756-IB16 digital input (**GND-0**) card using a wire. (Create a terminal connector using a crimping tool if you have a spring-clamp-type RTB.)
4. Now, we will connect our first momentary push button to our circuit by wiring one of the push button terminals to a terminal of the positive bus bar.
5. Finally, we will wire the other terminal of the momentary push button to terminal `1` (**IN-0** in the preceding diagram) of the 1756-IB16 digital input card. (Create a terminal connector using a crimping tool if you have a spring-clamp-type RTB.)

In the next section, we will use RSLogix to verify that we can see the input signal from our momentary push button.

Testing the digital inputs

In this section, we will test our digital input by verifying that we can see the signals when we go online in RSLogix:

1. Open the robot bartender RSLogix project and go online with the controller by selecting **Communications** | **Go Online**.
2. Once you are online with the controller, set the controller to run mode from **Communications** | **Run Mode**.

The key position on the controller CPU will need to be set to REM mode for you to remotely change the controller CPU to run mode.

3. Open the controller tags from the **Controller Organizer** pane, select the **Monitor Tags** tab at the bottom of the window, and expand the `Local:3:I.Data.0` tag value:

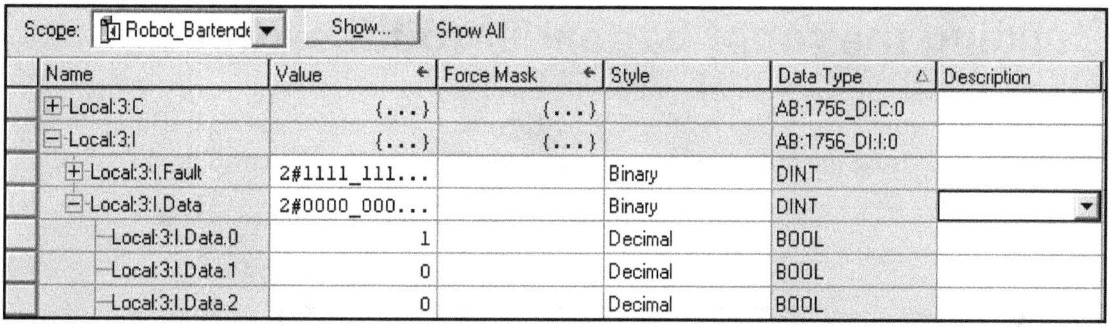

Name	Value	Force Mask	Style	Data Type	Description
+ Local:3:C	{...}	{...}		AB:1756_DI:C:0	
− Local:3:I	{...}	{...}		AB:1756_DI:I:0	
+ Local:3:I.Fault	2#1111_111...		Binary	DINT	
− Local:3:I.Data	2#0000_000...		Binary	DINT	
Local:3:I.Data.0	1		Decimal	BOOL	
Local:3:I.Data.1	0		Decimal	BOOL	
Local:3:I.Data.2	0		Decimal	BOOL	

4. Finally, press the momentary push button that you connected to `IN-0` and watch the value under **Monitor Tags** flip from `0` to `1`.

Next, you will need to repeat the same process for the other four push buttons (the drink selectors) and the one ESD button (used to stop all the pumps). We will connect these remaining push buttons to terminals `2` through `6` (`IN-1` to `IN-5`). Be sure to test each button after it has been wired up by going online in RSLogix and monitoring the tag value. It is important that we connect the ESD button to `IN-5` as later in the chapter, we will be using it in our logic to stop the pumps from running.

In the next section, we will begin writing the ladder logic for our drink recipes.

Writing the robot bartender ladder logic

In this section of the chapter, we will begin creating the logic that will dispense the ingredients for our robot bartender beverages. We will begin by creating the subroutine structure for our program and then we will fill in the logic for each routine. The program will be built around the main routine, which contains timer objects associated with each pump.

Each drink recipe will also have its own routine that will watch for a push-button input, modify the time for each pump timer, and then run the pumps. In the next section, we will create some empty place holder routines that we will populate later in the chapter.

Building the robot bartender routine structure

Let's start by creating some empty routines that will be executed by our main program. As you will recall from `chapter 8`, *Writing Ladder Logic,* we will need to create the jump to subroutine calls from the main program of our project so that the logic will be executed:

1. Right-click on **MainProgram** under **Tasks** | **MainTask** and select **New Routine...**:

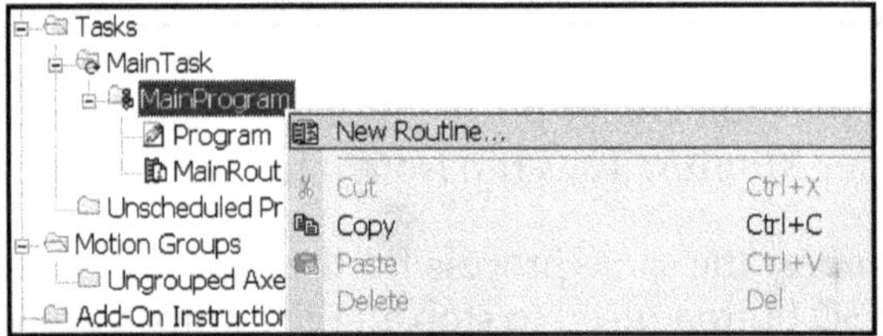

2. Create a new Ladder Logic routine called `Pump_Timers`:

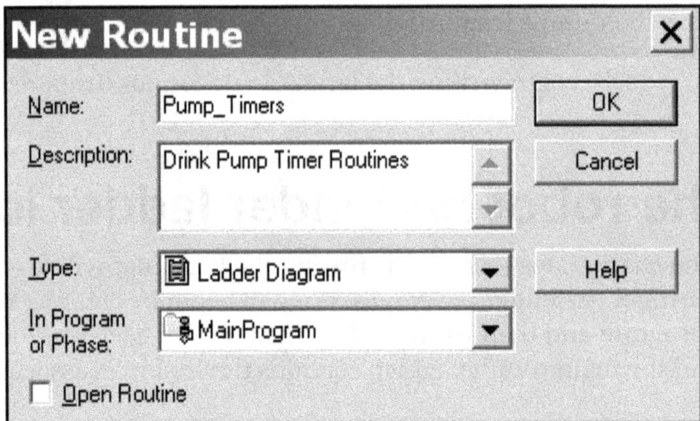

3. We will need to create several new routines for the robot bartender. Create the following additional Ladder Logic routines by following the previous steps again:
    - `Recipe_Old_Fashioned`
    - `Recipe_Boulevardier`
    - `Recipe_Manhattan`
    - `Recipe_Whiskey_Sour`
    - `Recipe_Mint_Julep`

4. Your **MainProgram** tasks should now look as follows:

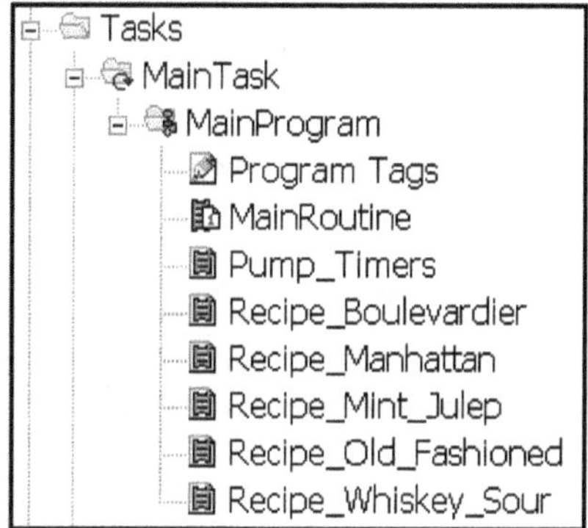

5. Next, we will connect **MainRoutine** to our newly created routines using the **Jump to Subroutine** (**JSR**) command. Open the **LadderLogic** tab of **MainRoutine**.
6. Under the **Ladder Logic** element tab labeled **Program Control**, select the **JSR** instruction and add it to the first rung of Ladder Logic.
7. In the **Routine Name** drop-down selection, select our newly created **Pump_Timers** routine.
8. Right-click on **Input Parameter** and select **Remove Instruction Parameter**. Do this for **Return Parameter** as well as we will not need to pass or return any parameters to our routine.
9. Repeat the same process and add the following routines as JSRs to **MainRoutine**:
    - **Recipe_Old_Fashioned**
    - **Recipe_Boulevardier**
    - **Recipe_Manhattan**
    - **Recipe_Whiskey_Sour**
    - **Recipe_Mint_Julep**

The following screenshot displays the required JSRs in our `MainRoutine` program:

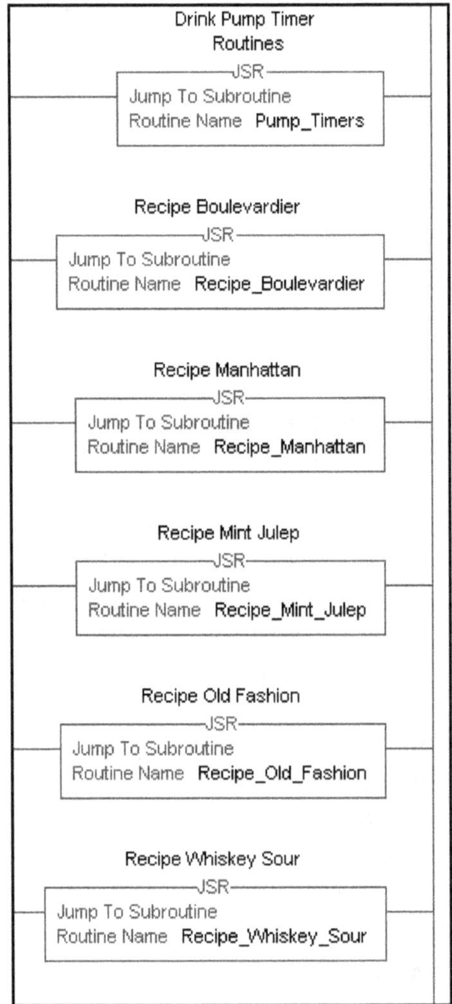

Now that we have created the routines for our robot bartender program and connected them to `MainRoutine` using the **JSR** instruction, we can start to build out the ladder logic for each routine. In the next section, we will create the heart of our program, which is the pump timer logic.

The pump timer ladder logic

In this section, we will be building the ladder logic for the pump timers that will handle the ingredient dosing for our robot bartender recipes.

The following steps will add and enable the ESD button so that it will stop the robot bartender's current recipe from pumping:

1. First, you will need to create the following five tags under the controller tags scope in the robot bartender project:

Tag Name	Data Type	Alias For
P01	BOOL	Local:2:O.Data.0
ESD	BOOL	Local:3:I.Data.5
Start_P01	BOOL	N/A
Running_P01	BOOL	N/A
Timer_P01	TIMER	N/A

Next, we will create the following ladder logic for the first pump in the pump timers routine:

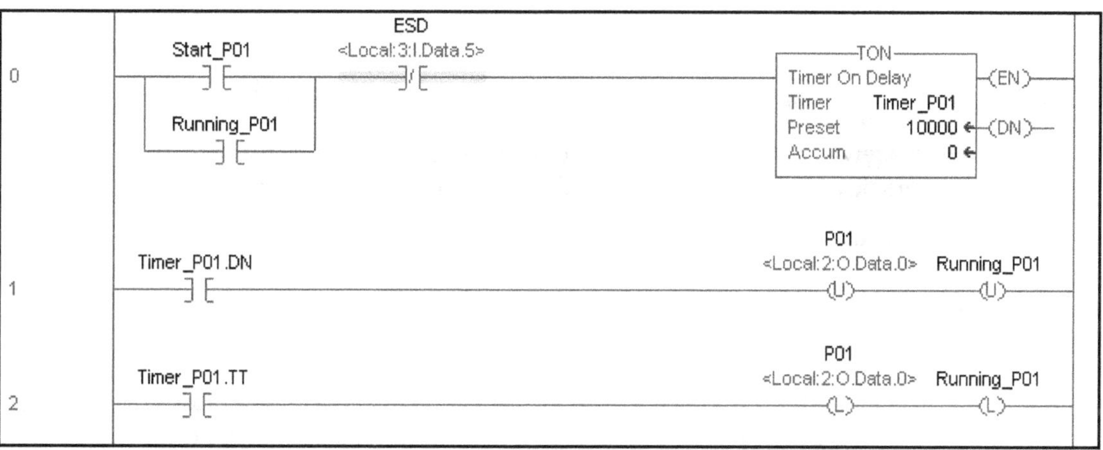

The preceding ladder logic manages the run timer for a single dosing pump. Rung 0 will trigger the start of the **Timer_P01** timer on delay.
The **Start_P01** controller variable will be used by our recipes' routines to start running the pump based on a predefined time limit. In order for the timer to run, the ESD button cannot be depressed.

2. As mentioned earlier, the ESD button will switch from `1` to `0` when pressed. We need to use an **Examine Off** instruction to stop the timer when the ESD button is pressed. `Start_P01` is only a momentary on signal, so to prevent the timer instruction from stopping as soon as the `Start_P01` value goes back to the off state, we have the `Running_P01` variable tag. The `Running _P01` contact is latched (on rung `2`) as soon as the timer starts and will unlatch (on rung `1`) once the timer has completed or is stopped early by the ESD button.
3. Finally, while the timer is running, the `P01` variable is latched, which is an alias for our first dosing pump at `Local:2:O.Data.0`.
4. Now that we have our code in place, we can test the logic by going online and downloading the program to our controller. By right-clicking on the **Start_P01** tag in the ladder logic and then selecting the **Toggle Bit** menu item, we can trigger the start of the pump. Once you toggle the **Start_P01** variable, you will need to immediately toggle it off again as it is meant to be momentarily on. If everything is working properly, you should see the pump you have connected at terminal `1` run for `10` seconds and then stop.

We have successfully created the timing logic for our first pump. In the next exercise, we will learn how we can export this logic and duplicate it multiple times with different variable names to save time and reduce the potential for mistakes.

Duplicating the pump timer ladder logic

In the following exercise, we will learn how to use the **Export Rung** feature in RSLogix and a text editor to quickly duplicate repeated ladder logic code with different variable names.

The steps in this exercise will demonstrate how we can duplicate ladder logic using the **Export Rung** and **Import Configuration** features in RSLogix/Studio 5000. This inevitably comes up in most automation projects and using this technique can save you a ton of time and reduce the risk of errors:

1. In the **Pump_Timers** routine, hold down the *Ctrl* key on the keyboard and select the far-left-side rungs, `0`, `1`, and `2`. This will select all of the logic for rungs `0`, `1`, and `2`.
2. Right-click on the left side of one of the rungs and select **Export Rung...**:

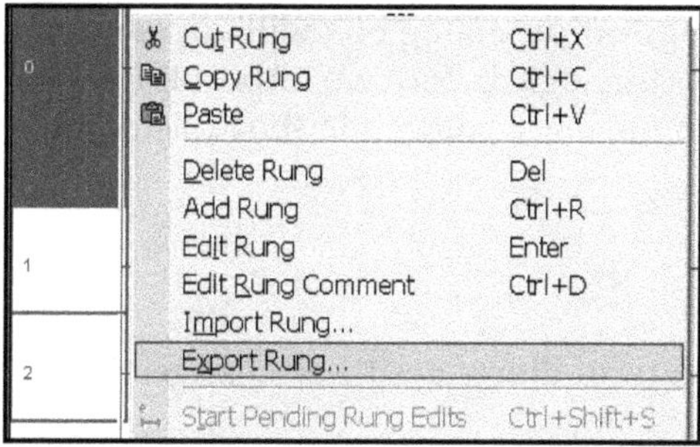

3. Save the file as `Pump_timers.L5X`:

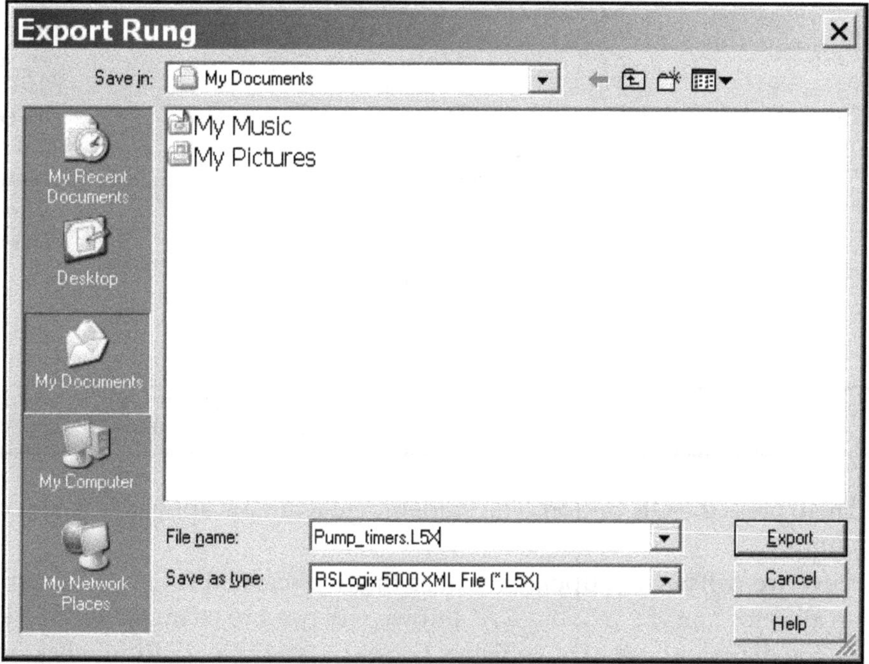

4. Next, right-click on the last rung (**End**) and select **Import Rung**.
5. Select the `Pump_timers.L5X` file.

6. An **Import Configuration** dialog box will appear that allows you to modify the variable names of the logic before we import the rung. You will need to modify the four values in the `Name` column in the table that has `P01` to `P02`:
   `P02`
   `Running_P02`
   `Start_P02`
   `Timer_P02`
   The following diagram illustrates these changes:

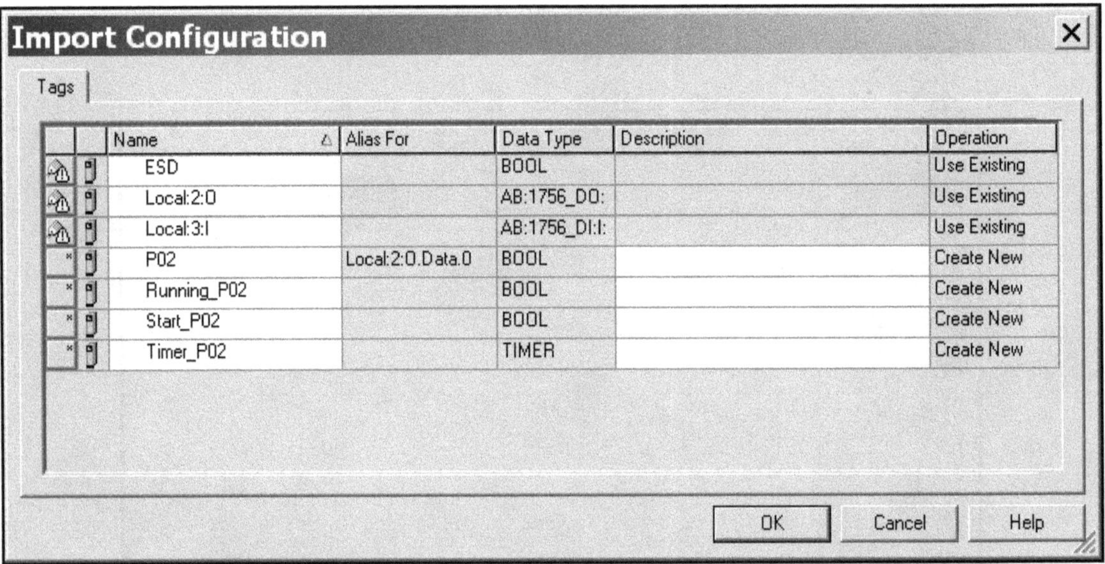

7. Then, press the **OK** button. The ladder logic will now appear for the second pump.
8. Next, we will need to update the alias that was created for `P02`. Currently, it is an alias for `Local:2:O.Data.0`, but we will need to change it to the next pump on the digital output card, which is `Local:2:O.Data.1`. Right-click on the **P02** variable tag in the ladder logic and select **Edit P02 Properties**.
9. Modify the **Alias For** field to be the next pump on the digital output card, `Local:2:O.Data.1`:

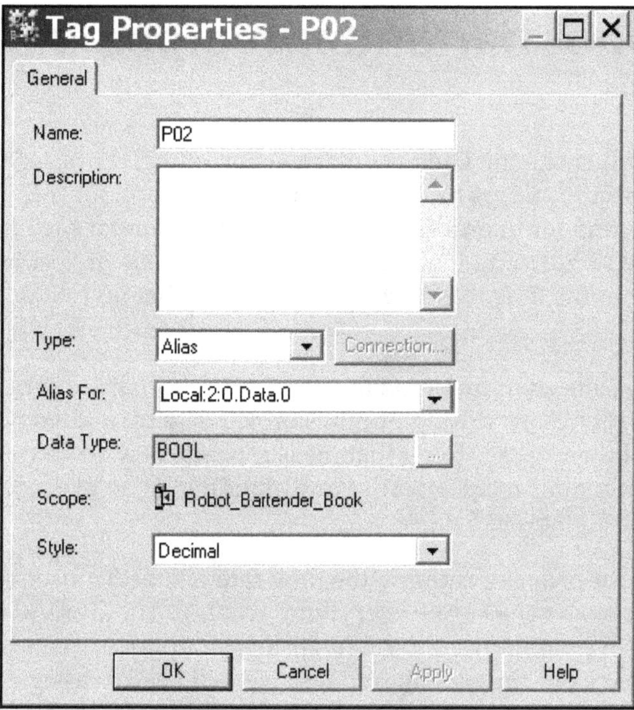

10. Now, repeat the **Export Rungs** and **Import Configuration** process detailed in the preceding steps for pumps `3` to `6`.

You should now have pump timer logic in place for pumps `1` through `6`. The logic should control the `Local:2:O.Data.0` through `Local:2:O.Data.5` digital outputs. You should test each pump timer by triggering the start of each one and ensuring each pump timer activates a different dosing pump.

Now that we have completed the core of our program, in the next section, we will focus on programming each robot bartender drink recipe in our ladder logic.

Writing robot bartender recipes in Ladder Logic

In this section, we will create the Ladder Logic version of our recipes. Our recipes are based solely on running specific pumps for a predetermined amount of time. But how long should we run the pump for in order to get the correct amount of each ingredient? The specifications for the 12 V dosing pump recommended for this project will pump between 170 and 460 ml per minute. The reason there is a range is that no two pumps are exactly alike.

It is likely that you will need to fine-tune the timings to get that 1-ounce shot consistently. The good news is that once the dosing pump is broken in a bit and you have that 1-ounce shot dialed in, it will then be able to hit that measurement very accurately. As we will need a good starting point for our recipes, let's start by landing on an average estimated flow rate of 300 ml/min, which equates to 5 ml/sec.

We will write all of our recipes assuming the flow rate will be 5 ml/sec with the expectation that we will field tune the values once everything is setup. There are 30 ml in 1 ounce of liquid, which means we would need to run a dosing pump for 6 seconds to pour a 1-ounce shot. Now that we have our timings figured out, we will need to assign pumps to specific bottles.

The following table contains the bottle and pump mapping that I will be using for the Ladder Logic recipes:

Dosing Pump	Bottle
`P01`	Maker's Mark bourbon
`P02`	Angostura bitters
`P03`	Campari
`P04`	Lemon juice
`P05`	Simple syrup
`P06`	Sweet vermouth

To make your life easier, you should assign the bottle names to the descriptions of the `P01` to `P06` variables to match the preceding table. We will also need to assign our momentary push buttons to the specific cocktails in order to complete our logic. The following table lists the push button aliases that you will need to create:

Cocktail Variable	**Alias For**
`Make_Old_Fashioned`	`Local:3:I.Data.0`
`Make_Boulevardier`	`Local:3:I.Data.1`
`Make_Manhattan`	`Local:3:I.Data.2`
`Make_Whiskey_Sour`	`Local:3:I.Data.3`
`Make_Mint_Julep`	`Local:3:I.Data.4`

The preceding variables will need to be added to the controller tags. Of course, earlier on in this chapter, we assigned the ESD button to `Local:3:I.Data.5`. Once you are finished, they should look as in the following screenshot in the controller tags table:

Scope: Robot_Bartende | Show... | Show All

Name	Alias For	Base Tag	Data Type	Style	Description
ESD	Local:3:I.Data.5	Local:3:I.Data.5	BOOL	Decimal	ESD Button
Make_Mint_Julep	Local:3:I.Data.4	Local:3:I.Data.4	BOOL	Decimal	
Make_Whiskey_Sour	Local:3:I.Data.3	Local:3:I.Data.3	BOOL	Decimal	
Make_Manhattan	Local:3:I.Data.2	Local:3:I.Data.2	BOOL	Decimal	
Make_Boulevardier	Local:3:I.Data.1	Local:3:I.Data.1	BOOL	Decimal	
Make_Old_Fashioned	Local:3:I.Data.0	Local:3:I.Data.0	BOOL	Decimal	

In the next section, we will create the Ladder Logic code for our cocktail recipes.

Writing a recipe for the Old Fashioned ladder logic

We will begin by creating the ever-popular old fashioned cocktail:

1. Open the empty **Recipe_Old_Fashioned** ladder logic routine we created earlier.
2. Add our newly created **Make_Old_Fashioned** tag as a contact for two new rungs. We will be using the move (**MOV**) instruction to set the timer preset value (`Timer_P0#.PRE`) to the desired number of milliseconds for each ingredient and then starting the timer using the `Start_P0#` variables.

3. Create your ladder logic to match the following screenshot for the old fashioned recipe:

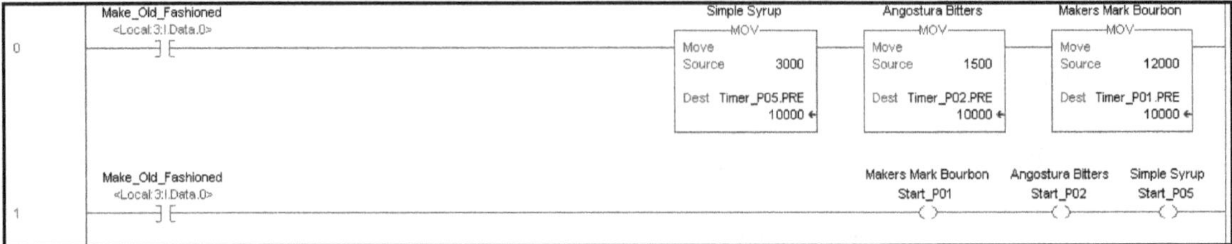

4. Now, save your project and go online with the controller, then download the program. Switch the controller to run mode and try pressing the **Old Fashioned** button. You should hear your dosing pumps running for the defined amounts of time.

In the next section, we will be creating the remaining recipes for our robot bartender.

Robot Bartender recipes

Now that we have our old fashioned recipe running correctly, it is time to create the others.

The following table can be used as a reference for the required timing of each recipe ingredient:

Recipe	Ingredients	Timing

Old fashioned	Maker's Mark bourbon
	Angostura bitters
	Simple syrup
		`Timer_P01.PRE = 12000`
		`Timer_P02.PRE = 1500`
		`Timer_P05.PRE = 3000`

Boulevardier	Maker's Mark bourbon
	Campari
	Sweet vermouth
		`Timer_P01.PRE = 8000`
		`Timer_P03.PRE = 6000`
		`Timer_P06.PRE = 6000`

Manhattan	Maker's Mark bourbon
	Angostura bitters
	Sweet vermouth
		`Timer_P01.PRE = 9000`
		`Timer_P02.PRE = 1500`
		`Timer_P06.PRE = 3000`

Whiskey sour	Maker's Mark bourbon
	Angostura bitters
	Simple syrup
	Lemon juice
		`Timer_P01.PRE = 12000`
		`Timer_P02.PRE = 1500`
		`Timer_P05.PRE = 4500`
		`Timer_P04.PRE = 6000`

Mint julep	Maker's Mark bourbon
	Lemon juice
	Simple syrup
		`Timer_P01.PRE = 15000`
		`Timer_P04.PRE = 6000`
		`Timer_P05.PRE = 3000`

The ladder logic for the Boulevardier recipe will set the timers for the sweet vermouth, Campari, and Maker's Mark bourbon pumps for an appropriate amount of time to get the correct ratios of ingredients. These values may need to be adjusted depending on the variance of dosing pump speeds and other factors, such as food-grade silicone line lengths:

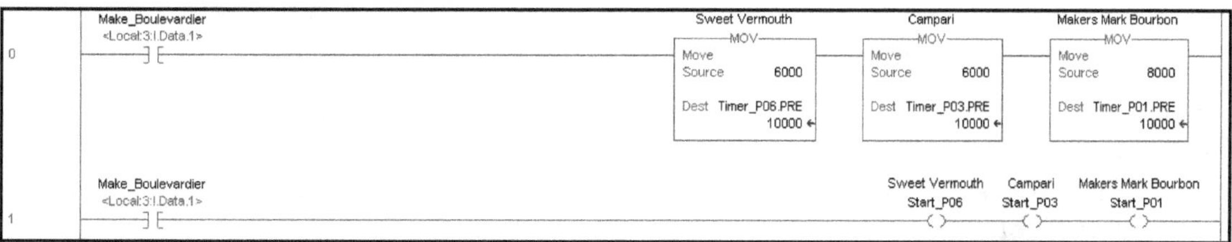

The ladder logic for the Manhattan recipe will deliver sweet vermouth, bitters, and bourbon by setting the timers for the appropriate dosing pumps and starting them:

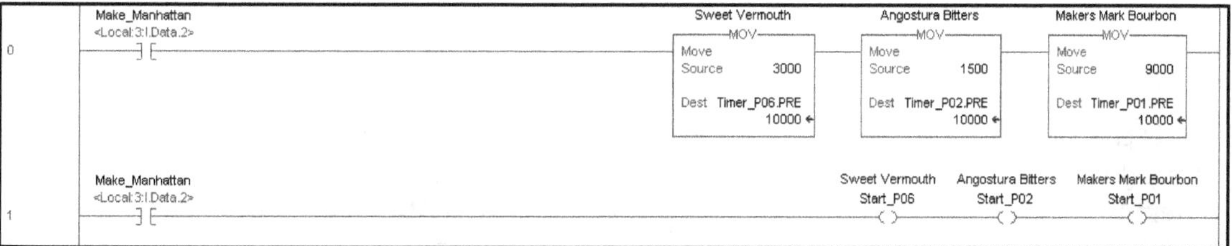

The ladder logic for the whiskey sour recipe will pump lemon juice, simple syrup, bitters, and bourbon:

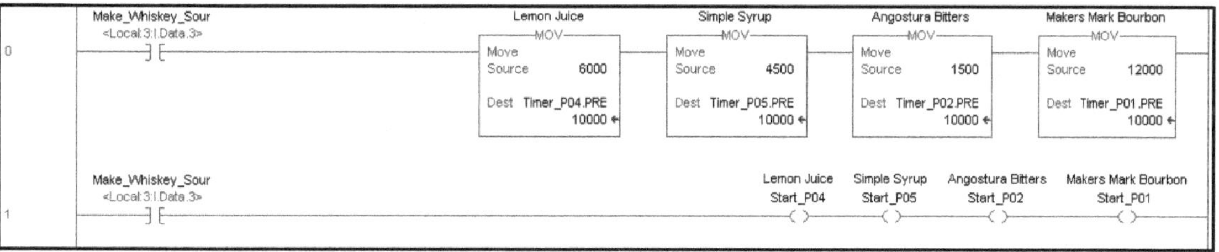

The ladder logic for the mint julep recipe will set the dosing pump timers for lemon juice, simple syrup, and Maker's Mark bourbon. Of course, you will also need to add mint to the Mint Julep after the recipe has executed:

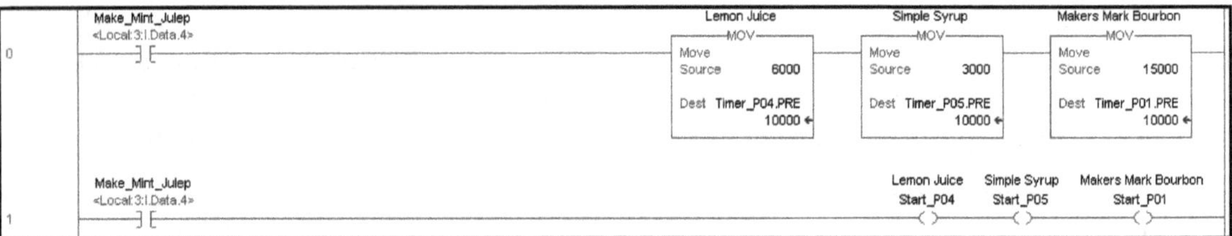

After completing the ladder logic for the recipes listed previously, it is time to start the testing and commissioning the robot bartender. It is a good idea to start with water and a measuring cup to ensure that the pumps and recipes are working when you press the different drink buttons.

Once you are confident that everything is working properly, it is time to start sampling some of the robot bartender recipes. Cheers!

Summary

In this chapter, we combined the skills we have learned throughout this book into a sample application. This chapter worked through building a complete robot bartender control system from scratch, including configuring the modules, writing the code, and downloading it onto our PLC. You now understand how to select the components required for a simple ControlLogix industrial control solution.

You have also learned how to wire digital input and output cards for a small control system project. You now have a deeper understanding of the entire industrial control system building, tuning, and troubleshooting process and can apply this knowledge to real-world control environments. Creating a robot bartender is a fun and gratifying experience.

Please do reach out to me on Twitter and send photos of your robot bartender creations at *@austin_m_scott*. I look forward to seeing them!

Questions

The following questions can be used to test your retention of the concepts introduced in this chapter. You can find the answers to these questions in the back of the book under *Assessments*:

1. What digital output module feature (denoted by an *E* in the product catalog identifier) protects the outputs from getting "blown" by using a fuse that can be reset in the RSLogix software?
2. What digital output module type (denoted by an *I* in the product catalog identifier) allows you to wire in a separate power source for each channel on the card?
3. What digital output module type provides a common (or shared) source for power to the individual digital outputs (and is the default type of digital output module)?
4. What digital output module type provides a common negative terminal, rather than a common source of power?
5. What digital input module feature (denoted by a *D* in the product catalog identifier) provides troubleshooting functionality that can detect when a wire is disconnected and can latch the value when an error occurs?
6. What is the name of the wiring systems that are attached to the front of Rockwell input and output cards and are used to connect wires to the card itself?
7. What is the name of the solution provided by Rockwell that contains a pre-wired cable system that moves the wiring from the card to a larger terminal on a DIN rail-mounted module?

Further reading

During the build process of our robot bartender, we covered a wide range of topics on I/O cards and wiring. For more details on how Rockwell cards and wiring work, please refer to the following Rockwell documents:

- 1756 ControlLogix I/O specifications: `https://literature.rockwellautomation.com/idc/groups/literature/documents/td/1756-td002_-en-e.pdf`
- Bulletin 1492 in-panel I/O wiring system modules and cables for Allen-Bradley programmable controllers: `https://literature.rockwellautomation.com/idc/groups/literature/documents/br/1492-br016_-en-p.pdf`
- Bulletin 1492 digital/analog programmable controller wiring systems: `https://literature.rockwellautomation.com/idc/groups/literature/documents/td/1492-td008_-en-p.pdf`
- Industrial Automation wiring and grounding guidelines: `https://literature.rockwellautomation.com/idc/groups/literature/documents/in/1770-in041_-en-p.pdf`
- Rockwell Automation digital I/O card wiring diagrams: `https://literature.rockwellautomation.com/idc/groups/literature/documents/um/1756-um058_-en-p.pdf`

Assessments

In the *Questions* section at the end of each chapter in this book, several review questions can be found. These questions provide the opportunity to test your ability to retain the knowledge learned and review some of the terminology from each chapter. The answers to the questions in each chapter can be found here.

Chapter 1

1. A water clock
2. Electro-mechanical relays
3. Allen-Bradley
4. Programmable Logic Controller (PLC)
5. The SLC-500
6. The ControlLogix platform
7. Integrated Architecture

Chapter 2

1. The ControlBus backplane
2. The ControlLogix L5 processor
3. The ControlLogix L7 processor
4. Program mode (`PROG`)
5. Remote mode (`REM`)
6. The GuardLogix controller system
7. The ControlLogix Extreme Environment controllers (Bulletin 1756 ControlLogix-XT)
8. Asynchronous operation cycle

Chapter 3

1. Small to medium size
2. 2001
3. CompactLogix 5480
4. The **Compatibility & Downloads** section of the Rockwell website
5. 5370 series
6. 2016
7. Compact GuardLogix controllers

Chapter 4

1. Both PC-based controller products provide a virtual rack and controller.
2. If you are looking for advanced debugging/logging features, Emulate 5000 would be a better option.
3. If you want a full-featured PC-based Logix controller for production use, rather than testing and debugging.
4. The SoftLogix chassis monitor.
5. The SoftLogix chassis monitor.

Chapter 5

1. The Emulate 5000 chassis monitor.
2. The virtual backplane driver.
3. 1789 SIM modules.
4. Logix Emulate 5000 is packaged with the Professional edition of Studio 5000. However, Emulate 5000 can also be purchased separately.
5. The 1789-MODULE Generic 1789 module (under **Other** in Logix Designer).

Chapter 6

1. Node
2. Segment
3. Tap
4. Terminating resistor
5. DeviceNet
6. ControlNet
7. EtherNet/IP
8. SynchLink
9. ODVA

Chapter 7

1. Rack
2. Slot
3. Channel
4. Address
5. Analog modules
6. Digital modules

Chapter 8

1. Ladder Logic
2. IEC 61131-3
3. Energized (`1`) and de-energized (`0`), or true (`1`) and false (`0`)
4. `AND` logic
5. `OR` logic
6. `NOT` Logic
7. Base tags
8. Alias
9. Controller level
10. Program Level
11. Buffering using program parameters

Chapter 9

1. Bytecode language
2. Function Block
3. Sheets
4. Analog wire
5. Digital wire
6. Textbox

Chapter 10

1. Non-retentive assignment operator
2. Logical operators
3. Arithmetic operators
4. An expression
5. The arithmetic instructions
6. The `CASE OF` construct
7. The `CASE OF` construct
8. The `FOR DO` construct

Chapter 11

1. **Sequential Function Charts** (**SFCs**)
2. SFC steps
3. SFC actions
4. SFC transitions
5. SFC branches
6. SFC stop element

Chapter 12

1. Controller tasks
2. Controller programs
3. Controller routines
4. Continuous tasks
5. Periodic tasks
6. Event tasks
7. Task watchdog time
8. System overhead time slice
9. An overlap
10. The Logix5000 **Task Monitor** tool

Chapter 13

1. Major fault
2. Minor fault
3. I/O fault
4. **Get System Value** (**GSV**)
5. **Set System Value** (**SSV**)
6. **User-Defined Data Types** (**UDTs**)
7. FactoryTalk TeamONE

Chapter 14

1. Source key protection or license protection
2. The Logix CPU Security Tool
3. FactoryTalk AssetCentre
4. **Converged Plantwide Ethernet** (**CPwE**) architectures
5. CIP security

Chapter 15

1. Electronically fused outputs
2. Isolated output modules
3. Sourcing modules
4. Sinking modules
5. Diagnostic modules
6. **Removable Terminal Blocks** (**RTBs**)
7. **Interface Modules** (**IFMs**) and pre-wired cables

Other Book You May Enjoy

If you enjoyed this book, you may be interested in this another book by Packt:

Embedded Systems Architecture
Daniele Lacamera

ISBN: 978-1-78883-250-2

- Participate in the design and definition phase of an embedded product
- Get to grips with writing code for ARM Cortex-M microcontrollers
- Build an embedded development lab and optimize the workflow
- Write memory-safe code
- Understand the architecture behind the communication interfaces
- Understand the design and development patterns for connected and distributed devices in the IoT
- Master multitask parallel execution patterns and real-time operating systems

Leave a review - let other readers know what you think

Please share your thoughts on this book with others by leaving a review on the site that you bought it from. If you purchased the book from Amazon, please leave us an honest review on this book's Amazon page. This is vital so that other potential readers can see and use your unbiased opinion to make purchasing decisions, we can understand what our customers think about our products, and our authors can see your feedback on the title that they have worked with Packt to create. It will only take a few minutes of your time, but is valuable to other potential customers, our authors, and Packt. Thank you!

Index

D

E

M

N

O

P

Q

R

S

T

U

V

W

www.ingramcontent.com/pod-product-compliance
Lightning Source LLC
Chambersburg PA
CBHW080611060326
40690CB00021B/4651

* 9 7 8 1 7 8 9 5 3 2 4 6 3 *